HOW THE
CLASSICS MADE
SHAKESPEARE

HOW THE
CLASSICS MADE
SHAKESPEARE

Jonathan Bate

PRINCETON UNIVERSITY PRESS

PRINCETON AND OXFORD

This book is published as part of the E. H. Gombrich lecture series, cosponsored by the Warburg Institute and Princeton University Press. The lectures upon which this book is based were delivered in October 2013.

Published by Princeton University Press
41 William Street, Princeton, New Jersey 08540
6 Oxford Street, Woodstock, Oxfordshire OX20 1TR

press.princeton.edu

LCCN: 2018957530
First paperback printing, 2020
Paperback ISBN: 9780691210148
Cloth ISBN: 9780691161600

British Library Cataloging-in-Publication Data is available

Editorial: Ben Tate, Hannah Paul, and Charlie Allen
Production Editorial: Natalie Baan
Text and Jacket / Cover Design: Leslie Flis
Production: Erin Suydam
Publicity: Jodi Price and Katie Lewis
Copyeditor: Hank Southgate

Jacket / Cover image: Titian, *Venus and Adonis*, c. 1555, oil on canvas. Courtesy of Shutterstock

This book has been composed in Minion and Trajan

Printed in the United States of America

CONTENTS

Ricardo Luckett
Paulo Hartle
Petro Holland
ob eruditionem et amicitiam
et in memoriam Francisci Kermode

PREFACE & ACKNOWLEDGMENTS

THIS BOOK GREW FROM the inaugural E. H. Gombrich Lectures in the Classical Tradition that I delivered in the autumn of 2013 at the Warburg Institute of the University of London, under the title "Ancient Strength: Shakespeare and the Classical Tradition." For the invitation, I would like to thank my dear friend Professor Peter Mack, who was at that time Director of the Warburg, and Al Bertrand of the European division of Princeton University Press. For comments, suggestions, and encouragement, I am grateful to the members of the Institute and others in the audience.

The "wide gap of time" between those happy occasions and this long-gestated book is due to a combination of the pressure of other commitments and the realization that I had far more to say on the topic than was possible in the brief span of three lectures. Those lectures form the basis of several chapters, but to further my argument I needed to incorporate both new research and additional material that was first essayed on other occasions: a Birthday Lecture given in 2010 at the Folger Shakespeare Library, Washington DC (with thanks to Gail Kern Paster), developed in a different form for the International Shakespeare Conference in Stratford-upon-Avon the same year (with thanks to Kate McLuskie); a lecture in the Bodleian Library of the University of Oxford on the exact four hundredth anniversary of Shakespeare's burial, which then became a Royal Irish Academy Discourse in Dublin; a segment of the British Academy Lecture at the 2016 Hay Festival; and even a few paragraphs from a Gladys Krieble Delmas Lecture delivered more than a decade ago for the Institute of English Studies at the University of London (with thanks to Warwick Gould).

Some of the preliminary reflections in chapter 1 were given a trial outing in an April 2016 essay in the *Guardian*, "Shakespeare: Who Put Those Thoughts in His Head?" The Epicurean aspect of the Horatian argument in chapter 9 further develops "Shakespeare the Epicurean," chapter 24 of my book *Soul of the Age: A Biography of the Mind of William Shakespeare* (Random House, 2009). Here and there, a few other thoughts from that book have been reformulated.

As this work was nearing completion, I became Gresham Professor of Rhetoric in the City of London. It is an honour to follow in the footsteps of such eminent Shakespeareans as Nevill Coghill, William Empson, and Jan Kott. The first lectures on rhetoric in the College that was Sir Thomas Gresham's former home were delivered in 1597–98, when Shakespeare was residing in the same parish of St Helen's, Bishopsgate: in the light of this pleasing coincidence, and given the centrality of rhetoric to my argument about the classical nature of Shakespeare's imagination, it seemed only fitting to devote my inaugural series of Gresham lectures to some of the ideas that I was finalizing for this book. Those ideas have been improved immeasurably as a result. For this opportunity, I thank Sir Richard Evans, Provost of Gresham College; Valerie Shrimplin, Academic Registrar; and the City of London Corporation and the Mercers' Company, joint trustees of the Gresham legacy.

E. H. Gombrich believed that it was perfectly possible, indeed thoroughly desirable, to present original academic research in such a way as to address large historical and cultural questions in a manner accessible to a broad general audience. Because I believe the same thing, and in order to honour the book's origin as public lectures, I have sought to retain the feel of a speaking voice and a tone that is sometimes informal. Equally, I have not assumed that all readers will have a prior acquaintance with, say, the Aristotelian principles of deliberative rhetoric, Cicero's notion of benefits, the "infirmity named *hereos*," and the early modern understanding of Epicurean philosophy. For this, I apologize to the *cognoscenti*, but I also hope that even the most experienced Shakespeareans will find things here that they did not know or had not noticed. To me, the wonder of Shakespeare is that I continue to find unseen depths in him even after forty years of studying, teaching, editing, watching, and writing about him.

Endnotes have been included in order to acknowledge sources, to engage with relevant scholarship, to suggest material for further reading, and occasionally to elaborate on contexts. They are, however, by no means comprehensive: this book is intended not as a full-scale survey of Shakespeare's knowledge of antiquity, but rather as an extended argument about the "classical" nature of his imagination. Latin texts are quoted from the Loeb Classical Library (https://www.loebclassics.com), unless otherwise stated; unattributed translations are my own. All Shakespearean quotations are from the Royal Shakespeare Company Edition, *William Shakespeare: Complete Works*, edited by Jonathan Bate and Eric Rasmussen (Modern Library, 2007), based on the First Folio (though with some minor textual variants). Unless otherwise stated, quotations from other authors follow the editions cited, thus offering a mix of modern and old spelling in the spirit of Shakespeare's own comingling of the antique and the contemporary. In old spelling quotations, typographic "i"/"j" and "u"/"v" are modernized for the convenience of the reader.

I thank my colleagues Peta Fowler and Scott Scullion for their help with some points of Latin and Laura Ashe for some medieval perspectives. My graduate student Adam Diaper scrupulously checked my Shakespearean references. I am deeply grateful to Barrie and Deedee Wigmore for establishing the fund that defrayed the costs of researching this book. My two generous and attentive anonymous readers for Princeton University Press saved me from assorted errors and offered many valuable suggestions, nearly all of which I was glad to implement. It has been a pleasure to work with the Press team of Ben Tate, Natalie Baan, Hannah Paul, and my superb copyeditor Hank Southgate. I am grateful to the Fellows of Worcester College, Oxford, for their desire to have an active scholar as their Provost. My exemplary personal assistant Dr Ilaria Gualino must also be thanked for guarding some precious spaces in my diary. I am able to say *beatus ille* of myself thanks to Dr Paula Byrne, Tom, Ellie, and Harry (*et canes*). And this is a fitting place to record that I am indebted to the late E. H. Gombrich for reading, and accepting for the *Journal of the Warburg and Courtauld Institutes*, an essay on Shakespearean allusion in English caricature in the age of Gillray, publication of which helped to launch my career.

ILLUSTRATIONS

HOW THE
CLASSICS MADE
SHAKESPEARE

1

THE INTELLIGENCE OF ANTIQUITY

WHAT DID SHAKESPEARE BELIEVE? We can only guess. He left neither a diary nor a philosophical treatise. His only recorded words are devoted to business transactions and legal cases.[1] His only surviving letters are conventional, if supremely elegantly phrased, pleas for patronage.[2] His will is orthodox and Anglican, but that is how wills were written in his England. It does not mean that he was orthodox and Anglican.

The only poems written in his own voice were the Sonnets. The man who wrote them clearly believed that love is a powerful and complicated thing, that poetry is an effective way of exploring its many dimensions, and—if his lines are to be taken at face value—that creative art is a way of achieving a kind of immortality for the beloved and perhaps for creative artists themselves. But his lines are not necessarily to be taken at face value. The "I" who speaks a poem, even an intimate love poem, is not synonymous with the person who writes the line. All poets rejoice in creating a *persona*. And if Shakespeare really believed that the purpose of writing love poetry was to immortalize the beloved, he might have taken the trouble to tell his readers the names of the addressees of his Sonnets.[3]

As for immortalizing himself, he was lackadaisical about publishing his works.[4] The Sonnets may well have been published without his permission, and half his plays were unpublished at the time of his death. As is often observed, had it not been for the diligence of his fellow-actors in seeing into print the First Folio of his collected comedies, tragedies, and histories in 1623, *Julius Caesar*, *Twelfth Night*, *Measure for Measure*, *Macbeth*, *Antony and Cleopatra*, *The Tempest*, and a dozen more would have been lost.

What kind of a thinker was Shakespeare? That is a better question.[5] The patterns of his mind may be traced in his work and from his education. Here we need not guess. We can say many things that are incontestable. He loved words and word play. He was fascinated by every variety of human character. He thought by way of dialogue and debate. He was sceptical of generalization about the ways of the world: almost every time a character in one of the plays gives voice to a piece of sententious wisdom, someone else says something that contradicts it—or a twist in the plot makes the seeming wisdom look foolish. "The gods are just," says Edgar in *King Lear*, yet within minutes the old king comes on bearing the hanged body of his beloved, virtuous daughter Cordelia, most unjustly murdered.[6]

The few moments in the plays where a sententious or philosophical discourse is vindicated rather than subverted by surrounding events tend to be those when a character says that life is like a play.[7] Most famously, there is Jaques's "All the world's a stage, / And all the men and women merely players" in *As You Like It*.[8] As if to prove he is right, he has hardly closed his mouth when young Orlando comes on bearing the frail body of a man approaching the seventh and last age of human life. He is pointedly named Old Adam: he is Everyman. It would be hard to controvert the view that Shakespeare believed that life is a kind of theatre and that theatre is, as Hamlet describes it, a mirror of life. But an actor turned dramatist would believe that, wouldn't he?

Sometimes "this great stage of fools" upon which we are born has an audience. "The gods look down," says Coriolanus as his mother kneels to him (inverting the orthodoxy whereby children would kneel nightly to their parents and ask for blessing), "and this unnatural scene / They laugh at."[9] These gods are plural because this is a play set in the polytheistic world of antiquity, but Shakespeare lived in a society where everybody, with a few wildcard exceptions such as the alleged atheist Christopher Marlowe, believed that the world was looked down upon by a singular God—albeit with aspects of three-in-one and one-in-three. In some of the civically performed Biblical plays of the fifteenth and early sixteenth centuries, the actor representing God would physically look down upon the "human" players. But in 1559, Queen Elizabeth published a proclamation forbidding the theatrical treatment of "matters of religion."[10] In 1569, the Corpus Christi plays were suppressed in York; the Coventry cycle was performed for the last time in 1579. The Elizabethan theatre has many vestigial traces of this religious tradition, most famously Hamlet complaining about players who out-Herod Herod, but Shakespeare never overtly dramatized Biblical matter.[11] There were strict laws proscribing stage blasphemy. Marlowe's fate hung over the stage-play world like an admonitory shadow. And the relationship between the church and the theatre became increasingly strained as "Puritan" polemicists voiced their disapproval of players, especially when adult male actors started kissing boys dressed as girls.[12] For all these reasons, Shakespeare was severely limited in his stage exploration and representation of Christian ideas, images, and doctrinal debates. He perforce handled such material cautiously, below the surface of the action; modern scholarship has unearthed rich polemical contexts and excavated subtle allusions, but it is not always clear that these would have been perceived by the original theatre audiences.[13]

In 1550, Parliament passed an Act "for the abolishing and putting away of divers books and images."[14] Extreme Protestantism, taking the Biblical Second Commandment literally, regarded all graven images—which is to say inventions of the human imagination—as idolatrous because they encouraged worship of the image of God as opposed to his ineffable Reality. When the Protestant revolution reached Stratford-upon-Avon, the treasurer of the town council, John Shakespeare, paid for workmen to whitewash over the image of the Last Judgment in the Guild Chapel across the road from the well-appointed house that his son William would purchase many years later. A poet and dramatist whose business was the making of images, in words and in stage pictures, would hardly have shared the Puritan relish for this kind of iconoclasm. Killjoy Malvolio in *Twelfth Night* is specifically described as a Puritan, while hypocritical Angelo in *Measure for Measure* is said to be "precise"—a "precisian" was another term for a Puritan.[15] The humiliation of both characters derives from the way in which their stand against sexual desire collapses under the force of sexual desire. One thing we can say for sure about Shakespeare's beliefs is that he was not a Puritan. His works may indeed be read as defences of the imagination and of the theatre against the strictures of Puritanism.

A tradition going back to the late seventeenth century affirms that he died a closet Papist. Yet despite three centuries of investigation and argument, there is no firm evidence, either internal to his plays or external in the biographical record, to confirm his recusancy or indeed that of his immediate family.[16] Perhaps he was a "Church-Papist," conforming outwardly but maintaining the old faith in his heart. Or he may have been an orthodox Anglican. It seems that his denominational allegiance could have been anything—other than "hot Protestant."[17] A play such as *King John* has at various times been used to "prove" that Shakespeare was a Papist and that he was an anti-Papist.[18] One suspects that throughout his career he had a vestigial love for the more theatrical aspects of the old faith—dressing up, ceremony, ritual. That was above all because of their theatricality, their appeal to the *imagination*—aspects of the old faith despised by Puritans.

We are unlikely ever to resolve the debate about Shakespeare's religious allegiance, or indeed the implicit religious attitudes within his plays. But there is no doubting his dependence on the pagan gods as an imaginative resource. The interest in resurrection and redemption that marks his last plays does not feel specifically Roman Catholic, or even specifically Christian: in *Pericles*, Thaisa expresses her gratitude for returning from the dead by becoming a priestess in the temple of Diana, while in *The Winter's Tale*, Hermione is reawakened under the aegis of Apollo's oracle and the influence of Ovid's Pygmalion through the agency of what Leontes calls Paulina's "magic," something that was regarded as the antithesis of "lawful" Christian faith.[19] Shakespeare's late plays, traditionally seen as his most spiritual works, take us to a number of temples, all of them ancient and pagan rather than Christian and modern: first those of Diana in *Pericles* and (by report) Apollo in *The Winter's Tale*, then a trinity of shrines—to Venus, Mars, and Diana—in the final act of his final play, *The Two Noble Kinsmen*. Add in the theophany of Jupiter in *Cymbeline* and the impersonation of Juno, Ceres, and Iris in *The Tempest*, and it becomes undeniable that Shakespeare's way of dramatizing divinity was more profoundly shaped by the humanist inheritance from ancient Rome than the modern contentions between Rome and Geneva.

Again, when it came to certain matters of ethical debate, the Shakespearean way of thinking was more akin to pagan reflection than Christian doctrine. The gravediggers in *Hamlet*, discussing the burial of Ophelia, remind us that suicide is a sin so mortal that Christian burial is not allowed. Hamlet himself knows this. The first thing he tells the audience once he is alone is that he wants his own life to end, in defiance of God's will: "O, that ... the Everlasting had not fixed / His canon gainst self-slaughter."[20] But where canon law was unequivocal about suicide, Hamlet regards it as a question without a clear ethical answer: "To be or not to be" is indeed *the* question. To debate the case for and the case against self-slaughter places Hamlet in a long tradition of Greek and Roman thinkers going back to Plato's dialogues on the last days of Socrates, the most famous suicide in history.[21] Furthermore, one of the principal ways in which such thinkers pursued the debate was by means of virtuous examples. The two most famous of these were Lucretia, who committed suicide after being raped, and Cato, who did so (in a botched and messy way) after losing the fight against Julius Caesar—he preferred to die than to live under a dictatorship. Shakespeare knew these cases well: he wrote an entire poem about *The Rape of Lucrece*, and he made a point of remembering Cato by introducing his son as a minor character in *Julius Caesar*, defining himself as an enemy of tyranny in the spirit of his father.[22] Brutus, whose wife, Portia, was Cato's daughter, expresses doubt about the compatability of Cato's Stoic code with the act of self-slaughter,[23] but he kills himself all the same—as did Seneca, the exemplar of Roman Stoicism. Most Stoics, notably Seneca, argued that suicide was an honourable way out when circumstances became such that the integrity of the self could no longer be sustained.[24] Given the noble examples of Lucretia and Cato, not to mention the number of honourable characters who commit suicide in Shakespeare's plays (one immediately thinks of Juliet, Enobarbus, Charmian, and the expressed intention of Kent in *King Lear*), it is clear that Shakespeare thought of the question of self-slaughter as an open, not a closed case. Canon law was firmly "fixed," whereas Shakespeare's imagination was always fluid.[25]

"What has Athens to do with Jerusalem?" asked Tertullian fourteen hundred years before Shakespeare. "Or the Academy with the Church?"[26] The compulsion of churchgoing and the habits of daily piety meant that the language of the Bible and Cranmer's *Book of Common Prayer* is echoed throughout the plays.[27] And religious faith is of the essence for such characters as Isabella of *Measure for Measure*, who wishes to be a nun, and Helen of *All's Well that Ends Well*, who goes on a pilgrimage. Yet there is suggestive evidence that Shakespeare's contemporaries especially associated him—or at least the poetic tradition in which he wrote—with pagan matter. Robert Southwell, in what many critics see as an allusion to *Venus and*

Adonis, complains of contemporary poets spending the sweet vein of their wit on "Paynim toyes" instead of lending their talents to "Christian works."[28]

In a different way, Shakespeare was not wholly enamoured of the claims of Athens. There is philosophy in his works, but he was not a philosopher. His three plays set in the ancient city of philosophers all turn on a movement away from the *polis* into some form of greenwood, strikingly rejecting the patriarchal tyranny of Theseus (*A Midsummer Night's Dream* and *The Two Noble Kinsmen*) and the philosophical cynicism of Apemantus (*Timon of Athens*).[29] As for *Troilus and Cressida*, the play with Shakespeare's largest cast of ancient heroes, it is hardly an advertisement for the virtue and clarity of Greek thought. We may conclude that, in response to the great debate between Athens and Jerusalem, reason and revelation, natural and divine law, Academy and Church, Platonic-Aristotelian and Judaeo-Christian world pictures, Shakespeare says not precisely "a plague on both your houses" but rather something to the effect of "I am sceptical of what we can know, more interested in how we react to what we experience." Or, as he put it in what may well have been his last words written for the stage,

> O, you heavenly charmers,
> What things you make of us! For what we lack
> We laugh, for what we have are sorry, still
> Are children in some kind. Let us be thankful
> For that which is, and with you leave dispute
> That are above our question. Let's go off,
> And bear us like the time.[30]

Every now and then in the plays, Shakespeare makes a glancing allusion to a theological "dispute" (the question of whether or not Purgatory exists, for example),[31] but for the most part he seems to have regarded metaphysics and ontology as "above our question." Though Hamlet's "To be or not to be" is on the surface a meditation in the neo-Stoic mold, laying out the cases for and against suicide, debating a question (*questio*) in the manner of an academic textbook,[32] in a deeper sense it is a mechanism for the unfolding of character and plot. It is an overheard soliloquy: a key question for the audience is whether or not Hamlet knows that he is being overheard, and if he does, whether he is putting on the act of being a student philosopher, just as he has previously claimed that he will put on an "antic disposition." "To be or not to be" may be a *performance* in a double sense. The very fact that it can be played so many different ways makes it into a species of utterance antithetical to the rigor of philosophical logic.

Shakespearean questions are only ever resolved dramatically, never philosophically. Because drama is an action unfolding in time, metaphysical generalization on stage is always liable to be subverted by context. And because drama involves characters in conflict, there is always another side to the question. What had Shakespeare to do with Athens or Jerusalem? His was neither the Academy's quest for truth nor the Church's for faith, but the Theatre's dream of mirroring and yet making sense of the multiplicity and the mess of life.

What fired Shakespeare's imagination? That is a very much better question than the one about what he believed. As the prologue to *Henry V* tells us, he sought to set alight his audience's *imaginary* forces. This book is about the formation of some key aspects of Shakespeare's imagination, and indeed about his distinctive valuation of the imagination, which, I argue, owed a huge debt to pagan antiquity.

The ancients bequeathed to Shakespeare a way of thinking, a form of intelligence. *Intelligentia* is defined in Thomas Thomas's Latin-English dictionary of 1587 as "A perceiving or understanding: intelligence: memorie, knowledge, sense, skilfullnes."[33] It is in these several senses that Shakespeare had a classical intelligence. One might even say that it was his intelligence (in the sense of *information about*) of antiquity that shaped his intelligence (in the sense of *cast of mind*). His memory, knowledge, and skilfulness were honed by classical ways of thinking: the art of rhetoric, the recourse to mythological exemplars, the desire to improvise within the constraints of literary genre, the ethical and patriotic imperatives, the consciousness of an economy of artistic patronage, the love of debate, the delight in images.

Where did he gain that intelligence? First when he crept, willingly or not, Latin textbooks in satchel, to school. There he was taught the art of memory and the skills of the writer. It was Stratford-upon-Avon grammar school that formed the mind of young William, to whom he surely nods in the scene in *The Merry Wives of Windsor* (his most English play), where a Welsh schoolmaster (he apparently had one himself)[34] gives a Latin lesson to a bright but cheeky schoolboy called William.[35] Sir Hugh Evans's declension of hig, hag, and hog in *The Merry Wives of Windsor* is a comic reminder of the tedium of Elizabethan early years education, which was all accidence and syntax. But once one had grasped the essentials of Lily's Latin grammar, there were rewards in store.

Play acting, for one thing. The dramatization of scenes from classical myth and history was a common schoolroom task of a kind evoked in the early play *The Two Gentlemen of Verona* when Julia, disguised as the boy Sebastian, imagines herself as a boy actor playing the "lamentable part" of "Ariadne, passioning / For Theseus' perjury and unjust flight," which she "so lively acted" with tears that her audience is moved to tears.[36] Emotional education—the art of "passioning"—is taught by way of a dramatization of one of the stories in Ovid's *Heroides*. The rhetorical art of persuading listeners to change their minds here becomes a dramatic art of moving an audience to tears—in anticipation of the player's speech to Hamlet.

Then there were exemplary stories. In *Titus Andronicus*, a schoolboy's book (albeit one received from his late mother, not his schoolmaster) is the device whereby the silenced and mutilated Lavinia reveals her own history:

> Soft, so busily she turns the leaves!
> What would she find? Lavinia, shall I read?
> This is the tragic tale of Philomel,
> And treats of Tereus' treason and his rape—
> And rape, I fear, was root of thine annoy.[37]

Storytelling was Shakespeare's method of making sense of the world, and no stories gripped him more fully than those of classical antiquity.

"What books readeth your master unto you?" asks the interlocutor's voice in a language textbook printed in 1591 by Shakespeare's schoolfellow Richard Field: "he readeth Terence, Virgil, Horace, Tully's *Offices*."[38] Shakespeare's encounters with these authors in grammar school laid the foundations of his art: Terence introduced him to comedy and scenic structure, Virgil to the heroic idiom, Horace to lyrical, occasional, and satirical poetry, and Tully (Cicero) to thoughtful reflection upon ethics, politics, and public duty. These classic authors, together with the more dangerous figure of Ovid, were formative of his thinking.

When we apply the label "Shakespeare's Roman Plays" to the quartet of *Titus Andronicus* and the three tragedies based directly on Plutarch's *Lives of the Noble Grecians and Romans*, we sometimes forget that no fewer than thirteen of Shakespeare's forty or so works are set in the world of ancient Greece or Rome. That constitutes one-third of his corpus, a body of work ranging from erotic and narrative poetry to tragedy to comedy to ancient history to satire to romance, covering a time-span from the Trojan war to fifth-century Athens to the early years of Rome to the assassination of Julius Caesar to the Roman Empire, with excursions into mythological narrative, Hellenistic seafaring romance, and more.

The Comedy of Errors is a free adaptation of the *Menaechmi* of Plautus, with embellishments from the same author's *Amphitryon*. *Titus Andronicus* is a tragedy in the style of Seneca that brings onto stage the *Metamorphoses* of Ovid. *Venus and Adonis* is also developed from the *Metamorphoses*, while *The Rape of Lucrece* is derived from a fusion of a story in Livy's *History of Rome* with that same story's retelling in Ovid's *Fasti*, along with a diversion into the siege of Troy. *A Midsummer Night's Dream* is set in the mythical Greece of Theseus and Hippolyta, whilst incorporating a dramatization of the Pyramus and Thisbe story that Shakespeare read in Arthur Golding's English translation of the *Metamorphoses*. *Julius Caesar*, *Antony and Cleopatra*, and *Coriolanus* all derive from Plutarch's *Lives* in the English translation of Thomas North. *Troilus and Cressida* draws on both classical and medieval narrations of the matter of Troy. *Timon of Athens* brings Plutarch's life of Alcibiades together with the Timon digression in his life of Mark Antony, perhaps mediated via a satirical dialogue by Lucian (known directly or indirectly). *Pericles* is in a tradition that dates back, via Chaucer's contemporary John Gower, to third-century Greek romance. The world of *Cymbeline* holds chronicle histories concerning the Roman occupation of Britain together with the appearance of Jupiter as a deus ex machina. *The Two Noble Kinsmen* returns to Theseus and Hippolyta via Chaucer's *Knight's Tale*, a story of the rivalry of the nephews of Creon, the mythical King of Thebes who is best known from the Oedipus and Antigone stories.

Among Shakespeare's characters are not only such famous figures from the classical tradition as Venus and Hymen, Theseus and Hippolyta, Achilles and Hector, Lucrece and Alcibiades, Caesar and Cleopatra, but also Soothsayers, Goths sacking Rome, and (offstage) the Delphic oracle of Apollo. Furthermore, all his works, wherever and whenever set, were shaped by the arts of classical rhetoric that he learned in school. All include frequent allusions to the mythology, literature, history, and culture of ancient Greece and Rome.[39] And his favourite books were either classical works or contemporary ones influenced by the classics.

In 1595, Richard Field, fellow-alumnus of the King Edward grammar school in Stratford-upon-Avon, printed *The lives of the noble Grecians and Romanes, compared together by that grave learned philosopher and historiographer, Plutarke of Chaeronea: translated out of Greeke into French by James Amiot, abbot of Bellozane, Bishop of Auxerre, one of the Kings privie counsell, and great Amner of France, and out of French into English, by Thomas North*. This was the book that got Shakespeare thinking seriously about politics: monarchy versus republicanism versus empire; the choices we make and their tragic consequences; the conflict between public duty and private desire. He absorbed classical thought, but was not enslaved to it. Shakespeare was a thinker who always made it new, adapted his source materials, and put his own spin on them. In the case of Plutarch, he feminized the very masculine Roman world. Brutus and Caesar are seen through the prism of their wives, Portia and Calpurnia; Coriolanus through his mother, Volumnia; Mark Antony through his lover, Cleopatra. Roman women were traditionally silent, confined to the domestic sphere. Cleopatra is the very antithesis of such a woman, while Volumnia is given the full force of that supreme Ciceronian skill, a persuasive rhetorical voice.[40] Timon of Athens is alone and unhappy precisely because his obsession with money has cut him off from the love of, and for, women (the only females in Timon's strange play are two prostitutes). Paradoxically, the very masculinity of Plutarch's version of ancient history stimulated Shakespeare into demonstrating that women are more than the equal of men. Where most thinkers among his contemporaries took the traditional view of female inferiority, he again and again wrote comedies in which the girls are smarter than the boys—Beatrice in *Much Ado about Nothing*, Rosalind in *As You Like It*, Portia in *The*

Merchant of Venice—and tragedies in which women exercise forceful authority for good or ill (Tamora, Cleopatra, Volumnia, and Cymbeline's Queen in his imagined antiquity, but also Queen Margaret in his rendition of the Wars of the Roses).[41]

Before he read Plutarch, he read Ovid, the author in whose work he found the things that made him a poet and a dramatist: magic, myth, metamorphosis, rendered with playfulness, verbal dexterity, and generic promiscuity. He acknowledged as much by bringing a copy of the *Metamorphoses* on stage in his first tragedy, *Titus Andronicus*; by basing his first published poem, *Venus and Adonis* (the book that made his name), on one of Ovid's tales; and by choosing another of them, the story of Pyramus and Thisbe, for the play within the play at the climax of *A Midsummer Night's Dream*. Ovidian strangeness and wonder weave a golden thread that runs all the way through his career from these early works to the late visions of *The Winter's Tale*, where the exquisite animation of Hermione's statue nods to the story of Pygmalion, and *The Tempest*, which alludes to the sinister magic of the sorceress Medea. Ovid was the master who taught Shakespeare that what makes great literary art is extreme human passion. Ovid showed him how to represent grief: in *Hamlet* it is learnt from Hecuba, in *Lear* from Niobe. And Ovid gave him the theme that is the driving force of all his comedies and several of his tragedies: erotic desire.[42]

A discovery that came some time after that of Plutarch was *The Essays of Lord Michael de Montaigne*, in the translation of John Florio, a prime example of an encounter with a very modern mind that was deeply shaped by the ancients. The more philosophical tenor of the works in the second half of Shakespeare's career can be attributed to his reading of this book when it was published in 1603, or maybe to a first acquaintance with parts of it in manuscript some time before—there is circumstantial evidence that he knew the translator Florio via his pursuit of the patronage of the Earl of Southampton. Shakespeare seems to have found an echo of his own intellectual growth in the progression of thought through the three books of Montaigne's endlessly re-readable meditative essays: a broad movement from attention to the Roman Stoical idea that "to philosophize is to learn how to die"[43] (which could stand as the set theme of *Hamlet*) to a severe scepticism about the Christian idea that God's providence is revealed through natural justice (the position that

Montaigne eviscerated in his lengthy "Apology of Raymond Sebond," which is echoed very closely in the deeply sceptical language of *King Lear*), to a coming to rest in a philosophy of acceptance associated with the ancient Epicurean tradition.[44]

There could be no better example of the rhetorical figure of *litotes*—understatement by way of ironizing negative—than to say that *Shakespeare was not unfamiliar with the classics*, whatever the formidably learned Ben Jonson might have been implying when he joked that his friend and rival was worthy to be named alongside the great dramatists of antiquity "Though thou hadst small Latin and less Greek."[45] As has often been remarked, the "small Latin" of a provincial grammar-school boy in the age of the first Queen Elizabeth would have been large by the standards of many a university Classics graduate in the age of the second.

⁓

There have been many admirable and thorough studies of Shakespeare and the classics.[46] Why add to the groaning shelf? Partly because certain aspects of Shakespeare's classical inheritance have been curiously neglected, perhaps because they are hiding in plain sight. It is always easier for a scholar to be "original" by positing a "hitherto unknown obscure source" than by remaining focused on the common currency of the canonical figures who shaped a tradition—in our case, most notably Cicero, Virgil, Ovid, Horace, and Seneca. Shakespeare's periodic adoption of a Horatian tone has rarely been discussed, despite the importance of Horace to Ben Jonson—or perhaps *because* of the importance of Horace to Ben Jonson, who from early anecdotes to modern criticism has been branded as Shakespeare's mighty opposite.[47] The exemplary force of Cicero, who actually appears as a character in *Julius Caesar*, has not been properly considered in the light of recent scholarship regarding the centrality of Ciceronian ideas to early modern humanist political thought. Little has been made of the significance of an allusion in *Love's Labour's Lost* to the neo-Latin pastoral poet Mantuan.

This list could be extended considerably, especially if we are willing to expand our notion of "influence" and "inheritance" beyond the realm of direct "sources." Shakespeare did not, we can be fairly sure, read deeply in Justus Lipsius, but there are traces in his work of the neo-Stoic frame of mind associated with Lipsius. Similarly with that vein of political thinking which intellectual historians call "Tacitism." And with the Epicurean tradition: we can be almost certain that he never read the *De Rerum Natura* of Lucretius, but we can be absolutely certain that he read many of the essays of Montaigne, who read, quoted from, and was profoundly influenced by Lucretius.[48]

The usual starting points for studies of Shakespeare and classical "influence" are direct quotations, verbal parallels, and explicit allusions. This was the approach exhaustively pursued by T. W. Baldwin in the two huge volumes of his *William Shakspere's Small Latine and Lesse Greeke*, which remains the most comprehensive work in the field.[49] Studies of this sort seek particular passages that provide firm evidence of Shakespeare's knowledge of particular classical texts. Typically, Baldwin sounds disappointed when he discovers that a Shakespearean echo of, say, "a verse in Horace," proves to be not prime evidence of Shakespeare's familiarity with the *Odes* but something of which the young dramatist might have said, as he makes Chiron say in *Titus Andronicus*, "I know it well: I read it in the grammar long ago."[50] The fallacy is to suppose that absence of evidence regarding Shakespeare's actual reading of Horace is evidence of absence of his awareness of what was understood by the Horatian idiom.

For educated Elizabethans, the names of Horace and Juvenal served as shorthand for satirical writing (Juvenal's being of the sharper kind): hence William Watson's reference in 1602 to "Horatian Satyriques" and Robert Greene's identification in his *Groatsworth of Wit* of Thomas Nashe as "Young Juvenal, that biting satirist."[51] But Horace's name was also synonymous with the trope of *beatus ille*: "happy is the man" who retreats from the political intrigue of the court to a healthy life in the country. To an educated Elizabethan, the character of Alexander Iden in *Henry VI Part 2* would have been instantly identifiable as a Horatian gentleman.[52]

Greene's coinage "He and Isabel ... began to be as Ciceronical as they were amorous" assumes that readers in the 1590s would have been familiar with the idea of Cicero as a model of prose style even if their own schoolday memories of Cicero's actual works were vague.[53] Similarly, a passage in Thomas Lodge's *Rosalynd*, the source for *As You Like It*, reveals that "Ovidian" was a shorthand term for the language of seduction: "Then, as the fishers put the sweetest bait to the fairest fish: so these Ovidians ... write that they be wrapped in an endless labyrinth of sorrow, when walking in the large leas of liberty."[54] Shakespeare was eminently capable of being—and recognized by his audience as being—Ciceronian, Horatian, or Ovidian without explicitly quoting or even naming Cicero, Horace, and Ovid.

Another limitation of the approach that confines Shakespeare's engagement with the classical tradition to his direct reading is that it forgets about his acting. He was, after all, in the cast of Ben Jonson's *Sejanus*, the most self-consciously classical drama of the age, played at court, probably during the Christmas 1603 season, then booed off the stage at the Globe in 1604. There is nothing like acting in a play, committing a part to heart, for gaining an intimate knowledge of its words and its world. Whether or not Shakespeare played the part of the Emperor Tiberius, as has often been conjectured,[55] his participation in *Sejanus* would have given him close acquaintance with a work that was based mainly on Tacitus but also steeped in Dio Cassius, Suetonius, and Juvenal. He would have either spoken in or heard a key piece of dialogue about the political power of historical writing:

> SEJANUS. Then is there one Cremutius
>   Cordus, a writing fellow they have got
>   To gather notes of the precedent times,
>   And make them into annals—a most tart
>   And bitter spirit, I hear, who, under colour
>   Of praising those, doth tax the present state,
>   Censures the men, the actions, leaves no trick,
>   No practice unexamined, parallels
>   The times, the governments; a professed champion
>   For the old liberty—
> TIBERIUS. A perishing wretch!
>   As if there were that chaos bred in things,
>   That laws and liberty would not rather choose
>   To be quite broken, and ta'en hence by us,
>   Than have the stain to be preserved by such.[56]

As a play about a notorious political conspiracy in ancient Rome, *Sejanus* was deeply influenced by *Julius Caesar*. Jonson wrote it, and Shakespeare acted in it, in full knowledge that Shakespeare's own Roman drama, though far less self-conscious in flagging its classical sources, was equally steeped in "parallels" between "precedent times" and the "government" of "the present state." In this sense, Shakespeare was a Cremutius Cordus to Jonson's Tacitus.[57] If that analogy holds, it is not beyond the bounds of possibility that Jonson saw a parallel between the arraignment of Cremutius Cordus forced by Sejanus—according to Tacitus, Cordus was the first person in Roman history to be charged with *maiestas* (treason) for writing a history (*editis annalibus*)—and the embroilment of both the Tacitean historian Sir John Hayward and Shakespeare's acting company some years earlier in the treason trial of the Earl of Essex.[58]

By considering the diversity of Shakespeare's direct *and indirect* encounters with the classics, this book attempts not only to fill some of those gaps in the existing scholarship but also to demonstrate more broadly that his imagination and his sympathies were shaped above all else by forms of thinking derived from what the character of Theseus in *A Midsummer Night's Dream* calls "antique" (or "antic") "fables."[59] In this, he was not alone. One purpose of this book is to contextualize Shakespeare within the wider "intelligence of antiquity" in England in the sixteenth century, for example by tracing the visual allusions to ancient Rome in Elizabethan London and by exploring the political and cultural imperatives that drove the urge to imitate Roman exemplars, none more important than Cicero. But the classical idea of *poiesis* ("making") presented a peculiar difficulty for Reformation culture, creating a need for what I will describe as "the defence of phantasms." Such defences are to be found in many places: I offer the examples of Sir Philip Sidney's theory of poetry as a golden world, the carefully chosen words in a song in *Cymbeline*, and the provocative dialogue between Poet and Painter in *Timon of Athens*.

This book argues that Shakespeare was almost always Ovidian, more often than is usually supposed Horatian, sometimes Ciceronian, occasionally Tacitean, an interesting mix of Senecan and anti-Senecan, and, I suggest, strikingly anti-Virgilian—insofar as Virgilian meant "epic" or "heroic." One key argument is that Shakespeare's form of classical fabling was profoundly *antiheroic* because it was constantly attuned to the force of sexual desire. When Shakespeare uses his classical inheritance most creatively, the Virgilian heroic brushes against the Ovidian erotic, poetry strives to outdo painting, and the muscular figure of Hercules is effeminized by love. The double meaning that the Elizabethans found in the word "heroic" (discussed in chapter 11) may provide a hidden key that unlocks the distinctive imaginative vision of a wide array of the plays and poems.

At the heart of the book, I propose an intimate relationship between the magical, the erotic, and the imaginative, or, in the terms of Theseus in *A Midsummer Night's Dream*, "The lunatic, the lover and the poet."[60] Shakespeare's imagination was magnetically drawn to dreams and visions, nightmares and ghostly apparitions, to the magic of theatre and desire, and thence to intimations of immortality. The question of survival beyond the grave leads me to consider Shakespeare's attitude to posthumous fame, and so into a closing argument about how his own immortality, seeded in his lifetime and coming to fruition in the eighteenth century, was assured when he began to function for modernity as the classics of antiquity functioned for him. Thus the arc of the book curves from Shakespeare *and* the classical tradition to Shakespeare *becoming* the classical tradition—precisely at the moment when, paradoxically, he was being praised for not being overlearned in the classics.[61] This brings my own work on Shakespeare full circle to its starting point, my studies of his eighteenth-century and Romantic *Nachleben*.[62]

〰️

In 1948, W. H. Auden won the Pulitzer Prize for a book-length poem called *The Age of Anxiety*. This (somewhat turgid) work is now little read, but the title phrase has endured and become shorthand for the ills of the late twentieth and early twenty-first centuries: in Auden's time, totalitarianism, world war, and the fear of nuclear annihilation; in ours, "the degradation of the environment, nuclear energy, religious fundamentalism, threats to privacy and the family, drugs, pornography, violence, terrorism"[63]—not to mention xenophobia, nationalism, and disillusionment with mainstream democratic politics. What is the place of the classics of literature, what hope is there for the future of humanist traditions, in a world dominated by anxieties such as these?

Studia humanitatis, that great intellectual movement which scholars would eventually call Renaissance humanism, was based on the belief that we may develop our understanding of humanity by studying the grammar, rhetoric, history, moral philosophy, and above all the poetry of classical antiquity. In Auden's age of anxiety, the ambition of the Warburg school of cultural historians was to study and preserve that tradition, which they believed was in danger of obliteration.

In the year that Auden's poem was published, a far greater book appeared in Switzerland. It too grew from a sense of anxiety—and the scholarly author was much closer than the fugitive poet to the nightmare of the previous decade. The book was *Europäische Literatur und lateinisches Mittelalter* (*European Literature and the Latin Middle Ages*) by Ernst Robert Curtius, dedicated to the memory of Aby Warburg.[64] Curtius acknowledged that his method owed a great debt to the approach to the history of art that was fashioned by Warburg, eldest son in the Warburg banking dynasty, who famously gave over to his younger brother the right to inherit the bank in return for a deal whereby he would be given enough money to buy books for the rest of his life. Aby Warburg duly devoted that life to scholarship and to the creation of his *Warburg-Bibliothek für Kulturwissenschaft*, the library that was moved to London in the year when Hitler became Chancellor of Germany and in which the great Jewish émigré scholars Friz Saxl, Edgar Wind, Erwin Panowsky, and E. H. Gombrich pioneered the study of the classical tradition.[65]

European Literature and the Latin Middle Ages made two lasting contributions to humanist scholarship. By drawing attention to the Latin writing of the Middle Ages, Curtius questioned the nineteenth-century historical model that imagined a development from Classical to Medieval to Renaissance, finding instead a continuity of literary devices and preoccupations. Secondly, Curtius pioneered the study of literary texts by way of themes, or *topoi*: the representation of the goddess *Natura*, the image of the hero, the features of the ideal landscape, the conception of the poet's divine frenzy, and so forth. His method proposed that literary creativity comes from a conjunction of continuity and change, convention and innovation, historicity and transcendence of history, tradition and individual talent, what one might call "presentness" and "pastness." In a crucial passage, Curtius proposed that literature possesses a freedom that is denied to visual art because "For literature, all the past is present, or can become so." He argued that Homer's *Iliad* can be "present" to its every reader in every age, whereas a painting by Titian is only truly present to the person standing in the room in front of it, and furthermore that

> The "timeless present" which is an essential characteristic of literature means that the literature of the past can always be active in that of the present. So Homer in Virgil, Virgil in Dante, Plutarch and Seneca in Shakespeare, Shakespeare in Goethe's *Götz von Berlichingen*, Euripides in Racine's *Iphigenia* and Goethe's. Or in our day: *The Thousand and One Nights* and Calderón in Hofmannsthal; the *Odyssey* in Joyce; Aeschylus, Petronius, Dante, Tristan Corbière, Spanish mysticism in T. S. Eliot. There is here an inexhaustible wealth of possible interrelations. Furthermore, there is the garden of literary forms—be they the genres ... or metrical and stanzaic forms; be they set formulas or narrative motifs or linguistic devices. It is a boundless realm. Finally, there is the wealth of figures which literature has formed and which can forever pass into new bodies: Achilles, Oedipus, Semiramis, Faust, Don Juan. André Gide's last and ripest work is a *Theseus* (1946).[66]

This is what we mean by "the classical tradition." For Curtius, it was the essence of civilized culture: "A community of great authors throughout the centuries must be maintained if a kingdom of the mind is to exist at all."[67] He never wrote at length on Shakespeare, but he could have found no better exemplification of the literature of the past being active in the present than in Shakespeare's reinvention of inherited narrative motifs, of figures such as Achilles and Theseus, and of the "garden" of literary genres—not to mention his adept deployment of a panoply of rhetorical techniques.

Curtius contended that "a historical consideration of European literature must begin at [its] darkest point"[68]—the point, that was to say, when the literature of antiquity was preserved only by means of manuscripts known to, and copied by, a small number of scholars and clerks, mostly monks. He was inspired by their curation of the classical tradition because he feared that Europe was on the brink of another dark age. As he explained in the foreword to the English translation of his book, "When the German catastrophe came I decided to serve the idea of a medievalistic humanism by studying the Latin literature of the Middle Ages. These studies occupied me for fifteen years." He made clear that his work was "not the product of purely scholarly interests": "it grew out of a concern for the preservation of Western culture."[69] The study of ancient works of culture was a way of responding to the barbarism of the present.

Given this ambition, it would be anachronistic to blame Curtius for ignoring the admonition of his contemporary Walter Benjamin that there is no document of civilization that is not also a record of barbarism, or for fixing his gaze on the Western tradition and failing to look East or South. It should, nevertheless, be acknowledged that he was a man of his time and that if a scholar in the twenty-first century were to retrace his steps, the perspective would need to be more globalized. Curtius was not interested in the fact that Terence, whom he rightly calls "one of the favorite school authors of the entire Middle Ages,"[70] was a slave, probably born in or near Carthage. He barely noticed the gendering of the classical tradition. And he was very thin on the role of Arabic scholars in preserving the ancient Greek foundations of Western thought. Averroes and Avicenna each get two passing mentions in a book of nearly seven hundred pages, and there is not a single reference to the eleventh-century Muslim-born physician Constantinus Africanus, writers who were formative in the transmission of classical thinking about many of Shakespeare's leading themes.[71]

Mercifully, we do not live in the world of book-burnings that Curtius inhabited in Germany as he was researching and writing his book between 1933 and 1945. We do, nevertheless, live in a world in which the classical tradition as he understood it is in danger of burial beneath the avalanche of the information revolution, and where its spirit of dialogue between different languages and cultures is ebbing rapidly away. Underlying my narrative about the creative regeneration of the classical tradition and the eventual emergence of Shakespeare as the modern classic are twin anxieties: for how much longer will his own classicism be recognizable to playgoers and students, who are no longer versed in the stories of Virgil and Ovid or a knowledge of Roman history? And will he continue to be a living classic in a future where attention spans are short and the long view of the past is flattened by the simultaneity of data derived from the digital world?

More information is now available at the push of a mouse to anybody in the world with an Internet connection than was ever available to the whole of history before our time. Shakespeare inherited a classical tradition that had been painstakingly constructed and reconstructed from manuscripts, fragments, broken statues, and other artifacts over several hundred years. We, by contrast, have an instantaneous and seemingly atemporal digital simulacrum of the whole of that tradition alongside the "modern classics" from Shakespeare to Milton to Modernism and far beyond. The question of the "immortal" Shakespeare's future survival—will he in fact prove mortal at some point between the four hundredth and the five hundredth anniversary of the burial of his physical remains?—is a synecdoche for the question of the future survival of any kind of "classical tradition" in the welter of the information age. These much-expanded E. H. Gombrich Lectures are accordingly a small contribution to the ongoing work of the Warburg school.

2

O'ER-PICTURING VENUS

"Venus, termed also Cytherea," explained Thomas Rogers in one of the "Annotations" to his *Celestial Elegies of the Goddesses and the Muses*, a sequence of fifteen sonnets or "quatorzains" published in 1598, was "poetically fained to be bred of the froth of the Sea." She "excelled all other Goddesses in beautie, she is the Goddesse of love, pleasures and lascivious delightes, she rideth in a chariot drawne by doves, she is the mother of Cupid and is accounted one of the seven planets."[1] Rogers was a gentleman-amateur among the many poets partaking of the vogue for sonnet writing in the 1590s. As love poems, sonnets are written under the sign of Venus, with whom Shakespeare had a particularly close association: for most secular readers and writers in the 1590s, the most celebrated and widely read poem about "the Goddesse of love, pleasures and lascivious delightes" was his *Venus and Adonis*. It went through no fewer than nine editions in the decade following its first publication in 1593, making it by far his most popular printed work. This was his signature work. Like Ovid, from whom he derived the story, he may accordingly be described as Venus's poet.

A poetry lover perusing the bookstalls in St Paul's Churchyard in the year 1600, perhaps having read the bestselling *Venus and Adonis* and heard gossip that Shakespeare was also the author of "sugared sonnets," could have alighted upon a slender volume published the previous year, entitled *The Passionate Pilgrime. By W. Shakespeare.* It included twenty poems, three of them lifted from *Love's Labour's Lost* and two subsequently published in *Shake-speares Sonnets* (1609). No fewer than four of the others, all sonnets, were on the theme of Venus and Adonis. Their authorship is disputed, with recent stylometric studies leaning towards the possibility that Shakespeare might well have written at least one or two of them.[2] The strongest case is for the first of them, which follows immediately upon three authentically Shakespearean poems:

> Sweet Cytherea, sitting by a brook
> With young Adonis, lovely, fresh and green,
> Did court the lad with many a lovely look,
> Such looks as none could look but beauty's queen.
> She told him stories to delight his ears,
> She showed him favours to allure his eye,
> To win his heart, she touched him here and there:
> Touches so soft still conquer chastity.
> But whether unripe years did want conceit,
> Or he refused to take her figured proffer,
> The tender nibbler would not touch the bait,
> But smile and jest at every gentle offer:
>> Then fell she on her back, fair queen, and toward:
>> He rose and ran away, ah fool too froward.[3]

In a sense, it is immaterial whether or not this sonnet is by Shakespeare: the point is that it was sold as being by him and its first readers would have assumed that it was by him. They would have read it as a retake of *Venus and Adonis* in miniaturized sonnet form. The inviting tumble in the closing couplet is a reversed reprise of a memorable couplet early in the original poem: "Backward she pushed him, as she would be thrust, / And governed him in strength though not in lust."[4]

The second of this group of four sonnets in *The Passionate Pilgrim* has Venus waiting for Adonis "Under an osier growing by a brook" on a hot day, in which "she is hotter" with desire; he arrives and strips off to bathe, provoking her to say "O Jove . . . why was not I a flood?"[5] In the third, she stands on a hill as Adonis approaches with his horn and hounds; she warns him of the dangerous boar in the wood where he is heading and tells him (proleptically) of a youth whom it has wounded in the thigh—she shows him whereabouts on the body she means, and upon seeing another "wound" (the gash of her genitals), he runs away, blushing. The fourth has Venus sitting by Adonis, clipping him in her arms, telling him the story of her seduction by Mars, beginning to undo his clothes as she describes how Mars undid hers; he runs away when she seeks to reenact Mars's kiss.

Each of the four sonnets thus offers an image of the encounter, the attempted seduction advanced to a greater or lesser extent, and a breakaway movement at the end—Venus's fall onto her back, ready to be made love to, in the first; Adonis's water-jump or flight in the others. It is as if each sonnet is a painting that suddenly bursts into motion. One inevitably wonders whether the author or authors were familiar not only with Shakespeare's *Venus and Adonis* and the original telling of the story in Ovid's *Metamorphoses*, but also with one or more of the many visual representations of it that were frequently created in the fifteenth and sixteenth centuries, whether by great artists or journeyman tapestry weavers.

"So much and such savored salt of wit is in his comedies," wrote the author of the epistle that precedes the first published text of Shakespeare's *Troilus and Cressida*, "that they seem (for their height of pleasure) to be born in that sea that brought forth Venus."[6] The birth of Venus, fully grown, from a shell in the sea is an ancient image of perfect beauty, while "height of pleasure" has a distinctly sexual aura. Though critics do not seem, as far as I am aware, to have noticed the fact, this comparison of Shakespeare's imagination to the birth of Venus was made in print hard on the heels of the first utterance on stage of his most memorable comparison of a human character to the goddess of love:

> For her own person,
> It beggared all description: she did lie
> In her pavilion, cloth-of-gold of tissue,
> O'er-picturing that Venus where we see
> The fancy out-work nature: on each side her
> Stood pretty dimpled boys, like smiling Cupids,
> With divers-coloured fans whose wind did seem
> To glow the delicate cheeks which they did cool,
> And what they undid did.[7]

This is Enobarbus's famous account of Cleopatra on her barge at Cydnus, elaborated out of a passage in Thomas North's translation of Plutarch:

> And now for the person of herself: she was layed under a pavillion of cloth of tissue, apparelled and attired like the goddesse Venus commonly drawen in picture: and hard by her, on either hand of her,

pretie faire boyes apparelled as painters doe set forth god Cupide, with litle fannes in their hands, with the which they fanned wind upon her.[8]

Plutarch alludes to paintings of Venus, in which she is usually attended by at least one Cupid, in order to paint a picture of Cleopatra in the imagination of his readers. Enobarbus does the same for the benefit of his onstage audience (Maecenas and Agrippa) and the auditors in the theatre, who have to imagine the scene because they are not allowed to see it. By saying that the person of Cleopatra beggars all description but then going on to describe her, Shakespeare seeks to outwork the work of painters. He adds colour, transforming the "little fans" of Plutarch's Cupids into "divers-coloured fans," and in the run of his verbs—"did seem / To glow ... did cool ... undid did"—he creates a sense of blowing hot and cold, of change, of the motion of the air.

Plutarch expects his reader to know that Venus is commonly drawn in pictures, whereas Shakespeare suggests the idea of a single picture of Venus as the archetypal example of art surpassing nature: "O'er-picturing that Venus where we see / The fancy out-work nature." In Shakespeare's time, the authoritative account of the origins of Western art was the thirty-sixth chapter of the thirty-fifth book of Pliny's *Natural History*, where the ancient Greek artist Apelles was praised as the perfect painter because of his ability simultaneously to be true to nature and to create beauty that outdid nature.[9] The high point of Apelles's art was said to be his "Venus Rising from the Sea, known as the Venus Anadyomene," which Augustus brought to Rome (Pliny reports that at the time of his death Apelles was working on a second, even more beautiful version, for the people of his own island of Kos).[10] The originals are lost, although a surviving mural in Pompeii gives an idea of what they probably looked like. Shakespeare did not see that; nor did he see the renderings of the subject by Botticelli and Titian that are among the masterworks of the Renaissance—nor indeed the exquisite bas-relief by Antonio Lombardo that was obtained for Wilton House by the family of the Earl of Pembroke, patron of the First Folio.[11] Shakespeare was not referring to a particular painting but to the idea of an Apelles-like depiction of Venus on the water as the archetype of beauty against which to match his verbal description of Cleopatra.[12] John Lyly's

Figure 1. Antonio Lombardo, *Venus Anadyomene* (marble bas-relief, Venice, c. 1510–15)

play *Campaspe*, one of the most reprinted dramas of the Elizabethan age, tells the story of how Apelles used Alexander the Great's favourite concubine, the lovely Campaspe, as the model for his Venus, and then fell in love with her. Shakespeare trumps Lyly and makes his point about "o'er-picturing" by imagining the goddess as the model for the mortal woman, instead of vice-versa.

Lombardo's bas-relief was inscribed with a line from Ovid's *Ars Amatoria*: "NVDA VENVS MADIDAS EXPRIMIT IMBRE COMAS" (naked Venus wrings out the spray from her hair).[13] The motif of the newly born and fully formed goddess drying her hair is common to numerous versions of the image: tracing the lineage of such details was the core business of the Warburg school of historians of the classical tradition.[14] "When we have isolated and named a literary phenomenon, we have established one fact," Curtius wrote in *European Literature and the Latin Middle Ages*:

> At that one point we have penetrated the concrete structure of the matter of literature. We have performed an analysis. If we get at a few dozen or a few hundred such facts, a system of points is established. They can be connected by lines; and this produces figures. If we study and associate these, we arrive at a comprehensive picture. That is what Aby Warburg meant by the sentence quoted earlier: "God is in detail."[15]

Warburg was fascinated by classical patterns, by the process of how artists keep the energy of antiquity alive through alluding to its stories. He was also fascinated by the relationship between poetry and painting. His doctoral thesis focused on Botticelli's two most famous paintings, *The Birth of Venus* and *Primavera*, exploring them in relation to their classical sources. Warburg's key questions are summarized by one of our own age's most formidable scholars of the classical tradition, Anthony Grafton:

> Two points in particular worried Warburg, one stylistic and one substantive. Why had Botticelli, a painter whose natural bent lay in the portrayal of still, dreamy figures, here [in these two paintings] used "bewegtes Beiwerk," fluttering hair and clothing, to give a sense of violent motion and emotions? And why had Botticelli decided to depict original combinations of myths drawn from Classical sources, like the *Homeric Hymns* and Ovid's *Metamorphoses*, on so grand a scale?[16]

Warburg discovered a particular connection that answered both questions. Angelo Poliziano, tutor to the Medici, wrote a poem in 1475 that included mythical scenes closely akin to Botticelli's. As Grafton puts it, "Like Botticelli, he combined his borrowings in new ways. And he described figures in motion—and the fluttering clothing and flying hair that expressed it—more obsessively and vividly than Ovid himself. Botticelli, whose deviations from the ancient sources matched Poliziano's, must have shared the poet's sensibility and relied on his advice in his mythological paintings."[17]

Warburg's thesis proposed that in both Poliziano's poetry and Botticelli's painting a Dionysian ancient world was brought alive in Renaissance Florence—in a manner very different from that of the austere forms which would in the seventeenth and eighteenth centuries come to be associated with "classicism." He was in this sense a child of Jacob Burckhardt, for whom, in the words of another modern scholar, "individualism, *virtù*, and the arts of statecraft, war, humanism, and the imagination identify themselves as 'Renaissance' by their participation in the reenactment of antiquity."[18]

For Warburg, as for Curtius, the bringing together of the past and the present was the key to our understanding of tradition. Ovid's *vitality* made him the most "present" of ancient poets. In a footnote to his thesis, Warburg elucidated the phenomenon of Venus's moving hair by way of an allusion to a wonderful image in the *Amores* that might be translated something like this: "Her lovely hair is ruined. Hair that Apollo would lust after. Hair that Bacchus would want for his own head. I might compare her tresses to those the painter once showed nude Dione supporting with her dripping wet hand."[19] A sense of movement, a focus on the body, an air of lightness, an interest in the relationship between poetry and painting: these are motifs that not only Poliziano and Botticelli in the fifteenth century but also Titian and Shakespeare in the sixteenth learned from Ovid. They too deployed them so sensuously as to bring the world of ancient myth into the presence of their audiences.

During the decade when John Shakespeare was working his way up through the Stratford-upon-Avon town council, prior to commissioning the workmen to cover over the images on the walls of the Guild Chapel, Philip II, king of Spain (and, for a time, England), commissioned Titian to execute a series of large paintings of highly erotic mythological scenes and allegories. In letters to his royal patron,

Figure 2. Titian, *Venus and Adonis* (original version 1554, this version by Titian and his workshop later in his career)

Titian described them as *poesie* or *favole*, "poetic inventions" or "fables."[20] The subjects are drawn from Ovid. Jupiter makes love to Danaë in a golden shower; the naked Diana is spied upon by Actaeon, and, in the sequel, he is metamorphosed into a stag; Callisto incurs Diana's wrath for becoming pregnant; Jupiter rapes Europa in the form of a bull; and, most famously, Venus tries to seduce Adonis—a painting that was dispatched to the king in London in 1554 at the time of his wedding to Queen Mary. It was copied in Titian's workshop on numerous occasions. For Titian and his peers, *poesie* and the pagan gods went hand in hand. His brush relished the flesh of both gods and humans. The royal eye was duly enchanted.

The contrast with Puritan iconoclasm could not be starker. Reformation ideology took to an extreme a hostile stance towards antique fables that Giorgio Vasari saw as the inevitable consequence of the coming of Christianity. In the preface to his *Lives of the Artists*, Vasari argued that "the fervent enthusiasm of the new Christian religion" inflicted "incomparably greater damage and loss on the arts" than the Visigoth invasions or the removal of the Emperor Constantine from Rome to Byzantium:

> After long and bloody combat, Christianity, aided by a host of miracles and the burning sincerity of its adherents, defeated and wiped out the old faith of the pagans. Then with great fervor and diligence it strove to cast out and utterly destroy every last possible occasion of sin; and in doing so it ruined or demolished all the marvelous statues, besides the other sculptures, the pictures, mosaics and ornaments representing the false pagan gods.[21]

The playful, polymorphous, polyamorous pagan gods were the very antithesis of Christianity's conception of the divine. In this respect, the iconoclasm of the Reformation was but a continuation and amplification of a process begun centuries before.[22] Those painters and poets who located the source of their creative imagination in the gods and fables of classical antiquity inevitably found themselves at odds with that iconoclasm.[23]

Shakespeare was not allowed to portray the Christian God on stage. He probably would not have wished to. His fascination with the human passions was such that pagan polytheism suited him well. He was interested in Juno as wronged wife, Venus as embodiment of erotic desire, Apollo as patron of art, Mercury as fleet-footed force of communication, and in the abusive power of the Jupiter to whom Falstaff comically compares himself in *The Merry Wives of Windsor*: becoming "a swan for the love of Leda" and "a bull for thy Europa."[24] Shakespeare loved to ring the changes on the old stories. To imagine a scene in which "Apollo flies, and Daphne holds the chase" (Helena in *A Midsummer Night's Dream*). To transpose the "heavy descension" from "a god to a bull" to the "low transformation" from "a prince to a prentice" (Prince Hal in *Henry IV Part 2*). To create a "Ganymede" who is female and in control of her destiny, instead of a boy who is abducted and made a catamite (Rosalind in *As You Like It*).

Or indeed to imagine a newly married couple enjoying sex by mutual consent as opposed to a god raping a girl: "he hath not yet made wanton the night with her, and she is sport for Jove" (Iago jealously imagining Othello and Desdemona consummating their love).[25] In order to create these imaginative variations, he required his audience to hold the antique fables in their minds. He accordingly wanted nothing to do with those polemical writers who made it their business to wipe out the memory of the pagan gods.

In Shakespeare's childhood, the homiletic message preached from the pulpit of Holy Trinity Church was the need to hold the commandments of God and the example of Christ constantly in mind, whereas the lesson learned from the Ovid first read in school was that the only constant is change. Shakespeare grew up to relish quick, bright changes as opposed to steadfast piety. Again and again, the metaphors and verb choices that he deployed in his allusions to the Ovidian fables evoke antique figures in motion.

The rhetorical term for this device was *energeia*. Sir Philip Sidney considered it a prime example of what he called the "forcibleness" of great writing.[26] Though some Renaissance theorists conflated or confused the two terms (both coined by Aristotle), *energeia* is distinct from *enargeia*, a key concept in Quintilian's classic account of the power of imagination: the orator, poet, or actor who has the gift (or skill) of *enargeia* will make the audience feel that they are not so much hearing as witnessing "the actual scene." The listener's "emotions will be no less actively stirred than if we were present at the actual occurrence."[27] Quintilian continues, in a later passage: "The speaker stimulates us by the animation of his delivery and kindles the imagination not by presenting us with an elaborate picture but by bringing us into actual touch with the things themselves; then all is life and movement and we receive the newborn offspring of his imagination with enthusiastic approval."[28] It is in these terms that Hamlet praises the player's ability to weep for the fictional Hecuba even as he castigates himself for failing to respond sufficiently powerfully to his own father's death.

Enargeia suggests the poet's ability to create visual images in the imagination of the reader or listener. It is thus in the same territory as Horace's memorable idea that poetry is like painting: *ut pictura poesis.*[29] *Energeia* is associated more with dynamism and motion. As one critic puts it, the terms "name a distinction between visuality and vitality, between clarity and energy."[30] Shakespeare's engagement with the classical tradition was at its most characteristic in the fusion of *enargeia* and *energeia*. He conjures images everywhere (*enargeia*), but he is at his most vital when he creates motion (*energeia*). Often this is when his classicism is playful and erotic, under the influence of Ovid.

The spirited pace of the *Metamorphoses* perhaps owes more to *energeia* than any other trope. A classic instance would be the closing line of the second book, where Europa is carried across the sea on the back of the bull-transformed Jupiter, her fluttering clothes twisting behind her in the breeze. Ovid's Latin, as so often, has supreme verbal economy. The image requires just four words: "tremulae sinuantur flamine vestes" (trembling clothes sinuous in the breeze).[31] Arthur Golding's English translation, the one known to Shakespeare, is less nimble and accordingly fails to catch the breezy motion: "The weather flaskt and whisked up hir garments being slacke."[32]

Clothing in Ovid is nearly always moving (and often being removed), but Poliziano and Botticelli recognized that his supreme example of *energeia* was the motion of hair. Poliziano imitated it, seeking to outdo his master, in poetry. Botticelli tried to capture it in still image. Shakespeare, intrigued by the capacity of poetry to outdo painting in its representation of figures in motion, was especially interested in hair. Cleopatra wants to know the colour of Octavia's hair in order to find out whether she is sexy or not. Golden hair is jokingly sexy and black hair ugly in *The Comedy of Errors* and *As You Like It*, and, famously, Shakespeare parodies the conventions of the love sonnet by way of "If hairs be wires, black wires grow on her head" in Sonnet 130. It is worth recalling that the wigmaker was a very important figure in the Elizabethan theatre. Indeed, at a key point in the middle of his career, Shakespeare took lodgings with a wigmaker—Mrs Mountjoy made wigs for the Court, and she may well also have done so for the theatre.

Shakespeare has his moments of formal *ekphrasis*—poetry about painting—in *Lucrece*, *Cymbeline*, and elsewhere, but it is *ekphrastic moments in motion* that are one of the key animating elements of his drama.[33] The effect is achieved through his particular gift of combining *enargeia* with *energeia*, conjuring the illusion of movement in a still image. Consider the attempt to stimulate the sexual imagination of Christopher Sly in *The Taming of the Shrew*:

> Dost thou love pictures? We will fetch thee straight
> Adonis painted by a running brook,
> And Cytherea all in sedges hid,
> Which seem to move and wanton with her breath,
> Even as the waving sedges play with wind.[34]

Running is the traditional posture of the hunter Adonis; here the epithet is transferred to the flow of water; breath and wind are then fused, wafting the sedges so that they subliminally merge with Venus's (Cytherea's) hair. A real picture—even one as great as Titian's *Venus and Adonis*—would freeze the moment, whereas Shakespeare's poetry creates a mental image of movement.

This is what in the next speech is called "lively" painting, the adverb suggesting not only "lifelike" but also "energetically":

> We'll show thee Io as she was a maid,
> And how she was beguilèd and surprised,
> As lively painted as the deed was done.[35]

It is a mistake to suppose that in these Ovidian images Shakespeare is necessarily describing paintings or other visual representations that he actually knew, not least because there are literary precedents—most notably Lyly's *Campaspe*—for the *topos* of a stage tour of an imaginary picture gallery displaying the erotic caperings of the pagan gods.[36] Of course, he may have been inspired by images he saw. Borachio's reference in *Much Ado about Nothing* to "the shaven Hercules in the smirched worm-eaten tapestry, where his codpiece seems as massy as his club" is a reminder that classical scenes were commonplace in Elizabethan tapestries and chimney-pieces.[37] When Shakespeare's acting company played at court and the Inns of Court, or in aristocratic houses, they would have seen paintings of mythological subjects on the walls. Essex House, for example, where there were private performances, displayed at least two pictures of Diana and Actaeon, two of Venus and Cupid.[38]

Shakespeare had ample opportunities to see images of Venus and Adonis, Venus and Mars, Apollo and Daphne, and the rest, without crossing the Channel. Attempts to match the "wanton pictures" in the *Shrew* Induction to particular Italian paintings have sometimes led conspiracy theorists along the primrose path to the anti-Stratfordian claim that the author of the play must have visited the Palazzo Te in Mantua, where Giulio Romano did his finest erotic Ovidian work.[39] That said, the naming of Giulio Romano as the sculptor of Hermione's statue in *The Winter's Tale* has never been fully explained. Vasari ranked Romano as one of the greats, alongside Michelangelo and Raphael. But Vasari was not available in English. There are passing references to Giulio in various books that Shakespeare might have known, and there is also the possibility of knowledge being picked up from a more learned colleague ("Give us the name of an Italian artist, Ben"). Jonson referred in his Venetian play, *Volpone*, to the pornographic sonnets of Aretino, which were accompanied by explicit images, drawn by Giulio, of an array of athletic sexual "postures."[40] In *Cymbeline*, Iachimo (who also delivers an erotically charged *ekphrasis*) speaks of unnatural "postures" in the context of "the shrine of Venus"; Cleopatra imagines a boy-actor impersonating her "i' the posture of a whore." Could it be that when Leontes describes Giulio Romano's statue as reproducing Hermione in "Her natural posture," Shakespeare is deliberately reversing the association of Romano with "unnatural" or "wanton" sexual postures, restoring the art of love to a purity that befits his redemptive ending?[41]

The purpose of the *ekphrasis* in the Induction of *Shrew* is not, however, to evoke particular paintings but to conjure up images in the imagination—of Sly and of the theatre audience—and then to bring them to life in a manner analogous to the way in which an actor brings a character to life. "Lively" acting is "lively painting" in three dimensions, with both motion and emotion. Julia in *The Two Gentlemen of Verona*, remembering (or inventing) her own performance as Ariadne in the Whitsun pastorals, claims that the part was "so lively acted" with tears that it created sympathetic weeping in her exemplary spectator.[42]

These examples are from the beginning of Shakespeare's career. Towards the end, Hermione's statue is equally "lively" and full of seeming "motion."[43] Motion creates emotion. Can a painting create motion? That is the question asked of the picture that is "Fair Portia's counterfeit" in *The Merchant of Venice*:

> What demigod
> Hath come so near creation? Move these eyes?

Or whether, riding on the balls of mine,
Seem they in motion? Here are severed lips
Parted with sugar breath, so sweet a bar
Should sunder such sweet friends. Here in her hairs
The painter plays the spider, and hath woven
A golden mesh t' entrap the hearts of men
Faster than gnats in cobwebs.[44]

The painter has no choice but to freeze the moment, capture the gnat in the cobweb. The poet's eye and the actor's voice, by contrast, can move with the dizzying speed of the gnat. As the actor uses his breath to speak the fluid rhythm of the enjambed pentameter, Shakespeare evokes in the imagination of his listeners the very movement not only of hair but also of "sugar breath" itself.

There is a strong probability that around the time he wrote this delicately woven and freshly animated *poesis* of a *pictura*, Shakespeare contributed the debate between Hieronimo and the Painter to his company's revision of Thomas Kyd's *The Spanish Tragedy*.[45] Here Shakespeare self-consciously challenges the idea that poetry is *like* painting.[46] No, he says, poetry can outdo painting by bringing the moment to life and to motion. Hieronimo asks his interlocutor, "Art a painter? Canst paint me a tear, or a wound, / A groan, or a sigh? Canst paint me such a tree as this?"[47] The claim is that the poetic dramatist can embody and enliven a tear, a wound, a groan, a sigh, the motion of a tree, in a way that the painter cannot.

The hair of Lucrece plays with her breath "like golden threads."[48] The horse in *Venus and Adonis* "vails his tail that like a falling plume / Cool shadow to his melting buttock lent."[49] And, in a moment that almost reads as Botticelli's *Birth of Venus* brought to life and motion, Venus says,

Bid me discourse, I will enchant thine ear,
Or like a fairy trip upon the green,
Or like a nymph with long dishevelled hair
Dance on the sands and yet no footing seen.
Love is a spirit all compact of fire,
Not gross to sink, but light and will aspire.[50]

These lines owe their enchantment to the way in which they are "all compact" of *enargeia* and *energeia*. They offer a momentary glimpse of magical motion, conjured into the mind of the listener or reader, then vanishing like Prospero's insubstantial pageant. The image of the dancing nymph who leaves no footprint on the sand was perhaps one of the inspirations of Percy Shelley's image of the divine spirit of poetry as an "evanescent visitation" with footsteps like those of the wind over the sea, whose "traces remain only as on the wrinkled sand which paves it."[51]

In 1593–94, the very period when he published *Venus and Adonis* and *The Rape of Lucrece*, the Stratford-born printer Richard Field was preparing a much larger book: an English translation of the six books of *Politicorum sive civilis doctrinæ* (*Politics or Civil Doctrine*) by Justus Lipsius, the Flemish philosopher and political theorist who sought to reconcile Christian doctrine with the Stoic wisdom of Cicero and Seneca. Lipsius set himself the task of gathering what he called the "certaine sparkles" of divine truth that "lye scattered here and there in prophane authors." This led him to a definition of God, derived from Cicero's *Tusculan Disputations*, as "A certaine spirit, or intelligence, which is free and in the greatest libertie, separate from all mortall and elementarie frame, and composition, giving all things life and moving, being not moved by any, but of it selfe in continuall motion."[52] There is no reason to believe that Shakespeare pored over Field's edition of the *Politics* of Lipsius, but there is something profoundly Shakespearean in this sense that by the "divine" we mean an animating intelligence, a spirit of freedom and especially of *continuall motion*.

The vital motion of Venus's hair worked for Aby Warburg as an image of how art endures and recreates across time, of how the particular speaks to the general, and of how "the poet's eye" may keep alive the dreams and visions that delighted the past and offer ways of seeing that take us beyond the constraints of our present. In the same spirit, this book seeks to augment our understanding of Shakespeare's quick-witted and fast-paced reanimation of the powers of the classical imagination, not least in order to celebrate a form of divinity that we may soon no longer appreciate or even understand.

3

RESEMBLANCE BY EXAMPLE

SHAKESPEARE'S SCHOOLING WAS SATURATED in the stories, character types, and literary genres of classical antiquity. Even more fundamentally, the public discourse of the age was based on the verbal skills that he was taught in the grammar school: the persuasive use of words, the elaboration of linguistic figures, the ability to argue both sides of a case. This art of rhetoric provided him, as it provided all his contemporaries, with the building blocks of his literary achievement. Rhetorical composition was his technique, his mode of writing.[1]

The core principles of rhetoric were much more profound, and more important to Shakespeare, than was the surface art of "ornament" that tended to dominate the style manuals of his age. He was far too clever to be content with the elaboration of ingenious verbal tropes and schemes to which this ancient art was often reduced in the schoolroom, in handbooks, and for that matter in some of the most popular literary works of his youth, notably the novels and plays of John Lyly. Rhetoric was the making of Shakespeare, but he also rejoiced in the parodying of pedantic figurative rhetoric.

When his characters speak of "figures," it is usually with comic intent. "It is a figure in rhetoric that drink, being poured out of cup into a glass, by filling the one doth empty the other," says Touchstone. The comedy comes from the statement of the very obvious in a formula that is very elaborate. And then there is Polonius, the exemplar of rhetoric art without substantive matter: "That he's mad, 'tis true, 'tis true 'tis pity, / And pity 'tis 'tis true: A foolish figure!" Quite so. Windy-worded Hotspur "apprehends a world of figures here, / But not the form of what he should attend," while Holofernes the pedant is full of figures: "This is a gift that I have, simple, simple; a foolish extravagant spirit, full of forms, figures, shapes, objects, ideas, apprehensions, motions, revolutions: these are begot in the ventricle of memory, nourished in the womb of pia mater, and de-

livered upon the mellowing of occasion."[2] And Berowne learns to
renounce them:

> O, never will I trust to speeches penned,
> Nor to the motion of a schoolboy's tongue ...
> Taffeta phrases, silken terms precise,
> Three-piled hyperboles, spruce affectation,
> Figures pedantical; these summer-flies
> Have blown me full of maggot ostentation:
> I do forswear them.[3]

And then there is the delicious verbosity of Don Armado, whose love
letter to the dairymaid Jaquenetta takes the question and answer
technique of rhetoric to something of an extreme:

> The magnanimous and most illustrate king Cophetua set eye upon
> the pernicious and indubitate beggar Zenelophon, and he it was that
> might rightly say, *Veni, vidi, vici*, which to annothanize in the vulgar,
> —O base and obscure vulgar!—*videlicet*, he came, see and overcame,
> He came, one; see, two; overcame, three. Who came? The king. Why
> did he come? To see. Why did he see? To overcome. To whom came
> he? To the beggar. What saw he? The beggar. Who overcame he? The
> beggar. The conclusion is victory. On whose side? The king's. The
> captive is enriched. On whose side? The beggar's. The catastrophe is
> a nuptial. On whose side? The king's. No, on both in one, or one in
> both. I am the king, for so stands the comparison: thou the beggar;
> for so witnesseth thy lowliness.[4]

Love's Labour's Lost might just as well have been called "rhetoric's
labours lost." It is passages such as this that come to the minds of
most playgoers and students when we speak of Shakespeare and
rhetoric. But the ornamental figures are just the froth on the surface.
Shakespeare mocks them precisely because they are a distraction
from the true substance of rhetorical art.

"*What is Rhetorique?*" "*Rhetorique* is an Arte to set foorth by
utteraunce of words, matter at large, or (as *Cicero* doth say) it is a
learned, or rather an artificiall declaration of the mynd, in the handling of any cause, called in contention, that may through reason
largely be discussed." Rhetoric is a tool for debate. What is "*The matter whereupon an Oratour must speake*"? "An Orator must be able to
speake fully of al those questions, which by lawe & mans ordinance

are enacted, and appointed for the use and profite of man, such as are thought apt for the tongue to set forwarde." What questions would these be? "Every question or demaund in things, is of two sortes. Either it is an infinite question, & without end, or els it is definite, and comprehended within some ende." Infinite questions are those that are not bounded by time, place, or person: the perennial questions for gentlemen such as "whether it be best to marrie, or to live single" and "Which is better, a courtiers life, or a Scholers life." Definite questions, by contrast, are those that are more historically specific, such as "Whether now it be best here in Englande, for a Priest to Marrie, or to live single" and "Whether it were meete for the [queen's] Majestie that nowe is, to marrie with a stranger, or to marrie with one of [her] owne Subjects." Such well-defined questions are "most agreeing to the purpose of an Orator" because they hone the art of debate, "the one affirming for his parte, and the other denying as fast againe for his parte."[5] A good rhetorician would be equally adept arguing both for and against the same proposition, *in utramque partem*.[6]

These precepts are to be found at the beginning of Thomas Wilson's *The Art of Rhetoric* (1560). This was the first vernacular treatise on a subject that had a history going back via Erasmus and Vives in the early sixteenth-century humanist educational revolution, through Quintilian and Cicero, to Aristotle and ultimately the Sophists of ancient Athens. The famous Sophist Gorgias said that a successful rhetorician could speak convincingly on any topic, regardless of his experience in that field. If you are a good enough orator, you can argue that Helen of Troy was not to blame for the start of the Trojan war. That was the kind of irresponsible line of argument of which Plato thoroughly disapproved. His strictures upon rhetoric led in turn to Aristotle's defence and codification of the art of rhetoric. And so the story continued through the centuries.[7]

What is rhetoric? It is, as Wilson has it, "the declaration of the mind" in persuasive, well-organized, and memorable words. What is the appropriate subject matter for rhetoric? Any question that is of "use and profit" for humankind. What kind of questions? Ultimately unanswerable (or "infinite") ones, such as the relative merits of the active and the contemplative life, or of the married and the single life. Certainly, too, such unanswerables as Hamlet's "To be or not to be, that is the question"—or, as William James rephrased the question, "Is life worth living?"[8] But also answerable (or "finite") ones, such as the religious question of priestly celibacy and the political one of royal marriages.[9] And especially legal questions. Lawyers—who resided in the Inns of Court and of Chancery, and many of whom attended the theatres, or commissioned special performances from Shakespeare's acting company, were trained in the art of rhetoric because it taught them the necessary skill of arguing on behalf of either a plaintiff or a defendant. The purpose of rhetoric was to be *persuasive*. Ever since Aristotle, it had been agreed that the successful rhetorician will "be able to reason logically, to understand human characters and excellences, and to understand the emotions."[10]

Once one sees rhetoric in these terms, it becomes clear that it is Shakespeare's essential tool. His plays explore all the big questions, such as the pros and cons of marriage, the rights and wrongs of monarchical behaviour, the case for and against revenge, the weighing of justice and mercy, the relationship between public and private selves. His characters are orators, each using language to affirm for his part as another denies as fast again for her part. Shakespeare's rhetoric runs the gamut from the razor-sharp banter of Beatrice and Benedick in *Much Ado about Nothing* to the formal orations of Brutus and Mark Antony in *Julius Caesar* to Hamlet's restless asking of the "infinite" questions.

Aristotle divided rhetoric into three classes, each of them appropriate for a particular purpose: *forensic* rhetoric for legal cases, *epideictic* rhetoric (the language of praise), which was especially useful for public ceremonies, and *deliberative* rhetoric.[11] We still have the English word "deliberate": it means to think carefully, to ponder a question, to weigh a case. For Aristotle and his most influential successor, Cicero in ancient Rome, deliberative rhetoric took place in the political arena: its purpose was to offer counsel about appropriate actions in pursuit of the public good.

Deliberation relied especially on a technique whereby an argument was made using examples from the past to predict future outcomes in order to illustrate that a given policy or action would be either harmful or beneficial. Aristotle made a key distinction when he wrote that "enthymemes are most suitable to forensic speeches" (the enthymeme is a form of syllogism, a mode of argument relying on logic), whereas "examples are most suitable to deliberative speeches; for we judge of future events by divination from past events."[12] Examples, for which Aristotle's Greek word was *paradeigmata*, are of two kinds: the mention of actual past facts (that is to say, historical examples) and the invention of facts by the speaker. Of the latter, there are two kinds: "the illustrative parallel and the fable (for example, the fables of Aesop)."[13]

The centrality of "examples" to deliberative rhetoric explains why in his rhetorical treatise *The Arte of English Poesie*, written just at the time Shakespeare was beginning his career in the theatre, George Puttenham gives a climactic place to the technique:

> **Paradigma, or a resemblance by example:** Finally, if in matter of counsell or perswasion we will seeme to liken one case to another, such as passe ordinarily in mans affaires, and doe compare the past with the present, gathering probabilitie of like successe to come in the things wee have presently in hand: or if ye will draw the judgements precedent and authorized by antiquitie as veritable, and peradventure fayned and imagined for some purpose, into similitude or dissimilitude with our present actions and affaires, it is called resemblance by example: as if one should say thus, Alexander the great in his expedition to Asia did thus, so did Hanniball comming into Spaine, so did Cæsar in Egypt, therfore all great Captains & Generals ought to doe it.[14]

Shakespeare parodies the pedantic use of the figure of *paradigma* as a form of argument when Fluellen compares King Henry V to Alexander the Great: "If you mark Alexander's life well, Harry of Monmouth's life is come after it indifferent well, for there is figures in all things."[15] The parody comes with such comparisons as Macedon and Monmouth both having rivers and there being "salmons in both."[16]

By contrast, when Titus Andronicus reads his daughter's fate through the memory of Ovid's Philomel, Shakespeare signals that "resemblance by example"—comparing "the past with the present" and drawing "judgements precedent and authorized by antiquity as veritable"—is one of his principal methods of storytelling. He would have agreed with Puttenham that "no one thing more prevaileth with all ordinary judgements than persuasion by *similitude*"—and that, if properly used, there is no more powerful similitude than a comparison with an exemplar from the past.[17] Such an art is applicable in any public forum, not merely a court or council, senate or parliament. Deliberative rhetoric thus had a very wide application. And in Shakespeare's London, the theatre was a new and democratic space for open debate about both public goods and private lives.

One might even go so far as to say that all the plays of Shakespeare and his contemporaries were exercises in deliberative rhetoric, in which the audience was invited to make up their own minds on matters of morality and politics.[18]

Shakespeare practiced the deliberative technique in almost everything he wrote. It is in this sense that his imagination was shaped by the art of rhetoric in general and "divination" from the classical past in particular. He learned the art in school, then heard and spoke it in action when he became an actor. No one was better at it than Christopher Marlowe, from whom he learned so much. To take a random example: when old Mortimer in *Edward II* reassures his son that he shouldn't worry about the young king's infatuation with Piers Gaveston because homosexuality is a phase he will grow out of, he makes his point by listing a string of classical exemplars:

> The mightiest kings have had their minions:
> Great Alexander loved Hephaestion;
> The conquering Hercules for Hylas wept;
> And for Patroclus stern Achilles drooped;
> And not kings only, but the wisest men.
> The Roman Tully loved Octavius;
> Great Socrates, wild Alcibiades.[19]

Uncomfortable as it was for strict Protestants schooled in the Biblical anathematizing of sodomy, these exemplary male-male pairings were familiar to anyone with a rudimentary classical education.

The uses of history, of illustrative parallel, of tale and fable: these were key weapons in Shakespeare's rhetorical armoury. More than this, at a very profound level, Shakespeare constructed his characters' selves by means of what I would describe as a *personalised rhetoric of illustrative parallel*. Let me demonstrate what I mean by considering the case of his most famous character, Hamlet.

The first occurrence in the play of the word "Hamlet" occurs during the opening scene, when Horatio names the ghost who has initially been identified as bearing "that fair and warlike form / In which the majesty of buried Denmark / Did sometimes march."[20] Horatio describes the dead king as "our valiant Hamlet."[21] The ghost appears to be wearing the very armour in which he killed old Fortinbras on the battlefield, in a war between Denmark and Norway. Old King Hamlet is thus set up as the archetype of the warrior hero. The audience then learns that there is also a "young Hamlet."[22] Horatio says they will go and tell him about his father's ghost.

The ghost—in a very literal sense, a figure from the past—is thus not only Hamlet's father, but also his paradigm, his illustrative parallel. However, when we see young Hamlet in the next scene, he is anything but a warrior hero. He is wearing black, which is not only a signal that he is still mourning when the rest of the court is not, but also the habitual dress of the melancholy man, the very opposite of the man of action. In addition, he is identified as a student, a scholar: a man of thought rather than action. And as a lover: Polonius believes that Hamlet is suffering specifically from love-melancholy, the malady of unrequited desire. In *The Anatomy of Melancholy*, Robert Burton would write of it symptoms: distraction, loss of appetite, sleeplessness, a disheveled appearance—exactly the way Hamlet represents himself to Ophelia.[23]

When the actors arrive later in the action, Shakespeare reminds his audience of the way that plays depend on character types: "He that plays the king shall be welcome: his Majesty shall have tribute of me; the adventurous knight shall use his foil and target; the lover shall not sigh gratis; the humorous man shall end his part in peace; the clown shall make those laugh whose lungs are tickle o' th' sere."[24] For the audience of *Hamlet*, these character types constitute a ready set of illustrative parallels within the theatrical repertoire: paradigms for the king, the warrior hero ("the adventurous knight"), the lover, the melancholy or "humorous" man, and the clown. The pleasure taken by Hamlet in his enumeration of these roles suggests that he quite fancies the idea of playing all of them—which in the course of the play he does, save that his reign as king lasts only a few seconds. But it also suggests that he does not know which role to play. Or, more precisely, that he detects a massive disjunction between the turmoil of his inner life and the public roles offered to him by history, custom, and theatrical example. As he says in his first substantial speech, "these indeed seem / For they are actions that a man might play; / But I have that within which passeth show."[25]

Hamlet cannot show us what he has within, but he can tell us. *Hamlet* is the play in which Shakespeare develops as never before the full art of soliloquy, the revelation of the individual mind to the listening audience. If we look at Hamlet's first soliloquy, we find that it is through the rhetorical art of illustrative parallel that he reveals himself. First he compares his father to his uncle, the old king to the new: "that was to this / Hyperion to a satyr."[26] Shakespeare expects his audience to know that Hyperion was the god of the sun (sometimes used as an alternative name for Apollo), the sun being the appropriate emblem for the majesty of a true king, and that a satyr was a mythical creature, half-man, half-goat, an emblem for the bestial element in man and especially for goatishness, which meant uncontrolled sexual desire. Then Hamlet compares Gertrude following her first husband to the grave to "Niobe, all tears."[27] Shakespeare expects his audience to know that Niobe was a mythical figure who wept uncontrollably for her many dead children, becoming "all tears"—but the audience would also know that Niobe then turned to stone, symbolically suggesting that after such grief she would forever be numb and incapable of further emotion. Here the comparison turns to contrast, in Puttenham's terms from similitude to dissimilitude: whereas Niobe turned cold, Gertrude has moved swiftly from watery tears to the heat of renewed sexual passion. Dissimilitude is also the ground of Hamlet's final illustrative parallel in his first soliloquy: Claudius, he says, is "no more like my father / Than I to Hercules."[28] Hercules was the archetypal action hero, the muscular demigod. "Hercules seemeth to be a general name, given to men excelling in strength all other of their time," noted an Elizabethan lexicographer.[29] By saying that he is not Hercules, Hamlet is identifying himself as a man of contemplation, not action, as a scholar and not a soldier.

Hamlet's method of thinking, then, is to find a paradigm in the repertoire of book learning that he has derived from his humanist education. The problem for a good student such as him is that there are so many possible models of behaviour that it is hard to choose between them. So, in his second soliloquy, he says that he will erase them all. He has just encountered the ghost, whose last words before disappearing were "remember me":

> Remember thee?
> Ay, thou poor ghost, while memory holds a seat
> In this distracted globe. Remember thee?
> Yea, from the table of my memory
> I'll wipe away all trivial fond records,
> All saws of books, all forms, all pressures past

That youth and observation copied there,
And thy commandment all alone shall live
Within the book and volume of my brain.[30]

"Saws of books" refers to the "sentences," the proverbial wisdom that one was supposed to write down in one's "table" or commonplace book—Polonius gives a whole list of them in his advice to Laertes ("neither a borrower nor a lender be," "to thine own self by true," and all that).[31] And among the "forms" and "pressures" past (mental impressions) would have been that repertoire of behavioural examples. Hamlet vows to wipe the slate clean and fill his mind with one image alone, that of his father's armoured ghost.

This creates a new problem for him. We need to remember here that Shakespeare's *Hamlet* was his distinctive reworking of an old tragedy of *Hamlet* that was in the repertoire at the beginning of his career. The old play is now lost, but the one thing that survives is the Ghost's catchphrase: it was "Hamlet, revenge!" Carried within that command is a rhetorical paradigm: if Hamlet were to ask "what do you mean by 'revenge'?" or "how shall I do it?," the answer would have been "behave like the past avengers you have read about or seen on stage"—classical literature and early modern drama are full of action heroes avenging their fathers' deaths. But by replacing the catchphase "Hamlet, revenge!" with "remember me," this ghost is depriving his son of his models and reducing him to brooding paralysis, since remembrance is a thought, not an action.[32]

So it is that in his next soliloquy Hamlet requires the stimulus of an actor to set him on the course of action. He witnesses the player weeping as he delivers a dramatic speech about Hecuba driven to madness by grief following the slaughter of her sons and her husband in Troy. The image of Hecuba is in itself a classical paradigm, but the presence of the Players adds a layer of complexity. The audience in the theatre witnesses the actor playing Hamlet witnessing the actor playing the actor playing the part of an actor in a play about the fall of Troy, describing Hecuba going out of her senses. The layers of performance are almost enough to make us go out of our senses, but at least the remembrance of the power of the imagined Hecuba play is enough to give Hamlet the inspiration for an action: namely, inserting a speech into another play in order to turn it into a "Mousetrap" to catch the conscience of King Claudius.

After Claudius's reaction to *The Murder of Gonzago* convinces Hamlet of his uncle's guilt, the young prince delivers another soliloquy in which he tries to turn himself into the embodiment of an avenger. The trouble is, he chooses the wrong paradigm. He should have remembered the revenge tradition that ran from Seneca's *Thyestes* to the drama of the 1590s and said something like "Let the soul of Atreus enter this firm bosom" or indeed "Let the soul of Andronicus enter this firm bosom." Instead, he says, "Let not ever / The soul of Nero enter this firm bosom." Tacitus and Suetonius had made Nero into the archetype of a tyrant: to mention his name is to summon up a paradigm for violent action. But Hamlet checks himself. Remembering in an instant that Nero secured his position by killing his mother, he modifies the comparison: "Let me be cruel," he says (that is to say, let me be like Nero), but then the modifier: "Let me be cruel, not unnatural" (that is to say, let me be unlike Nero—killing the person who gave birth to you is about the most unnatural thing imaginable). Hence Hamlet's conclusion: "I will speak daggers to her, but use none."[33] The personalised rhetoric of comparison and differentiation, similitude and dissimilitude, proceeds with the speed of thought.

Everywhere in Shakespeare, we find characters comparing themselves or others to figures from the mythology and history of Greek and Roman antiquity, in order to find positive or negative role models. What I am describing as his *personalisation* of deliberative rhetoric as a form of character creation does not always rely on *explicit* historical comparison. The technique of illustrative parallel can also be applied to a speaker's invention of his or her own imaginary past. Consider Lady Macbeth's scornful tirade of her husband, contrasting his backsliding with her resolution:

> I have given suck, and know
> How tender 'tis to love the babe that milks me.
> I would, while it was smiling in my face,
> Have plucked my nipple from his boneless gums
> And dashed the brains out, had I so sworn as you
> Have done to this.[34]

Our tendency on hearing this might be to ask a narrative question such as "how many children had Lady Macbeth?" But for Shakespeare and his audience, the speech is essentially a device of deliberative rhetoric. A past action is described: "I have given suck." The action is put to the service of an argument in favour of a future action: be a man and proceed with the bloody business. A supporting paradigm is then introduced in the form of an imagined history in the form of the past conditional image of a loving mother turned infanticide: "I would ... Have plucked my nipple ... And dashed the brains out." Notice how the delayed internal rhyme of "suck" and "plucked" links the two contrasting images of mothering. In processing the gruesome picture of a mother dashing out her baby's brains, rhetorically minded audience members of Shakespeare's original audience would have looked to the classical past for analogies. The obvious one would have been Medea: at the end of Seneca's tragedy about her, Medea, in furious vengeance for her husband Jason's infidelity, ascends the palace roof, kills their two children, and flings their bodies down to her husband below. Dashed brains indeed. At this point in Shakespeare's play, it seems to me that many of his original spectators would have thought "Lady Macbeth is turning into a Medea" rather than "are the Macbeths bereaved parents suffering from posttraumatic stress disorder?" (which is what Michael Fassbender and Marion Cotillard made them into in the 2015 film version of the play).

For further evidence that the memory of Seneca's *Medea* was knocking around in Shakespeare's brain while he was creating the character of Lady Macbeth, one only has to ask: which dark goddess presides over the "unsexing" of both women, their rejection of traditional female values? The answer is Hecate. Thomas Nashe famously mocked the author of "blood is a beggar" style plays for snaffling "whole Hamlets, I should say handfuls of tragical speeches" from English Seneca "read by candlelight."[35] It is not hard to imagine Shakespeare poring over some lines in which Seneca's Medea imagines an act of self-harm—mutilating her own breasts—as a way of embodying her unsexing. Here are the lines in the Elizabethan translation which Nashe had in mind:

> With naked breast and dugges layde out Ile pricke with sacred blad
> Myne arme, that for the bubling bloude an issue may bee made,
> With trilling streames my purple bloude let drop on th' aulter stones.
> My tender Childrens crusshed fleshe, and broken broosed bones
> Lerne how to brooke with hardned heart: in practise put the trade
> To florishe fearce, and keepe a coyle, with naked glittring blade.[36]

Given the decisive parallel in the concatenation of breast, dugs (nipples), and "children's crushed flesh and broken bruised bones," in the shared context of hardening the heart and committing oneself to the imagined dagger that leads one on to murder, we may say with some confidence that Medea was a "paradigm" for Lady Macbeth and that this is a formidable instance of the manner in which *paradigma* was one of the most frequently used weapons in Shakespeare's rhetorical armoury.[37]

Hamlet's naming of Nero brings the decadence of imperial Rome into paradigmatic play. But, as the Lady Macbeth example shows, the rhetorical use of the classical past for present and future political purposes does not always require a specific allusion. Late in the play, Hamlet adds to his roll call of charges against Claudius the claim that he "popped in between th' election and my hopes."[38] Most of Shakespeare's audience would have been very unlikely to know about the elective element in the Danish system of monarchical succession. But for those who had been to grammar school, the word "election" would in all probability have triggered a memory of one of the key themes of Livy and other Roman historians, which Shakespeare would place at the centre of *Coriolanus*: the role of the people's "voices" or "votes" in the election of consuls during the republican centuries between the expulsion of the Tarquins and the proclamation of Augustus as emperor.[39] Claudius confirms his Nero-like tyranny by way of his fear of the people (whether they be led by Laertes or Hamlet), whereas Hamlet's respect for the popular voice within the common weal is of a piece with his negative invocation of the soul of Nero. These allusions to the political vicissitudes of ancient Rome raise the question of the role of classical antiquity in shaping the politics of Shakespeare's age—and of his plays.

4

REPUBLICA ANGLORUM

IN THE DECADES BETWEEN THE BIRTH of John Shakespeare in about 1530 and the death of his son William in 1616, there was an unprecedented transformation in the role of poetry and drama in English culture. This change was a consequence of the increasing availability of printed books, but also of the birth of the popular theatre. And it was an essential part of the political self-analysis of the age.

The diplomat Thomas Smith, in an influential treatise on government written in the early 1560s and published posthumously in 1583, described the commonwealth of England, in true classical style, as the "Republica Anglorum."[1] But that commonwealth had a complex and many-layered structure. In the words of the historian Patrick Collinson, "Early modern England consisted of a series of overlapping, superimposed communities which were also semi-autonomous, self-governing political cultures. These may be called, but always in quotes, 'republics': village republics; in the counties, gentry republics; and at a transcendent level, the commonwealth of England, which Sir Thomas Smith thought it proper to render in Latin as *Republica Anglorum*."[2]

These "republics" were shaped not only by government, law, and social structure, but also through the images and ideas disseminated by the spoken and written word. Thus village republics were glued together by, for instance, the Homilies read from the pulpit of the parish church, while gentry republics were beginning to be dignified by county chorographies such as William Lambarde's *Perambulation of Kent*. Elizabethan writers and readers belonged to a series of overlapping, superimposed communities, each of which had its own distinctive literary styles and forms as well as shared habits of mind, values, and beliefs. To echo Collinson's terminology, these may be called, but always in quotes, "republics of letters": among them were Church of England, grammar school, university, Inns of Court, literate citizenry, country gentry household, aristocratic circle, and court. Most writers and readers belonged to at least three of these literary communities; for some, writing and reading were vehicles for moving into a more elite, prestigious "republic." The overlap between communities was especially visible in the public spaces of London, notably but not exclusively the new arena of the theatre. At the "transcendent level," by the end of Queen Elizabeth's reign, the commonwealth of England was, among other things, a "republic of letters" which derived its self-image from such sources as national history (Holinshed's *Chronicles*), national poetry (Spenser's *Faerie Queene*, Warner's *Albion's England*), and, partly for the benefit of the London unlettered, national drama (Shakespeare's history plays).

One of the most remarkable things about the writings of Shakespeare, especially given his lack of a university education, was the way in which they appealed to so many of the diverse reading and listening communities of his age. A grammar-school education was sufficient to allow him to create, even in the first few years of his literary career, the most popular poem among Oxbridge undergraduates (*Venus and Adonis*), a spectacular tragedy performed not only on the public stage but also in a gentleman's country household in Rutland (*Titus Andronicus*), a self-consciously classical comedy that appealed to the Inns of Court (*The Comedy of Errors*), and a chronicle history that brought cheers from thousands of London citizens (*Henry VI Part 1*).[3] As early as 1594, the reputation of his fellow-actors and the plays he wrote for them was such that they won the patronage of the Lord Chamberlain and, with it, regular invitations to play at court.

The only community of the word to which his poems and plays did not speak was the Church of England. And there's the rub. Imaginative writing—we call it "literature," whereas the Elizabethans called it "poesy" or "poetry"—was a key aspect of the process of nation building that was a core ambition of the Tudor regime and a consequence of King Henry VIII's break from Rome. The Elizabethans invented the idea of a distinctively national body of English literature.[4] Their extraordinary literary innovations—from national epic to biting satire to verse drama in the public theatre—were built on the classical tradition. In this respect, their model was ancient Rome. But because of the Reformation, their problem was modern Rome. And that created a tension with their inheritance from ancient Rome: the further the doctrinal shift from Catholicism, the greater the challenge to the free play of imagination and to creative delight in the world of pagan antiquity. Hence, for example, the contortions of Calvin's translator Arthur Golding in his attempt to "moralize" the stories of sex and violence in Ovid's *Metamorphoses*.[5]

Ever since Anglo-Saxon times, the English had told their national story in histories and legends, frequently drawing on comparisons with antiquity. In the late fourteenth century, Geoffrey Chaucer and John Gower defined themselves as national poets even as they imitated Italian and Roman models. Their double allegiance was unproblematic because until the early sixteenth century the polyglot literature of England was often explicitly and always implicitly part of something larger: the literature of Catholic Europe. This was especially true of the productions of those key literary communities, the monasteries. It was only after King Henry VIII dissolved the monasteries and proclaimed the supremacy of the English crown and the independence of the English church, that it became necessary to forge a new kind of national culture.

The process began as early as 1533, that year of such momentous events as Archbishop Cranmer's dissolution of the marriage with Catherine of Aragon, the King's marriage to Anne Boleyn and his pregnant bride's crowning as Queen, the fall of Sir Thomas More and the rise of Thomas Cromwell, and, not least, the Pope's excommunication of the Defender of the Faith. This was the year during which John Leland was commissioned to search the libraries of the cathedrals, abbeys, priories, and colleges of the land for evidence of the nation's antiquities and history. His exhaustive and exhausting antiquarian tour, extending to almost every corner of the kingdom, lasted into the early 1540s. He amassed a vast body of material and in 1545 dedicated to King Henry *A New Year's Gift*, in which he outlined his project. Though he gained substantial assistance from the radical protestant John Bale, Leland only ever succeeded in publishing odd fragments of the *Itinerary* of his research; the enormity of the task seems to have driven him out of his wits, and in 1550, a broken man, he was given over into the custody of his brother for safekeeping until his death.

Nevertheless, the groundwork was laid: as Livy's history (*Ab Urbe Condita Libri*) had served the Emperor Augustus by telling the story of Rome from its legendary foundation in 753 BCE to his own time, so Leland's successors would furnish Queen Elizabeth with a new history of England. His materials were acquired by London printer Reyner Wolfe, who hoped to create—and to publish in the English vernacular as opposed to the international (and Catholic) language of Latin[6]—a "Universal Cosmography of the whole world, and there with also certain particular histories of every known nation."[7] It was Wolfe who hired Raphael Holinshed and William Harrison to assist him in putting together the "particular histories" of the nations of the British Isles. The "Universal Cosmography" fell by the wayside, but the national history duly appeared in the *Chronicles* of 1577 and 1587. Holinshed was in effect the editor of "the English Livy"—and Shakespeare was the person who dramatized elements of those *Chronicles* more extensively and influentially than any other writer, making the nation's history available to the people of London, both literate and illiterate.

It was no coincidence that in the late sixteenth century the term "the nation" took on the meaning of "the collectivity of the people" and the word "national" entered the language, as did the grammatically absolute usage of "country" as a personification of the native land—as in Shakespeare's "Forgive me, country, and sweet countrymen."[8] In 1615, William Camden dedicated his *Annals* of Queen Elizabeth's reign to "God, my country, and posterity" ("DEO, PATRIAE, ET POSTERIS").[9] Such a trinity would have been inconceivable a century earlier. Both the notion of *patria* and the weight given to "posterity" are, again, marks of the influence of ancient Rome.

Nor was it coincidental that in the 1560s Laurence Nowell applied to chief minister William Cecil for aid in mapping the entire realm, county by county; in the next decade, Christopher Saxton completed the first comprehensive *Atlas* of England and Wales. The Elizabethans did not only "discover" new worlds across the ocean: they also discovered England. And, despite—or because of—a succession of rebellions and the constant persecution of Roman Catholic recusants, they unified England. By the end of the sixteenth century, the government's administrative machinery had put in place a nationwide network of civic and legal officers ultimately answerable to the crown, while the ecclesiastical settlement had established the supremacy of Anglicanism.[10]

Most importantly in relation to Shakespeare's place in his age, a national culture had come to full flower, thanks in large measure to the educational advances effected by the grammar schools, the translation into English of the foundation texts of Western culture (the Bible, Homer, and the major authors of classical Rome), the writing of national history, the increased availability of books of all kinds, and, for Londoners at least, the completely new cultural arena of the public playhouse. Anticipations of some of these individual factors may be found in earlier periods, but it was their concatenation in the aftermath of the break from Rome that marked the distinctively Elizabethan image of the nation. This said, it must be remembered that an idealized image is not a universal practice: the old religion persisted, as did many of the old cultural habits.[11] Thus Elizabethan England remained a script culture even as it became a print culture—and, for that matter, learned scholars such as Camden wrote in Latin as well as in English.

Ancient Rome derived its cultural identity from its poets as well as its historians such as Livy and its politicians such as Cicero. To be the true successor, whether as *republica* or *imperium*, Elizabethan England would accordingly need not only its *Chronicles* and *Annals* but also its poetic tradition, its equivalents of Virgil, Ovid, and Horace. To be properly classical, that tradition would have to be organized by genre.

Quintilian's *Institutio Oratoria* was at the heart of the humanist project: it exercised a profound influence on sixteenth-century thinking about how to achieve eloquence. It is structured for the most part as a treatise on the arts of rhetoric, but the tenth book concerns literary models. As a ship needs a steersman and an athlete a trainer, says Quintilian, so writers or public speakers need to develop their skill through their reading of literary exemplars. Read, he recommends, "reread a passage again and again if we are in doubt about it or wish to fix it in the memory," read the whole work and not merely the striking parts, inwardly digest, and then reread: "Our reading must be almost as thorough as if we were actually transcribing what we read."[12] And what we should read most often are the works of the best authors. Poets are high on the list, for they "give us inspiration as regards the matter, sublimity of language, the power to excite every kind of emotion, and the appropriate treatment of character." Furthermore, "Cicero recommends the relaxation provided by the reading of poetry."[13]

In enumerating the best poets for orators to have on their reading list, Quintilian proceeds by genre. Epic, known in the sixteenth century as *heroic* poetry, is preeminent, Homer being foundational for the Greeks, Virgil for the Romans. Then there is *elegiac* poetry, Callimachus best among the Greeks, Tibullus, Propertius, and Ovid among the Romans. Then *satire*, said to be uniquely Roman ("Satura quidem tota nostra est"—"satire indeed is entirely ours"),[14] with Horace and Persius as its exemplars. Horace is also lauded as the best for *lyric*, as Pindar was among the Greeks. In *tragedy*, according to Quintilian, the Romans had as yet failed to live up to the Greek example: Accius, Pacuvius, and Varius could not compare with Aeschylus, Sophocles, and Euripides (though Quintilian thought that it would have been a different matter if Ovid had continued writing tragedies in the vein of his—now lost—*Medea*, instead of indulging himself with eroticism). In *comedy*, too, Terence and Plautus were inferior to both the old Greek comedy of Aristophanes and the new of Menander, whom Quintilian regarded as the ideal author to read in order to discover human character and the texture of the everyday: "so perfect is his representation of actual life, so rich is his power of invention and his gift of style, so perfectly does he adapt himself to every kind of circumstance, character and emotion." In *history*, however, the Romans have the right to feel proud: Sallust is the equal of Thucydides, Livy of Herodotus.[15]

Quintilian, then, provided a model for those late sixteenth-century English writers who praised the new writing of their own age by way of similar comparative listings, ordered by genre. The usual approach was to enumerate eight genres, though there was varied belief as to what these were: the commonest classification, which we find in Sir Philip Sidney, then Francis Meres, was "Heroic, Lyric, Tragic, Comic, Satiric, Iambic, Elegiac, Pastoral."[16] This disposition derived from Horace's *Ars Poetica*, as refined by a Roman theorist of rhetoric called Caesius Bassus and enshrined in a popular mid-sixteenth-century humanist handbook published in Basel, Gyraldus's *Historia Poetarum tam Graecorum quam Latinorum*.[17] Quintilian was distinctive in excluding Pastoral and Iambic, but including History.[18] For Sidney and others, history was not a poetic genre because poesy was defined in opposition to history, offering a different kind of truth.

This vocabulary of literary "kinds" was widespread in late Elizabethan literary discourse. George Puttenham, for example, in his account of the origins of poetry in classical antiquity, wrote of how the ancient Greeks divided poets into the heroic, the lyric, the elegiac, and the epigrammatic. He also noted that there were poets who "wrote only for the stage ... to recreate the people with matters of disport"; these writers for the stage, he explained, were either comical—of which the most notable examples among the Greeks were Menander and Aristophanes, among the Latins Terence and Plautus—or they were tragical: "such were *Euripides* and *Sophocles* with the Greeks; *Seneca* among the Latins."[19]

In 1586, on the brink of Shakespeare's career, an Oxford-educated gentleman's tutor called William Webbe published *A Discourse of English Poetry*. It began with "A Preface to the Noble Poets of England" that observed the proliferation of recently published "English Books": the "infinite fardles of printed pamphlets, wherewith this country is pestered, all shops stuffed, and every study furnished." Webbe noted that the vast majority of these new low-cost publications were "poetical" in either matter or form—that is to say, they were works of fiction, of imagination, many of them written in verse. He made it his business to distinguish "between good writers and bad," to work out which of those among the "rude multitude of rustical rhymers who will be called Poets" actually practised "true Poetry." His "adventure" was to set down his "simple judgment of English Poetry."[20] Webbe professed that he would base his judgments on literary merit alone, not moral purport or dignity of matter: his *Discourse* is accordingly one of the earliest English works of what we now call literary criticism. His reasoning was that the humanist educators of the sixteenth century—from Colet, Erasmus, and More to Ascham in his *Schoolmaster*—had done sterling work in dignifying the national tongue, but that their principles had not yet been applied to poetry:

> Whereas all kind of good learning have aspired to royal dignity and stately grace in our English tongue, being not only founded, defended, maintained, and enlarged, but also purged from faults, weeded of errors, and polished from barbarousness, by men of great authority and judgment, only poetry have found fewest friends to amend it.[21]

"English Eloquence" was well established thanks to the humanist art of imitating the classics in moral, political, and historical discourses, but, for the most part, poets had "contented themselves with a base kind of fingering." Learning, argued Webbe, was by no means in a state of general decay in England, but poetry was held "in small price": the art of "versifying" was "rude," not to say "tinkerly," as witnessed by the way in which "the natural property of the sweet Latin verse" had been displaced by "a bald kind of rhyming." Poetry, in other words, was too vulgar, not to say dangerously lower class. Webbe was making the case for an elite "gentlemanly" poetry to match the emergent gentry class who were shaping the new English nation—people such as his patron Edward Sulyard, an Essex land-owner. In order to be truly dignified, English poetry would have to be "reformed" on classical principles. The analogy was overt: as the Protestant Reformation had got rid of the medieval accretions of the Catholic church and returned to a "pure" Biblical faith, so poetry would have to get rid of medieval inventions such as rhyme and re-turn to the pure quantitative metre of the ancients.

That was Webbe's thesis, laid out in his preface. The main body of his text began with a history of poetry organized, under the in-fluence of Quinitilian, by genre. It proceeds through the Greek and Roman traditions from the classical age down to the neo-Latin writ-ing of Palingenius and Mantuan. Webbe then turned his attention to the vernacular, and made an astonishingly bold assertion: "I know no memorable work written by any Poet in our English speech until twenty years past."[22] Admittedly he went on to establish a select canon of earlier poets—Gower, Chaucer, Lydgate, Skelton, and Surrey—but his main concern was to praise the new. He especially commended "those learned Gentlemen which took such profitable pains in translating the Latin Poets into our English tongue," notably Thomas Phaer for his version of the first seven books of Virgil's *Aeneid* (1558) and Arthur Golding for his Ovid's *Metamorphoses* (1567).[23] Spenser's *Shepheardes Calender* was held up as a model for the new English poetry, a foundation for the art of pastoral in imitation of the *Idylls* of Theocritus and the *Eclogues* of Virgil. But Virgil had pro-gressed from pastoral through georgic to epic. This, Webbe believed, was the necessary next step for English poetry: there was an urgent need for a national epic.

The idea of the *heroic* was central to his conception of the patri-otic role of poetry. "Heroical works," exemplified by Homer in Greek and Virgil in Latin, were, he claimed, "incomparably the best of all other," thanks to their representation of "the noble acts and valiant exploits of puissant captains, expert soldiers, wise men, with the famous reports of ancients times." As yet, he lamented, "we have no English work answerable in respect of the glorious ornaments of gallant handling, yet our Chroniclers and reporters of our Country affairs come most near them."[24] The source materials were there in the *Chronicles*, but they had not yet been turned into poetry. Webbe thought that John Lyly, who had mastered the art of eloquence in his *Euphues*, might be the man to do the job. The prediction was wrong: at this time, Lyly was turning his hand to court comedy. It was others—Warner in *Albion's England*, Spenser in *The Faerie Queene*, and Samuel Daniel in *The Barons' Wars*—who would develop the art of English heroical verse. The question of how Shakespeare related to this "heroic" tradition is one that I will address when I turn to Virgil in chapter 8.

Webbe also made a key innovation in his enumeration of the genres. Granting the variations between different sources, we may say that most Elizabethan literary theorists organized their new national literature into the broad categories of heroic poetry, elegy, satire, lyric, tragedy, comedy, pastoral, and history. But the *Discourse of English Poetry* made a significant innovation. Noting that there were "many sorts of poetical writings," but seeking to achieve "better understanding and briefer method," Webbe reduced the genres to just three: "Comical, Tragical, Historial."[25] In this arrangement, "*Epigrams, Elegies*, and delectable ditties" (the latter being synonymous with the genre of "lyric"), which Webbe describes as poems devised for the sole purpose of offering "delight," are subsumed within the category of comedy. Meanwhile, "whatsoever is poetically expressed in sorrow and heaviness" is placed in the domain of tragedy, and everything between the two is lumped together as history.

Webbe's move paved the way for John Hemmings and Henry Condell (in all probability with assistance from Ben Jonson) to classify Shakespeare's complete plays as *Comedies, Tragedies and Histories*. But his reduction of eight kinds to three also helps us to understand the fluidity of the Elizabethan conception of genre. It allows us, for example, to read *Venus and Adonis* and the *Sonnets* as comedy, *The Rape of Lucrece* and *A Lover's Complaint* as tragedy, even though their form is not dramatic.

In 1594, Shakespeare's *Tragedy of Titus Andronicus* went into print, and his *Comedy of Errors* was performed at Gray's Inn. In contrast to John Lyly, whose preeminence was in comedy, and Christopher Marlowe, whose greatness was in tragedy, Shakespeare was, "among the English," "most excellent in both kinds for the stage." These are the words of Oxford-educated Francis Meres, who in 1597 was lodging in Botolph Lane, Eastcheap, from where he kept a finger on the pulse of the contemporary literary scene. The following year he made this high claim for Shakespeare in the "Comparative Discourse of our English Poets, with the Greek, Latin, and Italian Poets" that he included in his book *Palladis Tamia: Wit's Treasury, being the Second part of Wit's Commonwealth*.[26] By comparing contemporary poets to classical and Italian Renaissance exemplars, Meres laid out a national literary canon. Eight English poets were identified as answering to eight great poets of ancient Greece and eight of Rome:

> As the Greek tongue is made famous and eloquent by Homer, Hesiod, Euripides, Aeschylus, Sophocles, Pindar, Phocylides and Aristophanes; and the Latin tongue by Virgil, Ovid, Horace, Silius Italicus, Lucanus, Lucretius, Ausonius and Claudianus: so the English tongue is mightily enriched and gorgeously invested in true ornaments and resplendent abiliments by Sir Philip Sidney, Spenser, Daniel, Drayton, Warner, Shakespeare, Marlowe and Chapman.[27]

"Abiliments" nicely implies both "abilities" and "dress"—an idea linked to notions of decorum that were of equal significance for social manners and the appropriate literary style for particular forms, occasions, and themes. Meres liked to think in eights: he enumerated "eight notable several kinds of poets" (that is to say, eight genres: heroic, lyric, tragic, comic, satiric, iambic, elegiac, and pastoral) and eight "famous and chief languages" (Hebrew, Greek, Latin, Syriac, Arabic, Italian, Spanish, and French). The reason he omitted his own language, English, from this list was that, like much of his book, the divisions were not his own but a borrowing from the *Officina* of J. Ravisius Textor.[28] In this sense, *Palladis Tamia* was an attempt to hold fresh patriotic claims together with the inherited wisdom of the European humanist tradition.

Meres was the first to give a "canonical" place to Shakespeare. At a time when both elite courtly and Puritan civic critics were expressing grave reservations about the vulgarity, licentiousness, and potential sedition of the theatre, it is remarkable to see Shakespeare and Marlowe hoisted into the company of Sidney and Spenser. For Meres, the wits who entered the marketplace by publishing their works or staging their plays commercially had earned their place in the commonwealth of England. They had dignified their nation by producing modern equivalents of the ancient classics: Sidney's *Arcadia* is taken to be a match for Xenophon's *Cyropaedia*, Spenser's *Shepheardes Calender* for the *Idylls* of Theocritus and his *Faerie Queene* for Homer's *Iliad*, Daniel's *Civil Wars* for Lucan's *Pharsalia*, Warner's *Albion's England* for the *Fasti* of Ausonius, Drayton's *Polyolbion* for the *Rudimentorum Cosmographicorum* of Joannes Honterus, and the works of William Shakespeare for a whole panoply of exemplars.[29]

Meres's particular praise of Shakespeare was his excellence across the genres or "kinds" of poesy:

> As the soule of Euphorbus was thought to live in Pythagoras: so the sweete wittie soule of Ovid lives in mellifluous and hony-tongued Shakespeare, witnes his *Venus and Adonis*, his *Lucrece*, his sugred *Sonnets* among his private friends, etc.
>
> As Plautus and Seneca are accounted the best for Comedy and Tragedy among the Latines: so Shakespeare among the English is the most excellent in both kinds for the stage. For Comedy, witnes his *Gentlemen of Verona*, his *Errors*, his *Love Labors Lost*, his *Love Labours Wonne*, his *Midsummers Night Dreame*, and his *Merchant of Venice*; For Tragedy, his *Richard the 2*, *Richard the 3*, *Henry the 4*, *King John*, *Titus Andronicus*, and his *Romeo and Juliet*.
>
> As Epius Stolo said that the Muses would speake with Plautus tongue if they would speak Latin: so I say that the Muses would speak with Shakespeares fine-filed phrase if they would speak English.[30]

Shakespeare is summoned as England's myriad-mused stylist. No other writer within the new nation's commonwealth of wits is credited with such range. For Meres, the grammar-school playwright without an Oxbridge degree is not only worthy of Seneca in tragedy and Plautus in comedy, but also the successor to Ovid in poetry, as exemplified by his *Venus and Adonis*, *Lucrece*, and the *Sonnets*.

Early readers took Shakespeare's poems to be Ovidian because their subject matter was Ovid's favourite theme: the power of erotic desire. As to the specific works that they emulate, Meres may be presumed to be associating *Venus and Adonis* with the *Metamorphoses* (its source), *Lucrece* with both the *Fasti* and the *Heroides* (the former its source, the latter the key precedent for the genre of female "complaint"), and the Sonnets with the *Amores* (the archetypal sequence of love-lyrics).[31] Their Ovidianism is above all attributed to their embodiment of the spirit of sweet wit, "mellifluous and hony-tongued" verbal play.

The metaphor of Shakespeare as a bee creating verbal honey was already becoming commonplace by 1598, as may be seen from Richard Barnfield's contemporaneous poem, "A Remembrance of some English Poets":

> And Shakespeare thou, whose hony-flowing Vaine,
> (Pleasing the World) thy Praises doth obtaine.
> Whose Venus, and whose Lucrece (sweete, and chaste)
> Thy Name in fames immortall Booke have plac't.[32]

Ever since antiquity, discourses on poetry and rhetoric had used the figure of the bee to represent not only verbal sweetness and flowing felicity, but also the successful art of assimilation. As a bee gathers pollen from many flowers and transforms them into its own honey, so the best writers emulate their sources but create works that are not servile to their origins. The bee is the opposite of the ape, which is the traditional figure for the poet who copies but does not assimilate.[33] In *Greene's Groatsworth of Wit* (1592), players in general and Shakespeare in particular are represented as "apes"—from English ape to Latinate *apis* is a nice image of the way in which Shakespeare's nondramatic poems transformed his reputation.

The desire to achieve literary respectability may have been a conscious riposte to Robert Greene's assault in his *Groatsworth* on "Shake-scene" as an "upstart crow" adorned with "borrowed plumes."[34] All but a tiny minority of scholars agree that "Shake-scene" is an allusion to Shakespeare, but it is hotly disputed as to whether the imagery of the "borrowed plumes" is intended to suggest copying, borrowing, imitation, even plagiarizing.[35] Greene, and other Elizabethans writers, were well aware of a passage in which Horace warned the poet Celsus "not to pilfer from other writers any longer, lest those he has robbed should return one day to claim their feathers, when like the crow [*cornicula*] stripped of its stolen splendour [*furtivus nudata coloribus*], he would become a laughing-stock."[36]

This passage is clearly fused with Aesop's crow in an earlier allusion of Greene's that is specifically about plagiarism:

> Your honor may thinke I play like Ezops Crowe, which deckt his selfe with others feathers, or like the proud poet *Batyllus*, which subscribed his name to Virgils verses, and yet presented them to Augustus. In the behalfe therefore of this my offence, I excuse my self with the answere that Varro made, when he offered Ennius workes to the Emperour: I give quoth he another man's picture but freshlie flourished with mine owne colours.[37]

At the same time, it must be remembered that Elizabethan ideas about novelty and indebtedness were very different from ours. Since the emergence of a poetics of "originality" in the late eighteenth century and the Romantic period, literary "imitation" has often been regarded as a sign of deficiency, whereas in the poetics of Shakespeare's time, *imitatio* of the acknowledged classics was a cardinal virtue.[38]

Meres was familiar with Shakespeare on both stage and page. He was the first to attribute to Shakespeare the play published anonymously in 1594 under the title *Titus Andronicus*, an invented story but one steeped in knowledge of, and allusions to, Roman literature and history. And he was just one of many late Elizabethan readers to express high admiration for the two narrative poems that were Shakespeare's first publications, printed with dedicatory epistles over the author's name. *Venus and Adonis* and *The Rape of Lucrece* established Shakespeare's reputation. They were the calling card with which he entered the commonwealth of wits. They exemplify the rival traditions of comedy and tragedy, myth and history, levity and gravity, youthful invention and graver labour, the Ovidian and the Virgilian.

About a year after the publication of *Palladis Tamia*, a more subtle discourse on the flowering of poetry in late Elizabethan England was written by an Inner Temple law student called William Scott. Entitled "The Modell of Poesye Or The Arte of Poesye drawn into a short or Summary Discourse," it was unknown to Shakespeare scholars until the twenty-first century.[39] Scott begins with the traditional classical view of the nature of poetry, bringing together the key terms of imitation, feigning, delighting, teaching, and moving, while also following Sir Philip Sidney's adoption of the *ut pictura poesis* trope derived from Horace and ultimately Simonides:

> All antiquity, following their great leader Aristotle, have defined poetry to be an art of imitation, or an instrument of reason, that consists in laying down the rules and way how in style to feign or represent things, with delight to teach to move us to good; as if one should say with the lyric Simonides (after whom Sir Philip Sidney saith) the poem is a speaking or wordish picture.[40]

Having established his terms, Scott focuses on two aspects of poetic art: first, the "kinds," among which he enumerates the Heroical or Epic, Pastoral, Tragedy, Comedy, Satire, and Lyric ("wherein we imitate and discover our affections"); and then, with many examples both classical and contemporary, the techniques of good writing, which he defines in terms of "proportionableness" (that is to say, propriety or decorum of language in relation to subject matter), "variety," "sweetness" (that term which was so often applied to Shakespeare), and lastly, following Sidney's *Defence*, that "*energeia*, force effectualness, or vigour, which is the character of passion and life of persuasion and motion."[41]

The supporting structure for the achievement of "elegancy of style" is rhetorical skill. Shakespeare is cited both positively and negatively in this regard. Thus Scott finds paradoxical propriety in a particular image in *Richard II*: "Sometime the person shall be so plunged into the passion of sorrow that he will even forget his sorrow and seem to entertain his hardest fortune with dalliance and sport, as in the very well-penned tragedy of *Richard the Second* is expressed in the King and Queen whilst 'They play the wantons with their woes.'" And John of Gaunt in the same play has a speech exemplifying admirable rhetorical amplification: "Sometimes our amplification is by heaping our words, and as it were piling one phrase upon another of the same sense, to double and redouble our blows, that by varying and reiterating may work into the mind of the reader." But there is criticism as well as praise. Scott finds an inelegant redundancy at one point in *The Rape of Lucrece*: "you must not have idle attributes only to fill up your meter (saith Scaliger): 'The endless date of neverending woe,' a very idle, stuffed verse in that very well-penned poem of *Lucrece her rape*."[42] The line is singled out precisely because it is a weak link in a generally very strong poem. There were precedents for treating Sir Philip Sidney and Edmund Spenser as exemplars of classical poetic art, but Scott seems to have been the first to give Shakespeare "classic" status by way of specific citations of his verbal skill and in particular his *energeia*.

By the end of the 1590s, then, the grammar-school boy from the provinces had established himself as one of the commonwealth of England's true "touchstones of wit."[43] Copious extracts from his plays and poems were to be found, alongside samples of more "heroical" poets such as Edmund Spenser and Sir John Harington, the translator of Ariosto, in such anthologies as *England's Parnassus; or, The Choicest Flowers of our Modern Poets* and *Belvedére, or the Garden of the Muses*, both published in 1600. These printed commonplace books gathered memorable quotations on a vast range of subjects. In *England's Parnassus*, excerpts attributed to Shakespeare appear under forty-seven topics, the largest number of them pertaining to "Love." *Bel-vedére* includes no fewer than 89 extracts from six Shakespearean plays that had appeared in print and a further 125 extracts from *Venus and Adonis* and *The Rape of Lucrece*. This makes him the most-quoted author in the book.[44]

In John Florio's English-Italian dictionary of 1598, *A World of Wordes*, the Italian word *mente* is defined as "the highest and chiefest part of the soule, the mind, understanding, wit, memorie, intent, will, advise, remembrance, counsell, prudence, judgement, thought, opinion, imagination, conceit, knowledge, hart, wisedome, providence or foreknowledge of man."[45] For the Elizabethans, "wit" signaled the concatenation of linguistic facility with a panoply of mental powers. Wit offered wisdom on matters of memory, counsel, prudence, opinion, providence, and much else, while good style was characterized by "pleasant wittines in wordes, merie conceites or wittie grace in speaking wit."[46] Shakespeare was praised from early in his career because, to deploy more of Florio's copious definitions in his Italian-English dictionary, he wrote with *accorgimento* ("warines, foresight, craft, wilines, wit"), *acutezza* ("sharpnes, policie, subtiltie, vivacitie of wit or sight"), and *intellétto* ("understanding, wit, discretion, capacitie, knowledge, skill, reason, discourse, perceiving, intelligence, sence, or judgement"). That is why his plays and poems were regarded as such a rich source of "wise saws and modern instances" for inclusion in both manuscript and printed commonplace books, some of which are still being discovered.[47]

"Wit" is the thread that runs through nearly all the early allusions to his work: "a reigning wit" (1610); "in plays thy wit winds like Meander" (1614); "all that he hath writ / Leaves living art but page to serve his wit" (1616).[48] Most prominently, Ben Jonson's poem accompanying Martin Droeshout's title-page image of the author in the First Folio offers the conceit that the engraver has drawn Shakespeare's face very well but that if he could have "drawn his wit" he would have produced a print that surpassed every engraving ever made in the whole history of art. But since it is impossible to create a visual reproduction of the inside of Shakespeare's head as well as the outside of it, the reader should turn the page and read the book instead of lingering over the picture. Jonson's own witty point is that the book itself is the imprint of the greatest wit the world has ever seen.

In his second, much longer poem for the First Folio, Jonson gave a self-consciously patriotic twist to this claim: "Leave thee alone for the comparison / Of all that insolent Greece or haughty Rome / Sent forth." Jonson asserts that his "Britain" may "triumph" because "all scenes of Europe homage owe" to Shakespeare.[49] By trumping the ancients, Shakespeare enabled his nation to stand apart from the rest of Europe. A national literature had been born, and he was at the centre of it.

5

TRAGICAL-COMICAL-HISTORICAL-PASTORAL

QUINTILIAN BELIEVED THAT A WRITER constantly needed to practice, and there is a sense that many of Shakespeare's early works are practice performances, where he is testing, and indeed showing off, his art. To reveal his command of the repertoire of kinds was part of this process. Thus in *The Two Gentlemen of Verona*, Proteus (for ulterior motives of his own) gives Turio a lesson in the art of writing a melancholy love elegy. He explains that "wailful sonnets" are a form of "lime" (viscous extract of holly bark used to snare small birds) laid down in front of the desired woman in order to "tangle her desires." The poet's rhymes are "serviceable," he implies, in several senses: they proclaim service to the beloved, in courtly fashion, but they are also useful, pragmatic—especially in leading to the desired end of sexual "servicing."[1] Proteus then launches into what is effectively a love elegy in sonnet form (unrhymed until the closing chime of "silence" / "grievance"):

> Say that upon the altar of her beauty
> You sacrifice your tears, your sighs, your heart.
> Write till your ink be dry, and with your tears
> Moist it again, and frame some feeling line
> That may discover such integrity:
> For Orpheus' lute was strung with poet's sinews,
> Whose golden touch could soften steel and stones,
> Make tigers tame and huge leviathans
> Forsake unsounded deeps to dance on sands.
> After your dire-lamenting elegies,
> Visit by night your lady's chamber-window
> With some sweet consort: to their instruments
> Tune a deploring dump. The night's dead silence
> Will well become such sweet-complaining grievance.[2]

"This discipline shows thou hast been in love," responds the Duke approvingly.[3] But what it actually shows is that Proteus, like his creator, knows the manipulative power of love elegy and lyric song: the poet claims that his "feeling line" is a mark of "integrity," but it is actually a performance. The poet's "line" becomes synonymous with the "lime" that tangles the bird. Shakespeare is simultaneously exemplifying and offering a critique of the function of "dire-lamenting elegies."

Shakespeare's casual usage of generic descriptors reveals his awareness of the fluidity of the discourse of literary kinds. "Dost though think I care for a satire or an epigram?" asks Benedick in *Much Ado about Nothing*. Orlando in *As You Like It* "hangs odes upon hawthorns and elegies on brambles; all, forsooth, deifying the name of Rosalind."[4] Later usage confined the term "elegy" to the poetry of mourning, but in Shakespeare's time it also referred to love poetry. That was partly because the Latin elegiac metre was frequently used for this subject matter, most notably in Ovid's *Amores*, which Christopher Marlowe translated under the title *Ovid's Elegies*. But it was also because of the association of unrequited love with a melancholy mood.

Any audience member who had been to grammar school and paid attention in class would have recognized instances of the lyric genres within Shakespeare's plays. The mode would have been recognized as elegiac both when a character speaks a love-poem and when an epitaph is voiced. Equally, the witty or cynical riposte would have been recognized as having an epigrammatic quality. We cannot be sure, but it is possible that Shakespeare composed a handful of epigrams himself: a pointed epitaph on John Combe, an infamous Stratford usurer, was attributed to him in a number of independent early sources, and he may have written the short poem that is on his own gravestone, which is both epitaph and epigram.[5] More significantly, theorists of genre in Shakespeare's time regarded the modern sonnet as a descendant of the ancient epigram. The twist in the tail that is so characteristic of the closing couplets of Shakespeare's sonnets thus owes an indirect debt to the long tradition that goes back, via Martial and Catullus, to the *Greek Anthology* of epigrams by Meleager, Simonides, Callimachus, and others. The curious pair of sonnets that bring Shakespeare's collection to a climax (Sonnets 153 and 154) are indeed imitations, via an unknown intermediate source, of an epigram in the *Greek Anthology* by the obscure fifth-century Byzantine poet Marianus Scholasticus. While Cupid is sleeping by a pool, nymphs steal his torch and use it to heat the water—an image of the burning force of desire and, in Shakespeare's variation, an allusion to the sweating tub treatment for sexually transmitted disease.[6] These two sonnets, together with various unsavoury passages of invective in *Troilus and Cressida*, constitute Shakespeare's primary engagement with the unbridled sexual explicitness of classical epigram.

So much for the lyric genres. What, then, of Shakespeare's place in Elizabethan and Jacobean thinking about the two enduring dramatic genres that were first established on the ancient Athenian stage, comedy and tragedy?[7] How might the dramatist himself have reacted to Meres's claim that he was "most excellent in both kinds for the stage"?

Meres's qualifying phrase "for the stage" may be intended to distinguish between plays written for public performance and those written "for the closet," that is to say, to be read in private (often penned by an aristocrat, Mary Sidney's 1595 *Tragedie of Antonie* being a classic example). But it may also imply that there is such a thing as most excellent comedy and tragedy in lyric or narrative form, written for neither the public stage nor closet drama's theatre of the imagination, but purely for the page. If so, then Meres, like Webbe, was thinking of comedy and tragedy as terms applicable to subject matter more than to medium. Elsewhere in his "Comparative Discourse of our English Poets with the Greek, Latin and Italian Poets," he described Shakespeare's Warwickshire contemporary Michael Drayton as "*Tragaediographus*" (writer of tragedies) "for his passionate penning the downfalls of valiant Robert of Normandy, chaste Matilda, and great Gaveston."[8] These were narrative poems, not plays. And it was indeed within a contemporaneous narrative poem of a similar kind, *The Rape of Lucrece*, that Shakespeare passionately penned an apostrophe to Night that doubles as a kind of programme note defining the domain of tragedy:

> O comfort-killing Night! Image of hell!
> Dim register and notary of shame!
> Black stage for tragedies and murders fell!
> Vast sin-concealing chaos! Nurse of blame!
> Blind, muffled bawd! Dark harbour for defame!

Grim cave of death! Whisp'ring conspirator
With close-tongued treason and the ravisher![9]

This stanza offers an epitome of the dark lexicon of tragedy, neatly suggesting a dramatic register ("image," "stage") even as *Lucrece* was not written for the theatre. "Black stage for tragedies": in Christopher Marlowe's tragedy that set the London theatre scene ablaze in the late 1580s, Tamburlaine pitches white tents for mercy on the first day of a siege, red tents for blood on the second, and black tents for death on the third. Sometimes in the Elizabethan theatre, the stage was hung with black drapes to indicate tragic matter. We now call *Henry VI Part One* a history play, but to its original audience, the opening line would have announced its genre as tragedy: "Hung be the heavens with black: yield, day, to night!"[10]

Soon after Francis Meres published his comparison between English poets and classical ones, praising Shakespeare as the equal of both Plautus in comedy and Seneca in tragedy, Shakespeare himself reworked an old tragedy that had become something of a joke in the repertoire because of its excessive use of the inflated style of Seneca. To quote Nashe's famous jibe more fully than I did before: "English Seneca read by candle-light yields many good sentences, as *Blood is a beggar*, and so forth; and if you entreat him fair in a frosty morning, he will afford you whole Hamlets, I should say handfuls of tragical speeches.... Seneca, let blood line by line and page by page, at length must needs die to our stage."[11] When Polonius says of the players "Seneca cannot be too heavy," Shakespeare is in all probability nodding towards the heavy Senecanism of the old (lost) play that scholars call the *Ur-Hamlet*.[12] But he may also be wittily acknowledging Meres's recent compliment. If so, he is hardly returning the favour: the implication would be that Meres's laboured recital of discrete genres is a piece of Polonian pedantry.

The comparison to Plautus in comedy is less contentious. Most of Shakespeare's tragedies call themselves tragedies—*The Tragedy of Hamlet, The Tragedy of Macbeth*, and so on—but only one of his comedies names itself as such: *The Comedy of Errors*. This title is a way of saying to the audience: "this play is a *comoedia*, written according to the classical conventions." It is filled with the classic devices that have been the staple of comedy since its invention in ancient Greece: mistaken identities, people getting the wrong end of the stick, clowns getting slapped about the head, politically incorrect jokes about fat people and sexy women, a vertiginous succession of characters coming in and out of doors. It also obeys the ancient rule of the "unities": unity of action (a single plot line, not a variety of subplots), unity of place (the sole location is the marketplace of Ephesus), and unity of time (the action is completed within a single day). The play was one of Shakespeare's earliest, and never again would he obey all the unities. *The Tempest* is the only other one to have unity of time, but it has some variety of action and place.[13]

"Comedy," then, from *comoedia*. The other half of the title is also classically derived. The word "error" comes from the Latin verb *erro*, which means not only to make a mistake (which twin is this? am I really talking to my wife?) but also to wander or stray. "We have *erred* and strayed from thy ways like lost sheep," Shakespeare and his audience would have recited in the general confession of sins every time they went to church. One of the Antipholus twins is erring in the sense of wandering into a new city, lost after a shipwreck. The other, going off to dine with a courtesan, is straying from his marriage vows.

The Comedy of Errors is indeed a formal imitation of a classical original. Educated members of its early audiences recognized it as such. When the play was performed before a festive gathering of London lawyers and their patrons in the Christmas season of 1594, it was instantly recognized as being "like to Plautus his *Menaechmus*." Some years later, the lawyer John Manningham made the same link, describing *Twelfth Night*, Shakespeare's later comedy of twins and mistaken identity, as "much like *The Comedy of Errors* or *Menaechmi* in Plautus."[14] To the classically trained, a work was good not because it was original, but because it resembled an admired classical exemplar, which in this case meant the comedy by Plautus about "The Menaechmus Twins."[15] Like *Venus and Adonis* and *The Rape of Lucrece*, *The Comedy of Errors* reveals the young Shakespeare self-consciously displaying his classical credentials, perhaps partly in order to prove just how wrong Robert Greene was to call him an uneducated, provincial "upstart crow."

The critical tradition that sprang from Aristotle's *Poetics* was very clear about the distinctive matter of tragedy and comedy. At grammar school, the boys' introduction to drama came via the comedies of Terence. Most editions of his plays included not only a prose account of his life but also an essay concerning tragedy and comedy, ascribed to the fourth-century commentator Aelius Donatus. It makes a rigid division of genres: comedies are concerned with private citizens and lowlife characters; tragedies with monarchs, rulers, and heroes. Comedies end in reversals for the better: recognition of children, happy marriages. Tragedies end in reversal for the worse: a mighty fall, a mournful death. As the playwright Thomas Heywood, who was familiar with Donatus, wrote in part 3 of his *Apologie for Actors*, "Comedies begin in trouble and end in peace. Tragedies begin in calm and end in tempests."[16] This structural definition was reiterated in Cockeram's *English Dictionary*, published in the same year as the Shakespeare First Folio: a Tragedy is defined first as "A history or play of death" and then, more colourfully, as "A Play or History beginning very friendly, but ended with great slaughter of blood." Comedy is the reverse: "A Play or Enterlude, whose beginning is full of trouble, the end thereof is mirth and joy."[17] According to this structural definition, Shakespeare's audiences would have had a confident expectation that if they went to see a tragedy it would end in a bloodbath, whereas if a play called a comedy began with a threatened execution, as *Errors* does, there would be a happy reversal and a quasi-magical escape from catastrophe before the show was over.

Whereas some commentators defined genre by structure in this way, others concentrated on character type and characteristic plot line. "The ground work of comedies," wrote Stephen Gosson, "is love, cozenage, flattery, bawdry, sly conveyance of whoredom; the persons, cooks, knaves, bawds, parasites, courtesans, lecherous old men, amorous young men."[18] That is a snapshot of the range of parts in Terence and Plautus. *The Comedy of Errors* includes excellent examples of the cook, the courtesan, the wife, and their amorous young men. They play out their misadventures in a city street or square. Ancient Roman *comoedia* was above all *city* comedy. Rome was the greatest city the world had ever seen. The busy world of its comedies reflected its crowded population, mingling patricians and plebeians, merchants and slaves. The streets and the marketplaces of Rome were as central to Terence and Plautus as the sidewalks and subways of New York are to Martin Scorsese and Woody Allen.

The comic imagination of Shakespeare, the farmer's grandson from deep in the shires, more often took flight in a pastoral world:

a wood or a forest (*The Two Gentlemen of Verona*, *A Midsummer Night's Dream*, *As You Like It*), a royal hunting park (*Love's Labour's Lost* and *The Merry Wives of Windsor*), a lady's house and its garden (*Twelfth Night*), a community of shepherds (*The Winter's Tale*), a magical island (*The Tempest*).[19] But although he did not write a string of London plays, as Ben Jonson, Thomas Middleton, and Philip Massinger would in the early seventeenth century, he was perfectly capable of writing urban comedy, as witnessed by the Eastcheap scenes of the two parts of *Henry IV*, the clever redeployment of classical character types (*mulieres* as dominant agencies, Falstaff as both *senex* and *miles gloriosus*) in *The Merry Wives of Windsor*, and the Vienna of *Measure for Measure* that doubles as London—Vienna not being noted for constables called Elbow, barflies called Froth, and brothel-keepers called Mistress Overdone.

The Comedy of Errors foreshadows this world. It is the play in which Shakespeare announces himself as a city comedian. The setting may be ancient Ephesus, but it is also modern London. The stage represents a London street, a London marketplace, as much as a Mediterranean one. Unusually for Shakespeare, the exit and entrance doors indicate specific locations: the Phoenix (Antipholus's and Adriana's house), the Porcupine (the courtesan's house), and the Priory. These are very English names, suggestive of the signs identifying taverns, lodgings, and businesses in Shakespeare's London. Shakespeare's own origins on the fringe of the forest of Arden drew his imagination back to the greenwood, to the pastoral mode, but his London career as a professional actor and scriptwriter, an entrepreneur and shareholder in the new and profitable entertainment industry, meant that he moved in an urban world that gave him rich resources for dramatic exploitation. Whether ostensibly a prison in Vienna (*Measure for Measure*) or a brothel in Mytilene (*Pericles*), Shakespeare's urban locations are peopled by knaves, bawds, businessmen, parasites, courtesans, lecherous old men, and amorous young men who are at once types out of Plautus and Terence and inhabitants of the London in which he lived and worked.

The Comedy of Errors turns on the great preoccupation of the city: money. Its starting point is a restriction on free trade with a financial or legal penalty attached: we learn that due to a law forbidding the presence of Syracusan merchants in Ephesus, the old Syracusan trader Egeon faces execution when he is discovered in the city.

He can only escape by paying a fine of a thousand marks. The implicit critique of trade protectionism is in its way an anticipation of the fundamental driver of modernity and globalization that had its origin in the maritime expansion of Shakespeare's time: the triumph of free trade. Throughout the play, money makes the city go round. On arrival in Ephesus, the first thing that Antipholus of Syracuse has to do is sort out his currency: he sends his slave Dromio to deposit cash at the inn called The Centaur. A key twist in the plot comes with the confusion over which of the Antipholus twins has ordered a chain from Angelo the goldsmith and whether it has been paid for. To Shakespeare's original audience, the name Angelo—used again in that later city comedy *Measure for Measure*—would have evoked the coin known as an angel, an item so central to the working of the economy and the oiling of social relations that many a tavern was named after it (as, for example, the Angel in Islington). Money gets you into trouble—though it can also get you out of it—with the law, with your partner, and with your family. Money for fines, money for bail, money for goods, money for sex, money exchanged by mistake, money shaping marriages, money bringing bad fortune and good: that is the story of *The Comedy of Errors*, that is Shakespeare's take on life in the city, that is a key part of his inheritance from Terence and Plautus.

In thinking about Shakespeare in the context of classical genre theory, it is important to distinguish between performance and print. When his acting company became the King's Men in 1603, they were licensed "freely to use and exercise the Art and faculty of playing Comedies, Tragedies, histories, Enterludes, morals, pastorals, stage plays and such other like."[20] The purpose of their playing, the royal licence added, was the "recreation" of the people and the "solace and pleasure" of the King, a clear indication of the new monarch's distance from the Puritan tendency.[21] The loose terminology of the license suggests that from the point of view of performance there was a relaxed view of genre in Elizabethan and Jacobean England.

When audience members went over the river to the Globe after 1599, did they have any particular expectation that they were going to see a tragedy, a comedy, a history, an interlude, a moral, or a pastoral? Or simply a "stage play"? This is a difficult question to answer because there are no surviving posters or theatre programmes from the period. The only full-scale listings we have of plays as performed in Shakespeare's England are the diaries and account books of Philip Henslowe, the manager of Shakespeare's rival company. And what is very striking in Henslowe's lists of box office takings and fees paid to dramatists is that he hardly ever describes his repertoire with the words "tragedy" and "comedy." The play that in print was called *The Spanish Tragedy*, and that exercised a huge influence on the genre, was always known by Henslowe as *Jeronimo*. He called another play *The Comedy of Jeronimo* not because he wished to define it generically but simply in order to distinguish it from the original, far more frequently performed, play.

There are a few appearances of the words "comedy" and "tragedy" in Henslowe's lists, which include over four hundred play titles, but they are the exception rather than the rule. He tended to use the terms specifically for plays that were named for a setting: *The Venetian Comedy*, *The Grecian Comedy*, *The French Comedy*, *The Spanish Comedy*; *The Chester Tragedy*, *The Bristol Tragedy*, *The World's Tragedy*. Just occasionally, a tragedy was named for a person, usually when it was based on a real-life murder story: *Baxter's Tragedy*, *Beech's Tragedy*, *The Tragedy of John Cox*. Two non-Henslowe plays that have found their way into the Shakespeare "apocrypha" also come into this category: *The Tragedy of Master Arden of Faversham* and *The Yorkshire Tragedy*. But Henslowe did not use the nomenclature of tragedy for the frequently performed and hugely influential Marlowe plays that were staged in his theatres: *Tamburlaine*, *The Jew of Malta*, and *Dr Faustus*.[22]

When it comes to the entry of plays in the Stationers' Register and to their title pages when printed, it was a very different story. Shakespearean drama went into print in the 1590s with such titles as *The Most Lamentable Tragedy of Titus Andronicus* (1594), *The True Tragedy of Richard Duke of York* (1595), *An Excellent Conceited Tragedy of Romeo and Juliet* (1597), and *A Pleasant Conceited Comedy called Loves Labors Lost* (1598, the first Shakespearean comedy to be printed). So too with Marlowe: *Tamburlaine the Great … Divided into Two Tragical Discourses* (1590); *The Tragical History of Dr Faustus* (1604). Reading texts, in other words, were given the classical label in a way that performance texts were not. The denomination "tragedy" or "tragical" was a way of saying that a play was worth reading, worthy of comparison with the ancients. Strikingly, generic labeling, notably for court performances, became more common in the seventeenth century—as a result, I would suggest, of an increasing sense of the neoclassical dignity of vernacular drama and indeed by way of a feedback loop with the more generically formal entitling practice of printed play texts.

In gathering Shakespeare's complete plays for posthumous publication, the team preparing the First Folio saw the opportunity to take this practice further. In calling the volume *Comedies, Tragedies and Histories*, they were self-consciously giving Shakespeare "classical" status. This is especially striking, given that when the self-consciously classical Ben Jonson had collected his works in 1616, he arranged them chronologically, not by genre. The decision of the Folio compilers, who may properly be called editors, to present the Shakespearean canon generically was of a piece with their imposition of a "classical" five-act structure on all the plays that had been published in the quarto simply as a succession of scenes.[23]

Prior to 1623, the only play collections dignified with the word "tragedies" on the title page were *Seneca his Tenne Tragedies, translated into Englysh* (1582) and *The Monarchicke Tragedies: Croesus, Darius, The Alexandraean, Julius Caesar* (1607) by Scottish aristocrat Sir William Alexander. That is to say, a classical work and a collection of strictly neoclassical courtly closet dramas.[24] To elevate Shakespeare's stage plays into such company was to make a bold claim for the status of public theatre. Similarly, the only book prior to the First Folio with "comedies" on its title page was *Flowers or eloquent phrases of the Latine speach, gathered out of all the sixe comoedies of Terence* (1575): to collect Shakespeare's comedies was thus to reaffirm his status as what John Davies of Hereford called him in a poem published in 1610, "our English Terence."[25]

Prior to the Folio, there were over a hundred English books with the word "histories" somewhere on their title page.[26] But none of them were collections of plays. The compilers of the Folio made a major innovation when they decided to arrange the complete run of Shakespeare's English chronicle plays in order of historical chronology as opposed to that of first performance or publication. They also renamed *The Tragedy of Richard the Second* and *The Tragedy of Richard the Third* as *The Life and Death* of those respective kings, and branded the entire sequence as Shakespeare's "Histories."[27] In so doing, they were not only elevating the history play as a genre to the same status as the narrative chronicles of Holinshed that constituted Shakespeare's primary source, but also further affirming Shakespeare's generic versatility. As William Webbe proposed back in the 1580s that all literary productions could be contained within the three genres of tragedy, comedy, and history, so the Folio editors announced that Shakespeare held in his hand a generic full house.

Shakespeare himself, however, was eminently aware that Webbe's tripartite division was a simplification of the complex matter of classical genre theory. Although he would have been taught in school about the rigid distinction between tragedy and comedy, he would not have discovered it in practice when he entered the theatre world. English popular drama conformed to the structural model of comedy versus tragedy—that theory of happy and unhappy endings transmitted from Donatus to Heywood and Cockeram—but it confounded the classical decorums of tone and character type. Sir Philip Sidney was complaining about this back in the early 1580s when he condemned stage "comedians" in his *Apology for Poetry*:

> all their plays be neither right tragedies, nor right comedies, mingling kings and clowns, not because the matter so carrieth it, but thrust in the clown by head and shoulders, to play a part in majestical matters, with neither decency nor discretion, so as neither the admiration and commiseration, nor the right sportfulness, is by their mongrel tragi-comedy obtained. I know Apuleius did somewhat so, but that is a thing recounted with space of time, not represented in one moment; and I know the ancients have one or two examples of tragi-comedies, as Plautus hath *Amphitrio*. But, if we mark them well, we shall find that they never, or very daintily, match hornpipes and funerals. So falleth it out that, having indeed no right comedy, in that comical part of our tragedy, we have nothing but scurrility, unworthy of any chaste ears, or some extreme show of doltishness, indeed fit to lift up a loud laughter, and nothing else: where the whole tract of a comedy should be full of delight, as the tragedy should be still maintained in a well-raised admiration.
>
> But our comedians ... in themselves they have, as it were, a kind of contrariety.[28]

It was precisely this contrariety, or breach of decorum, that Shakespeare and most of his theatrical contemporaries relished. In the eighteenth century, his "mongrel" form came to be regarded as the essence of a distinctive Englishness: while strictly neoclassical Frenchmen such as Voltaire fumed that Shakespeare was manifestly a barbarian because he included a joking lowlife gravedigger in *Hamlet*, Dr Johnson celebrated the very contrariety that Sidney condemned as the matching of hornpipes and funerals:

> Shakespeare's plays are not in the rigorous or critical sense either tragedies or comedies, but compositions of a distinct kind; exhibiting the real state of sublunary nature, which partakes of good and evil, joy and sorrow, mingled with endless variety of proportion and innumerable modes of combination; and expressing the course of the world, in which the loss of one is the gain of another; in which, at the same time, the reveller is hasting to his wine, and the mourner burying his friend.[29]

A precedent for this astute judgment in Johnson's preface to Shakespeare may be found in the prefatory epistle that appears in some copies of the quarto of *Troilus and Cressida*, a play notoriously difficult to categorize by genre. The printer's copy for the Folio text arrived so late in the day that the play is absent from the contents list of *Mr William Shakespeares Comedies, Histories and Tragedies*, and indeed some early copies were published without it. The printer eventually managed to squeeze it in between the histories and tragedies, which was a suitable position: the Trojan war, as represented in the *Iliad*, provides the foundation for Western tragedy, but the quarto edition of 1609 had called the play *The Famous History of Troilus and Cresseid Excellently expressing the Beginning of their Loves, with the conceited wooing of Pandarus Prince of Licia*, a title emphasizing a medieval romance accretion to the classical epic tale. The quarto preface performs a delicate balancing act, acknowledging that the play is "passing full of the palm comical," but emphasizing its serious literary content and praising Shakespeare's works for being "so framed to the life that they serve for the most common commentaries of all the actions of our lives."[30] This latter phrase catapults the play from the semimythical into the everyday world, Johnson's "real state of sublunary nature."

Johnson wrote of *Troilus and Cressida* that "the comic characters seem to have been the favourites of the writer.... They are copiously filled and powerfully impressed."[31] Although tragedy was traditionally considered the higher dramatic art, as heroic poetry was thought to be higher than elegiac, satiric, and lyric, the essential dramatic art of holding the mirror up to nature, "exhibiting the real state of sublunary nature" and "expressing the course of the world," is actually closer to the domain of comedy, which is why Dr Johnson, following Thomas Rymer, believed that Shakespeare's "natural disposition" led him to comedy.[32] In this respect, there is a direct line back to Quintilian's view that Menander, founder of "realistic" comedy, offered the best of all models because he was perfect in "his representation of actual life." There is *potential* for tragedy in the action of Shakespeare's comedies: Beatrice's "kill Claudio" in *Much Ado about Nothing*, Malvolio's threat of revenge in *Twelfth Night*, the darker moments in *All's Well that Ends Well* and *Measure for Measure*, and so on. But there is *actual* comedy in Shakespeare's tragedies because he wanted them to hold up a mirror to "actual life," in which there is no such thing as pure tragedy.

Sidney singled out Plautus's *Amphitryon*, which would be one of the sources of *The Comedy of Errors*, as a rare example of classical tragicomedy, but secular English drama was tragicomic from its earliest flourishing. One of the first vernacular stage tragedies to reach print was Thomas Preston's *A lamentable tragedy mixed ful of pleasant mirth, conteyning the life of Cambises king of Percia from the beginning of his kingdome vnto his death, his one good deed of execution, after that many wicked deeds and tirannous murders, committed by and through him, and last of all, his odious death by Gods Justice appointed* (1572). By Shakespeare's time, this play had become a byword for hoary old-fashioned overacting. Thus Falstaff: "Give me a cup of sack to make my eyes look red, that it may be thought I have wept, for I must speak in passion, and I will do it in King Cambyses' vein."[33] A byword, too, for generic impurity: the incongruity of "lamentable tragedy" and "pleasant mirth" on its title-page lies behind Theseus's incredulity in *A Midsummer Night's Dream*:

> LYSANDER. "A tedious brief scene of young Pyramus
>   And his love Thisbe. Very tragical mirth."
> THESEUS. "Merry" and "tragical"? "Tedious" and "brief"?
>   That is hot ice and wondrous strange snow.
>   How shall we find the concord of this discord?[34]

Save for a few generally unsuccessful experiments in the art of strict classicising (Ben Jonson's *Catiline his Conspiracy* of 1611 most notable among them), it was only in print, not on stage, that there was any appetite for the decorum of "pure" tragedy. *Tamburlaine* included a printer's preface that, as well as commending "the eloquence of the author" and "the worthiness of the matter" (standard terms from the rhetorical tradition), explained that

> I have purposely omitted and left out some fond and frivolous gestures, digressing, and, in my poor opinion, far unmeet for the matter, which I thought might seem more tedious unto the wise than any way else to be regarded, though haply they have been of some vain-conceited fondlings greatly gaped at, what time they were shewed upon the stage in their graced deformities: nevertheless now to be mixtured in print with such matter of worth, it would prove a great disgrace to so honourable and stately a history.[35]

A gentleman reader of a "tragical discourse" and "others that take pleasure in reading histories" would, it is implied, have different, more classical, expectations from those of the mixed audience, gaping "fondlings" among them, who saw the tragedy on stage. Similarly, when Ben Jonson brought *Sejanus his Fall* into print in 1605, his preface not only acknowledged certain features that did not conform to strict Aristotelian rules (no unity of time, no Chorus), but also mentioned that the printed text excluded certain passages in the stage version that emanated from a "second pen"—in all probability, these were comic or lighter elements contributed by another King's Men playwright, Chapman perhaps, or even (as has sometimes been proposed) Shakespeare.[36] By contrast, when Shakespeare went into print as the author of a self-proclaimed tragedy, *Titus Andronicus*, the scenes with the Clown were not omitted. The play very deliberately mingles king and clown, anticipating the encounters of Hamlet and the gravedigger, Lear and his Fool, and especially Cleopatra and the Clown who bears the asp in his basket of figs.

Shakespeare's own attitude to the attempts of grammarians and commentators to distinguish rigorously between literary kinds is revealed by way of the comedy he extracts from Polonius's praise of the versatility of the "tragedians of the city": "The best actors in the world, either for tragedy, comedy, history, pastoral, pastorical-comical, historical-pastoral, tragical-historical, tragical-comical-historical-pastoral, scene individible, or poem unlimited.... For the law of writ and the liberty, these are the only men."[37] The mingling of genres may in part be a dig not only at the theoreticians but also, as with Theseus's "tragical mirth," at the tendency of title pages to call printed plays "tragical histories" or "historical tragedies." The meanings of "scene individable" and "poem unlimited" remain elusive. The only contemporaneous occurrences of the word "individible" are with reference to the individability of atoms.[38] If Polonius is continuing his thought, he might mean "a play that cannot be chopped up into some scenes of tragedy, some of comedy, some of history, some of pastoral"; if he is turning his mind to classical dramatic theory more generally, he might alternatively mean "plays in which every scene has the same location, thus obeying the classical law of unity of place (and perhaps also the unities of time and action)." A "poem unlimited" (curiously, Shakespeare's only use of the word "poem") is presumably a play unconstrained by the rules of classical decorum. The players are thus said to be excellent in both rule-bound neoclassical drama and innovative works that take liberties with convention: hence "the law of writ and the liberty." Some editors, considering "the law of writ" to be clunky phrasing for a reference to "the rules of composition," emend to "the law of wit and the liberty."[39] Whatever the precise meaning, Shakespeare is implicitly defining the "liberty" of his own generic practice by measuring it against the "law" of the classical tradition.

Polonius's allusion to "pastoral" in the context of a company of players is perhaps surprising. In 1599, around the time *Hamlet* was being written, Philip Henslowe paid George Chapman, who is sometimes seen as Shakespeare's "rival dramatist," for a "Pastoral Tragedy," now lost.[40] But this was an outlier: the only two printed dramas of the Elizabethan era to be branded as pastorals were from the repertoire of the boy companies, whose rivalry with the "common players" is famously alluded to in the "little eyases" allusion in this scene in *Hamlet*.[41] Those two plays were George Peele's *The Araygnement of Paris: a Pastorall* (1584) and John Lyly's *Love's Metamorphosis: a Wittie and Courtly Pastorall* (1601). The latter was an old play revived by the Children of Paul's at exactly the time of *Hamlet*, so very germane to what Rosencrantz calls "the late innovation" of the new "fashion" for boy players that began with the re-establishment of that company around 1600.[42] Set in Arcadia, *Love's Metamorphosis* combines the story of Erisichthon in Ovid's *Metamorphoses* with an invented plot line involving three foresters falling in love with three nymphs in the service of the goddess Ceres, who are temporarily transformed into a rock, a rose, and a bird as punishment for rejecting their suitors, and only restored when they agree to marry them. As this suggests, Elizabethan dramatic "pastoral" takes us into the twin territories of Ovidianism and tragicomic romance.

It was as a result of Battista Guarini's *Il Pastor Fido: Tragicomedia Pastorale* (Venice, 1590) that the term "pastoral" became significant in the lexicon of dramatic genre in Shakespeare's time.[43] Also set in Arcadia, it was immensely popular in late sixteenth- and early seventeenth-century Italy. An edition was printed in London in 1591 and an English translation in 1602. John Fletcher's answering play *The Faithful Shepherdess* was published in 1610 with an address to the reader explaining that it had failed on stage a couple of years earlier because it did not conform to the audience's expectations of the genre: "It is a pastoral tragi-comedy, which the people seeing when it was played, having ever had a singular gift in defining, concluded to be a play of country hired shepherds in gray cloaks, with curtailed dogs in strings, sometimes laughing together, and sometimes killing one another; and, missing Whitsun-ales, cream, wassail, and morris-dances, began to be angry."[44] In response to what he sarcastically calls the common playgoer's "singular gift in defining," Fletcher offered his Guarini-influenced definition of tragi-comedy:

> A tragi-comedy is not so called in respect of mirth and killing, but in respect it wants deaths, which is enough to make it no tragedy, yet brings some near it, which is enough to make it no comedy, which must be a representation of familiar people, with such kind of trouble as no life be questioned; so that a god is as lawful in this as in a tragedy, and mean people as in a comedy.[45]

That same year Shakespeare was working on his most pastoral play, *The Winter's Tale*.[46] With its complement of "country hired shepherds" and dancing satyrs, it offered audiences the kind of material that Fletcher's play lacked, while also pushing at the limits of tragicomedy, what with Antigonus's death at the claws of the bear, the loss of the child Mamillius, and the seeming death of Hermione. If Hemmings and Condell had wanted to give a separate generic classification to Shakespeare's late plays—which twentieth-century scholars decided to call "romances"—they could not have done better than "Pastorals." Or "Tragicomedies." Or "Pastoral Tragicomedies." But perhaps that would have been too Polonian (Hemmings himself seems to have specialized in older men's roles, so he may well have been the original Polonius).

Perdita's line "Methinks I play as I have seen them do / In Whitsun pastorals" suggests a self-conscious engagement with the classification "pastoral" that is absent from Shakespeare's earlier shepherd play, *As You Like It*, set in the not quite English Arcadia of the forest of Arden.[47] There, the word does not occur. The difference is probably due to Guarini and Fletcher. *Pace* Polonius, prior to the turn of the century, "pastoral" was considered primarily a nondramatic form, though the notion of a pastoral interlude within a tragedy or comedy was understood. William Scott's 1599 *Model of Poesy* enumerated the varieties of pastoral writing (eclogues, bucolics, georgics) and put forward the proposition that the "vulgar persons" who made up the body of Chaucer's Canterbury pilgrims should be characterized as pastoral characters. He then added, "The gardner in like sorte, is with a passinge good Decorum brought on the stage in that well-conceipted Tragedye of Richard the seconde."[48] Scott's view that the gardener scene had "passing good Decorum" despite its introduction of lower-class characters was probably due to the fact that it was written in verse, as was the entire *Tragedy of King Richard II*. One suspects that he might not have passed quite such a favourable judgment upon the prose pastoral interlude in Justice Shallow's Gloucestershire orchard in *Henry IV Part 2*. But it is very interesting that he equates the presence of "vulgar" characters on the stage of tragedy with a shift into the pastoral mode. By this way of thinking, pastoral becomes a kind of Trojan horse, breaching the wall of classical generic constraint.

The geographical and temporal span of pastoral, together with the interweaving of multiple plot lines and the coming together (often via disguise) of aristocrats and shepherds, could hardly be further from the Aristotelian world of the unities of time, place, and action. In *Pericles Prince of Tyre*, written in collaboration with writer and brothel-keeper George Wilkins, Shakespeare followed the medieval freedom of John Gower in dramatizing the ancient story of Apollonius of Tyre, who wandered around virtually the whole of the Mediterranean world before what he had lost was restored to him. The sea, the voyage, the storm, the unlucky and lucky chances, the years of quest and grief, the child lost and found, the resurrection of the apparently dead: the Apollonius story was a classic exemplar of the literary genre that has come to be called "romance." That descriptive term is, however, a label imposed retrospectively by scholars. In Shakespeare's time, this kind of story was sometimes known as a "fable," occasionally as a "novel" (from the Italian word *novella*, something new and strange), and most often as a "tale."

The foundation text for this kind of story was a tale called, to use the title of its first English translation, published when Shakespeare was a child, *An Ethiopian History, written in Greek by Heliodorus, no less witty than pleasant.*[49] Heliodorus, of whom we know almost nothing, lived in the third century CE. The manuscript of his tale was lost for more than a millennium, but then recovered during the sack of Buda in the early sixteenth century, after which it was soon translated into Latin, French, Italian, and English. Sometimes considered the first "novel," it exercised a huge influence on Renaissance adventure-writing in both verse and prose.

It tells of a queen who, fearing that she will be accused of adultery, gives her baby daughter Chariclea into the care of a trusted follower, who takes her to Egypt and leaves her in the care of a priest. The girl is then taken to Delphi, where she falls in love with a nobleman called Theagenes, who has come to consult the oracle. Assisted by another loyal servant, they escape on a series of adventures, encountering pirates, bandits, and near-death experiences until Chariclea is finally reunited with her parents, revealed to be of royal birth, and happily married to her noble lover. In one particularly memorable scene, Theagenes discovers the dead body of a girl and believes that it is his beloved Chariclea—a twist borrowed by Shakespeare in *Cymbeline*, the tale he wrote after *Pericles*.

Shakespeare makes passing mention of *The Ethiopian History* in *Twelfth Night*, but we do not know whether his knowledge of the story was direct or indirect.[50] What is not in doubt is that this ancient romance was the shaping influence on Sir Philip Sidney's sprawling tale *Arcadia*, which is full of the same kind of outlandish adventures, mistaken identities, twists and turns. It was from the

Arcadia that Shakespeare borrowed the Gloucester subplot in *King Lear*, and, in all probability, it was under the influence of one of its heroes, Pyrocles, that he renamed Apollonius of Tyre as Pericles.

Another popular Elizabethan prose romance, Robert Greene's *Pandosto: The Triumph of Time*, also stitched together many different elements of *The Ethiopian History*—a trial, an oracle, a shipwreck— into a tale of children separated from parents, lovers, disguises, near misses, and an eventual happy ending. *The Winter's Tale*, written in 1610, after *Pericles* and *Cymbeline* but before *The Tempest*, is a dramatization of *Pandosto*. Although Shakespeare clearly had a well-thumbed copy of Greene's romance open on his table as he was writing *The Winter's Tale*, there are also traces of the *Arcadia*. There the hero Pyrocles, in cross-dressed disguise as an Amazonian princess, finds his friend Musidorus disguised as a shepherd and is invited to watch some pastoral festivities of dancing and singing, including a leaping dance of shepherds in honour of Pan and his Satyrs. Musidorus kills a bear, and there is a comic account of a cowardly clown who witnesses the scene.

A variant on the name of the man who kills the bear provided the title of what was, to judge by the demand for it in print, the most popular play of Shakespeare's age: the anonymous *Most Pleasant Comedy of Mucedorus*. This featured a prince disguised as a shepherd, a beautiful princess who challenges her father's will, a hapless but lovable clown, misapprehensions and mistaken identities, adventures in a pastoral world, including an encounter with a wild man of the woods, and a festive mood in which, despite some very dark moments, there is always the expectation, duly fulfilled, that all will end well. Originally produced in the 1590s, *Mucedorus* was revived by Shakespeare's acting company and played before King James I in his palace at Whitehall during the Shrovetide festivities of 1610 or 1611. That is precisely the time when Shakespeare was writing *The Winter's Tale*, which shares so many of these features, and *The Tempest*, which has its own wild man in the character of Caliban. Some of the alterations and additional scenes for this revival may have been crafted or overseen by Shakespeare himself.[51] At the very least, his eye must have been caught by one stage direction: "*Enter Segasto running and Amadine after him, being pursued with a bear*."[52] It has even been argued that both the King's Men revival of *Mucedorus* and their new play *The Winter's Tale* featured the same live polar bear cub, borrowed from King James's royal menagerie.[53] Whether or not that was the case, it is clear that *The Winter's Tale* was written and performed at a time when the fantastical tradition of romance was all the rage.

Othello falsely accuses his wife of adultery. The play is called *The Tragedy of the Moor*, so we know that it won't end well. It doesn't: he murders her, then commits suicide. In *Cymbeline*, Posthumous falsely accuses his wife of adultery. The play was eventually published among Shakespeare's tragedies, and there are moments when it doesn't look as if it will end well, but since so many romance elements are woven into the plot, it is not a surprise that the ending (though convoluted) is happy. Leontes falsely accuses his wife of adultery. But the play is called *The Winter's Tale*. Early on, Mamillius says, "A sad tale's best for winter," but the title indicates that this story is a romance, so we can be reasonably sure that everything will be resolved and "that which is lost" will be found. It will, however, be sixteen years before the resolution and reconciliation occur. This "wide gap of time" is another indication that we are in the sprawling, travelling world of romance, not the compressed intensity of tragedy.[54]

The eruption of Leontes's rage, the false accusation, the trial, the death of the boy Mamillius, and the apparent death of Hermione: all this seems like the matter of tragedy. But when good Antigonus deposits baby Perdita on the wild coast of Bohemia, we know that we are entering another world, one in which if a baby is left in such a place we can be almost sure that there will be a friendly animal or shepherd to bring it up. For a moment, we might wonder whether the bear will prove kind, but Antigonus is unlucky: he is ripped to pieces even as the mariners are drowned. When the Old Shepherd finds the baby, he signals the play's change of mood when he says to his son the Clown—who has lightened the tone by describing the bear and storm in comic style—"thou met'st with things dying, I with things newborn."[55] Winter is inevitably followed by Spring, and, following the intervention of Time, we are soon in the world of "Whitsun pastorals," ballads and flirtations, dancing Satyrs, and the shepherdess (who is really a princess) as queen of the feast.

Greene's *Pandosto* did not have an entirely happy ending. Parents are restored to their children and lovers to each other, but in Shakespeare's source the dead queen does not come back. This was where he made his most creative and magical innovation. Perhaps inspired by the story in Ovid's *Metamorphoses* of Pygmalion sculpting a statue of a girl so gorgeous and realistic that he falls in love with it and is rewarded by its coming to life when he kisses its lips, Shakespeare introduced the statue of Hermione and the character of Paulina as a kind of magician or stage director orchestrating the long-awaited ending. In a way, he had been here before: at the climax of *Much Ado about Nothing*, Hero, who has been supposed dead, returns in the guise of another woman—it's an ancient motif that can be traced back to the beautiful ancient Greek story of Alcestis, the wife who sacrifices herself for her husband only to be restored to life, giving the man a not-entirely-deserved second chance.

That idea of the second chance—of forgiveness and reconciliation instead of parting and death—is a deep human need that the romance of great art can indulge. When the eighteenth-century composer Gluck sought to reform opera by focusing on the profoundest of human passions while making the words and the music of equal importance, he turned—as Shakespeare did so often and as opera has throughout its history—to ancient Greece. Gluck dramatized two stories of wronged but beloved wives returning from the underworld: Orpheus and Eurydice was one of them, Alcestis the other. *The Winter's Tale* is set in a timeless world where there are kings in Bohemia and Sicilia, alongside a very English Elizabethan pedlar in the form of Autolycus, but at the same time, the ancient voice of Apollo—god of truth and prophecy, of music and poetry—still speaks through his oracle. Apollo was also god of something else that the genre of "tale"—or romance—seeks to bring: healing.

⌣⌢

Shakespeare's Warwickshire contemporary Michael Drayton once wrote a poem in which he explained that at the age of ten he asked his tutor to make him a poet. His teacher began the job by reading him "honest *Mantuan* / Then Virgil's *Eglogues*."[56] "Honest *Mantuan*" is the late fifteenth-century Carmelite monk Baptista Spagnuoli Mantuanus, whose eclogues (known as the *Adolescentia* or *Adulescentia* because they were written in his youth) constituted one of the most influential neo-Latin texts of the age.[57] Erasmus called him "the Christian Virgil" not only because both the ancient poet and his modern imitator came from Mantuan, but also because the explicitly Christian content of his eclogues avoided some of the problems that occurred when pagan texts were prescribed to schoolboys. As John Colet explained in the statutes of St Paul's School in London, Mantuan was the exemplar of "goode auctors suych as have the veray Romayne eliquence joyned withe wisdome, specially Cristyn auctours that wrote theyre wysdome with clene and chast laten." Mantuan was "clean," whereas the poets of Roman antiquity were sometimes "filthy."[58]

An early account of Tudor educational practice describes how every Monday and Wednesday afternoon students in the Elizabethan grammar school would take six lines per lesson of a given eclogue of Mantuan, commit them to memory, construe and parse them, write them down, turn them into English, and translate them back into Latin. The starting point was the opening of the first ecologue; subsequent focus was upon those ecologues that were "less offensive than the rest," such as the ones that recommended a religious life, espousing the kind of instant conversion that Duke Frederick undergoes at the end of *As You Like It*.[59] In a similar vein to the *Ovide moralisé* tradition that sought to render the erotic stories of the *Metamorphoses* respectable for Christians by reading them allegorically, Mantuan moralised and Christianised the pastoral tradition. Thus he begins his first eclogue with the explanation that the only reason for talking about love affairs is to keep yourself awake and alert to danger: "Faustus, while the cattle all lie chewing their cud in the cool shade, I pray you let us tell a little about our loves of old, lest, if sleep perchance overwhelm us, any of the wild beasts that now lurk secretly in ambush within the ripened wheat fields should rage against the herd. Watchfulness is better than sleep."[60] Pastoral dialogue on the subject of love becomes a pretext for a nugget of moral advice in the form of a "sentence" to be committed to memory: "melior vigilantia somno"—it is better to be alert and vigilant than somnolent and idle.

These opening lines of Mantuan's first eclogue were among Shakespeare's very first encounters with poetry. Later in his education, Mantuan would also have been used as the starting point for his instruction in poetic scansion and the art of prosodic composition. In *Love's Labour's Lost*, when the illiterate Jaquenetta asks Parson Nathaniel to read Don Armado's love letter, the pedantic schoolmaster Holofernes is inspired by her choice of verb, "beseech" (which in

Latin would be *precor*), to quote—or maybe misquote—those first lines of the first ecologue with which, year after year, he would have introduced his pupils to the art of poetry:

> *Fauste, precor gelida quando pecus omne sub umbra ruminat,*—and so forth. Ah, good old Mantuan, I may speak of thee as the traveller doth of Venice: *Venetia, Venetia, / Chi non ti vede non ti pretia.* / Old Mantuan, old Mantuan! Who understandeth thee not, loves thee not? *Ut, re, sol, la, mi, fa.*[61]

Most modern editors assume compositorial error and follow the Second Folio in correcting the Latin to match Mantuan's opening line, but the Quarto and Folio texts actually read "Facile precor gellid quando pecas omnia." A minority of editors retain the errors, notably "Facile" (easily) for "Fauste" (O Faustus), on the assumption that the error is deliberate, that Holofernes is such a bad schoolmaster that he makes the most "facile" mistake imaginable—forgetting the first line of the first poem taught in every grammar school. The argument is plausible, given that at the end of the speech, his mind wandering from the teaching of basic prosody via Mantuan to elementary musical instruction via the gamut, he gets the order of his *ut, re, me* wrong.[62] Interestingly, a few years before the first performance of *Love's Labour's Lost*, the first words of the first ecologue of Mantuan were used as shorthand for very low-level learning when Gabriel Harvey mocked Thomas Nashe for having a "Grammer-schoole witte" that was only "as deepelie learned as *Fauste precor gelida*."[63]

As for Holofernes's closing question, one obvious answer is Jaquenetta, who, being both a girl and from the laboring class, would not have understood Mantuan, since she would not have gone to school. Shakespeare himself, and those members of his audience who had been through a grammar-school education, would certainly have understood Mantuan, who was prescribed as the poet for beginners precisely because his Latin was elementary. Whether they would have *loved* him, given his association with pedantic early years learning of the kind mocked in the figure of Holofernes, is another matter.

Even so, the allusion to the dialogue in the first ecologue between Fortunatus and Faustus on the subject of "honourable love and its happy outcome" introduces the matter of pastoral into the world of *Love's Labour's Lost*. Faustus's immediate reply to Fortunatus's opening injunction evokes his beloved, Galla, a figure very like Jaquenetta: she has "a ruddy and stout face" and is "almost blind in one eye," but that does not stop Faustus marveling at her good looks and comparing her to the goddess Diana.[64] Furthermore, a later eclogue, disputing the relative merits of city and country life, often used as a theme for debate in the schoolroom, begins with an evocation of winter that is very similar to the song of *Hiems* (Winter) that ends *Love's Labour's Lost*. Thus Mantuan:

> Ningit hiems, mugit Boreas, a culmine pendet
> Stiria; depositis bobus requiescit arator,
> Dormit humus; clauso pastor tunicatus ovili
> Cessat iners, sedet ante focum fumosa Neaera
> atque polenta coquit.

> Winter's snows have come, the north wind is bellowing, and icicles hang from the roof. Having bedded his oxen the plowman is resting, and the ground lies asleep. His sheepfold shut up, the shepherd, snug in his cloak, idly beguiles the time, and seated before the hearth, sooty Neaera is cooking polenta.[65]

And Shakespeare:

> When icicles hang by the wall
> And Dick the shepherd blows his nail
> And Tom bears logs into the hall
> And milk comes frozen home in pail,
> When blood is nipped and ways be foul ...
> While greasy Joan doth keel the pot.[66]

There is no polenta in Shakespeare, but greasy Joan does seem to be standing in for sooty Neaera. Shakespeare's dairymaids, shepherdesses, and goatherds, his Jaquenetta, Phoebe, and Audrey, are firmly in a line of descent from Mantuan's unromantic countrywomen. More pervasively, the eclogues of Mantuan introduced Shakespeare to the non-Arcadian "hard" version of pastoral: the sixth eclogue is uncompromising on the question of the expropriation of land, anticipating Shakespeare's acknowledgment that it is tough for Corin in *As You Like It* to be "shepherd to another man" who is of "churlish disposition" and is in the process of selling up his "flocks and bounds of feed."[67]

In this respect, Mantuan was more realistic than his classical forbears Theocritus and Virgil. But in other respects, he was more moralistic. Where classical pastoral frequently indulged amorous infatuation, Mantuan warns against it. His third eclogue is entitled "De insani amoris exitu infelici" (the unhappy outcome of mad love). Here desire is a folly, a plague. The poem makes frequent use of the language of Virgil's second eclogue, to which there is a somewhat coy allusion towards the end: "Nec melius cecinit pugnas ac tristia bella, / Hordea et agrorum cultus et pascua noster / Tityrus a magno tantum dilectus Alexi" (Nor did Tityrus sing better of battles and unhappy war, of barley and pastures and the care of the fields— Tityrus, our fellow, greatly beloved by mighty Alexis).[68] "Tityrus" is Virgil, Mantuan's poetic authority ("auctor").[69] The close of the allusion reminds the Christian reader of a major problem that follows from the reading of the poem's model: whereas the shepherd Amyntas in Mantuan's third eclogue has been driven mad by his unrequited love for a girl, Corydon in Virgil's second is aflame with desire for the boy Alexis, his master's pet: "Formosum pastor Corydon ardebat Alexim, / delicias domini."[70] In the Christianity of Mantuan's day, extreme erotic desire for a woman was bad enough. Homoerotic desire was utter anathema. His third eclogue was a self-conscious heterosexualising of what was perceived as a dangerous tradition.

Mantuan's poetry sought to de-eroticise and in particular to de-homoeroticise the pastoral. It was also characterized by a vein of misogyny in which women were seen as dangerous distractions from proper male behaviour. This is one of the reasons why Shakespeare was keen to tease him by way of Holofernes's fondness for him. After all, *Love's Labour's Lost* offers the very antithesis of Mantuan's movement through his eclogues away from desire into monastic seclusion. The play begins with the ambition to establish a cloistered academe, but the folly of the scheme is revealed as soon as womankind becomes present. Eros prevails and—as will be discussed in chapter 12—pleasure is chosen over what a puritan sensibility would regard as virtue.

Virgil was the most admired of pagan poets not only because the *Aeneid* was the model heroic poem, but also because his fourth eclogue, with its promise of the birth of a child who would save the world, could be read as a prophecy of the coming of Christ. But although Elizabethan schoolmasters tried to direct their pupils to that fourth eclogue, they could not make them avert their eyes from the second, with its male on male plea for a "lovely boy" ("o formose puer") to "live with me" ("o tantum libeat mecum").[71] When Shakespeare addresses a sonnet to "thou, my lovely boy," or when Marlowe's "passionate shepherd" sings, "Live with me and be my love" in a poem that first appeared in print in a little book with Shakespeare's name on its title-page, they are evoking Virgil's Alexis.[72] To enter the world of pastoral was to confront various desires that were unexceptionable in pagan antiquity but profoundly contrary to the teachings of the church. Shakespeare, whatever his own personal proclivities may have been, had a bisexual imagination. He knew where his allegiance lay: his mockery of Mantuan by way of Holofernes was a subtle way of removing shame from the pastoral convention, of a piece with his affection for the unashamedly lusty Jacquenetta and his idealization of the lovely boy Adonis.

6

S. P. Q. L.

In November 1597, the local tax collector in the city parish of St Helen's, Bishopsgate, reported the names of a number of local residents whose payments had been due a year before and who were in default. Among them was a certain William Shakespeare. He was assessed again, in October 1598—thirteen shillings and fourpence due on his goods valued at five pounds, payment required the following winter. One wonders what those goods were: books, perhaps? Again, he did not pay. In 1600, the overdue sum was referred to the Bishop of Winchester, who had authority in the liberty of the Clink, on the south side of the river in Bankside and thus outside the jurisdiction of the city sheriff.[1]

The logical inference is that from 1595 or 1596 to 1598 Shakespeare had a London residence in Bishopsgate, but that by the turn of the century he had crossed the water to Bankside. This is consistent with what we know of the movements of his acting company, the Lord Chamberlain's Men. Upon their formation in 1594, they played at the modestly named Theatre in Shoreditch; in 1597, following problems with their landlord, they moved to the nearby Curtain. Then, between Christmas and New Year 1598, they stole back to the deserted Theatre by night, accompanied by an accomplished carpenter called Peter Street and some dozen workmen, dismantled the structure and put the timbers into storage in Street's yard near the Bridewell jail. In the spring, they shipped the materials across the river and built the Globe, not far from the site of the reconstruction that stands beside the river today, near Southwark Cathedral.

The authorities in the city of London did not approve of playhouses. Theatre in the afternoon meant absenteeism on the part of apprentices and mischief among merchants' wives. The theatres were accordingly located in the "liberties" on the margins of the city. The walk from St Helen's Church, Bishopsgate, to Curtain Road, Shoreditch, the site of those first two theatres, takes just under fifteen minutes: an easy commute for Shakespeare, during which he could mull over the plays he wrote for his company in these pre-Globe years: *A Midsummer Night's Dream* and *Romeo and Juliet*, *Love's Labour's Lost* and the lost *Love's Labour's Won*, *The Merchant of Venice*, and *Much Ado about Nothing*; *Richard II* and the two parts of *King Henry IV*, in which the Boar's Head tavern on Eastcheap, a ten-minute walk in the opposite direction, is the key location.

It made sense for Shakespeare to move across the river in 1599, in order to be close to his new theatre, for which he wrote a new comedy, a new history play, and a new tragedy: *As You Like It*, *Henry V*, and *Julius Caesar*. He was out of reach of the taxman—though a couple of years later, he moved back into the city, where he lodged in Silver Street in the home of a French Huguenot called Mountjoy and his wigmaker wife, a dwelling-place now buried somewhere beneath the Barbican.

Shakespeare could have been fined for not paying his taxes. He could also have been fined for failing to attend church, as his father had been back home in Stratford-upon-Avon. Records are patchy, so we do not know whether he was marked for nonattendance at St Helen's. But given the duration of his assessment as a resident of the parish, it would be highly unlikely for him never to have darkened its doors. What would he have found inside?

St Helen's survived the Great Fire and the Blitz, though it was badly damaged by IRA bombs in the early 1990s. The first thing one notices going into it today is a distinctive double nave. That is because in the Middle Ages it was a two-for-the-price-of-one place of worship. There was a wall down the middle. One side was for the lay people of the parish. The other was for nuns: this part of Bishopsgate was originally occupied by a Benedictine priory. Following the dissolution of the monasteries, the refectory became the livery hall of the Leathersellers, and the curtain wall between the two naves was removed, giving the whole of the church over to the parish. The rest of the priory fell to ruin. As may be seen from an eighteenth-century engraving, here in the heart of the city, not just in the countryside, Shakespeare's England was a place where you could go—as a Goth soldier somewhat incongruously does in *Titus Andronicus*—to "gaze upon a ruinous monastery" and where a metaphor for the ravages of time and the decay of all things could be found in "Bare ruined choirs, where late the sweet birds sang."[2]

SOUTH EAST VIEW OF THE NUNNERY OF ST HELEN, BISHOPSGATE STREET.

Figure 3. "Bare ruined choirs …": eighteenth-century engraving of the remains of the nunnery in Shakespeare's parish in Bishopsgate

A place, that is, where reminders of the old faith were ever present. In *Hamlet*, the ghost of the father speaks of residence in Purgatory, a Roman Catholic idea abolished in Protestant thought, while the son goes to university at Wittenberg, alma mater of Martin Luther, architect of the Reformation. In *Measure for Measure*, a Puritan called Angelo is pitted against a novice nun called Isabella. One element in the authorial background of that play is the fact that Shakespeare had an aunt called Isabella who was the prioress of a Benedictine nunnery at Wroxall in Warwickshire, just thirteen miles from Stratford. Another might be Shakespeare's imagination setting to work as he sat or knelt, probably bored, one Sunday in St Helen's church during his years of residence in the parish: as he thought of the old curtain wall, the embodiment of the boundary between an enclosed priory and a bustling city of commerce, legal dispute, and sexual intrigue, the seed might have been sown for a dark comedy in which a pimp visits a nunnery in the heart of a steamy city.

But that is speculation. What we can say for sure is that there were a number of monuments in the church. Among them, just above an imposing altar tomb in the nave of what was originally the nun's half of the church, there was a memorial to William Bond, who died in 1576, flanked by Corinthian columns and bearing an inscription, split across the two sides of the mural and laid out as Latin hexameter verse:

Flos mercatorum, quos terra Britanna creavit,
Ecce sub hoc tumulo Gulielmus Bondus humatur.
Ille mari multum passus per saxa per undas
Ditavit patrias peregrinis mercibus oras.
Magnanimum Græci mirantur Iasona vates
Aurea de gelido retulit quia vellera Phasi.

Græcia docta tace, graii concedite vates.
Hic jacet argolico mercator Iasone Major
Vellera multa tulit magis aurea vellere Phruxi
Et freta multa scidit magis ardua Phasidos undis.
Hei mihi quod nullo mors est superabilis auro;
Flos mercatorum Gulielmus Bondus humatur.

Flower of merchants produced by the land of Britain,
Behold, William Bond is buried beneath this tomb.
That man, having endured much on sea, over rocks, over waves,
Enriched this country's shores with foreign wares.
The Greek poets admire great-hearted Jason
because he brought back the golden fleece from chilly Phasis.

Learned Greece, be silent, and Greek poets, make way:
Here lies a merchant greater than Argive Jason.
He brought back many fleeces, more golden than the fleece of
    Phrixus,
And he rapidly cleaved through many straits, higher than the waves
    of Phasis.
Alas for me that death cannot be overcome by any amount of gold:
Alas that the flower of merchants, William Bond, lies buried.[3]

To take the key points from this: Bond, buried here, is the "flower" of merchants. Born of Britannia, he has sailed the seas, braving great dangers, in order to enrich his native land with foreign merchandise.

Figure 4. The Bond monument in Shakespeare's parish church in Bishopsgate: merchant adventurer as Jason in search of the Golden Fleece (sculpted shortly after his death in 1576, probably by Garat Johnson the Elder)

As ancient poets have praised Jason for winning the Golden Fleece from the king of Colchis (Phasis was the main river in Colchis), so Bond must be praised because he is a new Argonaut, a greater Jason, who has won many fleeces, vast quantities of gold. The poets of antiquity have to make way for the neo-Latin poet of the present, because his hero is superior to Jason in his achievements by virtue of the fact that he was more widely travelled, over many seas, and not one river, and that he imported fleeces galore, not simply one. Bond was an alderman and sheriff of the city who, as the monument makes clear, accumulated great wealth as a "merchant adventurer." He was the brother of Sir George Bond, who became Lord Mayor in the Armada year, which happens to be the first year when William Shakespeare is recorded in London, acting for his family in a legal case.[4]

I am intrigued by the thought of Shakespeare reading this inscription on Bond's monument. Or, if not Shakespeare himself, then certain members of the theatre audience at the Curtain doing so—or indeed readers of the scripts of Shakespeare's plays that were available from the booksellers a fifteen-minute walk away in St Paul's churchyard. For two reasons: first, the obvious fact that it is in Latin. The monument itself shows Bond and his wife and their six sons and one daughter kneeling, at prayer, to reveal their piety and the sure hope of his eternal salvation.[5] But the flanking Corinthian pillars and the language of the inscription are reminders to the viewer that, even (or maybe *especially*) though church and state had broken from the Roman church, the culture of Elizabethan England measured itself by—forged itself in the image of—ancient Rome. Latin was the language of the grammar school: anyone with even a rudimentary education would have been able to read the inscription.

The second matter of interest is the comparison used to praise William Bond and assert his fame. He is described as another Jason, and his merchant sailors are seen as new Argonauts. The comparison is a perfect example of a way of thinking that was utterly characteristic of the age of Shakespeare: understanding and judgment in the present are shaped and bolstered by measurement against the classical past, evocation of the exemplars of ancient Greece and Rome. How do you praise a merchant adventurer? By comparing him to Jason.[6]

We may date *The Merchant of Venice* with a degree of certainty. Francis Meres listed it among Shakespeare's comedies in 1598. In July of that year, it was registered for publication. A reference to a ship called the Andrew suggests a date of late 1596 or early 1597, because that was the time when a Spanish vessel called the St Andrew was much in the news, having been captured during the assault on Cadiz. Shakespeare's merchant adventurer play, then, was written whilst he was resident in the parish of St Helen's.

In the opening scene, Bassanio conjures up an image of highly desirable goods in the form of Portia:

> In Belmont is a lady richly left,
> And she is fair and, fairer than that word,
> Of wondrous virtues ...
> Nor is the wide world ignorant of her worth,
> For the four winds blow in from every coast
> Renownèd suitors, and her sunny locks

Hang on her temples like a golden fleece,
Which makes her seat of Belmont Colchos' strand,
And many Jasons come in quest of her.[7]

Then, after Bassanio has achieved the rich prize of Portia's fortune, his fellow-adventurer Gratiano proclaims:

How doth that royal merchant, good Antonio?
I know he will be glad of our success,
We are the Jasons, we have won the fleece.[8]

I am not suggesting that Shakespeare made the comparison between Bassanio and Jason as a result of reading the words on the monument in the church comparing Bond to Jason (though it is a nice coincidence that the term "bond" is at the very heart of the play: thirty-nine of the seventy-three Shakespearean occurrences of the word are in *The Merchant*, mostly in the context of the bond between Antonio and Shylock over a loan and a pound of flesh). My point is rather that Shakespeare the dramatist and the anonymous author of the Latin hexameter epitaph on Bond's funeral monument share a frame of mind in which they reach instinctively for the example of Jason as they extol the exploits of a modern merchant adventurer. During the 1560s, while Bond was making his fortune by land and sea, Arthur Golding was at work on the English translation of Ovid's *Metamorphoses* that would be read by Shakespeare and in which the story of Jason and the Argonauts was transmitted to an Elizabethan readership. In his prefatory epistle, Golding explained that

The good successe of Jason in the land of Colchos, and
The dooings of Medea since, do give to understand
That nothing is so hard but peyne and travail doo it win,
For fortune ever favoreth such as boldly doo begin.[9]

"Travail" is a pun on "hard work" and "travel." As far as the writer of the encomium to Bond was concerned, his arduous labours by land and sea, like those of Jason, proved the adage that fortune favours the brave. The message of Shakespeare's play is rather more complicated, as is hinted by the counterbalancing presence in a later scene of the name of Medea, but that is something we will come to later.

The Merchant of Venice, with its argosies at sea, its commercial bonds and legal disputes at home, is very much a play of commerce, trade, and the modern city. As often in the drama of the period, an Italian setting is used as a kind of body double for an English one. The powerful men of the city of London were suspicious enough of the world of theatre without adding to their hostility by coming too close to home. The contentious matter of usury, lending money at interest, was best displaced to Venice and the Jew. But the displacement invites reflection upon the parallels. When the dispute with Shylock over the bond is referred to the courts, Antonio says,

> The duke cannot deny the course of law,
> For the commodity that strangers have
> With us in Venice, if it be denied,
> Will much impeach the justice of his state,
> Since that the trade and profit of the city
> Consisteth of all nations.[10]

A London audience hearing these lines spoken at the Curtain in 1597 or 1598 would have thought of their own city: the "trade and profit" of London, in the first age of globalization, depended on "strangers" (traders from abroad, but also resident aliens) having full confidence in the legal system, particularly when it came to the enforcement of contracts. For Shakespeare's original audience, there was a clear sense in which the conduct of business on the Rialto mirrored that in the Royal Exchange in London. So it is, to say the least, suggestive that Shakespeare hatched the play when he lived in Bishopsgate: for in St Helen's church he would also have seen the tomb of the most famous Merchant of London, Sir Thomas Gresham. It is indeed the altar tomb just below the monument to William Bond.[11] Furthermore, one of the principal landmarks in Shakespeare's parish was Gresham's mansion.[12]

Five hundred yards down the road there stood the building that was visited by Queen Elizabeth I in January 1571, on a site provided by the City of London Corporation and the Worshipful Company of Mercers. "The next thing worthy of note," wrote a tourist in the 1590s, "is the Royal Exchange, so named by Queen Elizabeth, built by Sir Thomas Gresham, citizen, for public ornament and the convenience of merchants. It has a great effect, whether you consider the stateliness of the building, the assemblage of different nations, or the quantities of merchandise."[13] At the suggestion of his factor, Gresham had the vision of a commercial centre for the city. Having made his money as a businessman in the Low Countries, he had a model to hand: the design of the Royal Exchange was based on that of the *bourse* in Antwerp, the city that had been Europe's greatest trading centre throughout the first half of the sixteenth century. So it is that in the second part of Thomas Heywood's play *If You Know Not Me, You Know Nobody*, which combines the story of the building of the Exchange with the defeat of the Spanish Armada, a Lord is imagined standing in front of the new building, saying that he has never seen a "goodlier frame" in all his life:

> yet I have been in Venice,
> In the Rialto there called St Mark's:
> 'Tis but a bauble if compared to this.
> The nearest that which most resembles this,
> Is the great Burse in Antwerp, yet not comparable
> Either in height or wideness, the fair cellarage,
> Or goodly shops above: O my Lord Mayor,
> This Gresham hath much graced your city London,
> His fame will long out-live him.[14]

As indeed it has, largely because of his foundation of the Royal Exchange.

A contemporary engraving of the *bourse* that was Gresham's model bears a tabular inscription headed with the initials "S. P. Q. A."[15] That is to say, *Senatus Populusque Antverpiae*, in allusion to the famous abbreviation S. P. Q. R. (*Senatus Populusque Romanum*). Rome was the centre of the ancient world. Thus Antwerp proclaims itself the centre of the modern world. For a time, the boast was justified: the historian Fernand Braudel argues that by the mid-sixteenth century Antwerp had become not merely the richest city in Europe but "the centre of the *entire* international economy."[16] In this, it was the true successor to Venice. But, as Venice had begun its long slow decline, so Antwerp's moment passed: the religious wars in the Low Countries broke out in the 1560s, and in 1576 the city was sacked in a fit of Spanish fury. Gresham's timing was impeccable: if Venice was Antwerp's predecessor, London was its successor. As the *bourse* had taken over from the Rialto, now the Royal Exchange took over from the *bourse* as the engine room of the world economy. Each great trading city in early modern Europe thus sought to outdo the others in claiming to be the modern descendant of ancient Rome. So it was

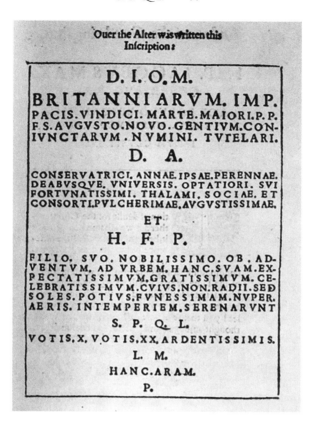

Figure 5. "S. P. Q. L.": inscription over the altar in the Temple of Janus erected for the coronation triumph of King James in 1604

that the altar of the Temple of Janus built for the 1604 coronation procession of King James was emblazoned with the initials "S. P. Q. L."— *Senatus Populusque Londinensis.*[17]

Shakespeare lived in a neo-Roman world.[18] He was drilled in that idea from an early age. His own plays were part of a national project to invent a new cultural heritage on the model of ancient Rome, not least as a form of resistance to the Catholic authority of modern

Rome. Look around Shakespeare's London. His culture—visually, verbally, and in its customs—was as steeped in the examples of antiquity as it was in the habits of Christianity. The skyline of the famous Visscher panorama of London is dominated by the tower of old St Paul's and dozens of church spires, but the engraving's inscriptions are in Latin. The title is "Londinum Florentissima Britanniae Urbs, Emporiumque Toto Orbe Celeberrimum" (London, the most renowned city in Britain and the most celebrated marketplace upon the entire globe), alluding to London's claim to have surpassed Antwerp as the leader in world trade.[19] This caption is also a clever reworking of a well-known line in Virgil. The first of his eclogues ends with the idea of exile from a beloved native plot; Meliboeus speaks of going to the distant corners of the earth, to Africa, Scythia, Crete, and to the Britons wholly cut off from all the world: "penitus toto divisos orbe Britannos."[20] For Virgil, "toto orbe" signifies Britain's isolation as a northerly outpost of the empire, marooned from the mainland of Gaul. The Visscher caption reclaims the phase and makes the British capital into a destination of choice rather than exile. The marginal wasteland has become the hub of international trade, London the new Rome with "Thamesis Fluvius" flowing through the middle, imagined as the modern Tiber.

The theatres in the foreground of the panorama are of a form that, as Johannes de Witt put it when sketching the Swan, "seems to bear the appearance of a Roman work."[21] Indeed, in labeling the parts of the theatre for the benefit of a friend back home in the Netherlands, de Witt used Roman terms: *proscoenium* for the stage, *mimorum aedes* for the tiring-house, *ingressus* for the entrance, *planities* or *arena* for the yard or pit. The most prominent signaling of the classical inheritance comes in the form of the pair of marbled Corinthian columns that support the stage canopy. Elsewhere in his *Observationes Londiniensis*, which only survives in fragmentary form, de Witt noted that London had four theatres, which he called *amphiteatra*, a classical term that he probably derived from Justus Lipsius's treatise *De Amphiteatro* (1584), which attempted to reconstruct the Colosseum in Rome.

All the surviving evidence about the architecture of London's theatres in the age of Shakespeare confirms that each of them had, as a backdrop to the stage, the façade of the tiring-house, or backstage area, divided into three bays, with an entrance door in each of

Figure 6. The Swan drawing: Elizabethan theatre as neo-Roman edifice, labeled with Latin terms (copy by Aernout van Buchel of drawing made by Johannes de Witt in 1596)

the outside bays and a "discovery space" in the centre one. In this respect, theatre design mirrored the classical style that was becoming fashionable throughout Elizabethan England. As the historian Jean Wilson points out, "It was through smaller, comparatively portable, artefacts, such as monuments and items of furniture, rather than through the great prodigy houses which were erected at this period, that the Elizabethan classical style was first disseminated, not only geographically but also socially; furnishings are available to the prosperous middle classes when prodigy houses are not."[22] The monumental three-bay façade, divided by classical pillars, was a design visible on numerous mural memorials in churches, but also on domestic objects such as wooden chests.

If we follow another European tourist around London in the period when Shakespeare was a resident in the heart of the city, we find allusions to ancient Rome everywhere. The man in question is Philip Hentzner, a tutor accompanying a minor German aristocrat, the son of Duke Karl of Silesia, on a Grand Tour of Europe. They arrived in England in the summer of 1598. Hentzner kept detailed notes on everything they saw, supplementing the testimony of his eyes with material from William Camden's compendium of national history and antiquarian lore, *Britannia*, which had appeared in Latin in 1586 as a conscious attempt to "restore antiquity to Britaine, and Britain to his antiquity."[23] Hentzner duly wrote up his *Itinerarium*, and it was published at Nuremberg in 1612.[24] It is the most evocative surviving tourist account of Shakespeare's London. The fact of its being written in Latin is a reminder that, despite the religious break from Rome, England remained very much a part of a common European culture with an international language and deep roots in classical antiquity. Furthermore, Hentzner's way of seeing reveals some of the multiple respects in which Shakespeare's world was modelled on the example of Rome.

So, for example, during a tour of Westminster Abbey, Hentzner observes "the chair on which the kings are seated when they are crowned." In it is enclosed a stone, which has a sacred power attributed to the Judaeo-Christian tradition: it is said to be the stone on which the patriarch Jacob slept when he dreamed he saw a ladder reaching up to heaven, angels descending upon it. But the Latin verses "written upon a tablet hanging near it" not only tell this story but also inform the visitor that "Edward I, the Mars and Hector of England, having conquered Scotland, brought it from thence." The military heroism that enabled King Edward to steal the Stone of Scone is defined by a comparison of him to the Roman god of war and the exemplary Trojan hero, Hector.

Again, among the many memorials of famous men in the Abbey, Hentzner especially noted the monument to Thomas Linacre, King Henry VIII's physician, "a man learned in the Greek and Latin languages" who "translated with extraordinary eloquence many of Galen's works into Latin; and published, a little before his death, at the request of his friends, a very valuable book on the correct structure of the Latin tongue." Hentzner and his master subsequently visited Linacre's university, Oxford, described in the *Itinerary* as the "famed Athens of England; that glorious seminary of learning and wisdom, whence religion, politeness, and letters, are abundantly dispersed into all parts of the kingdom." In Oxford, it was obvious that the world of learning was a wholly classical edifice, but—through everything from grammar lessons to Galenic medicine—the influence of the ancient reached far beyond the realm of the highly educated.

When Hentzner visited the Tower of London, he noted that the "very ancient and very strong" White Tower, enclosed with four others, "in the opinion of some, was built by Julius Caesar." The Tower that we see (correctly) as a symbol of the Norman conquest, the Elizabethans (fancifully) construed as a vestige of the Romans in Britain. Towards the end of *Richard II*, with the deposed king about to enter under guard, Shakespeare gives some lines to the Queen, the purpose of which is to inform his audience that the scene to be imagined is a London street:

> QUEEN. This way the king will come. This is the way
> To Julius Caesar's ill-erected tower,
> To whose flint bosom my condemnèd lord
> Is doomed a prisoner by proud Bullingbrook.[25]

"Flint" economically plays on the materiality of the White Tower and the harshness of the prison conditions within.

Richard II is not the only Shakespearean royal to be taken to the Tower. Here is one of the boy Princes on the way to his fate in *Richard III*:

> PRINCE EDWARD. I do not like the Tower, of any place.—
> Did Julius Caesar build that place, my lord?
> BUCKINGHAM. He did, my gracious lord, begin that place,
> Which, since, succeeding ages have re-edified.
> PRINCE EDWARD. Is it upon record? Or else reported
> Successively from age to age, he built it?
> BUCKINGHAM. Upon record, my gracious lord.[26]

It is a shame that the Prince is about to be slaughtered. He is clearly a clever schoolboy, a budding historian eager to question his sources and warn against the unreliability of oral tradition, otherwise known as legend. Here, Shakespeare was gently poking fun at the "Romans in Britain" tradition that he would explore in a multifaceted way— sometimes historical and political, at other moments bizarre and fairytale-like—near the end of his career in *Cymbeline King of Britain*.

"London," writes Hentzner, is "the head and metropolis of England." He then enumerates its names in a range of classical sources: "called by Tacitus, Londinium; by Ptolemy, Logidinium; by Ammianus Marcellinus, Lundinium." He continues,

> It is the seat of the British Empire, and the chamber of the English kings. . . . It is built on the river Thames . . . and was originally founded, as all historians agree, by Brutus, who, coming from Greece into Italy, thence into Africa, next into France, and last into Britain, chose this situation for the convenience of the river, calling it Troia Nova, which name was afterwards corrupted into Trinovant. But when Lud, the brother of Cassibilan, or Cassivelan, who warred against Julius Caesar, as he himself mentions (lib. v. *de Bell. Gall.*), came to the crown, he encompassed it with very strong walls, and towers very artfully constructed, and from his own name called it Caier Lud, i.e. Lud's City.[27]

The name "Civitas Lud," Hentzner explains, eventually evolved into London. King Lud was buried in Ludgate, which Hentzner observes as the oldest entrance into the city. "Though others," he notes, imagine rather that the gate was originally "named Fludgate, from a stream over which it stands, like the Porta Fluentana at Rome." Whichever story you buy into, ancient Rome is the point of comparison.

In chapter 8, I will discuss the importance of the legend of Brutus and the name "Troia Nova" for the idea of "the British Empire" as the true successor to Rome. The point to note here is that Hentzner's gathering of widespread Elizabethan beliefs about London's connections to ancient Rome is predicated on a notion of succession through resistance. Julius Caesar is represented as an invading imperialist, while Cassibilan, warring against him, is regarded as a local hero.

Cassibilan's nephew Cunobelan, otherwise known as Cymbeline, fought the Roman invaders during the era of Augustus.[28] He was especially important to the Tudor chroniclers because it was believed that he was king of Britain at the time of the birth of Christ (though in fact he died some time earlier) and because he was supposedly brought up in Rome, thus being the first to combine Roman civility with British ethnicity. These traditions fed into Shakespeare's *Cymbeline*, with its shuttling of the action between Rome and the Romans in Britain. At the end of the play, Roman Jupiter descends to bless British Cymbeline, and there are such resonant lines as "To the majestic cedar joined, whose issue / Promises Britain peace and plenty" and (the closing couplet) "Never was a war did cease, / Ere bloody hands were washed, with such a peace."[29] Critics have persuasively linked this conclusion to King James's self-image as a modern Augustus, his project to unify England and Scotland as a new Britain, and his attempts to bring peace to the warring Catholic and Protestant factions across Europe.[30]

But that is to jump ahead in time. What King James was seeking to resolve were the problems he inherited from his Tudor predecessors: the ancient grudge between the houses of York and Lancaster, the tensions between the great earls of the north and the newly centralized court, the absence of an heir to Queen Elizabeth, and, above all, the resistance to modern Rome that came with Henry VIII's divorce and the wider Reformation. How did the example of ancient Rome shape the approach of Shakespeare and his contemporaries to these contentious matters?

7

But What of Cicero?

From the time of Shakespeare's birth until he reached artistic maturity in the late 1590s, there were religious wars between Catholics and Huguenots in France. Ben Jonson served as a soldier and Christopher Marlowe seemingly as a spy in the religious wars in the Low Countries. In 1569, the Catholic nobility of northern England, led by the Earls of Northumberland and Westmorland, attempted to supplant Queen Elizabeth I and place Mary, Queen of Scots on the throne in her place. For these reasons, the fear of civil unrest was pervasive. That is why Shakespeare began a play about the rebellion of an earlier Earl of Northumberland with the king conjuring up sanguinary images of English soil daubing "her lips with her own children's blood," of the "intestine shock / And furious close of civil butchery."[1]

The second half of the fifteenth century had been a time of aristocratic division—of, to follow the title page of one of the first of Shakespeare's plays to appear in print, "The Contention of the Two Famous Houses of York and Lancaster." In his historical novel *Ann of Geierstein*, published in 1829, Sir Walter Scott coined the term "The Wars of the Roses" as a description for those contentions. He did so under the influence of Shakespeare's famous (invented, unhistorical) scene in *Henry VI Part One* when representatives of the rival households of Lancaster and York pluck red and white roses in the garden of the Temple Church in the city of London. The notion that Henry Richmond's victory at the Battle of Bosworth Field and his marriage to Elizabeth York had reconciled the two houses, united the nation, and established a new dynasty, was essential to the self-fashioning narrative of the Tudor monarchs.

Their chroniclers accordingly deployed a new term to describe the previous century's divisions. Though the reality was that "the Wars of the Roses" were confined to the great lords and their retinues, with life in much of England carrying on as if nothing had changed, it suited the Tudors to describe the immediate past as a national catastrophe so as to make their people think better of the present.[2] Make them think long and hard, too, about resistance to the reformed regime, which would inevitably bring new broil. In order to press this argument, they looked to ancient Rome, as may be seen from the opening paragraph of the hugely influential book that was a starting point for Shakespeare's thinking about history, politics, and government:

> What mischiefe hath insurged in realmes by intestine devision, what depopulacion hath ensued in countries by civill discencion, what detestable murder hath been committed in citees by seperate faccions, and what calamitee hath ensued in famous regions by domestical discord and unnaturall controversy: Rome hath felt, Italy can testifie, Fraunce can bere witness.... Scotlande maie write, Denmarke can shewe, and especially this noble realme of Englande can apparantly declare and make demonstracion. For who abhorreth not to expresse the heinous factes comitted in Rome, by the civill war betwene Julius Cesar and hardy Pompey by whose discorde the bright glory of the triumphant Rome was eclipsed and shadowed? ... Who can reporte the misery that daiely hath ensued in Fraunce, by the discorde of the houses of Burgoyne and Orliens: Or in Scotland betwene the brother and brother, the uncle and the nephew? ... But what miserie, what murder, and what execrable plagues this famous region hath suffered by the devision and discencion of the renouned houses of Lancastre and Yorke, my witte cannot comprehende nor my toung declare nether yet my penne fully set furthe.[3]

So began Edward Hall's chronicle history, published in 1548 with its argument blazoned in its title: *The Union of the Two Noble and Illustre Famelies of Lancastre [and] Yorke, beeyng long in Continual Discension for the Croune of this Noble Realme, with all the Actes done in bothe the Tymes of the Princes, bothe of the one Linage and of the other, beginnyng at the Tyme of Kyng Henry the Fowerth, the First Aucthor of this Devision, and so Successively proceadyng to the Reigne of the High and Prudent Prince Kyng Henry the Eight, the Undubitate Flower and Very Heire of both the sayd Linages.* It was a paragraph that burned itself into Shakespeare's political consciousness: he set out to show that what Hall variously called "intestine division," "civil dissension," and "domestical discord" was the worst form of strife. Uncle is set against nephew in *Hamlet*, brother against brother at the beginning of *Titus Andronicus*; the fraternal bond between the thanes is broken in *Macbeth*, and the division of the kingdom in *King Lear* leads to war. These are horrors of the kind that, in Hall's phrasing, the wit cannot comprehend nor the tongue declare. Macduff uses the same idiom on discovering that King Duncan has been assassinated, "O horror, horror, horror! / Tongue nor heart cannot conceive nor name thee!"[4]

For Hall, the classic exemplar was the "civil war" between Julius Caesar and Pompey. The emotive term at the core of his argument was first recorded in writing by Cicero: *bellum civile*, "civil war."[5] Soon after Cicero gave currency to the idea of civil war as a distinctive category of strife, Julius Caesar began his *Commentarii de Bello Civili*, giving his version of his conflict with Pompey and the Senate. A century later, the poet Lucan wrote antiquity's most influential treatment of the theme, *Bellum Civile*, which began with the claim that "no foreign sword has ever penetrated / so: it is wounds inflicted by the hand of fellow-citizens that have sunk deep."[6] Or, as Christopher Marlowe put it in his translation:

> Fierce Pyrrhus, neither thou nor Hannibal
> Art cause; no foreign foe could so afflict us:
> These plagues arise from wreak of civil power.[7]

A century after Lucan, the Greek historian Appian would survey the whole history of Rome, making a key distinction between its "foreign" and its "civil" wars.[8] The English translation of 1578 was entitled *An Auncient Historie and Exquisite Chronicle of the Romanes Warres, both Civile and Foren*: it provided Thomas Lodge with the plot for his play *The Wounds of Civil War* (published in 1594) and possibly gave Shakespeare the raw material for Mark Antony's funeral oration on Julius Caesar.[9]

Contemporaneous accounts of "the wars of the Roses" did not use the term "civil war." That appellation only emerged when the Tudors borrowed from Cicero and Caesar in order to redescribe the wars that Henry VII brought to an end. Thus Roger Ascham, the future Queen Elizabeth's tutor, writing just a few years before the publication of Hall's chronicle:

> The bloudy Civil warre of England betwixt the house of Yorke and Lancaster, where shaftes flewe of bothe sydes to the destruction of

mannye a yoman of Englande, whome foreine battell coulde never have subdewed bothe I wyll passe over for the pyttyefulnesse of it, and yet maye we hyghelye praysc GOD in the remembraunce of it, seynge he of hys provydence hathe so knytte to gether those two noble houses, with so noble and pleasunte a flowre.[10]

Shakespeare made powerful use of this figure of knitting as political reunion at the end of *Titus Andronicus*: "O, let me teach you how to knit again / This scattered corn into one mutual sheaf."[11] The narrative engrained in the young Elizabeth by her tutor was repeated again and again, not least in the official record of her royal progress to Westminster for her coronation in 1558: "Therfore as civill warre, and shede of blood did cease / When these two houses were united into one."[12]

Shakespeare's history plays, both ancient and modern, are all marked with the Ciceronian idea of the peculiarly heinous nature of civil war. In his Roman world, there are the civil wars of *Titus Andronicus* and *Julius Caesar*: "Domestic fury and fierce civil strife / Shall cumber all the parts of Italy." In his English histories, "civil strife" is the linking theme. *Richard II* introduces it: "the dire aspect / Of civil wounds ploughed up with neighbours' sword." The two parts of *Henry IV* act out "the intestine shock / And furious close of civil butchery" in a "poor kingdom, sick with civil blows!" *Henry V* temporarily suspends it, by means of foreign war, but the shadow is always there, as the King recognizes: "Now, beshrew my father's ambition! he was thinking of civil wars when he got me." In *Henry VI*, it is back. *Part One*: "Civil dissension is a viperous worm / That gnaws the bowels of the commonwealth." *Part Two*: "Methinks already in this civil broil / I see them lording it in London streets." *Part Three*: "Conditionally, that here thou take an oath / To cease this civil war." But it only does cease with Henry Tudor's victory at the end of *Richard III*: "Now civil wounds are stopped, peace lives again."[13]

There was an unintended consequence of the mid-Tudor propagandists' invocation of the Roman idea of "civil war" in the context of the history that brought the dynasty to power. "Civil war" implies another Ciceronian term: *civitas*, the social body of the *cives*, or citizens, united by law.[14] To redescribe the contention between two noble houses as a civil war was to create an arena for the corporate voice of the *civitas* and thus the notion of the public good (*res publica*). Cicero, after all, was in the business of defending the Roman *republic*, which had been founded—as Shakespeare reminded the

Elizabethans in his *Lucrece*—on the explusion of a monarchy. Binding the nation together after the civil dissension of the fifteenth century was all well and good, but in leaning on the Roman example in its vocabulary of state building, Tudor political discourse was opening the way for the *civitas* to turn against the monarchy—and thus, in the next century, for a genuine civil war.

In the last years of the ageing Queen, there was fierce debate not only about who the next monarch should be, but about the balance between the divine right of the sovereign and the wellbeing of the people, the "common weal." Sir Thomas Smith's *De Republica Anglorum* had articulated the idea of a mixed constitution. Whereas the fiction of Albion as a "new Troy," which I will discuss in relation to Virgil, was always invoked in support of an idea of royal lineage and monarchical authority, a very different narrative, deriving more from Roman history than "antique fable," was also propagated in late Elizabethan England.

In this tradition, there is an abstracted conception of the public realm—*res publica*, that other key Ciceronian term, usually translated as the common weal—in which the wellbeing of the body politic matters more than anything else. So it was that Ancient Rome provided a template for the exploration of different conceptions of the "common weal." It offered both an imperial and a republican model.

Texts such as Sir Henry Savile's translation of Tacitus, published contemporaneously with *Titus Andronicus*, had given prominence to the pessimistic idea of imperial power descending into tyranny. Among Tacitus's methods of condemning the decadent Roman emperors such as Nero, whom the Saturninus of *Titus* resembles, was the contrasting of their savagery and corruption against the wholesome, pastoral Germans, who fed on berries, roots, goatsmilk, curds, and whey, as Aaron in *Titus* plans to have his baby fed among the Goths.[15] One of Shakespeare's key devices in that play was to question the commonplace that Rome stood for civilization and the Goths for barbarism: the final act proposes that a Goth invasion led by Lucius will save ancient Rome from decadence. Might that also mean that the German religious Reformation would save Albion from the decadent influence of modern Rome?

In this respect, there was alignment between Reformation ideas and classical thought. John Calvin had influentially argued that rebellion against a tyrant was justified within the civil law: God may use those in positions of lesser authority, such as magistrates, as "avengers" who will "punish the tyranny of vicious men and deliver the oppressed from their wretched calamities."[16] Was it always a crime against God and nature to kill an anointed monarch? Not if he was a tyrant, came the answer—immediately bringing to mind *Richard III*, *Macbeth*, and Claudius in *Hamlet*. And was it only the nobility, the patricians, or the magistrates who had the right to depose a tyrant? What about the plebeians?

The tragedy of *Coriolanus* turns on the "ancient malice" between the noble warrior Caius Martius and the "commoners." This internal "ancient malice" of Rome is never fully resolved. Shakespeare also uses the phrase "ancient malice" to refer to the external conflict between Rome and the Volscians, as embodied in the "ancient envy" between Coriolanus and Aufidius. That malice is rooted out when the rival warriors join in martial brotherhood after Martius's exile.[17] As in so many of Shakespeare's plays, and in accordance with the Elizabethan anxiety over civil strife, internal division proves a greater threat than external assault.

The notion of the "common weal" is debated throughout *Coriolanus*.[18] Menenius argues that the public good is nourished by the "counsels" and "cares" of the senators, telling the unruly plebeians that if they "digest things rightly / Touching the weal o' the common," they will discover that every "public benefit" they receive comes from the patrician class. But a voice is also given to the opposite point of view. In Shakespeare's source, Plutarch noted that the life of Caius Martius, surnamed Coriolanus, coincided with the appointment of Rome's first tribunes of the people, Sicinius and the tellingly named Brutus. As "voices" of the people, the tribunes proclaim Coriolanus "a traitorous innovator, / A foe to the public weal." Menenius riles the first citizen by calling him the "big toe" of the commonwealth, whereas the Tribunes argue that Coriolanus should be thrown from the Tarpeian rock by the "rigorous hands" of the people, that he should feel the full "severity of the public power / Which he so sets at nought." Base toe or controlling hand? The compromise is Coriolanus's exile from Rome upon the charge that "he affects / Tyrannical power," and this ultimately leads to his demise among the Volscians. Back in Rome, once he has gone, the tribunes enter with an Aedile (magistrate) and instruct him to dismiss the people to their homes with the assurance that "they stand in their ancient strength."[19]

But how much strength do the people have? The word "ancient" in each of these particular instances in *Coriolanus* primarily means "former" or "longstanding," but it is very important for the ethos of the play that it is set at a particular time in ancient Rome, close to the dawn of the republic. Caius Martius captured Corioli and gained his name a mere seventeen years after the expulsion from Rome of its last king, Tarquin II. According to Dionysius of Halicarnassus, that tribune in the time of Coriolanus was originally called Lucius Junius, but he added the name "Brutus" in order to associate himself with Lucius Junius Brutus, who was instrumental in the downfall of the Tarquins and the establishment of the republic.[20]

To speak, therefore, of both the "common weal" and the "ancient strength" of the people was inevitably to conjure up the idea of ancient *Libertas*.[21] The Roman goddess of that name was created along with the republic and always associated with the overthrow of the Tarquins. She was worshipped by the family of the Junii, that is to say, by the Brutus who claimed descent from Lucius Junius Brutus and who joined the assassination plot against Julius Caesar in order to defend the republic. Given the republican associations of *Libertas*, it is striking that in *Henry VI Part 2* the appeal to "ancient freedom" is transposed to an English setting and put in the mouth of Jack Cade, Shakespeare's most dangerous but also most risible revolutionary.[22] *Libertas* referred both to the freedom from tyranny that came with the overthrow of the Tarquins and to the desirable condition of not being a slave. Cade, or at least Shakespeare, is clearly aware of this latter sense, in that his reference to "ancient freedom" is followed by the accusation that his fellow rebels "delight to live in slavery to the nobility."[23] Do such associations mean that there is a vein of Roman-influenced republican thought in Shakespeare?[24]

Among the most widely read classical texts of Shakespeare's age were Livy's account of the expulsion of the Tarquins and Cicero's many defences of the Roman republic. The former was one of Shakespeare's sources for *The Rape of Lucrece*. As for Cicero, he actually appears as a character in *Julius Caesar*. And it is to his profound influence on early modern perceptions of the ancient Roman political order that I now turn.

What were the options for the ordering of a state? When Cominius launches into a formal encomium, praising the track record of Coriolanus and arguing that "valour is the chiefest virtue," his evidence for the martial hero's supremacy ("The man I speak of cannot in the world / Be singly counterpoised") takes the form of a memory of the young warrior's initiation in battle:

> At sixteen years,
> When Tarquin made a head for Rome, he fought
> Beyond the mark of others: our then dictator,
> Whom with all praise I point at, saw him fight,
> When with his Amazonian chin he drove
> The bristled lips before him: he bestrid
> An o'er-pressed Roman and i' the consul's view
> Slew three opposers: Tarquin's self he met,
> And struck him on his knee: in that day's feats,
> When he might act the woman in the scene,
> He proved best man i' th' field and for his meed
> Was brow-bound with the oak. His pupil age
> Man-entered thus, he waxed like a sea,
> And in the brunt of seventeen battles since
> He lurched all swords of the garland.[25]

This is an extraordinarily rich speech, creating a cast of politically diverse characters. Tarquinius Superbus represents tyranny marching against Rome: in striking him, Coriolanus is defending the republic. The on-field witness is a consul (elected representative of the republic), who has temporarily been given the absolute authority of a "dictator," under the Roman equivalent of an "emergency powers" act. Coriolanus himself is a boy of sixteen, smooth-chinned and thus perceived as feminine ("Amazonian"), undergoing military pupilage; but such is his valour that he immediately enters manhood and wins a civic crown (*corona civica*) for his action of saving an "o'erpressed Roman," which is to say a soldier who represents the threatened *civitas*. The dual invocation of Tarquin and the Amazons adds a layer of complexity. In the very act of proving his masculinity by defending the newly established republic, Caius Martius meets "Tarquin's self," raising the fleeting fear that he may one day become a second Tarquin, a permanent as opposed to a temporary "dictator."

At the same time, the image of an "Amazonian" saviour of Rome foreshadows the saving grace of female authority that will be exercised by Volumnia later in the play.

The dilemma in *Coriolanus* is that to be successful in war a state needs strong leadership, but that the restless man of military action has no time for the inglorious arts of peace.[26] This question of what to do with the returning soldier was all too familiar from the case of the Earl of Essex. The classic example was, of course, the story that Shakespeare put on stage in 1599, possibly as the opening show for the new Globe Theatre, even as Essex was leading an English army in Ireland. The success of Gaius Julius Caesar in his Gallic wars, including his invasion of Britain, gave him supreme military power; fearing the consequences of this, the Senate ordered him to relinquish his command and return to Rome; he refused, and crossed the Rubicon with the thirteenth legion, precipitating civil war; his victories over Pompey at Pharsalus and Scipio at Thapsus meant that he could be proclaimed *dictator perpetuo*. This was the constitutional turning point. *Dictator* was meant to be a temporary role in times of crisis: a dictator in perpetuity was effectively an absolute ruler, who might as well be crowned emperor or monarch. The *Oxford English Dictionary*'s earliest example of the word "dictator" in the sense "absolute ruler," as opposed to "chief magistrate with absolute power, appointed for a limited period," is Christopher Marlowe in *The Massacre at Paris*: "Guise, wear our crown.... And as Dictator make or war or peace."[27] And it is with the offer of a crown to Julius Caesar during his triumph that Shakespeare's 1599 tragedy begins.

Julius Caesar's great political opponent, the principal defender of the values of the republic, the most eloquent orator arguing the case against the idea of a *dictator perpetuo*, was Marcus Tullius Cicero. Plutarch noted in the "Life of Julius Caesar" that the man whom the Elizabethans often called "Tully" saw the danger from very early in Caesar's meteoric career: "Cicero like a wise shipmaster that feareth the calmnes of the sea, was the first man that mistrusting his [Caesar's] manner of dealing in the common wealth, found out his craft and malice, which he cunningly cloked under the habit of outward curtesie and familiaritie."[28] Cicero's climactic statement of the republican position came after the event, in his second *Philippic*, in which he poured the blame on Mark Antony for "offering the kingdom to Caius Caesar, perpetual dictator" during the Lupercalia, and thus destroying "laws and courts of justice ... by the substitution of kingly power": "Was it for this that Lucius Tarquinius was driven out; that Spurius Cassius, and Spurius Maelius, and Marcus Manlius were slain; that many years afterwards a king might be established at Rome by Marcus Antonius though the bare idea was impiety?"[29]

For the Elizabethans, Cicero was the embodiment of the Roman republic. As consul, he was responsible for the suppression of the conspiracy of Catiline, which was read—and dramatized by Ben Jonson—as a victory for the principles of the constitution over the ambition of the aristocracy.[30] In denouncing Julius Caesar and then Mark Antony, he risked and eventually lost his life in the name of the republic. It is intriguing, therefore, that Shakespeare plays down his role in the conspiracy of Brutus and Cassius against Caesar. Early in the play, we hear of him as a looker-on with "such ferret and such fiery eyes." Then Cassius asks Casca whether Cicero said anything in reaction to Caesar's initial refusal to accept the offer of a crown. "It was Greek to me," replies Casca, setting up the image of Cicero as a learned and loquatious intellectual, a thinker and not a man of action.[31]

In the following scene, the character of Cicero speaks his only four speeches in the entire play. First, he greets Casca: "Good even, Casca. Brought you Caesar home? / Why are you breathless, and why stare you so?" Casca replies by describing the stormy weather, suggesting that it portends either "civil strife in heaven" or impending destruction of the earth. Cicero pushes him further: did he see any other strange events? Yes, says Casca, a panoply of unnatural occurrences: the hand of a slave flaming like a torch but remaining unscorched; a lion strolling peacefully past the Capitol, ignoring the passers-by; a hundred women looking like ghosts because they thought they had seen men all on fire walking through the streets; and an owl hooting at midday. "Indeed, it is a strange-disposed time," replies Cicero, in his only speech of real substance, "But men may construe things after their fashion / Clean from the purpose of the things themselves." His last speech is merely a goodnight and a suggestion that it might not be wise to walk out under such a "disturbed sky."[32] The irony of giving so few lines to the embodiment of ancient eloquence is typical of the witty irreverence for tradition which Shakespeare combined with his reliance upon the classical inheritance that shaped the thinking of his age.

We do not see Cicero again, but he is the subject of two further exchanges. When Cassius and his co-conspirators go to the brooding Brutus the night before the ides of March, to discuss who will join them in carrying out the assassination on the morrow, he asks "But what of Cicero? Shall we sound him?" Cassius is convinced that "he will stand very strong with us," an intuitive view in the light of Cicero's track record of defending the republic. Casca and Cinna strongly agree, and Metellus Cimber comes up with a powerful argument of the buck-passing kind:

> O, let us have him, for his silver hairs
> Will purchase us a good opinion
> And buy men's voices to commend our deeds:
> It shall be said, his judgment ruled our hands;
> Our youths and wildness shall no whit appear,
> But all be buried in his gravity.[33]

Brutus slaps down the suggestion: "O, name him not: let us not break with him; / For he will never follow any thing / That other men begin." Cassius and Casca defer to his view and agree to "leave him out," Brutus having swiftly shown that "he is not fit."[34] But nonparticipation in the actual assassination does not save Cicero: on the eve of the battle of Philippi, he is singled out as one of the seventy senators who have been put to death by the opponents of Brutus and Cassius, the triumvirate of Octavius, Lepidus, and Mark Antony.

How are we to read this brief sketch of Cicero? His speaking Greek, his gnomic remark about misconstrual of the signs in the skies, his exclusion from the conspiracy, and his death by order of Caesar's supporters, one of whom will eventually become the Emperor Augustus, another of whom is the Mark Antony against whom the historic Cicero delivered his blistering philippics? In the "Life of Marcus Brutus," Plutarch claims that the conspirators did not include Cicero because they were afraid that he was "a coward by nature," made more cowardly by old age, and that he might "quenche the heate of their enterprise, the which speciallie required hotte and earnest execucion, seeking by perswasion to bring all things to such safetie, as there should be no peril."[35] Shakespeare could very easily have given Brutus a versification of this line of reasoning. We might imagine him composing a speech along the following lines:

> Born a coward, his fear increased by age,
> He'll quench the heat of this our enterprise,
> Which requires earnest execution:
> Let him not persuade in name of safety
> When this necessity calls for peril.[36]

Instead, he offers an explanation based on vanity: Cicero would be unwilling to play second fiddle in another conspirator's orchestra. The purpose of this is to reflect well on Brutus: his agonizing over whether or not to join the conspiracy is entirely out of principle; his doubts have nothing to do with a desire not to play second fiddle to Cassius.

His line of reasoning in this key scene goes something like this. I have nothing personal against Caesar, but absolute power will corrupt him. I owe it to my forefathers to defend the republic: "My ancestors did from the streets of Rome / The Tarquin drive when he was called a king."[37] I hesitate, because my state of uncertainty is a nightmarish form of inner "insurrection."[38] I hesitate still more because the conspirators come under the cover of darkness, suggestive of duplicity and evil. I do not like the idea of binding ourselves to the deed by way of an oath, because I believe that if we are to do it we should do it out of "honesty" (integrity) and inherent Romanness. No, don't involve Cicero. No, don't kill Antony as well as Caesar, for that will make us seem too bloody and vengeful.

The conspirators then depart without Brutus making an explicit commitment to join them. Portia's entrance raises the possibility that his wife might dissuade him, but before he has the opportunity to share with her the secrets of his heart, he is interrupted by a knock at the door and the entrance of Caius Ligarius, who says that Brutus's participation will cure him of his sickness. This is the thing that finally persuades Brutus: he will participate not out of his own ambition, but in order to cure a close friend. He has said of Caius Ligarius, "He loves me well, and I have given him reasons."[39] The cure of Ligarius serves as synecdoche for the salvation of the state. Shakespeare is nearly always careful when making the choice of which lines to give to which character. It is Metellus Cimber who has the idea of involving Caius Ligarius as a way of winning over Brutus. And he has it in his next speech after the one in which he suggests involving Cicero. Metellus is clearly thinking: get Cicero and we'll have both the dignity of age and the leading voice of the republican ideal on our side, and that will be enough for Brutus. Brutus, however, recognizes that Cicero is "ambitious, and desirous of praise,"[40] so rejects the idea of his involvement; the image of him standing aloof and speaking Greek has also suggested his arrogance and the sense that he is not a team player. Metellus is accordingly forced to come up with the alternative idea of using Ligarius. If Brutus won't be persuaded in the name of Ciceronian ideology, he will in the name of friendship. When Ligarius appears, he credits Brutus with his instant recovery:

> By all the gods that Romans bow before,
> I here discard my sickness! Soul of Rome!
> Brave son, derived from honourable loins!
> Thou, like an exorcist, hast conjured up
> My mortified spirit. Now bid me run,
> And I will strive with things impossible;
> Yea, get the better of them. What's to do?[41]

Kill Caesar, and redeem the state, that's what to do, Brutus replies. Cicero was often regarded as the soul of Rome: in 63 BCE, after the Catiline affair, the Senate conferred upon him the title *pater patriae*, father of the fatherland. Here, though, it is not his idealism but the spirit of personal friendship that spurs the action forward. Brutus construes Ligarius's psychosomatic transformation as a sign that it is his destiny to restore Rome from sickness to health, yet Cicero's earlier words still echo: "men may construe things after their fashion, / Clean from the purpose of the things themselves." Shakespeare leaves open the possibility that there is in fact no causal logic in the connection that Brutus makes. Just as Cicero questions Casca's assumption that the signs of the skies are signs of the times, so it may occur to the audience that Brutus is removing the cure of Ligarius clean from its purpose.

The second half of the play tells the story of the unraveling of the conspirators' hopes for Rome and their bond of friendship in action more than speech. We move swiftly to the battle of Philippi, with no time for the delivery of the *Philippicae* in which Cicero tarred

Antony with the brush of Caesar's ambition and tyranny. The irony is that in the course of his campaign against Antony, Cicero, who by this time bitterly regretted that Brutus and Cassius had not killed Antony as well as Caesar, legitimized the private army of Octavius, thus inadvertently hastening the eventual demise of his beloved republic that came with Octavius's assumption of the title *princeps* and the name Augustus Caesar. Although Cicero does not appear again, his death is invoked as a symbol of the death of the republic. Like the dismemberment of Cinna the poet, mistaken for Cinna the conspirator, and indeed the suicides of Cassius and Brutus, it is a reminder to the audience that insurrection brings only chaos. Though Shakespeare does not use the detail, it is notable that in Plutarch's "Life of Brutus," immediately after the passage about the exclusion of Cicero from the conspiracy, there is a marginal note giving the reason proffered by the followers of Marcus Cato—Cicero's right-hand man in putting down the Catiline conspiracy—for not participating: "Civill warre worse than tyrannicall government."[42] Cicero would not have agreed, but, on balance in the 1590s, with the shadow of the past century's civil wars and religious divisions, it might just have been politic for Shakespeare to offer his implicit assent.

Shakespeare derived the detail of Brutus's cure of Ligarius from his principal source, Plutarch's "Life of Marcus Brutus," but there is no doubt that he also read the "Life of Julius Caesar." So, for example, Caesar's "Cowards die many times before their deaths. / The valiant never taste of death but once" (Nelson Mandela's favourite lines in Shakespeare)[43] is clearly derived from what was marked in the margin of North's translation as "Caesar's saying of death": "it was better to dye once, th[a]n always to be affrayed of death."[44] By the same account, it is hard to imagine a mind as inquiring as Shakespeare's ignoring the life of Cicero in his copy of North. There he would have found the outline of Cicero's life and thought.

Born on the margins of Rome, outside the political class, as a child Cicero was noted for his wit, but also for being thin and physically weak. He studied in Greece and declaimed in Greek, and was thus the embodiment of the importation into republican Rome of Greek politics and ethics. He studied the actor Roscius in order to turn himself into an orator. A fine taunter, he was noted on the one hand for diligence, justice, and lenity, on the other for ambition and the desire to be praised. He had the sweetest of tongues, which is why

Suffolk in *Henry VI Part 2* calls him "sweet Tully."[45] He was the exemplar of the man who could argue both sides of a case, refute any argument, move between praise and invective, eviscerate by irony and by forensic logic. He was famous for his "subtile and pleasant sayings"—none better known than the oft-quoted tag on the decline of the times, *O tempora, O mores.*[46] He turned to philosophy in moments of exile and defeat, his career in politics and the active defence of the republic having had mixed success. His hostility to Mark Antony was his eventual undoing, and in that sense there is deep irony in Shakespeare giving Antony the most effective piece of Ciceronian rhetoric in his entire canon: "Friends, Romans, countrymen, lend me your ears...."[47]

The irony is doubled by the fact that Cicero had addressed his history of Roman eloquence to Brutus, whose prose oration is so much less effective than Antony's superbly structured sequence of set pieces in verse. Plutarch gives no details of Antony's funeral oration. Scholars usually assume that Shakespeare took some hints for it from Appian's *Civil Wars*, but verbal parallels are lacking, and there is no firm evidence that he knew this source.[48] From a structural point of view, the ultimate debt is to Cicero. Antony's argument progresses from ironic praise of Brutus to sincere praise of Caesar's generosity towards the people to emotive action—the display of Caesar's bloody clothing, which is the final straw that provokes the plebeians into violent reaction against the conspirators. This follows Cicero's account of how Antony's oration progressed from *laudatio* (praise) to *miseratio* (condemnation of Brutus's betrayal of Caesar's friendship) to *cohortatio* (the incitement of riot).[49]

Shakespeare would also have found in Plutarch's life of Cicero the backstory explaining Metellus's lines "Caius Ligarius doth bear Caesar hard, / Who rated him for speaking well of Pompey."[50] Caesar had accused Ligarius of treason for having supported Pompey during the civil wars, and the only thing that saved him from execution was the persuasive power of his defence counsel, Cicero. "The force of Ciceroes eloquence, how it altered Caesar," as the marginal note has it in North's translation.[51] Plutarch's account of this moment is one of his most memorable instances of the transformative power of rhetoric:

> Ligarius being accused to have bene in the field against Caesar, Cicero tooke upon him to defend his cause: and that Caesar sayd unto

his frendes about him, what hurte is it for us to heare Cicero speake, whome we have not heard of long time? For otherwise Ligarius (in my opinion) standeth already a condemned man, for I know him to be a vile man, and mine enemie. But when Cicero had begonne his Oration, he moved Caesar marvelously, he had so sweete a grace, and suche force in his words: that it is reported Caesar changed divers colours, and shewed plainly by his countenance, that there was a marvelous alteracion in all the partes of him. For, in thend when the Orator came to touche the battell of Pharsalia [in which Caesar had defeated Pompey], then was Caesar so troubled, that his bodie shooke withall, and besides, certaine bookes he had, fell out of his hands, and he was driven against his will to set Ligarius at libertie.[52]

There could be no better example of the manner in which courtroom oratory has theatrical power: Caesar's mind is troubled, his face changes colour, and the persuasive words provoke a bodily reaction, the dropping of his book. These are exactly the kinds of effect that Shakespeare's characters strive for in their on-stage orations.

That Ligarius owes his life to Cicero's rhetorical genius binds the two characters together and reinforces the significance of Metellus's invocation of them one after the other. It is noteworthy, then, that Ligarius is the one conspirator who is not actually present for the assassination. His absence stands in for Cicero's exclusion. And yet, after Antony's rhetoric persuades the plebeians to "Revenge! About! Seek! Burn! Fire! Kill! Slay!" having torn Cinna the poet to pieces (mistaking him for Cinna the conspirator), they set off with brands to set fire to the houses not only of the conspirators who stabbed Caesar, but also to that of Ligarius.[53] Cicero the orator, Cinna the poet, and Ligarius, the man whose life is saved by Cicero's rhetoric and who later rises from his sickbed and has "heart new-fired," are thus joined as men of words who will lose their lives as a result of the actions of the conspirators.[54]

The importance of Cicero in Shakespeare's classical imagination is not dependent on his breadth and depth of reading in the actual sources: all educated men and women in the sixteenth century knew something of his life, death, talents, and ideas.[55] This was an influence transmitted by osmosis as well as by education. After all, Cicero had articulated the very basis of the kind of mixed constitution under which the Elizabethans believed they lived. In *De Re Publica*, the key precedent for Thomas Smith's *De Republica Anglorum*, he argued that *potestas* resides with the magistrates (upholders of the law), *auctoritas* with the senate (the makers of law), and *libertas* with the people (*in populo*, the beneficiaries of the law, whose elected representatives were the tribunes). Despite the difference between the Roman legislative code and the English common law tradition of precedent, this division provided a model for the separation of powers: *potestas* resided in the law courts, *auctoritas* among the aristocracy, and *libertas* in the House of Commons. This model was inevitably in tension with the idea of monarchy: as Cicero frequently reminded his listeners, the republic was built on the expulsion of King Tarquin, and the proclamation of Julius Caesar as *dictator perpetuo* signaled the beginning of its end. Prudent as it was for Shakespeare to marginalize Cicero in *Julius Caesar*, the structural analogies between the Roman and the English state meant that his republicanism inevitably shadows the play, heightening the sense that there are alternative models to the one in which a supreme leader wears a crown.

The republican virtue espoused by Cicero was not only bound up with the matter of representative government against the idea of an *imperium*. It was also, in some ways more centrally and certainly more influentially, a code of civic duty. The core argument of *Pro Ligario*, his oration in defence of Ligarius, was that the state depended on reconciliation and clemency, with no place for vengeance, a code that, says Cicero, belongs to "fickle Greeks and savage barbarians," not Roman citizens.[56] This distinction was frequently made in Cicero's speeches; in Shakespeare's *Titus Andronicus*, the carrying out of revenge killings in Rome is a sign that the distinction between civilization and barbarism has broken down, that republican values have degenerated. As an exemplary plea for clemency, argued with extreme eloquence, *Pro Ligario* is a classic precedent for Portia's courtroom speech in *The Merchant of Venice*, "The quality of mercy is not strained."[57] Though she Christianises the argument, she makes the same move as Cicero: acknowledging the authority of "temporal power" but then suggesting that "mercy" (*misericordia*) is positively godlike: "Of all your many virtues, there is none more admirable, none more beloved than your mercy, for there is no action by which men make a nearer approach to the gods, than by conferring safety on others."[58]

The underlying thrust of *Pro Ligario* is the desire for reconciliation between the rival powerful families of Rome. How should those relationships among the powerful be regulated? Unquestionably the most influential of Cicero's treatises was *De Officiis*, "of benefits," his last major work before his denunciations of Antony. Though written in the form of a letter of advice to his son, its target audience was all young men of the ruling class. In Shakespeare's England, it was widely read in schools and universities. The task that Cicero sets himself is in the realm of practical ethics: to balance individual integrity and social integration.

Book 1 argues that actions should be judged according to whether they are *honestus* (honourable) or *turpis* (immoral). A good man will be judged by his public reputation (*eudaimon*, prosperity, good fortune). His key attributes are *fides* (trustworthiness, loyalty), *societas* (commitment to the bond of fellowship), *decorum* (seemliness), *dignitas* (dignity and good standing), and *gravitas* (seriousness, respect). These qualities should be exercised both in personal friendship (*amicitia*, another of Cicero's core values) and in service to the state. What Cicero promulgates is essentially the code of the gentleman that was inculcated in the education of the English elite for centuries. Mark Antony's repeated mantra "Brutus is an honourable man" derives its ironic force from this idea of *honestas*: the subtext is that if he truly were honourable, he would have been loyal to his friend Caesar. In another part of the forest, Othello's outsider status means that he fails to recognize how Iago is undermining him by faking the gentlemanly values of *fides* and *societas*. The audience is tempted to scream out, "No, Iago is *not* an honest man."

In books 2 and 3 of *De Officiis*, Cicero sets out to show how the code of honour may be translated into social relationships by means of the practice of giving and receiving *benefits*. This is the meaning of the noun *officium*: it denotes a voluntary service, a kindness, favour, courtesy, obligation, or duty. Harmony between powerful families, friends, political allies, and participants in a network of patronage operated through the exchange of services: the act of helping someone creates a bond whereby he will be obliged to offer reciprocal help in the future. Often, the benefit would take the form of an appointment to a position of public service, for which the term was also *officium*. With such benefits came duties or responsibilities, for which, again, the term was *officium*. This sense of public duty was the absolute basis of what may properly be described as the Ciceronian ethos of the ruling class from Shakespeare's time until the mid-twentieth century. Shakespeare uses the word "duty" nearly two hundred times and "office" nearly three hundred. One of his great themes is indeed that of *De Officiis*: the potential for division between person and office, often with the particular spin provided by his monarchical culture, where, as he explores so acutely in *Richard II* and *Henry IV*, the king has two bodies, a double self as both an individual and the embodiment of the realm, sanctioned by God.[59]

When Brutus and Cassius fall out, it is precisely over breaches in the code of benefits. Cassius accuses Brutus of condemning Lucius Pella for taking bribes and in so doing "slighting off" Cassius's letters "praying on his side."[60] Cassius's assumption is that Brutus owes him a benefit that he wishes to pass on to Lucius Pella. Brutus responds that it is Cassius who has broken the code: "You wronged yourself to write in such a case."[61] Furthermore, Cassius himself has defied *officium* by selling and marting his "offices" for "gold."[62] To bring bribery within the system of benefits is *turpis*, and especially reprehensible because if one begins to wonder "what is the difference between a favour and a bribe?" the answer might be "not very much." Cicero devotes a whole section of *De Officiis* to exactly this question.[63] His conclusion is that bribery is abhorrent because it is motivated by avarice. The public official should be Spartan in private life, subordinating personal greed to service of the state. Bribery is a fault akin to flattery: Cicero warns against susceptibility to sycophants (*adulari*).[64] They are only out for themselves; they do not participate in the reciprocal culture of benefits, as Shakespeare's Timon of Athens discovers when he runs out of money.

Brutus has a further accusation. He says that he is "so strong in honesty" (*honestas*) that he cannot be hurt by insults, but that what riles him is Cassius's failure to confer a benefit:

> I did send to you
> For certain sums of gold, which you denied me.
> For I can raise no money by vile means.

He is so exercised by this that he says it twice:

> I did send
> To you for gold to pay my legions,
> Which you denied me: was that done like Cassius?[65]

This failure is castigated as supremely un-Roman because the practice of benefits is so central to the working of Roman society. It may not be coincidental that news of the murder of Cicero comes just a few minutes later, as if to symbolize the desecration of the old republican code of mutual obligation that he had recently anatomized in *De Officiis*.

Cunningly, Shakespeare forever holds opposing forces and ideologies in balance, never openly advocating insurrection or assassination, mocking the plebeians even as he gives them voice, and ultimately subordinating systematic Ciceronian republicanism to his fascination with the interior life of the self, as his patrician characters wrestle with *honestas*, *amicitia*, and *officium*. He preserves his neutrality, never speaking for a particular faction. But by dramatizing breaches of the code of obligation—on the London stage and, when called upon, in commissioned performances in great houses or at court—and showing how such breaches lead to personal humiliation and civil broil, he was implicitly offering warnings as to the dire consequences of division between present-day patricians such as Leicester and Burghley, Essex and Cecil. In this, Shakespeare was the Cicero of his age.

8

PYRRHUS'S PAUSE

TO FORGE A NATIONAL IDENTITY, you need a narrative of origins. A good example in modern times is the story of the "founding fathers" of the United States of America: banknotes, monuments, place names, teaching in schools, and many other cultural allusions all reinforce a narrative about resistance to empire, foundational documents, and the birth of a nation. Equally, when a nation is under threat, a heroic image of its history becomes all the more important. That is why Laurence Olivier, with the full support of Winston Churchill, made a highly patriotic film of Shakespeare's *Henry V* during the Second World War. Ever since the eighteenth century, the English have looked to Shakespeare as their "national" poet. They have gone to his history plays for their myths of origin and union. But what about the Elizabethan age itself, when the nation was constantly under threat from the power of Spain?

At the end of Queen Elizabeth's reign, the theatre was a new medium for the popularizing of national history, but the more traditional and elevated literary form for the narration of national origins was the heroic poem, the Elizabethan term for what we call the epic. Sir John Harington, in the preface or "apology" to his translation of *Orlando Furioso in English Heroicall Verse* (1591), noted that the heroical was "by all men's consent" the chief of all poetic kinds. "The reading of a good heroical poem," says Harington, "may make a man both wiser and honester."[1] Humanist educators, following such classical literary theorists as Quintilian, had no doubt that Homer was the fountain from which all eloquence and learning issued forth:

> For in his books be contained, and most perfectly expressed, not only the documents martial and discipline of arms, but also incomparable wisdoms and instructions for politic governance of people, with the worthy commendation and laud of noble princes; where-

with readers shall be so all inflamed that they most fervently shall desire and covet, by the imitation of their virtues, to acquire semblable glory.[2]

As the Greeks had Homer, so the Romans had Virgil. For the Elizabethans, *The Aeneid* was like two Homers for the price of one: the first six books offered a voyage narrative akin to the *Odyssey*, while the second told of martial deeds in the manner of the *Iliad*. To Edmund Spenser, Aeneas was the fully rounded hero: in the letter addressed to Sir Walter Ralegh published with *The Faerie Queene*, he proposed that Homer "ensampled" a good governor in the person of Agamemnon and a virtuous man in that of Ulysses, but that Virgil combined both in Aeneas.[3] *The Aeneid* was the exemplary poem because it combined its narrative of the growth of an individual to heroic stature with the public matter—*res publica*—of Rome's legendary identity. "Pius Aeneas" becomes symbolic of the values of Rome itself.

Educated Elizabethans were well versed in the essentials of the life and times of the great author (or *auctor*, authority) Publius Virgilius Maro. Indeed, what has been called "the early modern construction of the Author-as-massive-presence" was built on the example of Virgil.[4] The idea of an author as a great man, and of a body of literary work as an organism that grows with that man's career, can be traced back to the first-century *De viris illustribus* of Suetonius, in which Virgil was singled out for particular luster.[5] Suetonius tells of how "While he was in his mother's womb, she dreamt that she gave birth to a laurel-branch, which on touching the earth took root and grew at once to the size of a full-grown tree, covered with fruits and flowers of various kinds."[6] *Laurus nobilis* was of course the classical tree of poetic champions. The most widely read Elizabethan translation of *The Aeneid* included an Englishing of Aelius Donatus's fourth-century expansion of Suetonius, which quoted Cicero's famous remark about Virgil being "the second hope of Rome" and Sextus Propertius claiming that *The Aeneid* had outstripped Homer's *Iliad* even when it was "scarce yet begun."[7]

Virgil was also seen as exemplary because his lifetime (70–19 BCE) coincided with what was regarded as the most momentous period in the history of Rome—the era dramatized in *Julius Caesar* and *Antony and Cleopatra*, and Jonson's *Catiline* and *Poetaster*, that included such events as Cicero's triumph over Catiline; the crossing of the Rubicon and the assassination of Julius Caesar; Brutus and Cassius losing the battle of Philippi to the triumvirate of Mark Antony, Lepidus, and Octavian; Antony and Cleopatra being defeated at the battle of Actium, and Octavian becoming sole master of Rome, taking the name Augustus, garnering the praise of poets and assuming the title *princeps*, meaning "chief" or "leader."

Augustus was granted a *majus imperium* over the senatorial provinces; he took control of the army, the legislative and judicial systems, and a considerable proportion of the state revenues. He developed an imperial civil service and exercised wide powers of patronage. He also launched a new cultural and social policy: the restraint of luxury and the restoration of what was supposed to be the austere ancient morality of the Roman race. Virgil's lifetime was also marked by the effective completion of the long process of cultural unification of the Italian landmass under the influence of Rome. That he himself became the Roman poet par excellence, despite being born far to the north, in Mantua, was symptomatic of this development. The Augustan project outlined here was in almost every respect a model for the Elizabethan process of state building.

Virgil's poetry itself played a major part in the formation of this Augustan culture. Like Horace, he benefited from the patronage of Maecenas, one of Octavian's most trusted counsellors. In his *Georgics*, he celebrated "labor," that characteristically Roman industriousness which was necessary to replenish the land after the long years of civil war. The *Georgics* also imagined the age of Augustus as a return of the golden age. Having begun his literary career in the imaginary persona of a shepherd singing pastoral *Eclogues*, then progressing in the *Georgics* to the arts of cultivation, Virgil finally addressed the high martial theme that went back to Homer. He devoted the last eleven years of his life to the writing of his *Aeneid*, an edited text of which began to be circulated soon after his death. It was rapidly established as the national epic, the archetypal celebration of the origin and growth of the Roman Empire. At the heart of its narrative is a prophecy, spoken by Aeneas's father Anchises, of Rome's future greatness under Augustus as an imperial power holding the world under the rule of law.

Because Rome dominated Europe for so long, and because Virgil came to be regarded as the supreme Roman poet, the influence of the *Aeneid* permeated the Middle Ages. As early as the fourth century CE, the commentator Servius coined the word *polysemus* to designate the multiplicity of meanings—historical, philosophical, philological—that radiated out from the Virgilian texts. The classic example is that mysterious, much-discussed passage in the fourth of his *Eclogues* that predicted the return of the Golden Age under the aegis of a newborn child who would rule a pacified world in the spirit of his virtuous father, which Christian commentators inevitably read as something it could not have been: a prophecy of the birth of Jesus some forty years after the poem's composition. Virgil thus became the most honoured of pagans—hence his role as Dante's guide in the *Divine Comedy*. The *Aeneid* was also read allegorically, always moralized, and sometimes Christianized. Mediaeval commentators suggested that classical authors wrote *sub integumento*, wrapping truth in the veil of fiction. Scholiasts with the ingenuity to turn Ovid's polymorphously perverse and polytheistically packed *Metamorphoses* into a moral and Christian allegory had an easy task with the more high-minded Virgil. The life of "pius Aeneas" was seen as symbolic of the growth of the virtuous man from youth through maturity to old age. In this reading, Dido becomes the sexual temptress distracting the hero from the path of moral rigor and public service.[8]

The prestige of Virgil was such that the translation of the *Aeneid* into the vernacular became a sign of the maturation of a national literary culture. If Elizabethan England were to be a second Rome and Elizabeth herself a second Augustus, then a new Virgil would be required. A first step was taken with the "Englishing" of the *Aeneid*. Several highly distinctive translations were duly produced: since there is no firm evidence of Shakespeare's direct knowledge of them, I discuss them in an appendix, by way of context.[9] The second task was the act of creative imitation whereby poets set out to write the mythic origins of their own nation with a sweep comparable to that of Virgil.

Think back for a moment to the tourist Philip Hentzner, whom we met in chapter 6: he noted that London was known as "Troia Nova." Here he was alluding to the foundational myth that modern London shared with ancient Rome: its self-image as a new Troy. A key dimension of the Elizabethan process of nation building was the theory of *translatio imperii*: the westward shift of imperial dominion from Troy to Greece to Rome to England, with a new English empire beginning to stretch further westward as a colony was planted in Virginia.

The prevailing myth of the origins of the British race had long been modelled on the example of the *Aeneid*. Ancient Rome had trumped Greece by proclaiming its mythic origins in Aeneas's escape from Troy. After the fall of the Roman Empire, British chroniclers deployed the same tactic as a means of asserting their own venerable pedigree. The story is first encountered in the ninth-century *Historia Brittonum* of Nennius; it was told most influentially in Geoffrey of Monmouth's twelfth-century *Historia Regum Britanniae*, retold again and again by the Tudor chroniclers. As Edmund Spenser put it in Queen Elizabeth I's national epic, *The Faerie Queene*, explaining the old name of London, "For noble *Britons* sprong from *Trojans* bold, / And *Troynovant* was built of old *Troyes* ashes cold."[10]

Spenser offered a parade of ancient British kings in *The Faerie Queene*,[11] but the most sustained Elizabethan attempt to create a vernacular heroic poem that told the mythical story of Britain's origins, and in so doing to emulate for England the achievement of Virgil for Rome, was William Warner's *Albions England*. First published in 1586, this had the elaborate subtitle *Or Historicall Map of the same Island: prosecuted from the lives, Actes, and Labors of Saturne, Jupiter, Hercules, and Aeneas: Originalles of the Brutons, and English-men, and Occasion of the Brutons their first aryvall in Albion. Continuing the same Historie unto the Tribute to the Romaines, Entrie of the Saxones, Invasion by the Danes, and Conquest by the Normanes. With Historicall Intermixtures, Invention, and Varietie: proffitably, briefly, and pleasantly, performed in Verse and Prose*. Thomas Nashe described it as an "absolute" poem, while Francis Meres was fulsome in his praise: "As Homer and Virgil among the Greeks and Latins are the chief Heroic Poets, so Spenser and Warner be our chief heroical makers." Meres reported that Warner "hath most admirably penned the history of his own country from Noah to his time, that is to the reign of Queen Elizabeth. I have heard him termed of the best wits of both our universities our English Homer."[12]

Warner's dedication to Henry Carey, Baron of Hunsdon, Lord Chamberlain of Her's Majesty's Household, explains that the whole island which at that time contained the two kingdoms of England

and Scotland was "anciently called Brutaine," and "more anciently Albion," but he would call his poem "Albion's England" to distinguish English history from Scottish ("which is from us remote," he adds). The poem would "write the gests of Brutons stout and acts of Englishmen."[13] Though it proposes a lineage for Albion that stretches all the way back to Noah's ark, the tower of Babel, the battle of the Titans, ancient Thebes, and the Trojan war, the tipping point of the narrative is the story of how Aeneas was "a Patriarke of our Brutones."[14] The story goes that, having deserted Dido in Carthage, Aeneas came to the land of Latinus, fought with Turnus, married Lavinia, and died leaving her pregnant. She then gave birth to Silvius Posthumus, "so called of his being born amongst the woods, after the death of his father."[15] Posthumus inherits the kingdom of Latium, but whilst hunting is mistakenly killed by his son Brute or Brutus, who as a result leaves Rome in sorrow, embarks with other Trojan gentlemen, and sails to Albion, which they rename Brutaine.

Warner traces the line of Brutus through such ancient British kings as Locrine, Lear, and Gorboduc, all of whom were also the subject of contemporaneous stage-plays. By the time he reached his third edition in 1592, he had brought the story up to date with an account of the Tudor kings. It was in this edition that his chronological narrative reached the Reformation. This historic rupture was a problem for Warner, since his whole narrative of his nation's origins was premised on continuity with ancient Rome via the Aeneas-Brutus connection. The solution was to paint Albion as a return to pure origins: to a "true Religion" that was "Primative," in contrast to the ways of "new Rome" (the Roman Catholic church) that had decayed into corruption:

> Now Rome fell sicke in England, but how long she lay in traunce
> We list not write, alonly death to her did never chaunce:
> For old Rome never lackt that durst their lives for her bestoe,
> Not new Rome that to Hell for her dare soules and bodies goe.
> Then true Religion might be sayd with vs in Primative,
> The Preachers and the people both then practively did thrive:
> Our decent Church-Rites, still in print, not practise.[16]

By this account, the "print" of Cranmer's prayer book and the English Bible was the route back to a spiritual purity that had been lost amidst the flummery of priestly Catholic rites and doctrines. The argument is anchored by the idea of the recovery of a "primitive," pre-Roman faith in Albion that was true to the noble Trojan spirit of Brut(us).

In Shakespeare, the name Brutus always refers to the assassin of Julius Caesar, the Lucius Junius Brutus of the Lucrece story, or the tribune in the time of Coriolanus, never to the Trojan founder of Britain. He does, however, allude to the legend of Britain as another Troy. When Richard II's queen conjures the image of her husband as an authentic king robbed of his royal identity, she describes him as both a "map of honour" and "the model where old Troy did stand."[17] When King Henry VI bids farewell to the Earl of Warwick as the latter goes into battle, he describes him as his Hector and thus "my Troy's true hope."[18] And in a notably powerful speech in *Henry VI Part 2*, Queen Margaret slips seamlessly from "England's blessèd shore" and "Albion's wishèd coast" to the story of Aeneas and his descendants that "commenced in burning Troy."[19]

At the end of *Titus Andronicus*, a Roman Lord asks who has been responsible for the betrayal of the city that has led to the collapse of the imperial regime into bloodshed and mayhem:

> Speak, Rome's dear friend, as erst our ancestor,
> When with his solemn tongue he did discourse
> To love-sick Dido's sad attending ear
> The story of that baleful burning night
> When subtle Greeks surprised King Priam's Troy,
> Tell us what Sinon hath bewitched our ears,
> Or who hath brought the fatal engine in
> That gives our Troy, our Rome, the civil wound.[20]

This is the most explicit of Shakespeare's allusions to the second book of *The Aeneid*, evoking as it does the listening Dido as well as the story of Sinon and the Trojan horse. *Titus* is a play about the troubled question of succession to the imperial crown. For a London theatre audience in the 1590s, the question has a subtext. The *translatio imperii* implies "our Troy, our Rome, our Albion": if "this England" cannot sort out the succession to the childless Queen Elizabeth, she too will be struck with civil wound. The question, then, would be whether the imperial or the republican Roman example was of more value. Lucius, who inherits the Roman Empire at the end of *Titus*, shares a name with the first Christian king of Britain. Shakespeare seems to imply that his alliance with the Goths will bring a reign of peace and perhaps a reconciliation, if only a temporary one, between northern and southern Europe, Protestant and Catholic. But, like all his tragedies and histories, *Titus Andronicus* is suffused with a sense of the fragility of any political order, the transience of every regime, and the destruction that precedes and follows every triumph. Can we be sure, the allusion asks, that Lucius will not prove an inadvertent Sinon? After all, the arrival of the Goths in the seat of power is an inevitable reminder of the eventual decline and fall of the Roman Empire.[21]

The monument to Shakespeare in Holy Trinity Church, Stratford-upon-Avon, erected shortly after his death in 1616, bears a Latin inscription proclaiming that the earth holds his body, the people mourn him, and his spirit is on Mount Olympus. It praises his judgment as that of Nestor, the wise old man in Homer's *Iliad*, his mental powers as those of Socrates, the greatest philosopher of the ancient world, and his literary art as that of Virgil, the most admired of Roman poets.[22] At the time of his birth in 1564, it would have been inconceivable that a provincial glover's son who started his career as an actor, turned playwright for the public stage, and never published an epic or heroic poem could end his life being regarded as an English Virgil, a genius of Olympian proportions. In his lifetime, he was more aptly compared to Terence, Plautus, Seneca, and Ovid. In his extant works, he never mentions Virgil by name, in the way that he refers to Ovid, Seneca, Plautus, Horace, Cicero, and Mantuan. The claim that he had the art of Virgil ("arte Maronem") is shorthand for "he was the best" and perhaps "he is, or will come to be seen as, our national poet," not "his works were in the Virgilian style."

Although Shakespeare never named *The Aeneid* or its author, the passage at the end of *Titus* is by no means his only allusion to Aeneas. The character is remembered—as most educated Elizabethans remembered him—for three things: escaping from Troy with his father on his back, falling in love with Dido Queen of Carthage and then deserting her, and becoming the "great ancestor" of the Romans. Thus Cassius's simile for his action in rescuing the drowning Caesar from the Tiber: "as Aeneas, our great ancestor, / Did from the flames of Troy upon his shoulder / The old Anchises bear."[23] The bearing of Anchises—an image widely represented in engravings and emblem books—is explicitly reimagined on stage, though with the father dead, at the end of the battle of St Albans at the climax of *Henry VI Part 2*. Young Clifford exits carrying the body of his father, who has been slain on the field in combat with Richard Duke of York:

> Come, thou new ruin of old Clifford's house:
> As did Aeneas old Anchises bear,
> So bear I thee upon my manly shoulders:
> But then Aeneas bare a living load,
> Nothing so heavy as these woes of mine.[24]

As for the desertion of Dido, this is remembered in *Cymbeline* and *The Tempest*—"False Aeneas," "Widow Dido! / What if he had said 'widower Aeneas' too?"[25]—and, most memorably, *The Merchant of Venice*:

> In such a night
> Stood Dido with a willow in her hand
> Upon the wild sea banks and waft her love
> To come again to Carthage.[26]

In its dramatic context, this allusion is highly ironic: it is supposed to be a romantic moonlit scene with lovers (Lorenzo and Jessica) at the beginning of their relationship. A broken-hearted woman about to commit suicide is not exactly an auspicious augury. This suggests that Shakespeare just might have had what could be described as a counter-Virgilian, or at least an antiheroic, imagination.[27]

Consider his closest approximation to a "heroic" poem. In William Scott's critical account of Elizabethan poetry in the light of classical genre theory, written in 1599, "*Lucrece's Rape*" is numbered among the works that "are to be comprehended under the Heroicke, that of late are soe gratiously entertayned of our gracelesse age, and which in solemne verse (not fitt for Musick) handle narratyvely the mysfortunes of some unhappely raysed or famous person, thorough error, vice, or malice overthrown."[28] Modern criticism does not usually classify *The Rape of Lucrece* as a heroic poem, presumably because it is not quite two thousand lines long (the equivalent of only a fifth of *The Aeneid*), is not divided into books, and is written in rhyme-royal stanzas as opposed to verse paragraphs in a metre that seeks some equivalent of Virgilian hexameters. Nor does it have a hero.

And yet: it tells the story of the origins of the Roman republic; it is written in a self-consciously elevated style; it contains lengthy discourses and laments by its characters. These are indeed characteristics of the heroic poem. Shakespeare himself describes *Lucrece* as his "graver labour," clearly implying an ascent from light Ovidian matter (*Venus and Adonis*) to heavy Virgilian narrative.[29] "Labor" is one of Virgil's most important words: it is the opposite of the *otium* afforded by the *locus amoenus* of the *Eclogues*, the essence of the agricultural ardour of the *Georgics*, and a defining term for the combination of hardship and sorrow endured by the hero of the *Aeneid*.[30] Indeed, one might go so far as to say that the progression from "omnia vincit Amor"—love conquers all—in the final eclogue to "labor omnia vicit"—work conquers all—in the first *Georgic* was for the Elizabethans the key marker of a Virgilian sensibility.[31] Once this is recognized, the counter-Virgilian nature of *Lucrece* immediately becomes apparent: Aeneas renounces his erotic desire for Dido in order to go on and establish Rome, whereas the encounter between the rapacious *Amor* of Tarquin and the chastity of Lucrece, with her virtuous *Amor* for Collatine, leads to a Roman revolution. According to Shakespeare's way of seeing, *Amor* conquers *labor*. Or, to put it another way, the Ovidian trumps the Virgilian.[32]

Virgilian language is again and again inverted: in the fourth book of the *Aeneid*, Dido kills herself with Aeneas's sword, but this does not prevent him from going on to triumph in battle after battle in the second half of the poem. Rome is thus established by the sword, whereas Tarquin uses his sword to strike a torch into flame as he strides to Lucrece's chamber: "As from this cold flint I enforced this fire, / So Lucrece must I force yield to my desire." Once in the bedroom, he "shakes aloft his Roman blade" over her supine body—the imagery is threateningly phallic, the sword turned from a martial hero's weapon to an instrument of sexual subjugation.[33] Virgil's hero is "pius Aeneas," whereas Tarquin's conscience tells him that his act is "impious" and it is Lucrece who is "the picture of pure piety" (something that could not be said of Dido).[34]

Furthermore, *The Rape of Lucrece* includes an extended *ekphrasis* describing the siege of Troy. The extended description of a visual work of art as an interlude within a long poem is a marker of the heroic idiom, the archetypal example being Homer's description of the shield of Achilles in the *Iliad*. Shakespeare may be nodding to this tradition when, in telling of how the original epic hero was depicted in Collatine and Lucrece's painting of Troy, he pointedly substitutes a martial accoutrement for the human figure: "That for Achilles' image stood his spear, / Gripped in an armèd hand, himself behind / Was left unseen."[35] Whether or not that is the case, there is no doubt that the painting's account of Troy is a reprise of Aeneas's "discourse / To love-sick Dido's sad attending ear" in Virgil's second book.[36] In numerous respects, notably its focus on paternal Priam, cruel Pyrrhus, and despairing Hecuba, it anticipates the Player's speech in *Hamlet*, to which we will come.

In *The Rape of Lucrece* painting's epitome of the matter of Troy, nearly all the heroes on both side of the war are mentioned: Priam, Hecuba, Hector, Helen, Troilus, Ajax, Ulysses, Nestor, Achilles. The one who is conspicuous by his absence is the man who told Dido the tale of burning Troy: Aeneas himself. The focus switches instead to the traitorous Sinon. In the poem's most brilliant stroke, Lucrece scratches out the eyes of his figure: in her mind's eye, his "painted image" has become Tarquin.[37] For Virgil, Aeneas's escape meant that Rome would rise phoenix-like from the ashes of Troy; for Shakespeare, Tarquin's symbolic descent from Sinon signals not only the need for a change to a mixed form of government, but also the fall of the heroic idiom as poetic model.

⌒

Yet on returning to the theatre after the period of plague closure that gave him the opportunity to write *Venus and Adonis* and *The Rape of Lucrece*, Shakespeare had to recognize that the audience wanted martial heroes:

> How would it have joyed brave Talbot, the terror of the French, to think that after he had lain two hundred years in his tomb, he should triumph again on the stage, and have his bones new embalmed with the tears of ten thousand spectators at least (at several times) who in the tragedian that represents his person imagine they behold him fresh bleeding. I will defend it against any collian or clubfisted usurer of them all, there is no immortality can be given a man on earth like unto plays.[38]

To set this in context and parse it: brave Sir John Talbot was a heroic figure during the Hundred Years' War against France in the time of Joan of Arc, early in the ill-fated reign of the boy king, Henry VI.

He won victories against the odds at Pontoise, Harfleur, and on the Somme, gaining high renown, being created the first Earl of Shrewsbury, and becoming known as the English Achilles. Eventually, though, he was defeated and killed in Bordeaux during the battle that marked the end of English rule in Aquitaine. A century and a half after his death ("two hundred years" is a rhetorical exaggeration), his heroic deeds were celebrated on stage in a play called *Harry the Sixth*, performed to packed houses in the Rose theatre on London's south bank in 1592. His death scene was so powerful that spectators imagined that the actor who played Talbot really was the heroic warrior, "fresh bleeding." They were moved to tears, and those tears were a metaphoric embalming of his body. The stage thus became a second tomb, closer to home than his actual tomb in faraway Bordeaux. Noble warriors were traditionally buried with their military "achievements"—sword, shield, and helmet—above their tomb, as a way of immortalizing their deeds (in Shakespeare's time, you could see those of King Henry V in Westminster Abbey). In the case of Talbot, by contrast, it is the retelling of his story on stage that gives him renown: "there is no immortality can be given a man on earth like unto plays."

As that nickname "the English Achilles" suggests, ever since ancient times, epic poetry was a medium for immortalizing heroic deeds on the battlefield: Homer's *Iliad*, with the death of Achilles on the field of Troy, was the foundation stone of Western literature. When Talbot urges his men into battle, the hearts of an English theatre audience in the war-torn 1590s would have been truly stirred:

> How are we parked and bounded in a pale,
> A little herd of England's timorous deer,
> Mazed with a yelping kennel of French curs!
> If we be English deer, be then in blood;
> Not rascal-like, to fall down with a pinch,
> But rather, moody-mad and desperate stags,
> Turn on the bloody hounds with heads of steel
> And make the cowards stand aloof at bay:
> Sell every man his life as dear as mine,
> And they shall find dear deer of us, my friends.
> God and Saint George, Talbot and England's right,
> Prosper our colours in this dangerous fight![39]

The listener may sense Shakespeare getting into his stride. In retrospect, the speech reads as a dry run for the language of King Harry the Fifth, in whose rhetoric the deer gives way to the greyhound:

> I see you stand like greyhounds in the slips,
> Straining upon the start. The game's afoot:
> Follow your spirit, and upon this charge
> Cry "God for Harry, England, and Saint George!"[40]

The theatre loves an action hero, whether it be Harry at Agincourt or Martius Caius in primitive Rome, penetrating the city of Corioles alone, and emerging to win the name Coriolanus:

> If you have writ your annals true, 'tis there,
> That, like an eagle in a dove-cote, I
> Fluttered your Volscians in Corioli:
> Alone I did it.[41]

But wait. In Shakespeare's case, the story is always more complicated.

The account of the thousands of spectators cheering and weeping at the figure of Talbot on stage quite probably refers to a version of the play *Harry the Sixth* that was performed before Shakespeare had a hand in it. We cannot be sure about this, but for over two hundred years scholars have been fairly certain that the majority of the play we now call *Henry VI Part 1* is not by Shakespeare.[42] It seems to have been a collaborative work, with a leading part in the writing undertaken by Thomas Nashe—who just happens to be the man who wrote the passage about the stunning success of the play. He was almost certainly engaged in a piece of self-promotion. There is, however, little doubt that the bulk of act 4 in the surviving text of the play, including the "God and Saint George, Talbot and England's right" speech, *was* written by Shakespeare. We don't know what Talbot's death would have been like in the original version by Nashe and others. What is striking about Shakespeare's version of it is that he mingles the heroic rhetoric with another kind of language, much more tender and elegiac. Talbot's son fights alongside him, and dies before him. My guess is that the son was a Shakespearean innovation in the script. Talbot's last lines are those of the father, not so much the warrior:

> O, thou, whose wounds become hard-favoured death,
> Speak to thy father ere thou yield thy breath!

> Brave death by speaking, whether he will or no;
> Imagine him a Frenchman and thy foe.
> Poor boy! he smiles, methinks, as who should say,
> Had death been French, then death had died to-day.
> Come, come and lay him in his father's arms:
> My spirit can no longer bear these harms.
> Soldiers, adieu! I have what I would have,
> Now my old arms are young John Talbot's grave.[43]

There is a gentleness, and a wit, here that draws the audience away from the image of the valiant hero and towards consciousness of the human cost of war. The young should not die before their parents: few images are more poignant than that of a father bearing his dead child in his arms. Thinking forward in Shakespeare's career, we look to eighty-year-old King Lear, carrying onto stage the dead body of his beloved youngest daughter, Cordelia, who has been executed in prison after she and her father's forces have been defeated in a bloody civil war.

Civil war—that great fear in the Elizabethan age—is, as we have seen, a recurring theme in Shakespeare's plays. A scene in *Henry VI Part 1* that is certainly attributable to Shakespeare is the encounter in the Temple Garden in the city of London, where representatives of the houses of York and Lancaster pluck white and red roses, and symbolically prepare the way for the civil strife that will rip England apart in *Henry VI Parts 2 and 3*. The rupture in the fabric of the nation is nowhere more powerfully visualized than in a scene in *Part 3* when first there enters a son who has killed his father and then there follows a father who has killed his son. The division of the kingdom brings the division of families. When the father realizes that the body he is bearing is that of his son, he delivers a reprise of Talbot's elegy over his dead boy, though here with the added poignancy of the inadvertent filicide, the fact that they have been fighting against each other, not standing together for their country:

> These arms of mine shall be thy winding-sheet;
> My heart, sweet boy, shall be thy sepulchre,
> For from my heart thine image ne'er shall go;
> My sighing breast shall be thy funeral bell;
> And so obsequious will thy father be,
> Even for the loss of thee, having no more,

As Priam was for all his valiant sons.
I'll bear thee hence; and let them fight that will,
For I have murdered where I should not kill.[44]

Personal loss leads this soldier to reject the pursuit of military glory. The argument turns on the simile "As Priam was for all his valiant sons." According to Homer, King Priam of Ilium had fifty sons, the vast majority of whom were slain on the field of Troy by the Greeks. Priam is the archetype of the father who has the horror of witnessing the death of his sons in battle. This process of comparison with an example from classical antiquity—that rhetorical figure of *paradigma*—is one of Shakespeare's strongest ways of revealing his complex, critical attitude to heroism.

Consider the most Virgilian speech he ever wrote. It comes in *Hamlet*. The players have arrived at Elsinore. Hamlet welcomes his old friend, the lead actor. He asks for an instant taster of the Players' quality, "a passionate speech."[45]

"What speech, my lord?"

O, says Hamlet, one from a play that was either never acted or that bombed after a single performance, because it was too sophisticated, "caviar to the general." "One speech in it," he continues, "I chiefly loved: 'twas Aeneas' tale to Dido, and thereabout of it especially where he speaks of Priam's slaughter."[46] Then off he goes, Hamlet beginning it, and the Player picking up from him: "The rugged Pyrrhus, he whose sable arms, / Black as his purpose, did the night resemble.... With eyes like carbuncles, the hellish Pyrrhus / Old grandsire Priam seeks."[47] Pyrrhus is the son of Achilles, determined to avenge his father's death on the battlefield. The Player takes up the narrative:

> Anon he finds him
> Striking too short at Greeks: his antique sword,
> Rebellious to his arm, lies where it falls,
> Repugnant to command. Unequal matched,
> Pyrrhus at Priam drives, in rage strikes wide,
> But with the whiff and wind of his fell sword
> Th' unnervèd father falls. Then senseless Ilium,
> Seeming to feel this blow, with flaming top
> Stoops to his base, and with a hideous crash
> Takes prisoner Pyrrhus' ear, for, lo, his sword,

Which was declining on the milky head
Of reverend Priam, seemed i' th' air to stick:
So as a painted tyrant Pyrrhus stood,
And, like a neutral to his will and matter,
Did nothing.
But as we often see against some storm
A silence in the heavens, the rack stand still,
The bold winds speechless and the orb below
As hush as death, anon the dreadful thunder
Doth rend the region, so, after Pyrrhus' pause,
Arousèd vengeance sets him new a-work,
And never did the Cyclops' hammers fall
On Mars his armour forged for proof eterne
With less remorse than Pyrrhus' bleeding sword
Now falls on Priam.[48]

Certain details such as Priam's "antique sword ... repugnant to command" seem to be taken from Virgil's second book ("inutile ferrum")[49] and others from the dramatization of Aeneas telling his tale in Marlowe and Nashe's *Dido Queen of Carthage*, notably the image of Priam being knocked to the ground by the "whiff and wind" of Pyrrhus raising his sword.[50] But the particular verbal parallels are of little importance; the significant aspects of the speech are the contrast between its style and that of the surrounding play, and a particular Shakespearean innovation that is without precedent in either Virgil or the Marlowe-Nashe play.

In Virgil, Pyrrhus's actual slaying of Priam is dispatched in two swift lines: "implicuitque comam laeva, dextraque coruscum / extulit ac lateri capulo tenus abdidit ensem," translated by Thomas Phaer as "And with his left hand wrapt his lockes, with right hand through his side / His glistringe sworde outdrawn, he did hard to the hiltes to glide."[51] In Aeneas's speech in Marlowe and Nashe's play, there is a delay whilst soldiers remove Hecuba, who has sought to protect her aged husband by attaching her fingernails to Pyrrhus's eyelids. But then, as soon as Priam is felled by the air-rush of the whirring sword, the end is equally swift: "Then from the navel to the throat at once / He ripped old Priam" (and in so doing presumably gave Shakespeare the hint for Macbeth unseaming Macdonald "from the nave to the chaps").[52] But in the Player's recitation to Hamlet, Pyrrhus's raised sword is held suspended in an effect anticipating a cinematic freeze-frame: during the imagined suspension, Pyrrhus "Did nothing." Even the beat of the iambic pentameter is interrupted: this is a much-abbreviated line. The hearts of Pyrrhus, the reciting Player, the listening Hamlet, and the audience skip several beats, just as the pentameter can only be filled by missing beats.

The gap before the fall of the sword is filled by two lengthy similes: a five-line analogy with a lull before a storm and then, picking up on the thunder clap with which the storm breaks, a comparison with the noise of the hammer of the Cyclops as they forge the armour of Mars. The elaborate comparison to the storm is what is known as an epic simile. Because epic poetry is an extended form that moves at a leisurely pace, the narrative is frequently punctuated by such comparisons. There is a good example in Aeneas's tale to Dido where he speaks of Priam's slaughter. When Pyrrhus arrives at Priam's door in his "brazen harness bright with burnished brand," there is a five-line comparison to a serpent raising itself up in readiness to strike:

> Before the porch all ramping first at th' entry dore doth stand
> Duke *Pyrrhus* in his brasen harneis bright with burnisht brand.
> And glistring like a serpent shines whom poysonid wéedes hath fild.
> That lurking long hath under ground in winter cold ben hild.
> And now his cote of cast all fresh with youth renewd and pride
> Upright his head doth hold, and swift with wallowing back doth glide
> Brest high against the sunne, and spits with toongs thre-forked fier.[53]

At the end of the Pyrrhus speech, which is the second longest in the play, longer than all but Hamlet's longest soliloquy (forty-two lines to the fifty-nine of the Hecuba soliloquy), Polonius has the immortal line: "This is too long." This is not an entirely foolish observation: Hamlet agrees that the speech will have to be trimmed if it is to be performed: "It shall to th' barber's, with your beard."[54] This is Shakespeare's way of saying that he recognizes that there is something inherently undramatic about the heroic idiom exemplified by Virgil: to pause for an epic simile is inevitably to slow down the action. The effect works brilliantly for the deliberate freeze-frame of Pyrrhus's pause in the embedded narrative, but for a character to keep stopping to speak in lengthy similes and metaphors runs the risk of boring the audience. Given the parallels with Marlowe's rendition of Aeneas's tale in *Dido Queen of Carthage*, which actually incorporated chunks of direct translation from Virgil, Shakespeare may even be teasing his dead rival over the excessive length and poetic elaboration of his speeches. The Virgilian style of *Dido Queen of Carthage*, written for court performance in the 1580s, is now, at the end of the 1590s, implicitly condemned as distinctly old-fashioned. Shakespeare's idiom may have aspired to the heroic in parts of *Henry VI* and indeed, more recently, in *Henry V*, but in *Hamlet* he deliberately brackets out the epic voice by giving it to the Player, contrasting it with his own more subtle style that switches between stretches of everyday prose and supple blank verse that moves with the rhythm of thought and the beat of conversational speech.

There is further significance to Pyrrhus's pause. Shortly after the king breaks up the play within the play, the audience is presented with the powerful stage image of Claudius kneeling in penitential prayer and Hamlet standing over him with sword drawn. This is a clear echo of Pyrrhus standing over Priam. It enacts precisely the freeze-frame moment that the Player has described. But Hamlet does not follow his role model. At this point, the classical inheritance clashes with the Christian, and in particular the Protestant, belief system: Pyrrhus plunges in the sword and sends his adversary to Hades, but Hamlet stops to reflect that to kill a man at prayer would be to send him straight to Heaven, which would be no requital for the murder of old Hamlet, taken "full of bread, / With all his crimes broad blown" as he slept, deprived of the opportunity of deathbed penitence. The added twist here is that old Hamlet appears to be in Purgatory, a Catholic imagining, whereas Hamlet's education at Wittenberg has presumably led to him to accept the Protestant abolition of the idea of Purgatory and the idea of instant salvation as the reward for true penitence. Though, of course, the further irony is that Claudius's "words fly up" while his "thoughts remain below," since "words without thoughts never to heaven go."[55]

Hamlet's rejection of the pattern offered by Pyrrhus is of a piece with the play's broader questioning of the ethos of revenge. When we see Hamlet standing over the praying Claudius, he resembles for a moment the "painted tyrant" to whom Pyrrhus was compared in the

Player's speech.[56] The problem Hamlet wrestles with throughout the play is that to become a revenger, he must be a murderer, and that potentially makes him a tyrant no better than Claudius. It is this thought that sparks his conscience—a key Christian idea. In this regard, it is notable that Hamlet's most famous soliloquy begins with canon law's proscription of suicide, "self-slaughter," and ends with the idea that conscience makes cowards of us all.[57] The coward is the opposite of the hero. But, strikingly, in this soliloquy, for once, Hamlet does not measure himself against an exemplar—whether Hercules or Nero, the Player or Fortinbras. He represents himself as the quintessence of the individual, alone with his "conscience," a man thinking, making decisions for himself without the crutch of precedent or example.[58] Ultimately, Shakespeare seems to be saying, we cannot rely on comparisons. Each of us must, as Polonius's sententious statement has it, to our own self be true. In this regard, Hamlet is a new and very modern, we might as well say an *existential*, hero.

The hero is traditionally, as is said of Ajax in *Troilus and Cressida*, "a very man *per se*, and stands alone." Macbeth is increasingly isolated as his play progresses: as he himself says, he ends up like a lone bear tied to the stake in a baiting ring. Upon stabbing King Henry VI, Richard III announces himself with the words "I am myself alone," and in his last soliloquy, delivered upon starting out of his dream of the ghosts of those he has slain, he uses the word "myself" no fewer than twelve times.[59] So perhaps in his self-absorption and his isolation, Hamlet is not so different from the warriors who are his antitype. Hector says farewell to Andromache, Aeneas to Dido, Coriolanus to his wife. The warrior-hero stands alone in single combat; his closest bond is, paradoxically, with his adversary—in *Coriolanus*, Caius Martius and Aufidius almost treat each other as bride and groom. Hamlet, too, says goodbye to love (thus sending Ophelia to despair, madness, and death), stands alone in his soliloquies, then goes on his journey to England effectively alone, since he knows that his companions Rosencrantz and Guildenstern have been suborned to betray him. He escapes alone, then goes alone into the fencing arena that takes the place of the battlefield. But he does have the close friendship of Horatio and, in regretful retrospect, the memory of his love-affair with Ophelia. And always he has his father's injunction to remember. Shakespeare knows that the self depends on a network of connections, those of family, pair bond, and friendship above all.

In this regard, he redoubles his doubts about the heroic idiom of the man per se who stands alone. We have seen in detail how Hamlet is not like Virgil's Pyrrhus. Consider also the way that the supposedly exemplary Trojan and Greek heroes are represented in Shakespeare's play about the war that Homer remembered in the *Iliad* and Virgil in the *Aeneid*: Hector is hen-pecked, Ajax is a blockhead, Ulysses is a scheming politician, and Achilles is less interested in fighting than in playing charades with his camp lover Patroclus. As for Aeneas himself, he is reduced to the status of a glorified messenger, whose messages often get things wrong: he marches into the final scene, announcing that the Trojans are "masters of the field," only to be followed by Troilus with the news that Hector is dead and all is lost. Heroic masculinity does not get a good press in this play.[60] Shakespeare seems to be self-consciously mocking the heroic idiom of George Chapman's recently published translation of seven books of *The Iliad* into high-sounding English verse. The play, moreover, is named not for the Trojan and Greek heroes, but for the lovers: *Troilus and Cressida*.

Troilus and Cressida is called a history on the title page of its quarto, a tragedy in the Folio, and a comedy in its dedicatory epistle, where it is indeed compared to "the best Commedy in *Terence* or *Plautus*."[61] But in its treatment of the heroic, it might best be called a satire. It is the supreme example of Shakespeare as proponent of generic and stylistic hybridity, its language veering from the sublime to the intricately argumentative to the obscene. Shakespeare had no desire to be the Elizabethan Virgil; as he had multiple styles, so he had multiple masters. In this, he was in sympathy with the spirit of a different Augustan poet, one who was equally adept in the arts of lyric, panegyric, and satire, and who defied the idea that a poet should have a single model: "Nullius addictus iurare in verba magistri, / quo me cumque rapit tempestas, deferor hospes" (I am not bound to swear allegiance to a single master: / where the storm drives me I turn in for shelter).[62] That poet was Horace.

9

THE GOOD LIFE

THE ELIZABETHANS REGARDED VIRGIL, Ovid, and Horace as the three great poets of ancient Rome. They were the centre of a literary education then, as Shakespeare is now. In mapping the ancients onto the moderns, our tendency—for which there is ample precedent in both self-image and Elizabethan criticism—is to associate Virgil with Spenser (author of a national epic, poet whose career progression went from pastoral via georgic to epic), Marlowe and Shakespeare with Ovid (composers of erotic poetry, creators of playful stage metamorphoses), and Jonson with Horace (satiric temperament, translation of *Ars Poetica* and other poems, self-representation in *Poetaster*).[1] Shakespeare's contemporaries associated him with Ovid, and Jonson saw himself as Horace. However, the fact that Shakespeare was not a self-proclaimed Horace in the manner of Jonson does not mean that Horace could not also have been a formative influence upon his mind and work.

One of the principal arguments of this book has been that the influence of the classical tradition on Shakespeare's culture was so pervasive that an understanding of the shaping of his own mind by the classics should not be confined to the influence of his schoolroom education and his direct reading of such works as Golding's Ovid and North's Plutarch. Horace arguably exercised a stronger influence than any other writer on what might be called "gentlemanly sensibility" in the sixteenth century. In the light of that claim, and given Shakespeare's aspiration to become a "gentleman," owning property and obtaining a coat of arms for his family, it is astonishing how little scholarship has been devoted to the subject of Horatianism in Shakespeare.[2]

Horatianism should be understood as an idiom, a frame of mind. It is typified by the lyric "In Hortos Eiusdem" ("On His Gardens") by the early seventeenth century's most famous English poet in Europe, Elizabeth Jane Weston. The opening lines have been rendered in English as follows:

> Here is a garden richly cultivated with aromatic plants,
>> cultivated and nourished by Barvitius's assiduous care.
> Here you relieve your wearied breast of its cares, whenever
>> Caesar's court releases you in a state of exhaustion.
> This place welcomes your trusted friends as well;
>> here is an opportunity for seeing and conversing.[3]

A carefully cultivated garden as a retreat and relief from the cares of court, as a place for friendship and conversation, a haven free from the envy and competition that inevitably accompany virtue and status: this is the Horatian idyll, and it is pervasive in the poetry of the age, through to its apogee in the garden poems of Andrew Marvell.

There is no better example of this pervasive Horatianism than the case of the book that came to be known in the nineteenth century as *Tottel's Miscellany*. It includes three loose translations, one of them by the Earl of Surrey, of Horace's ode to Licinius in praise of a life devoted to moderation, the "the golden mean."[4] In addition, there are several imitations of Horace, most notably by Thomas Wyatt: one of them adapts the fable of the town mouse and the country mouse from the sixth poem in the second book of the *Satires*, while another, "Mine own John Poyns," is a superbly rendered Englishing of the Horatian idyll of retreat from the turmoil of the court to the peace and liberty of a rural estate:

> Say he is rude that cannot lie and feign;
> The lecher a lover; and tyranny
> To be the right of a prince's reign.
> I cannot, I; no, no, it will not be!
> This is the cause that I could never yet
> Hang on their sleeves that way, as thou mayst see,
> A chip of chance more than a pound of wit.
> This maketh me at home to hunt and to hawk,
> And in foul weather at my book to sit;
> In frost and snow then with my bow to stalk;
> No man doth mark whereso I ride or go:
> In lusty leas at liberty I walk.[5]

Given that Shakespeare knew Tottel's *Songs and Sonnets* very well, as is clear from the allusion to it in *The Merry Wives of Windsor,* he did not need to read Horace's epodes and satires to absorb this Horatian attitude. It may even be the case that the John Poins poem gave him the name for Prince Hal's companion in *Henry IV*: although Ned Poins is associated with the world of Eastcheap as opposed to that of rural Kent (we do, however, meet him on Gadshill), he is intimately associated with Hal's period of retreat from the court.

However much or little of Horace Shakespeare read once he had left school, where he would have had his first exposure to a range of the poems, he could not have avoided being aware of the perception of Horace. In Thomas Cooper's *Thesaurus,* Quintus Horatius Flaccus is described as "A famous Poet born at Venusium":

> a man excellent in sharpenesse of wit, and quicknesse of sentence: he was addict to Epicures sect, somewhat wanton in maners, though he with great libertie of speeche noted the vices of other men in his verses called Satyræ. In balades to sing to the harpe (which were in xviii. sundrie kindes of verses) he passed all other that wrote in Latine. He was in good fauour with the Emperour Augustus, by the meanes of Mecœnas the Emperors minion, who tooke in him for his myrth and wit much delectation: to whome, and to Augustus, he wrot diverse Epistles in verse, comprehending great wisdome in compendious sentences: and dyed when he was 57 yeares olde, as Eusebius writeth.[6]

This brief character sketch strikes to the quick of the Renaissance image of Horace: he was notable for his witty use of words and especially for his creation of memorable phrases ("sentences"); he was associated with "liberty" in both speech and action ("liberty" shading into the libertinism of "wantonness"); he was gifted with great generic and metrical variety, as adept in satire and epistle as in lyrical ode; he won the favour of Augustus through his patron Maecenas (a whispered hint that, as Maecenas was Augustus's "minion," so Horace was perhaps Maecenas's toyboy); and, in philosophical disposition, he was an Epicurean—though, as we shall see, Epicureanism meant something more complicated than the crude pursuit of bodily pleasure.

A fuller biographical sketch of him in the "Lives of the Poets" that accompanied Suetonius's *Lives of the Twelve Caesars* highlighted both positive and negative aspects of Horace's Epicureanism. Negatively, "It is said that he was immoderately lustful; for it is reported that in a room lined with mirrors he had harlots so arranged that whichever way he looked, he saw a reflection of venery"; such was his sexual appetite that Augustus affectionately called him his "purissimum penem" (purest penis). More positively, Horace is seen, paradoxically in the light of his association with Augustus and Maecenas, as the exemplification of an Epicurean life of *otium*, a withdrawal from the pressing demand to please patron and emperor: "He lived for the most part in the country on his Sabine or Tiburtine estate, and his house is pointed out near the little grove of Tiburnus."[7] "As for me," he wrote with ironic self-deprecation, "when you want a good laugh, you will find me, in a fine state, fat and sleek, a true of hog of Epicurus' herd."[8]

Horace was associated above all with a series of tags. These became proverbial, with the result that critics have been reluctant to assume that Shakespeare engaged directly with the Horatian idiom. In the early modern period, you did not have to be a close reader of Horace himself to be familiar with phrases such as *carpe diem* ("seize the day"), *nil desperandum* ("never despair"), *nunc est bibendum* ("now is the time for drinking"), *ira furor brevis est* ("anger is a brief madness"), *beatus ille* ("happy the man"—who retreats to his own country estate), *dulce et decorum est pro patria mori* ("it is sweet and fitting to die for one's country"), *aequam memento rebus in arduis servare mentem* ("in adversity, remember to keep an even mind"), *auream quisquis mediocritate diligit* ("whoever cultivates the golden mean" avoids both the poverty of a hovel and the envy of a palace), *exegi monumentum aere perennius* ("I have made a monument more lasting than bronze"), *pulvis et umbra sumus* ("we are but dust and shadow"), *ut pictura poesis* ("poetry is like painting"), *dulce et utile* (the task of the poetry is to be both "sweet and useful"), *delectando pariterque monendo* (and thus "to instruct and to delight"). In this respect, Horace was to the Elizabethans what Shakespeare became to the English in later generations: a collection of memorable phrases and quotations, familiar even to those who have never read the poems or seen the plays.

Horace also provided the Elizabethans with a paradigm for a poetic career of generic diversity. His example shaped the understanding of the terms ode and satire. Thus when Dumaine in *Love's Labour's*

Lost announces "Once more I'll read the ode that I have writ," or when one of the offerings for the wedding festivities in *A Midsummer Night's Dream* is "some satire, keen and critical, / Not sorting with a nuptial ceremony," there is an implicit nod to Horace.[9] Such was the familiarity of Horace that he did not have to be named to be evoked: "They say, my lords, *Ira furor brevis est*, / But yon man is ever angry."[10] Conversely, the idea of Horace as a source of proverbial tags does not necessarily require a tag to be quoted: "Under pardon, sir, what are the contents? or rather, as Horace says in his— What, my soul, verses?"[11]

The fact that so many of Horace's phrases had become proverbial did not make them any less Horatian. Consider the particular case of the trope of *beatus ille*, the happy man content in his country life, freed from the turmoil of the court. Shakespeare quietly, sometimes indirectly, alludes to this on numerous occasions. Early in his career, we witness Titus Andronicus telling his son Lucius that he is a "happy man" because he has been sent into exile. The city of Rome "is but a wilderness of tigers," and "Tigers must prey," so "how happy art thou, then, / From these devourers to be banished!"[12] Late in his career, we witness Innogen on her way to the happy rural retreat of Milford Haven: "this same blessed [*beatus*] Milford": "Tell me how Wales was made so happy as / To inherit such a haven."[13] In such cases, Horace himself does not have to be invoked in order to establish the idiom of his second epode.

Consider the following lines of Alexander Iden, the country gentleman in *Henry VI Part 2*:

> Lord, who would live turmoiled in the court,
> And may enjoy such quiet walks as these?
> This small inheritance my father left me
> Contenteth me, and worth a monarchy.
> I seek not to wax great by others' waning,
> Or gather wealth I care not with what envy:
> Sufficeth that I have maintains my state
> And sends the poor well pleasèd from my gate.[14]

The turmoil of the court against the quiet of the country; rejection of the vicissitudes of fortune's wheel and the quest for wealth; the verbs *content*, *suffice*, and *please*: these details would have been recognized, consciously or unconsciously, by genteel audience members as Horatian in their sentiment, very much in the manner of Wyatt's verse epistle to John Poins. Furthermore, Shakespeare's semi-ironic attitude to Iden's comfortable stance is equally Horatian. The irony of Horace's second epode is that the *beatus ille* praise of the life of rural retreat turns out to be spoken by a moneylender called Alfius who is about to make a financial gamble in the city. The irony of Iden's vision of his personal rural Eden is that he claims that his own modest almsgiving will be sufficient to send the poor "well pleased" from his gate, but in the very next instant he encounters a poor man in his garden and kills him. The man is Jack Cade, who has led the poor in their uprising against the social order that allows the wealthy their rural leisure, while others have to content themselves as servants and still more are beggars. As he dies, Cade curses the garden. Iden's England will no longer be an Eden, a demi-paradise, as is amply demonstrated by the ravaging of the land still to come in the following plays in the cycle of violence.

There is a similar ironic juxtaposition in *Henry VI Part 3*. In the middle of a battle, amidst alarums and excursions, the King enters alone and delivers the play's longest speech, an extended *beatus ille*—"O God! methinks it were a happy life, / To be no better than a homely swain"—that elaborates the trope of living a "sweet" and "lovely" life moment by moment, hour by hour, day by day, and year by year until one reaches "a quiet grave." How much better, he says, this would be than to be a king in an opulent court "When care, mistrust, and treason waits on him."[15] No sooner does he finish the speech than there is another alarum and a son enters with the body of the father that he has killed. King Henry's attempt to stop the clock of political time is a singular failure. The same motion is repeated more economically and subtly in *Henry IV Part 2*. The sleepless king attaches the *beatus ille* motif to the lowly—"then, happy low, lie down! / Uneasy lies the head that wears a crown"—but is then interrupted by Warwick and Surrey, whose entrance provokes a meditation on the cycle of revenge and the "rank diseases" growing on "the body of our kingdom." If one could "read the book of fate" and "see the revolution of the times," then even "the happiest youth" (*beatus ille*) "Would shut the book and sit him down and die."[16] It is almost as if the metaphoric book at this moment is a work of

Horatian comfort that must be closed because such sentiments as *beatus ille* and *carpe diem*, let alone *dulce et decorum est*, are insufficient coping mechanisms in time of war.

⌒

The Elizabethan and Jacobean writer most closely associated with Horace was Ben Jonson. By writing poetry that self-consciously offered profit and delight, by praising his Maecenas-like patrons, by excelling in the art of satire, and by translating *beatus ille* and the *Ars Poetica* (as well as many more poems, with commentaries, all lost in his library fire), Jonson presented himself as the English Horace. In *Poetaster*, the boys' company play in which he laid out an Augustan model for the future of English poetry, he identified with Horace, the poet-moralist who was more measured than the "whipping satirists" (Juvenal and Persius in ancient Rome, rival poet-dramatist John Marston in the early seventeenth-century *poetomachia* or "poets' war").[17] *Poetaster* is Jonson's critique not only of harsh satire, but also of love-poetry—Ovid and thus Shakespeare—on the grounds that it cannot shape the social order and indeed that it potentially undermines public morality.

We know from Jonson's "Apologetical Dialogue" that the adult actors, possibly including Shakespeare, were offended by the portrayal of them in *Poetaster*. The Chamberlain's Men entered the *poetomachia* when they staged a riposte called *Satiromastix* ("the whipping of the satirist") in which Horace (i.e., Jonson) is presented as a craven and sycophantic time-server. This was Shakespeare's closest encounter with Horace: he almost certainly acted in a play in which a purge is delivered to Horace. As company dramatist, he may also have overseen, even intervened in, the writing of it.[18]

We are unlikely ever to establish Shakespeare's precise role in the creation of *Satiromastix*. What can be said with much more certainty is that he went on, albeit in collaboration with the more satirically inclined Thomas Middleton, to mock the idea of a Horatian (or Jonsonian) poet in pursuit of patronage in another play, *Timon of Athens*. That play is an extension of the *poetomachia*, but transposed from Rome to Athens perhaps because the Augustan self-image of King James made it too dangerous to continue the debate in Rome. The play is a satire on the pursuit of patronage in the Jacobean court. The sycophantic Poet in the opening scene is not specifically Jonson, but rather a stand-in for all those writers who sought patronage in the Jacobean court, as Horace sought the patronage of Maecenas. The Poet's debate with the Painter is a testing of the Horatian theme of *ut pictura poesis*. And the satire he is writing for Timon sounds like a very Horatian effort: "I am thinking what I shall say I have provided for him: it must be a personating of himself, a satire against the softness of prosperity, with a discovery of the infinite flatteries that follow youth and opulency."[19]

As the ironic twist at the end of the second epode reminds us, Horatianism always has one eye on advancement, the other on retreat. In a sense, the arc of *Timon* is to split these two elements apart, focusing in the first half on the flatterers seeking preferment and in the second on Timon's retreat from the city to the woods, from court to country. This structural movement is a typically Shakespearean one, in comedy (*As You Like It*), tragedy (*King Lear*), and pastoral (*The Winter's Tale*). By the same account, Shakespeare's own commuting between London and Stratford-upon-Avon mimics Horace's movement between competitive Rome and the rural peace of his farm at Tivoli. Where Jonson was forever seeking a seat at the table of the great, Shakespeare was content to return to New Place, Horace to his Sabine farm.

For all that Shakespeare sought to replicate the verbal pyrotechnics and the erotic entanglements of Ovid, he also had a voice of calm, autonomy, and detachment that may be properly described as Horatian. The satirical and patronage-seeking aspect of the Poet in Timon may be a hit at Jonson and his like, but the self-description of the process of composition is more Shakespearean: "A thing slipped idly from me," he says, in sharp contrast to Jonson's frequent emphasis on poetic *labor*:

> Our poesy is as a gum, which oozes
> From whence 'tis nourished. The fire i' th' flint
> Shows not till it be struck: our gentle flame
> Provokes itself and like the current flies
> Each bound it chafes.[20]

These images of natural productivity and spontaneous combustion sing the autonomy of art. The artist is not to be bidden by the mere exigencies of the patronage system. Poetry must come from within. Horace wrote of distilling poetic honey.[21] Shakespeare's language of creativity is similarly sweet, progressing from oozing gum to the "free drift" of the Timon poet that "Halts not particularly, but moves itself / In a wide sea of wax," where there is a suggestion not only of the motion of a wave and the imprint on a waxed writing tablet, but also of a honeycomb.[22] As countrymen, both Horace and Shakespeare took inspiration from the example of honeybees.

The very structure of Shakespeare's life enacted a Horatian move from *negotium* back to *otium*. At the conclusion of my intellectual biography of him, *Soul of the Age*, I suggested that this could be described as an Epicurean progress.[23] What I failed to see there is the Horatian dimension of the journey.

What did Shakespeare really value? What did he imagine were the principles of a good life, a well-lived life? In the year 306 BCE, a man named Epicurus took up residence in Athens. He was an enemy of Platonism. He bought a house and a little garden, and he cultivated his pupils there. He argued against the idea, shared by Plato and Aristotle, that happiness and the good life were linked to active citizenship. Epicurus suggested instead that political ambition leads only to misery. Instead, we need to find inner happiness, and our models for finding true happiness are to be discovered by looking at the cycles of birth and decay in nature in that garden. We need to accept the mortality of all things. Life, according to this way of living, must be lived in the present. Whereas Aristotle said that the cultivation of civic virtue should be the basis of philosophy, that we are political animals and indeed that anyone who is not political, not interested in civic life, is an idiot, Epicurus replied by extolling the virtues of radical idiocy, of a rejection of the political life.[24] He proposed instead that we need to seek peace of mind, inner tranquillity. We find this by discovering the true nature of things.

The true nature of things is as follows. All that exists are atoms and the void. The soul is mortal. There is no such thing as divine providence. The gods do not intervene in human affairs. We should overcome our fear of death and the unknown through the knowledge that there is no afterlife. We have nothing to fear, because when we die all that happens is that our atoms are dispersed back into the cosmos. Philosophy, argues Epicurus, accordingly means a pursuit of the good life, and the good life is achieved through the cultivation of pleasure. The word he used was *hēdonē*, from the Greek, *hedus*, which means "sweet": the sweet or good life. This idea of "Hedonism" in subsequent centuries has been much frowned upon. We associate the word with the indulgence of our appetites. If we think of the idea of the "Epicurean" in the context of the drama of Shakespeare's age, the first character who will come to mind is Sir Epicure Mammon in Ben Jonson's comedy, *The Alchemist*, a huge Falstaffian man, whose life revolves around money, food, and sex. That, however, is not what Epicurus was recommending when he told us to pursue the good life. He argued instead that the chief virtue that we should cultivate is friendship. It is friendship that provides us support in time of need. Epicurus suggests that the basis of human relations should be good conversation, because conversation embodies friendship. We should cultivate an agreeable personality. Cicero liked that idea. He wrote of *suāvitās*, the idea that an Epicurean way of being is to be agreeable. Sometimes, the agreeable Epicurean was contrasted to the supercilious Platonist, the dour Stoic, and the boorish Cynic. The Epicurean shows consideration for others, is ruled by honesty and by nonaggression, and, above all, has a particular hatred of flattery, sycophants, and parasites. Epicureanism believes in patience in the present, hope for the future, and gratitude for the past. "Ingratitude" is a special demon, corrosive of the soul.[25]

Epicureanism was much frowned upon in Shakespeare's time because of the hostility to both the idea of the indulgence of the flesh and the atheism of the world-system encoded in the *De Rerum Natura* of Lucretius, the poetic codifier of Epicurus's materialist philosophy. However, largely through the example of Horace, the ethical code of Epicureanism filtered through from antiquity: the notion that moderation as opposed to excess was the way to true pleasure; the belief in friendship as the cardinal virtue; the conviction that one should not allow oneself to become involved in anything which is potentially outside one's control; hence the resistance to participation in political and civic activities; the preference for everyday practical matters over unproductive metaphysical speculation; above all, a turning away from worldly ambition and the gaining of solace from oneself alone, perhaps as one cultivates one's garden. In reflecting on the example of Horace, as in reading Montaigne's essays in the translation of John Florio, published in 1603, Shakespeare would have found many images of a virtuous Epicurean life, not least that of the country gentleman sitting in his library or scratching the earth in his cabbage patch. Or cultivating his farm at Tivoli.

There is a strong vein of anti-Stoicism running through Shakespeare. In *Titus Andronicus*, the most appalling things happen to Titus. His daughter is raped, her hands are cut off, her tongue is cut out, his sons' heads are cut off. In response to all this, his brother, Marcus, a very good Roman Stoic, tells him to have patience. That is what the stoical Roman does. But Titus does not have patience: at his nadir, he laughs. He demonstrates through action the thought that Marcus expresses but does not follow through, namely that emotion must be expressed physically: "Sorrow concealed, like an oven stopped, / Doth burn the heart to cinders where it is."[26] If we repress our emotions, eventually they will explode within us. Patience is an act of the will; laughter is a reaction of the body, as are tears. Shakespeare is Epicurean, not Stoic, when he recognizes that we always live in our bodies. He partly learned that through his early experience as an actor and his witnessing of his colleagues' manner of acting: the player works with the body, breathing from the stomach, gesturing with the hands, moving limbs and muscles in tune with the thought.

Stoicism proposed that we should cultivate our reason and subdue the desires of our bodies. The academe in *Love's Labour's Lost* is in this sense a Stoic project, a three-year commitment to the renunciation of bodily desire in the pursuit of wisdom. The foolishness of this aspiration is revealed by the fool, Costard: "Such is the simplicity of man to hearken after the flesh."[27] The body intrudes; we cannot deny the reality of bodily need. This train of thought is precisely the Epicurean response to the Stoic idea that only the mind matters. In Shakespeare's plays, again and again, the body, its emotions, and its desires, are there to question those who think that the vicissitudes of life can simply be kept in check through the processes of reason. "The world must be peopled," as Benedick reminds us in *Much Ado about Nothing*. Or, as the learned poet George Chapman put it in highly Epicurean fashion in "Eugenia," his poem about good breeding: "For God's love and good life yet, as too true / We prove, our bodies means have to imbue / Their powers with carnal love."[28]

Shakespeare is traditionally praised for his capacious sympathy for all his characters, but he manifestly loved some of his characters more than others, and those he relished most are often the ones who embrace their carnality, Cleopatra and Falstaff foremost among them. Falstaff is Sir Epicure Mammon's match, but with a key difference: to Prince Hal, he embodies the true Epicurean virtue of friendship that he has not found in family or court, but does find in a riotous tavern. Falstaff embodies friendship every bit as much as he is an eater, a drinker, a deceiver, a self-server, and a seeker after pleasure. Fluellen unwittingly reveals in *Henry V* that one respect in which King Harry resembles Alexander the Great is that he causes the death of his best friend: as Alexander stabbed Cleitus in a drunken argument, so Hal causes Falstaff to die of a broken heart.[29]

Horace's much-imitated fable of the town mouse and the country mouse follows hard on the heels of a discussion, at his Sabine farm, of the nature of true friendship and its relation to the good life.[30] The Renaissance idealization of friendship is a theme with numerous classical antecedents, Cicero's *De Amicitia* foremost among them, but Horace's treatment was the most influential in two respects: its linkage to the idea of rural retreat, *otium* in opposition in *negotium*, and its blurring of the borders between the bond of male friendship and the force of homoerotic passion. Horace often extols the virtues of nonsexual male friendship, but the beautiful youth Ligurinus in the odes is an object of desire. The short ode "O crudelis" is so explicitly homoerotic that for centuries it was omitted from English translations of Horace.[31] The lovely youth is chided for his cruelty, warned that he will regret it when he looks at his reflection in future years and sees that his beauty has begun to fade. The art of simultaneously praising and condemning, yearning and admonishing, refusing to idealise the beloved boy, is exactly that of Shakespeare's more bitter sonnets such as "They that have power to hurt and will do none ... They are the lords and owners of their faces."[32]

The sense that time will ravage the face of the lovely boy links the poetry of homoerotic desire to the theme of *carpe diem*. In *Twelfth Night*, Feste offers Sir Toby and Sir Andrew the choice of a "a song of good life" or "a love song." Sir Toby opts for a love song and Sir Andrew concurs because he cares not for the "good life."[33] The good life is the Horatian ideal. But Feste's love song is equally Horatian. It is a classic lyric of *carpe diem*:

What is love? 'tis not hereafter;
Present mirth hath present laughter;

What's to come is still unsure:
In delay there lies no plenty;
Then come kiss me, sweet and twenty,
Youth's a stuff will not endure.[34]

Shakespeare suggests that a love song and a song of the good life are one and the same Horatian thing. Furthermore, in the wider context of the play, the "youth" that is desired, the wished-for object of a kiss, is above all Viola-Cesario, who, as if in homage to Horace's bisexual imagination, is master-mistress of the passions of both Orsino and Olivia.

Given that Shakespeare was born on the fringe of the forest of Arden and had a mother called Mary Arden, we may reasonably say that one of the plays that must have been particularly close to his heart was *As You Like It*, in which he transposes his source from Ardennes to Arden and introduces references to Robin Hood, not to mention a cameo appearance from an English country bumpkin pointedly called William. Its pastoral embraces another song of *carpe diem*: "Therefore, take the present time ... for love is crownèd with the prime."[35] The play's thesis is laid out in the exiled Duke's opening oration to the effect that the life of exile is "more sweet" (*dulce*) than that of the "painted pomp" of the court. The absence from Arden of "envy" and "flattery," two of the aspects of court and city life that Horace again and again excoriates in his satires; the sense of exemption "from public haunt"; the ability to find "sermons in stones, and good in everything": all these tropes are indicative of a Horatian idiom. The winter wind blows harshly—this is no soft *Eclogue*-like pastoral—but the weather is "not so unkind as man's ingratitude": in the Horatian-Epicurean code, ingratitude is the worst of vices. "A friend remembered not," as a result of the jostling for preferment at court, is a far worse thing than a little physical hardship in the countryside.[36]

At the same time, Shakespeare challenges the Horatian idyll— just as Horace sometimes did himself. Jaques is a satirist who follows the Horatian precept of speaking "invective" against human folly in general, as opposed to attacking an individual in the abrasive manner of Juvenal:

Thus most invectively he pierceth through
The body of the country, city, court,

Yes, of this our life, swearing that we
Are mere usurpers, tyrants, and what's worse,
To fright the animals and to keep them up
In their assigned and native dwelling place.[37]

Jaques vents his spleen in speaking against not only the city and the court, but also the life of the country, indeed all of human life. In this, he is sometimes seen as a parody of Jonson, but it is more likely that he is intended as a generic satirist—who is himself satirized by his fellow sojourners in Arden. Often wrongly described as one of the Duke's courtiers, he is a gentleman who has sold his lands in order to become a "traveller,"[38] a wry, detached observer of manners and morals, very much in the manner of Horace.

Jaques and Touchstone—characters invented by Shakespeare, without precedent in his source, Thomas Lodge's *Rosalynd*—spar with each other because the satire of the former and the witty foolery of the latter are rival modes of mocking courtly pretensions such as Orlando's highly romanticized language of love-service. Touchstone argues that what Arden offers is in some respects "a good life," in other respects not.[39] Horatian rural ease depends on the kind of "plenty" that Ben Jonson celebrated in his praise of the groaning table of Sir Robert Sidney at Penshurst. Shakespeare the realist, who lived so much of his life in the country, knew that many of his neighbours had to endure empty stomachs. The "natural philosopher" Corin replies to Touchstone with an ethic of common sense: he knows the harshness of the elements and the grounding reality of the physical body, he knows poverty and the need to work, in a manner from which sophisticated courtiers are insulated.[40]

Shakespeare aspired to be a gentleman like Horace. He succeeded in retiring to the country and becoming a landowner. But throughout his plays he continued to give voice to ordinary working men and women—gardeners and tapsters, hostesses and whores, servants and countrymen, shepherds and pedlars—as if to remind himself that the Horatian "good life" is a privilege, not a right.

10

THE DEFENCE OF PHANTASMS

FRANCIS MERES'S "COMPARATIVE DISCOURSE of our English poets with the Greeke, Latin, and Italian poets," with its nationalist agenda and its high claims for Shakespeare, was published as "*the Second part of Wit's Commonwealth*." The first part, by a London grocer and literary patron called John Bodenham, entitled *Politeuphuia: Wit's Commonwealth*, is much less well known. It consists of a vast array of commonplaces—equal weight being given to classical and Christian sources—on subjects ranging from divinity to morality to the passions. Bodenham has much to say about the virtues of wit when it comes in the form of Ciceronian eloquence and humanist wisdom, but his chapter "Of Poetry" is full of anxiety.

It begins with a definition: "A Poet was called *Vates*, which is as much as Diviner, Fore-seer, or Prophet, and of this word *Carmina*, which was taken for Poesy, came this word *Charms*, because it is as a divine enchantment to the senses, drawing them by the sweetness of delightful numbers, to a wondrous admiration."[1] The divinity and the prophetic power of the poet are read as a form of witchcraft, an enchantment that seduces the senses and draws the reader away from the spirit of reverence and piety. Poetry may inculcate honour and virtue, it may "quickneth the wit, sweetneth the discourse, and tickleth the ear," but too often it is "lascivious" and "full of feigned sighs, lewd allegories, immodest metaphors, and incredulous descriptions." Plato, Bodenham reminds his readers, "drove Poets out of his commonweal, as those that make the common people effeminate." Poets are too often driven by love or anger, emotions that overheat the brain (a sentiment derived from Juvenal). They are also too often impious, making "*Clio a Thais*" (the Muse of history turned to a *hetaira* or concubine), "Helicon a brothel-house, and themselves contemptible."[2]

Ironically, given that Bodenham sponsored the publication of a number of poetic anthologies such as *Englands Helicon* and *Bel-*

vedére, or the Garden of the Muses, his vituperative language here is highly reminiscent of Puritan attacks on the stage and on love poetry. This brings us to the central problem faced by Elizabethan boosters of the new national literature: the irreconcilable difference, especially in matters sexual, between paganism and Christianity.

Webbe's *Discourse of English Poetry* established a model of the nation's literary history that became commonplace. Three years later, George Puttenham's *Art of English Poesy* picked up on the idea that the English literary Renaissance only began in the mid-sixteenth century:

> In the latter end of [King Henry VIII]'s reign sprung up a new company of courtly makers, of whom Sir *Thomas Wyatt* th'elder and *Henry* Earl of Surrey were the two chieftains, who having travelled into Italy, and there tasted the sweet and stately measures and style of the Italian Poesy, as novices crept out of the schools of *Dante, Ariosto*, and *Petrarch*, they greatly polished our rude and homely manner of vulgar Poesy from that it had been before, and for that cause may justly be said the first reformers of our English metre and style.[3]

Though Puttenham did not agree with the idea that English verse should be written in quantitative metres, he followed Webbe in removing the word "reformers" from its ecclesiastical origins and giving it over to a purely literary phenomenon. Literary history became a means to dignify the art of the nation—a necessity, as the choice of the word "reformer" reveals, because the break from Rome had created the imperative for the forging of a national cultural identity.

Herein lay the problem. The writing of national history was inspired by the classical inheritance, as embodied in the example of Livy and other Roman historians. But it was also shaped by the ideology of the Reformation—the trajectory of the *Chronicles* was a providential progression towards the establishment of the reforming Tudor dynasty, a story seen as a sign of God's choice of the English nation as the instrument of his work. John Foxe's *Actes and Monuments* (1563 and many subsequent editions), popularly known as the "Book of Martyrs," was the extreme version of this narrative. But the relationship between Protestantism and poetry, as opposed to history, was a fraught one. Poetry involved the making of images, whereas the destruction of images, on the grounds that they were idolatrous, was one of the primary impulses of sixteenth-century "reformers" who espoused the more radical—the pure, or Puritan—versions of Protestantism.

In addition, poetry had an unfortunate tendency to celebrate rather than seek to restrain sexual desire. In the later sixteenth century, and throughout the seventeenth, numerous religious writers and preachers complained, as George Herbert put it in a sonnet attacking the conventions of sonneteering, of poetry's tendency to "wear *Venus'* livery" and "only serve her turn" (the sexual *double entendre* in the latter phrase is intended as an example of the lascivious style that is to be renounced). Herbert asks God, "Why are not *Sonnets* made of thee?"[4] Is it not time, he demands, for the Dove of the Holy Spirit to replace the winged Cupids of secular, pagan-inspired poetry?

The historian Johan Huizinga ventured the paradox that the Middle Ages knew only "applied art," religion in its manifold aspects being the foremost application.[5] In Huizinga's interpretation of fourteenth- and fifteenth-century culture in northern Europe, the purpose of an artwork predominated over its aesthetic value; indeed, he argued, the very idea of pure aesthetic value only emerged with the luxury of Renaissance courts and the superabundance of artistic production associated with them. This was a highly questionable generalization about the "Middle Ages," but its notion of the primacy of "applied art" in an intensely religious culture remains valuable—particularly in the context of a cultural revolution such as that precipitated by Henry VIII's break from Rome. The primary purpose of most of the major literary achievements between the fractious year of 1533 and the accession of Queen Elizabeth I in 1558 was something other than aesthetic pleasure.[6] The foremost of those purposes were religious and national.

The late Henrican and Edwardian printing press "knew only applied art" because it was predominantly an agent of Protestant revolution. By the end of the century, however, a book culture had developed that was much more varied in its genres and purposes. Let us take the example of a single representative year. In 1594, the year in which a Shakespearean play appeared in print for the first time, only about one-third of the total number of titles published in London were religious texts (Bibles, prayer books, versions of the Psalms, commentaries, sermons, devotional manuals, antipapist propaganda). About a quarter of them were what we would now call "literary" or "artistic" works (poetry, plays, prose romances, satires, travel narratives, translations of the classics, and musical part-books).

The religious works, whether the five imprints of the Geneva Bible which appeared that year, the eleven volumes of sermons, prayers, and exhortations by the indefatigable popular preacher Henry Smith, or an elementary handbook such as Edward Vaughan's *How to Read all the Books in the Holy Bible*, were by their nature devoted to spiritual, doctrinal, and homiletic ends. They continued the work of the Protestant Reformation in the vernacular. As at all times in the history of print, the year 1594 also witnessed a substantial body of publications devoted to the dissemination of useful information. A practical handbook such as Vincentio Saviolo's translation of Muzio's *Il Duello* or a legal textbook such as the seventh (enlarged) edition of William Lambarde's *The Duties of Constables, Borsholders, Tithing-Men*, or a political pamphlet such as *A Brief Note of the Benefits that grow to this Realm by the Observation of Fish Days* may be of considerable interest in illuminating such works of imagination as Shakespeare's *As You Like It* (Touchstone on the duello), *Much Ado about Nothing* (the character of Dogberry), or Thomas Nashe's *Lenten Stuff* (with its parodic discourse on red herrings), but their prime function was to be instrumental towards certain immediate ends in the everyday world.

The sixty or so volumes of verse, drama, prose fiction, and music published in London in 1594—Shakespeare's *Lucrece*, *Titus Andronicus*, and reprinted *Venus and Adonis* among them—stand in a different relation to that world. Each of them asks to be read as a world of its own. Unlike the other one hundred and seventy or so volumes, they are not, as Sir Philip Sidney put it in his *Defence of Poetry*, "wrapped within the fold of the proposed subject."[7] They take the course of their own invention; they play serious games whose rules have to be learnt. The end of the game may well be ideological—a moral point, a spiritual exhortation, a patriotic sentiment—but the distinction of such books is that the reader is invited to take a particular interest in the means as opposed to the end. An interest, that is, in style and indeed stylishness. Such works are "poesy": they ask to be judged for their artfulness, or indeed for the quality that Castiglione called *sprezzatura*, the art that conceals art.

"A Poet is as much to say a maker," wrote Puttenham in the first sentence of *The Arte of English Poesie*, in allusion to the Greek *poiesis*, making.[8] Poetic writers are valued for their *making* more than their teaching. They are praised for pleasing as opposed to profiting their readers. Their works are not ostensibly practical or instrumental. According to this way of thinking—shared by Puttenham, Sir Philip Sidney, and many other Elizabethan literary theorists—the world of a poetic text is a thing in itself, not the means to a direct moral, spiritual, or political end. Of course, a true poem or play may be patriotic, or may conform to the new orthodoxies of Protestantism, but to do so is not its primary purpose, as would be the case with a homily, a sermon, or a narrative of providential history.

According to this definition, "poetry" is not confined to verse: the word refers to all writing of the kind that we would now call "creative" or "imaginative." Sir Philip Sidney was the most illustrious Elizabethan exponent of the view that "poetry" or "poesy" is that kind of writing which constitutes a "second" or "golden" world distinct from the realms of history and philosophy. "Verse," he believed, was "but an ornament and no cause to Poetry, since there have been many most excellent poets that never versified, and now swarm many versifiers that need never answer to the name of poets."[9]

"Poesy," wrote Sidney in his defence of the art, is "a representing, counterfeiting, or figuring forth—to speak metaphorically, a speaking picture." The poet is characterized by the art of "feigning notable images of virtues, vices, or what else."[10] Language cannot present the world as it is; it is perforce a re-presentation or a "figuring." By this account, poesy is a kind of writing that is especially finely attuned to its own figurality. It takes peculiar delight in its own feignings, its status as "counterfeit." Sidney considered the best poesy to be that which figures forth "another nature," an alternative world to the Nature that is described by astronomers, geometricians, philosophers, lawyers, historians, physicians, and the like.[11]

In this poetic, feigning is also faining, as in "I would fain," meaning "I desire." The art of pretending, imagining, inventing, and deceiving is linked to desire and delight. It is never far from the erotic and the gratification of the senses. Like so much of the most sophisticated Renaissance visual art, Elizabethan poetry at its best creates worlds within worlds: the Shakespearean play or Spenserian poem or Sidneyan romance presents to its spectator or reader a feigned/fained imaginary world within which there is another feigned/fained world—the play within the play, the faery landscape within the poem, Arden, Illyria, Arcadia.

The critic Harry Berger proposes that serious delight in feigning was an historical novelty in the Renaissance and was indeed symptomatic of a sea-change undergone by the mind of Europe between the fourteenth and the seventeenth century: "As nature loses its Aristotelian substantiality, as the lines between subjective and objective forms of phenomena become more sharply drawn, as physical reality becomes more closely identified with atoms, forces, and mathematics—as, in general, man by retracting his projected self-images confers new otherness on both God and nature, the mind-made orders increase in dignity and importance." The artwork becomes its own place, "the playground, laboratory, theatre, or battlefield of the mind, a model or construct the mind creates, a time or place it clears in order to withdraw from the actual environment."[12] The movement away from "application" highlights the force and, from a Protestant point of view, the danger of what Berger calls "the second world" of Renaissance fiction-making.

From the point of view of a Puritan sensibility resistant to play, to image-making, and to the delights of *otium* as opposed to *negotium*, second worlds are dangerous, not to say scandalous. The only communal place where one should go in order to retreat from the business of the world (*negotium*) was the church. Certainly not the playhouse. And in one's private closet, one should be praying and reading holy books, not poring over "ill and undecent provocations," "lascivious Poems ... such as are Ovid's love Books and *Elegies*, Tibullus, Catullus, and Martial's works, with the Comedies for the most part of Plautus and Terence."[13] Delight was all too close to sexual indulgence and transgression. "Reforming" English verse to make it more classical and to dignify the national culture was one thing, dwelling in the garden of poetic delights quite another. For Stephen Gosson, to whose attack on poetry Sidney's defence was a reply, the world of "feigning" was *The School of Abuse*. His book of that title was subtitled *A pleasant invective against Poets, Pipers, Players, Jesters and such like Caterpillars of a Commonwealth*.[14] The whole motley crew of disreputable entertainers was regarded as a danger to both religion and the state.

And yet Hamlet says that the purpose of playing is and ever was "to hold as 'twere the mirror up to nature: to show virtue her feature, scorn her own image, and the very age and body of the time his form and pressure."[15] Where amidst all the feignings and counterfeits, it may be asked at this point, is *mimesis*, the ancient idea—also invoked by Sidney in his *Apology for Poetry*—that art should properly be an imitation of nature? What might, for shorthand, be described as the "Reformation" and the "Renaissance" reading of Hamlet's image are radically opposed to each other. A Reformation reading will be just that: the images of virtue and vice you see in the mirror of art are intended to reform you. The *Mirror for Magistrates* was so called because it provided a series of negative *exempla* that were intended to bring the reader to just political *praxis* and an amendment of moral life. A Renaissance reading will be more multilayered and sceptical: it will be aware that "playing" is and is not "being," that a mirror is bound by a frame, is not a work of nature but an elaborate human artifice (from 1507 onwards consisting of glass backed with an amalgam of tin and mercury, manufactured under monopoly in Venice), that the world inside the mirror is an illusion, since it has left-right reversal and projects three-dimensional reality onto a two-dimensional space, that its image is perceived according to the laws of perspective and may be contrived to produce various dioptric distortions, and that the human faces it reflects are only external appearances which may well be adept in the art of counterfeiting, of concealing the vice beneath the skin. Precisely for these reasons, "Reformation" poetics were extremely suspicious of "Renaissance" ones. Sidney wrote his defence of poesy in reply to a Reformation attack on it, while "Puritan" hostility to the feignings of the stage was widespread. The touchstone of Renaissance poetics is Touchstone's Sidneyan principle that "the truest poetry is the most feigning," a truth-claim scandalous to the Reformation sensibility.[16]

The hostility of Protestantism to the feigning imagination is especially apparent in the first English-language mythography, which manages to condemn the vanity of imagination and counterfeit creation even in its title: *The golden booke of the leaden goddes Wherein is described the vayne imaginations of heathe[n] pagans, and counterfaict Christians: wyth a description of their several tables, what ech of their pictures signified. By Stephen Batman, student in divinitie.* Batman, author of such works as *A Christiall Glass for Christian Reformation, treating on the 7 deadly Sinns*, enumerates the symbolic meaning of some forty pagan gods.[17] Thus, for example, Venus is "figured in a Garden of Flowers, naked.... Her Garland of Roses doth signifie the superfluity which wantons require," while the lion skin of Hercules signifies not only his valour but also the prudence through which he "subdued his outragious affections." Each figure is then followed by a summary of a story or stories that "The Poets fayne" about the god under examination. Having dispatched the pagan gods in this way, Batman then turns to "A Recapitulation of the Sectarian Gods, by whose Heresies, much harme hath growen, to Gods true Church," in which deviants from the true faith, ranging from Papist saints to the Anabaptist John of Leiden ("this Rustical hedge god"), are given similarly hostile treatment on the grounds of their predilection for lying symbols and imaginings.[18]

A principal source of the imaginative power of the literature of the period is the paradox whereby the Renaissance delight in feigning was exercised and celebrated by writers who were at the same time ideologically committed to the building of a reformed English nation. Edmund Spenser wrote with greatest intensity when inventing places such as the Bower of Bliss where his Reformation and his Renaissance sensibilities were stretched in creative tension.[19] His pagan temples and earthly paradises offer at one and the same time sensuous delights and anticipations of heavenly bliss. Bottom's experience in Titania's bower similarly brings together immediate sexual gratification of an Ovidian kind and, by way of garbled quotation from St Paul's letter to the Corinthians, a suggestion of the delights that God has prepared for his believers in the kingdom of heaven.[20]

The poet's art of feigning is a recurrent *topos* in Shakespeare. Touchstone's quip is only the most obvious instance. Others include Richard of Gloucester's "all that poets feign of bliss and joy," Lorenzo's "therefore the poet / Did feign that Orpheus drew trees, stones and floods" in *The Merchant of Venice*, Egeus's "Thou hast by moonlight at her window sung, / With feigning voice verses of feigning love" in *A Midsummer Night's Dream*, and Olivia's response to Viola/Cesario's announcement early in *Twelfth Night* that her message from Orsino is "poetical": "'Tis the more like to be feigned."[21]

The most explicit and extended treatment of the theme occurs at the beginning of *Timon of Athens*.[22] The Poet who is seeking wealthy Timon's patronage describes his latest work, in which he has "upon a high and pleasant hill / Feigned Fortune to be throned."[23] This introduces the familiar figure of poetry as feigning. There may also be a subliminal pun on "fane," meaning temple, conjuring up an image of Fortune enthroned within a hilltop temple: it is hard to visualize the throne plonked in the open air. A little later, the ancient animosity between the poet and the philosopher is rekindled when Apemantus throws the association of feigning with falsehood in the unnamed Poet's face:

> APEMANTUS. How now, poet?
> POET. How now, philosopher?
> APEMANTUS. Thou liest.
> POET. Art not one?
> APEMANTUS. Yes.
> POET. Then I lie not.
> APEMANTUS. Art not a poet?
> POET. Yes.
> APEMANTUS. Then thou liest: look in thy last work, where thou
>   hast feigned him a worthy fellow.
> POET. That's not feigned; he is so.
> APEMANTUS. Yes, he is worthy of thee, and to pay thee for thy
>   labour. He that loves to be flattered is worthy o' the flatterer.[24]

Apemantus, who has the philosopher's (which is also the Fool's) mode of always beginning with a question, then coming to a clever conclusion, claims that his kind are truth-tellers, whereas poets create flattering fictions—feignings—for money.

Apemantus is a Cynic, whose case against poetry is one part philosophical and the other part social. By contrast, Shakespeare's awareness of the high religious stakes around the idea of poetic "feigning" is apparent from an infrequently noticed comparison in *Cymbeline*, a play much concerned with the tensions between classical and Christian inheritances, set as it is in Britain at the moment during the reign of the Emperor Augustus when Jesus Christ was born. In a curious exchange, Guiderius says to Arviragus that because he has a tin ear ("I cannot sing"), he will merely "word" the elegy that the two brothers once sang for their late mother and that they propose to repeat for the supposedly dead Fidele, who is really the sleeping Innogen. "For notes of sorrow out of tune are worse," he says, "Than priests and fanes that lie." Arviragus then agrees that they will "speak" rather than sing the words of "Fear no more the heat o' th' sun."[25] It is not clear whether there was a symbolic reason for this choice (an allusion to controversies about music in the liturgy?) or merely a pragmatic one (an actor who genuinely couldn't sing? a desire not to bring into this Welsh country scene the musicians who earlier played for Cloten in a court scene, or to hold them back for the "solemn music" of the visions in act 5 scene 3?). Whatever the reason, the exchange gives Shakespeare the opportunity to juxtapose a jibe at religious hypocrisy with an idea of poetic decorum (the need for the artistic note to be in tune with the emotional mood). According to the Puritan way of thinking, priests and places of worships offer the only way to truth; it is poets and singers who "lie." A "fane" is a temple: the pun on "feign," unavoidable given the proximity to "lie," reverses the thought: secular poetry, not ecclesiastical liturgy, is offered as the truest obsequy in honour of a deceased loved one.

What is more, the words of the spoken song—"Golden lads and girls all must, / As chimney-sweepers, come to dust"—echo only the "dust to dust" aspect of the funeral service in Archbishop Cranmer's prayer book.[26] Nothing is said of the idea of the soul of the virtuous and innocent Innogen/Fidele going to heaven. In this dispensation, everything ("scepter, learning, physic") comes to dust, an idea far more Lucretian-Epicurean than Christian.[27] The only immortality is that provided by the elegy itself: the spoken song's closing line, "renowned be thy grave," is in the tradition of Horace's "Exegi monumentum aere perennius."[28] "No exorcizer harm thee, / Nor no witchcraft charm thee," chant Guiderius and Arviragus: here the lying priest is more the juggler, the dangerous conjuror, the caterpillar of the commonwealth, whereas the plain-speaking poet is the truth-teller.[29]

The debate about the truth status of poetry became especially acute as a result of Reformation hostility to the "idolatry" of images, but its history was ancient. "The Author of truth [i.e., God] loves no falsehood," proclaimed the church father Tertullian in an attack on stageplays and circuses written at the end of the second century CE:

> All that is feigned is adultery in His sight. The man who counterfeits voice, sex or age, who makes a show of false love and hate, false sighs and tears, He will not approve, for He condemns all hypocrisy. In His law He denounces that man as accursed who shall go dressed in women's clothes; what then will be His judgement upon the pantomime who is trained to play the woman?[30]

Tertullian condemned the theatre not only because actors were counterfeits and the whole institution of public performance was idolatrous and derivative from pagan rituals, but also on Platonic philosophical grounds. Famously, in his *Sophist* Plato argued that works of art are a questionable form of imitation because they tend to reproduce not an exact likeness (*eikon*) of a real form but a semblance (*phantasma*), in which the artistic image is manipulated in order to appear beautiful.[31] The Puritan abhorrence of theatre echoed an ancient quarrel. Plato argued that poets should be banned from the ideal republic not only because plays stirred up unhealthy emotions, but also because if, philosophically speaking, the day-to-day world is a "shadow" of the true Reality of ideal forms (as on the wall of a cave by flickering firelight), then plays, imitations of those "shadows," are shadows of shadows, at two removes from Reality.[32] From Aristotle to Plotinus to the Florentine neo-Platonists such as Ficino, there was an answer to this critique which proposed to the contrary that poetry bypasses the particularities of history and nature, and provides direct access to the ideal, even the divine.[33] The true poet or maker is accordingly a kind of second deity.

Sidney answered Plato by giving the *eikon/phantasma* distinction a moral twist: "I ... not say that Poetry abuseth man's wit, but that man's wit abuseth Poetry. For I will not deny but that man's wit may make Poesy, which should be *eikastike*, which some learned have defined, 'figuring forth good things,' to be *phantastike*, which does contrariwise infect the fancy with unworthy objects."[34] Puttenham, by contrast, offered a qualified defence of the fantastic. He proposes that the art of creating phantasms is praiseworthy provided that the created images are beautiful, good, or true. But there is danger if they are disordered, corrupt, or perverse:

> Even so is the phantastical part of man (if it be not disordered) a representer of the best, most comely, and beautiful images or appearances of things to the soul and according to their very truth. If otherwise, then doth it breed *Chimeras* and monsters in man's imagination, and not only in his imaginations, but also in all his ordinary actions and life which ensues.[35]

For both Sidney and Puttenham, the moral purpose remains paramount. In their different ways, they both resort to an ethical argument in defending poetry's image-making power against the Puritan denunciation of the idols of invention. There is still a deference to Protestant hostility to "the school of abuse."

Anxiety about the fictive—the delusional—quality of phantasms persisted well into the seventeenth century. Thomas Blount's 1656 *Dictionary* defined "phantasm" as "a vain Vision, or false Representation ... an imagination of things, which are not indeed, and doth proceed of the sences being corrupted."[36] The terms "vain," "false," and "corrupted" leave no doubt that a judgment is being passed even as a phenomenon is being described. Shakespeare, by contrast, delights in phantasms and mocks those who complain of abuse. Bottom's "most rare vision" is at once paradisal and monstrous, while the extravagant word-mongering of such "phantasimes"—the word itself seems to be a Shakespearean coinage—as the "lisping, affecting" Tybald, so-called "prince of cats," and Don Armado, "the man of fire-new words," is a cause for mirth, not moralizing.[37] In Shakespeare, although the interim "Between the acting of a dreadful thing / And the first motion" is "Like a phantasma, or a hideous dream," it is such moments of meditation and internal "insurrection" that are the occasion for the most intensely realized and dramatic soliloquies of a Brutus or a Hamlet.[38] Macbeth's phantasmic dagger ("fatal vision," "dagger of the mind," "false creation, / Proceeding from the heat-oppressèd brain") is morally and politically dangerous, but what matters more to Shakespeare is that it is psychologically and dramatically compelling.[39] Phenomena traditionally considered to be mere phantasms—ghosts and spirits, dreams and visions—are regarded by Shakespeare as manifestations (and not necessarily "tricks") of "strong imagination," the very essence of his own art.[40]

In this regard, an important aspect of Shakespeare's classical inheritance might be described as "the defence of phantasms." In an influential passage of the *Institutio Oratoria*, Quintilian wrote,

> There are certain experiences which the Greeks call *phantasiae*, and the Romans visions, whereby things absent are presented to our imagination with such extreme vividness that they seem actually to be before our very eyes. It is the man who is really sensitive to such impressions who will have the greatest power over the emotions.... When the mind is unoccupied or is absorbed by fantastic hopes or daydreams, we are haunted by these visions.... Surely, then, it may be possible to turn this form of hallucination to some profit.[41]

This is Shakespeare's art bound in a nutshell: turning multiple forms of hallucination to maximum profit.

As for the Puritan idea that the inventive work of "man's wit" may "infect the fancy with unworthy objects," one only has to consider the case of Malvolio. He is explicitly identified as a Puritan; he disapproves of laughter, song, cakes, and ale; he is self-consciously "virtuous." But the witty interventions of Maria and Feste turn his world upside down, leading him to do all the things that Puritans disapproved of—dressing up, acting a role, smiling, breaching decorum, and indulging his sexual fantasies. Invention and dissembling— the arts of imaginative play—reduce him to humiliation. When Malvolio says (more than once) that "there was never man so notoriously abused," Shakespeare, via Feste, is rubbing the face of the Puritan in the fact that the theatre genuinely *is* a "school of abuse."[42] But Shakespeare being Shakespeare, when Olivia repeats the sentiment ("He hath been most notoriously abused"),[43] there is a moment of pity, a recognition of the cruelty of the schooling. His sympathy extended even to the Puritan sensibility that sought to constrain or even extirpate the very imaginary power that was the essence of that sympathy.

When was Shakespeare most Shakespearean? Perhaps when he was inventing a play from scratch, rather than reworking an existing source in the form of an old play or story or something from a history book. Perhaps, too, when he could self-consciously display his own "art"—a word, as Prospero reminds us in one of those plays invented from scratch, that could also be applied to magic.[44]

Towards the end of Shakespeare's most magical play, Theseus Duke of Athens reflects on the strange events that have taken place in the forest during the night. He thinks they are "More strange than true," setting up an opposition between imagination and reason:

> I never may believe
> These antique fables, nor these fairy toys.
> Lovers and madmen have such seething brains,
> Such shaping fantasies that apprehend
> More than cool reason ever comprehends.
> The lunatic, the lover and the poet
> Are of imagination all compact.

One sees more devils than vast hell can hold:
That is the madman. The lover, all as frantic,
Sees Helen's beauty in a brow of Egypt.
The poet's eye, in fine frenzy rolling,
Doth glance from heaven to earth, from earth to heaven,
And as imagination bodies forth
The forms of things unknown, the poet's pen
Turns them to shapes and gives to airy nothing
A local habitation and a name.
Such tricks hath strong imagination,
That if it would but apprehend some joy,
It comprehends some bringer of that joy.[45]

"Don't believe it," Theseus seems to be saying. "The events that you have seen on stage, the story of the night in the wood narrated by the lovers are fanciful lies"—which in a sense they are, since it is all a fiction, a play. Perhaps the whole thing has just been a dream, an illusion: Theseus doesn't believe in antique fables and fairy toys. Yet he is himself an antique fable, a creature of myth (and, at another level, an actor feigning a part). Besides, we have witnessed the work of the fairies: if we willingly suspend our disbelief to make ourselves imagine we are listening to Theseus, then by the same rule we must believe in the fairies. Indeed, the combination of antique fable in the form of mythical matter taken from Ovid with fairy toys and native folk traditions has been the play's distinctive achievement.

Theseus makes "shaping phantasies" synonymous with "imagination," the word he uses three times in the speech and ascribes to the three agencies of lunatic, lover, and poet. *Phantasia* was the Aristotelian term for what we call the imagination.[46] Our senses perceive ("apprehend," as Theseus has it) things that are real; our "cool reason" then "comprehends" them. But lovers and madmen see things that are not: this is the trick of "strong imagination," the thing of which these three peculiar kinds of person are "all compact." Though editors do not gloss it, there is a telling pun in the latter term.[47] The lunatic, the lover, and the poet are entirely made ("all compact") of imagination; in this sense, "compact" means composed, framed, or closely knit. But a compact is also a contract, a bond, as in the phrase "joined in compact."[48] Lunatic, lover, and poet are fellows, brothers as it were, sharing fealty to imagination as opposed to everyday reality.

They do not see as others see. Edgar in *King Lear*, feigning lunacy, pretends to see devils. The lover sees "Helen's beauty in a brow of Egypt": beauty is in the eye of the beholder: it resides in the mental image of the beloved, not the physical reality of their appearance. To others, you might be in love with someone perceived (in the colour-coded stereotyping of the time) as dark, not fair, but you, the lover, see the most beautiful woman in the history of the world. The poet, with a similar kind of madness, uses imagination to body forth "the form of things unknown." The poet can apprehend the joy of love, or for that matter the joy of sex. The imagination will then trick you into rationalising it, comprehending it by creating out of an airy nothing a bringer of that joy, who might be a mischievous god called Cupid or a puckish spirit called Robin Goodfellow. Through the voice of Theseus, Shakespeare describes exactly what he is doing in the play, exactly how his art works. In so doing, he implicitly ac-knowledges that theatre is a conjuring trick, a piece of magic.

Again and again at key pressure points in the plays, we find Shakespeare defending the power of mental images, of phantasms. "Horatio says 'tis but our fantasy," says Marcellus of the ghost, "And will not let belief take hold of him."[49] Horatio's suspicion may be owed to the Protestant environment of his university at Wittenberg. Shakespeare delights in upsetting his conviction: he will soon ask both Horatio and the audience to let belief take hold of them. Ham-let has already seen the ghost in his mind's eye, his imagination. The "apparition" of the Ghost—like the apparitions in *Macbeth*—embodies the phantasms of the mind, in the manner of which the Poet speaks when he is praising the Painter at the beginning of *Timon of Athens*:

> What a mental power
> This eye shoots forth! How big imagination
> Moves in this lip![50]

Shakespeare is at his most Shakespearean when he bigs up imagina-tion, projecting mental images to the eye of the spectator and through the lips of the actor.

He pondered deeply on the route from the eye to the mind and vice-versa. A sequence of scenes in the anonymously published his-tory play of *Edward III* in which King Edward attempts to seduce the married Countess of Salisbury are, nearly all scholars would now

agree, by Shakespeare.[51] In that work of seduction, the king enlists
the assistance of a courtier called Lodowick who is well versed in
poetry. He commissions Lodowick to use poetry to win over the
Countess. Lodowick makes it quite clear that the purpose of poetry
is the art of seduction, a lesson learned from Ovid and also taught
in the scene in *The Taming of the Shrew* in which a courtship takes
place by means of a lesson in the translation of the *Heroides*.

Lodowick begins, "I might perceive his eye in her eye lost." That
is what it means to be captured by desire, as we see on stage when
Puck works his magic in *A Midsummer Night's Dream*.[52] Lodowick
then proceeds with an anatomy of the workings of *eros*:

> I might perceive his eye in her eye lost,
> His ear to drink her sweet tongue's utterance,
> And changing passion, like inconstant clouds
> That rack upon the carriage of the winds,
> Increase and die in his disturbèd cheeks.
> Lo when she blushed, even then did he look pale,
> As if her cheeks by some enchanted power,
> Attracted had the cherry blood from his.[53]

Erotic attraction is here represented as magical transformation, an
enchantment whereby the physiology of Edward is changed by the
appearance of the Countess. As she blushes, he looks pale: she provokes a reaction in his blood. The King is lovesick: he recognises
that the beauty of the Countess is the ground of his infirmity, but the
true cause is his own desire. It is not her true nature but the image
of her beauty that has been planted in his mind.

This mental image is what in Shakespeare's time would have been
called a phantasm. Aristotle's theory of how human cognition works
had held sway for two millennia. He used the word "phantasm" to
refer to what we would now call a mental image. That is to say, we
perceive through the senses, but we create mental images in our
imagination.[54] Aristotle suggests that desire is at the centre of that
creation of mental images. When some desirable object is not actually present to our sense, exerting its pull on us directly, our motivation to strive to obtain it is driven by our awareness of either our
memory or our fantasy of the image. This might as well be an account of what it is like to be in love. And the power to create mental

images in the mind of the reader or the spectator is the particular gift of the poet. Hence "the lover and the poet." We will return to the lunatic.

King Edward tells Lodowick to "bring thee hither an enchanted pen / That may for sighs set down true sighs indeed."[55] Once again, writing is represented as a form of enchantment; at the same time, there is a challenge to the Platonic and Puritan idea that the words of poets are lies because they are at a remove from the phenomena that they describe. Lodowick is tasked with writing *true* sighs, re-creating rather than merely representing the experience of love. A paradigm for the possibility of doing so is then presented:

> For if the touch of sweet concordant strings
> Could force attendance in the ears of hell,
> How much more shall the strains of poets' wits
> Beguile and ravish soft and human minds?[56]

The archetypal poet Orpheus conjures music of such sympathetic power that the concord of his strings binds and subdues—exercises magical control over—even Cerberus, the dog of hell.

There follows a step-by-step explication of the poet's art of conjuring up mental images: "Write on while I peruse her in my thoughts." Lodowick is asked to turn the voice of the Countess into that of a nightingale, her hair into silk. At the same time, the king practices the art of paradigmatic criticism that he has no doubt learned from some handbook of rhetoric. He stops Lodowick from producing a nightingale image because he remembers that this bird is, according to Ovid, the metamorphosed form of the raped Philomel: "The nightingale sings of adulterate wrong," and that, he says, is too close to the bone of his own desire with respect to the Countess.[57]

On a similar note, Lodowick then makes a mistake. The king asks him to reread one of his lines. It includes the phrase "More fair and chaste":

> I did not bid thee talk of chastity,
> To ransack so the treasure of her mind,
> For I had rather have her chased than chaste.[58]

Poetry, the king demands, should be put in the service of erotic pursuit, not the praise of chastity. A reference to the "constancy" of Judith proves equally displeasing. In the book of Judith, which was part of the Catholic Old Testament and the Protestant Apocrypha, the eponymous beautiful Hebrew widow enters the camp of Holofernes, a general of Nebuchadnezzar who is besieging the Jews, and starts to seduce him verbally. They have a party and all get drunk; Holofernes thinks that this is a prelude to sleeping with her, but as he lies in an intoxicated stupor, she chops off his head. This is one of the rare occasions when Shakespeare makes an allusion to a Biblical story rather than a myth in a classical source such as Ovid's *Metamorphoses*. It is hardly surprising that the king objects to it, since the outcome he desires with the Countess is the one that Holofernes does not obtain. The deeper significance is that Shakespeare is in the position of Lodowick. He seems to have made his contribution to *Edward III* around the same time that he was writing love sonnets, probably for a patron. One line in the play, "Lilies that fester smell far worse than weeds," is shared with Sonnet 94. Because the lover and the poet are of imagination compact, he perforce owes allegiance to Orpheus and the art of seduction, not Judith and the strength of chastity.

When King Edward eventually enlists the help of the Countess's father in trying to seduce her, there is a sequence very close to the attempted seduction in *Measure for Measure* that climaxes with Angelo's demand for Isabella to yield up her body to his will. In both scenes, Shakespeare reflects deeply on the intimate relationship between poetry and erotic desire, between writing and seduction, and on the transgressive enchantment that follows from those associations. In the later play, he turns the puritanical aversion to any representation of such matters on the inventor's head by putting the voice of "sharp appetite" and "sensual race" into the mouth of an avowed "precisian." "My false o'erweighs your true," says Angelo in his final line in the scene: as a Puritan, he should be committed to the "true," regarding the conjurations of poetry and love as "false," but the force of his own desire is such that he reverses the trope.[59]

Another reason for the Puritan suspicion of theatre was the conjuring of devils, as portrayed in Marlowe's *Dr Faustus* (c. 1592) and Robert Greene's *Friar Bacon and Friar Bungay* (c. 1592). For Shakespeare, and for subsequent dramatists such as Thomas Middleton and John Webster, possession by evil spirits, for which another word was lunacy, was an idea full of dramatic potential, as seen definitively in the feigned madness of Edgar as Poor Tom in *King Lear*. Theatre relishes those moments that seem to say, "It's a mad world, my masters." In *The Comedy of Errors*, a play replete with strange events and mistaken identities, the town is "full of cozenage":

> As nimble jugglers that deceive the eye,
> Dark-working sorcerers that change the mind,
> Soul-killing witches that deform the body.[60]

Dr Pinch is a mad doctor, and the wandering Antipholus is led to believe that he is mad. The lover, the poet, and the lunatic are all compact.

Magic, like love, has power to deceive the eye and change the mind. In *Antony and Cleopatra*, erotic attraction is a form of enchantment ("I must from this enchanting queen break off"); in *As You Like It*, Rosalind's orchestratation of the love plot of the play is managed under a fictive self-description as the niece of a magician who lives in the forest. Towards the end of *Henry V*, King Harry, a soldier not a lover, complains that he cannot "conjure up the spirit of love" in Princess Kate.[61] Once again, the idea is that love is a form of magic that requires conjuring, the creation of a change in the mental state of a person so that she will see you differently and fall in love with you. Burgundy offers some direct advice:

> Pardon the frankness of my mirth, if I answer you for that. If you would conjure in her, you must make a circle: if conjure up love in her in his true likeness, he must appear naked and blind. Can you blame her then, being a maid yet rosed over with the virgin crimson of modesty, if she deny the appearance of a naked blind boy in her naked seeing self? It were, my lord, a hard condition for a maid to consign to.[62]

There are numerous *double entendres* in this passage. In particular, "make a circle" means both "draw a magic circle" and "open her vagina." Conjurors such as Dr Faustus, Prospero, and the combined team of Roger Bullingbrook the conjuror and Margaret Jordan the witch in *Henry VI Part 2* all make circles in order to conjure up spirits. Burgundy finds an occult connection between this process and the power of naked, blind Cupid to inaugurate an alteration of mental states that will eventually lead to the physical action of a hymen being broken, which is what is implied in the image of "a maid yet rosed over with the virgin crimson of modesty."

Shakespeare's sustained imagery of conjuration suggests that he saw both *eros* and magic as forms of manipulation. Helena in *A Midsummer Night's Dream* describes male desire as a process that will "conjure tears up in a poor maid's eyes" and "extort / a poor soul's patience": that is to say, an enchantment that both causes a physical reaction and, in the manner of a succubus, extorts a virtue from the soul.[63] Similarly, Brabantio accuses Othello of enchanting his daughter: by making her fall in love with him, he is binding her "in chains of magic."[64] Othello responds by saying that the only charms and conjuration, the only "mighty magic," he used were his words.[65] All he did was tell a story. All he did was use poetry. But his poetry is the charm. He has used a form of magic: the magic of art. The tragedy of Othello derives from the way that Iago also uses the enchanting power of words in order to persuade Othello of Desdemona's infidelity. His method of persuading is, of course, the handkerchief, of which Othello believes there is magic in the web. But the real magic is not in the web of the handkerchief but in the weave of Iago's enchanting art, his language, the effect that that has on Othello's love for Desdemona. Iago uses language to conjure love into hate.

If Othello is the great tragedy of how the enchaining force of erotic love can lead to destruction to death through jealousy, *The Winter's Tale* is the play where the same thing seems to be happening until the action breaks and then resumes on a path to a redemptive conclusion. Leontes, like Othello, condemns his wife for an infidelity that she has not committed. But after a wide gap of time, their love is redeemed through the magic of the animation of Hermione's statue by Paulina, whose language turns the Faustian pact of conjuration through one hundred and eighty degrees. Leontes says to the statue,

> There's magic in thy majesty, which has
> My evils conjured to remembrance, and
> From thy admiring daughter took the spirits.[66]

Then, through the art of Paulina, who is at once a conjurer and a dramatist, the statue comes to life or seems by theatrical magic to come to life: "O, she's warm! / If this be magic, let it be an art / Lawful as eating."[67] This moment of feigned resurrection, influenced by

Ovid's story of the animation of Pygmalion's statue, is another of Shakespeare's rebukes to the Puritan prohibition against both magic and image-making.

Eros and magic are as one because of their shared effect on the imagination. What is love? The romantic Silvius in *As You Like It* would agree with the unromantic Mercutio in *Romeo and Juliet* that to love "is to be all made of fantasy, / All made of passion and all made of wishes." It is to be totally dominated by the phantasm, the mental image, and that is like a dream, as Mercutio says of Queen Mab: "True, I talk of dreams, / Which are the children of an idle brain, / Begot of nothing but vain fantasy."[68]

Shakespeare knew that *eros* is not always as evanescent as a dream. In response to Theseus's speech condemning the story of the midsummer night as an unreal fantasy, Hippolyta replies that the transfiguration of the minds of the lovers "More witnesseth than fancy's images / And grows to something of great constancy."[69] Violent ends do not always follow from the violent delights of *eros*, for sometimes desire is transformed into a more enduring, selfless kind of love, a "constancy" of the kind exemplified by the Countess of Salisbury in *Edward III*. But constancy does not make for interesting drama. The thing that compels Shakespeare is the dangerous force of desire.

The Renaissance Neoplatonic philosopher Marsilio Ficino, in his treatise *De Amore*, made the startling claim that

> The whole power of Magic is founded on Eros. The way Magic works is to bring things together through their inherent similarity. The parts of this world, like the limbs and organs of the same animal, all depend on Eros, which is one; they relate to each other because of their common nature. Similarly, in our body the brain, the lungs, the heart, liver, and other organs interact, favor each other, intercommunicate and feel reciprocal pain. From this relationship is born Eros, which is common to them all; from this Eros is born their mutual rapprochement, wherein resides true Magic.[70]

Ficino believed that the world is made of a series of interconnected forces, sympathetic powers, and the force that holds them all together is *eros*. He went on to argue that what a magician can do is take control of those forces and thus bind the objects of his desire. Magic, he suggests, can work through all sorts of media, from music to poetry, to works of art, to incantations and spells, to talismans that draw down particular powers from the stars. Ultimately, the magician is able to control all the attractive forces throughout the cosmos, just as a lover binds and creates a magic web around his love. The lover and the magician both do the same thing, Ficino suggests: "They cast their nets to capture certain objects to attract and draw them to them."[71]

Ficino envisages the true magician unifying his audience in a variety of chains, arousing in them hope, compassion, fear, love, hate, indignation, anger, joy, patience, and disdain for life and death and the vicissitudes of *Fortuna*. This image of the magician manipulating his audience could as well be an account of what the poet and the dramatist do to their audience. The ambition of the Shakespearian theatre is to offer its audience the experience of being enchanted.

What is the greatest of all the interconnected forces that the magician can summon under his command? According to Ficino's disciple who visited England, Giordano Bruno, "The bond of bonds," *vinculum vinculorum*, is indeed love: "All bonds are reduced to the bond of love and depend on the bond of love. Love is the foundation of all feelings."[72] *Eros* is magic based on the power of enchaining; it is also, Bruno argued, the foundation of *all* human feeling.

In Shakespeare's time, magic was essentially a form of psychology, closely bound to the psychology of the arousal of sexual feelings. As the Warburg scholar D. P. Walker put it,

> The use of transitive magic directed at animate beings constitutes an overlap with practical psychology; such magic is meant to control and direct other people's emotions by altering their imagination in a specific and permanent way. There is a marked tendency for such magical techniques to be centred on sexual feelings, both because they were probably recognized to be especially powerful and fundamental, and because they are in fact more closely linked with the imagination than other natural appetites. Treaties of witchcraft came near to being a pornographic *genre*; and Bruno made a remarkable attempt to outline a technique for controlling all emotions which is explicitly based on sexual attraction.[73]

Following Walker, the émigré Romanian scholar Ioan Couliano, who in 1991 was assassinated by the Romanian security forces in the Divinity School of the University of Chicago, noted that Bruno applied the phrase *vinculum vinculorum* not only to *eros* and *phantasia*—

which, as I have been suggesting, are in some sense synonymous—but also to religious faith. The priest or prophet is a kind of magician who has the power to alter the mental state of his congregation, to make them into believers.[74] Couliano argues provocatively that this idea of the quasi-sexual enchanting power attributed to the Renaissance magician still lives on in the powers of mass psychology: it accounts for the working not only of evangelical preaching but also of advertisements, psychoanalysis, and media spectacle. These are all ways of manipulating mental images for the purpose of exercising power over people.[75]

For our purposes, the more relevant point of comparison is the case of Christopher Marlowe, inventor of the most famous magician on the Elizabethan stage. Consider the notorious Baines accusations against him. They focus very specifically on *eros*: the allegation that he claimed that Jesus had an "extraordinary love" for John, that he slept with the "whores" Martha and Mary Magdalene, and that Mary the mother of Jesus was "dishonest." And on magic: "Moyses was but a Jugler" and "esteming [St] Paul a Jugler." And on religion as manipulation ("That the first beginning of Religion was only to keep men in awe") and quasi-theatrical spectacle (notice the key word "performed"): "That if there be any god or any good Religion, then it is in the papistes because the service of god is performed with more Cerimonies, as Elevation of the mass, organs, singing men, Shaven Crownes, etc. that all protestant are HypoCriticall asses."[76] For Marlowe, the conjuror, the dramatist, and the Roman priest are of imagination all compact.

According to Bruno, "All affections and bonds of the will are reduced to two, namely aversion and desire, or hatred and love. Yet hatred itself is reduced to love, whence it follow that the will's only bond is Eros. It has been proved that all other mental states are absolutely, fundamentally, and originally nothing other than love itself."[77] The point here—and Iago provides the perfect example—is that the manipulative force that someone uses to conjure up hate is exactly the same as the force used to conjure up love. It relies on this process of enchantment or enchaining. That is why Bruno says that love was described in the Platonic tradition as the Great Demon:

> There where we have spoken of natural magic, we have described to what extent all chains can be related to the chain of love, are dependent upon the chain of love or arise in the chain of love.... As regards

all those who are dedicated to philosophy or magic, it is fully apparent that the highest bond, the most important and the most general belongs to erotic love: and that is why the Platonists called love the Great Demon, *daemon magnus*.[78]

If erotic love is the great demon and love is the favoured matter of the playhouse, it was hardly surprising that the hotter kind of Protestant viewed the drama with fear and loathing.

Love's Labour's Lost has plausibly been read as Shakespeare's play about the debate between this Neoplatonic tradition, expressed most forcefully in the writings of Ficino and Bruno, and the humanist educational tradition that held sway in England.[79] "When Love speaks," says Berowne, "the voice of all the gods / Make heaven drowsy with the harmony."[80] Love subdues all other gods. At the climax of his speech, Berowne says, "Who can sever love from charity?"[81] Traditionally in Christianity, there is a separation between erotic love and divine love: one answer to Berowne's question would therefore be St Paul, in the third chapter of his epistle to the Colossians, where "fornication, uncleanness, inordinate affection and evil concupiscence" are condemned as "idolatry," which must be put away so that the believer may "*put on* love, which is the bond of perfectness."[82] To a Pauline sensibility, the claim for the synonymity of *eros* and *caritas* is as dangerous an idea as the conjunction of art and magic, a step on the slippery path towards the Marlovian heresy that religion is but a trick of the imagination.

The conjuror-poet-dramatist Prospero's renunciation of his rough magic is perhaps Shakespeare's shying away from those dangers. Having devoted his career to the creation of phantasms, he dismisses them as the stuff that dreams are made on. The epilogue to *The Tempest* seems to turn instead to Christian orthodoxy:

> Now I want
> Spirits to enforce, art to enchant,
> And my ending is despair,
> Unless I be relieved by prayer,
> Which pierces so, that it assaults
> Mercy itself, and frees all faults.[83]

Yet having moved to this Christian lexicon, away from any vestige of a Neoplatonic allegiance to magic, Prospero concludes by saying, "As you from crimes would pardoned be, / Let your indulgence set me free."[84] This is not a prayer to the living for indulgence on behalf of the dead; it is a request to the audience for applause. Shakespeare is still enchanting us: in demanding applause, he is manipulating the audience one last time, subtly retaining loyalty to the very magic of art that he has pretended to abjure. Prospero has vanished his phantasmic apparitions, but is still enchaining his audience with the power of poetry.

11

AN INFIRMITY NAMED *HEREOS*

WHERE DO WE GET OUR IDEA OF ROMANTIC LOVE? For the last hundred years, the answer has probably been: from Hollywood, from romantic fiction, and from popular music. Where action movies are about heroes—the modern equivalents of those figures such as Hector and Achilles, Aeneas and Alexander the Great—RomComs and tearjerkers are about lovers. *Casablanca* and *Brief Encounter*, *Love Story* and *Love Actually*. Then there has been the huge industry aimed predominantly at a female audience, exemplified in fiction by Harlequin and Mills and Boon romances. And then of course there are the songs that have provided the soundtrack of the love lives of most people since the invention of radio and the gramophone record: "What is this thing called love?," "Have I told you lately that I love you?," "You're the one that I want," "She loves you yeah yeah yeah."

Where did Shakespeare's original audiences get their idea of romantic love? Just as novels, movies, and pop songs have shaped the idea in the last hundred years, so poets and creative artists past and present shaped the idea in the sixteenth century—and duly had their romantic notions questioned by the authors of conduct books, the equivalent of modern magazine columnists offering marital advice and agony auntery. Ophelia's love-madness is expressed through her singing of ballads—Elizabethan pop songs—such as "How should I your true love know?" and "For bonny sweet Robin is all my joy."[1] Thomas Morley's setting of "It was a lover and his lass" from *As You Like It* was what we would now call a "hit."[2] The literate, meanwhile, purchased love poems. In a pair of plays called *The Return from Parnassus*, performed by Cambridge students, a lovesick character called Gullio starts quoting in what he calls "Mr Shakespeare's vein." Another character, Ingenioso, accuses him of "monstrous theft" from *Romeo and Juliet* and says, "We shall have nothing but pure Shakespeare and shreds of poetry that he hath gathered at the theatres."

"I'll worship sweet Mr Shakespeare," says Gullio, "and to honour him will lay his *Venus and Adonis* under my pillow."[3] The language of love is learned from *Romeo and Juliet* and *Venus and Adonis*. To judge by number of reprints and frequency of allusions, the latter was the bestselling volume of single-authored poetry of the Elizabethan age. I say single-authored because an even more popular volume was the anthology called *Songs and Sonnets* that gathered together the love-poetry of Thomas Wyatt, the Earl of Surrey, and others—modern scholars name it for its publisher as *Tottel's Miscellany*. That book is the vade mecum of one of Shakespeare's less imaginative lovers, Abraham Slender in *The Merry Wives of Windsor*: "I had rather than forty shillings I had my Book of Songs and Sonnets here."[4] Books of sonnets were handbooks for wooers, and the theatre was a school of love.

Romantic love was everywhere in the literature of the 1590s. Giles Fletcher teased the reader in the preface to his 1593 sonnet sequence *Licia* by refusing to say whether the sonneteer really is "in love" or whether he is playing an elaborate game—an interesting context for Shakespeare's sonnets.[5] Robert Greene in the *Groatsworth of Wit*, famous for its attack on Shakespeare, described how a character called Lucanio is "so far in love as he persuaded himself [that] without her grant he could not live."[6] And, in a hostile vein, Dr John Rainolds, President of Corpus Christi College, Oxford, warned in his *Overthrow of Stage Plays* that, since love enters by the eyes (witness the Old Testament example of "Potiphar's wife, who cast her eyes on Joseph, and fell in love with him"), the very act of seeing boys dressed as girls in the theatre ran the risk of inflaming perverted desire.[7] Above all, romantic love pervaded the theatrical repertoire. Here is a simple-minded cobbler called Strumbo, in love with a wench called Dorothy, in the comic subplot of *The Tragedy of Locrine*, published in 1595 with an attribution to one W. S. on the title page: "the little god, nay the desperate god Culprit [his malapropism for Cupid], with one of his vengible bird-bolts, hath shot me unto the heel.... I burn, I burn, and I burn, ah, in love, in love, and in love."[8] And here is Shakespeare's Rosalind, a few years later in *As You Like It*: "O coz, coz, coz, my pretty little coz, that thou didst know how many fathom deep I am in love!"[9]

A phrase such as "I am in love with you" has in some sense to be learned. When we say it, we are imitating the archetypal lovers from page and screen who have said it before us. For Shakespeare's audience, it was readily learnt from the stage. If one searches online databases of sixteenth-century texts for the phrase "I am in love," the (surprisingly few) results are clustered among the comedies of the 1590s, such as John Lyly's *Gallathea*, Robert Greene's *Friar Bacon and Friar Bungay*, Anthony Munday's *Fedele and Fortunio; or, The Deceits in Love*; and Shakespeare's *The Two Gentlemen of Verona, Love's Labour's Lost, As You Like It*—along with *Romeo and Juliet*, the play that takes the conventions of romantic comedy (union of young lovers against the opposition of their parents) and turns it to tragedy.

The stage was a new public arena for the open exploration of love, sex and marriage. A certain Henry Crosse fumed in *Vertue's Commonwealth* (1603) that the players were getting rich and buying land on the proceeds of "adulterous Playes."[10] One of the reasons why Puritans didn't like the theatre was the fear that housewives would start getting romantic ideas from the plays that they went to see, such as *Arden of Faversham*, in which a genteel married woman has a passionate affair with a man from the servant class. This is a play in which, according to the most recent stylometric scholarship, Shakespeare may well have had a hand.[11] Arden says to his wife early in their play,

> Sweet love, thou knowst that we two, Ovid-like,
> Have often chid the morning when it 'gan to peep,
> And often wished that dark night's purblind steeds
> Would pull her by the purple mantle back
> And cast her in the ocean to her love.
> But this night, sweet Alice, thou hast killed my heart:
> I heard thee call on Mosby in thy sleep.[12]

"Ovid-like" because Ovid was known as "Cupid's poet"[13] and, more particularly, because in one of his most famous poems he pleads to Aurora, goddess of dawn, to hold back her horses so that he can spend more time in bed with his girlfriend—"O lente lente currite noctis equi" (run slowly, slowly, O horses of the night).[14] Shakespeare's Juliet will beautifully reverse the image, urging the fiery-footed steeds of the sun to race towards the west and usher in "love-performing night."[15] But for Arden the marital bed has become a place of heartbreak: he has heard his wife moaning the name of another man as she dreams. A tragedy of adultery, jealousy, murder, and revenge is about to unfold. Having instigated the murder of Arden, Alice and her lover are duly punished with death. Their demise ensures that the story conforms to public morality: as the title page has it, this is a play "Wherein is showed the great malice and dissimulation of a wicked woman, the insatiable desire of filthy lust and the shameful end of all murderers." But what an audience remembers is not the rough justice of the ending but Alice's boldness and strength of character—"Love is a god and marriage is but words," she says, "And therefore Mosby's title is the best."[16] Not what a woman was supposed to say in a vigorously Protestant culture that took seriously St Paul's injunction that the only proper place for sex is within marriage.

Sir Philip Sidney's defence of poetry against the strictures of Puritanism makes it clear that the enflaming of desire was one of their main anxieties. He noted how the antitheatrical polemicists claimed that poetry "abuseth mens wit, training it to wanton sinfulnesse, and lustfull love": "They say the Comedies rather teach than reprehend amorous conceits. They say the Lirick is larded with passionat Sonets, the Elegiack weeps the want of his mistresse, and that even to the Heroical, Cupid hath ambitiously climed."[17]

For physicians in Shakespeare's time, erotic desire was unhealthy in a more literal sense: it was regarded as a form of sickness, of mental aberration. In a *Treatise of Melancholy*, published in 1586, Richard Bright noted that "love, which upholdeth the propagation of kinde, and is the onely glue to couple the joynts of this great frame of the world together" induces a state in which "reason is often times failed of the passion, and (carried captive) submitteth where it should have preeminence and rule."[18] Love is not rational; indeed, desire captivates the soul and thus suppresses the ability to think clearly. It is easy to see how an overlaying of this empirical observation upon the story of Eve leads to misogyny: woman as sexual temptress leads to the overthrow of reason. Some of the foundational myths of classical antiquity were read in a similar way: the female enchantress Circe ensnares Odysseus and his crew, while the sexual allure of Dido diverts Aeneas from his heroic destiny.

Five years after Shakespeare's death, Robert Burton published the first edition of his *Anatomy of Melancholy*. In its "Third Partition," called "Love Melancholy," Burton writes of how love tyrannizes over men: it is "a disease, Frensie, Madnesse, Hell." He contrasts "honest love," which we would call affection and upon which he argues that marriage should be based, with what he calls "heroical love," which he considers to be a form of melancholy. Heroical love "is a wandring extravagant, a domineering, a boundlesse, an irrefregable passion: sometimes this burning lust rageth after marriage, and then it is properly called *Jelousie*, sometimes before, and then it causeth this *Heroicall* melancholy ... sometimes it produceth rapes, incests, murders ... [it] is confined within no termes, of yeares, sexe or whatsoever else."[19] Crazed jealousy, rape, incest, murder: one immediately sees how this raging form of desire is a rich source of raw material for tragedy—the jealousy of Othello, Posthumus, and Leontes; the rape of Lavinia in *Titus Andronicus* and Angelo's near-rape of Isabella in *Measure for Measure*; the by-some-accounts (Hamlet's, certainly) incestuous passion of Claudius and Gertrude; the murder in *Arden of Faversham*.

Burton quotes the medieval Arabic scholar Avicenna, who defined the state of being in love as "a disease or melancholy vexation or anguish of mind, in which a man continually meditates of the beauty, gesture, manners of his mistris, and troubles himselfe about it." He also quotes a passage from Cicero's *Tusculan Disputations* in which love is said to be "a furious disease of the mind," and another from Ficino, the Renaissance commentator on Plato, where it is "a species of madness."[20] Most physicians, Burton reports, regard it as a species of melancholy. He goes on to list the symptoms: paleness, leanness, hollow eyes, loss of appetite, insomnia, groans, tears, the kind of distracted symptoms that lead Polonius to believe that Hamlet has been driven mad by his love for Ophelia:

> his doublet all unbraced,
> No hat upon his head, his stockings fouled,
> Ungartered, and down-gyvèd to his ankle,
> Pale as his shirt, his knees knocking each other ...
> He raised a sigh so piteous and profound
> As it did seem to shatter all his bulk
> And end his being.[21]

Here Hamlet is acting the part. Troilus has the symptoms for real: he is constantly sighing, he proclaims himself "mad / In Cressid's love," "giddy," whirled round because all he can think of is what it would be like to taste the nectar of Cressida's love, which he thinks will be akin to death: "Swooning destruction, or some joy too fine, / Too subtle-potent, tuned too sharp in sweetness" for the capacity of normal mortal powers. He will come to horrible disillusionment, for this is a play that satirizes the medieval code of courtly love as vigorously as it does the Homeric code of martial honour. The chief engine of the plot is the unprincely prince Pandarus, whose name speaks for itself, who compares the art of love to breadmaking, with its progression from grinding to bolting to kneading to leavening to cooling, while on the Greek side the warrior heroes are persistently undermined by the foul-mouthed Thersites, who brings the play to the resounding conclusion that "all the argument is a cuckold and a whore."[22]

Troilus idealizes his love in courtly language, but at the same time compares his desire to a wound: "the open ulcer of my heart."[23] The term "heroical love" initially seems a puzzling epithet for this condition. Hamlet's appearance in Ophelia's closet could hardly be less heroic. Indeed, for Shakespeare's Troilus, Virgil's Aeneas, and many another warrior hero, a love affair is the principal impediment to heroic action. Burton tried to offer an explanation of the term by suggesting that this kind of love is particularly associated with heroes, with knights and noblemen. But a medical treatise published on the cusp of Shakespeare's career offered a different explanation. In *The Breviarie of Health* (1587), there is a short chapter that "doth shew of an infirmitie named *Hereos*." "*Hereos* is the greke word," the author explains. "In latin it is named *Amor*. In English it is named love sicke." The cause of this infirmity is "amours which is a fervent love, for to have carnal copulacion with the party that is loved, and [if] it can not be obtayned, some be so folish that they be ravished of their witte." The proposed remedy is "muse not, but use mirth and mery company," which is to say, take your mind off it.[24]

Not heroes, then, but *hereos*. Shakespeare would have come across the term when he read Chaucer's *Knight's Tale*, the source for *The Two Noble Kinsmen*, his final play, coauthored with John Fletcher. Chaucer tells us that Arcite suffers from "the loveres Maladye / Of Hereos," which is engendered of melancholy and leads to those symptoms of sleeplessness, loss of appetite, and so forth. In Speght's 1598 edition of Chaucer, probably the one that Shakespeare used, there is a helpful note explaining that the term is synonymous with

Eros or Cupid.[25] In his 1602 edition, Speght actually emended *Hereos* to *Eros*.[26] The term *hereos* was transmitted from ancient Greece to medieval and Renaissance Europe via Arab commentators such as Avicenna, Constantinus Africanus, and the *Hayât al-Hayawân* of Ad-Damîrîs. The latter describes how "the imagination of the ardent lover is never free from the object of his ardent love, and consideration and remembrance of the object of love are never absent from his thoughts and mind; the mind is diverted ... and the lover is prevented from eating and drinking ... and also from thinking, remembering, imagining and sleeping."[27] This passage is especially valuable in reminding us that *hereos* is a disease of the imagination: the lover's mind is filled with the *image* of the beloved. In many respects, the extreme lover of this kind is in love with an idealized image, not a reality: Elizabethan literary representations of the malady of *hereos* are almost always informed by the Petrarchan tradition of suggesting that the beloved is perfect in beauty, unattainable, set upon a pedestal—the kind of love-worship that Shakespeare so memorably parodies in his sonnet "My mistress' eyes are nothing like the sun."[28]

Hereos, then, is an aberrant mental condition provoked by the mischievous little god that the Greeks called *Eros* and the Romans Cupid. His arrow is symbolic of the pain that comes with desire, the sense that love is a wound which makes us feel incomplete until we possess the beloved, while his blindness—more characteristic of Renaissance art than the classical pantheon—is symbolic of the arbitrariness whereby there is no predictability or reason in the act of falling in love.[29] In *A Midsummer Night's Dream*, the agent of *eros* is the mischievous vernacular spirit Puck, or Robin Goodfellow, and Cupid's dart is displaced into the juice of the plant named love-in-idleness. As Oberon explains to Puck,

> Yet marked I where the bolt of Cupid fell.
> It fell upon a little western flower,
> Before milk-white, now purple with love's wound,
> And maidens call it "love-in-idleness."
> Fetch me that flower; the herb I showed thee once:
> The juice of it on sleeping eyelids laid
> Will make or man or woman madly dote
> Upon the next live creature that it sees.[30]

We no longer imagine falling in love as a transformation precipitated by an external agency—Cupid's dart or the juice of love-in-idleness—but the underlying model of the psychology of the process is not so very different from our own. It is just the language that is different: the Elizabethans' mythological narrative of desire has been replaced by our neurochemical one, which goes roughly as follows. We are programmed with a biological imperative to reproduce. The hypothalamus therefore stimulates the sex hormones testosterone and estrogen. But reproduce with whom? This is where the laws of chemical attraction come into play: the dopamine rush, the release of a related hormone, norepinephrine, which makes us giddy, energetic, euphoric, obsessive, wide-eyed, even unable to eat or sleep. Sooner or later, probably sooner, some pharmacologist will distil the essence of testosterone, dopamine, and norepinephrine into a drug that will have precisely the same effect as Puck's love-in-idleness, and we will say, as we so often do, that Shakespeare got there four hundred years before us.

However, the sexual arousal that comes with these hormones has a downside: they appear to shut down those parts of the prefrontal cortex that regulate critical thinking, self-awareness, and rational behaviour. It is presumably out of an instinctive understanding of this, along with the experiential knowledge that being madly in love is usually a state that lasts for a maximum of about eighteen months, that most cultures for most of human history have taken the view that "romantic love" is not a good basis for marriage and parenthood.

The idea of erotic love as a kind of madness is everywhere in Shakespeare, nowhere more variously and sustainedly than in *A Midsummer Night's Dream*, where, as discussed earlier, Theseus asserts that the lover is as "frantic"—a word that means deranged—as the madman. Lovers have "seething brains" and "shaping phantasies." Their way of seeing is the opposite of "cool reason." Erotic love is a trick of "strong imagination." And it is especially associated with poets.[31] The word "poet," from the Greek *poiesis*, making, could refer to any act of imagination. This takes us back to the idea that creative types—poets and songwriters, romance writers and moviemakers—are the inventors of romantic love. And that idea has a history going all the way back to Plato. As a philosopher, an apostle of "cool reason," he was very sceptical about both poets and lovers: he regarded poetry and love as forms of madness, in which the rational mind was struck by a mania-inducing force from without.[32] In poetry, you call it the Muse; in love, you call it *Eros* or Cupid. But Plato also recognized that we are all susceptible to the power of *Eros*, and in his *Symposium* he put the case that the desire that is consummated in sex might be a rung on the ladder to divine love. As part of that argument, we find the suggestion that the love of a man for a beautiful boy might be a purer thing than a man's desire for a woman, because the endpoint of the latter is mere bodily conception, whereas the former has a spiritual quality. That distinction would appear to be one of the keys to Shakespeare's love sonnets, with their differentiation between "the marriage of true minds" which is the aspiration of those addressed to the "lovely boy" and the self-disgust that marks many of those addressed to the "dark lady" ("The expense of spirit in a waste of shame / Is lust in action").[33]

But now let us go back to the beginning of his career and ask where he got his ideas for the dramatization of romantic love. Consider what may have been his first comedy. *The Two Gentlemen of Verona* sets up an opposition to which Shakespeare will return again, most notably in his sonnets and in his final play, *The Two Noble Kinsmen*: the conflict between the bond of male friendship and the force of erotic desire. Cicero's essay on friendship, *De Amicitia*, was hugely influential in the sixteenth century, underlying scores of conduct books and literary works, including John Lyly's *Euphues*, the most popular English novel of the age. Another book that was hugely influential throughout Western Europe in the second half of the sixteenth century was a Spanish pastoral romance called *Diana Enamorada*.[34] Shepherds in love, disguises that cross the boundaries of rank, strong cross-dressed heroines, the administration of a magic potion that makes its victims either forget they are in love or fall in love with someone new: all these elements, so familiar to us from Shakespeare, are found in the *Diana*. The particular detail that caught his eye when he was preparing the script of *The Two Gentlemen of Verona* was a plot line in which one of the heroines, Felismena, disguises herself as a page and enters the service of her lover, who has been sent away by his father to gain an education in the world.[35] She overhears him wooing another woman. Shakespeare makes this second woman into the beloved of the main character's best friend, enabling him to fuse the *amicitia* tradition and the *enamorada*, thus setting up the battle between love and friendship.

There is a schematic quality to this early comedy, as witnessed by Shakespeare's choice of names. One of the gentlemen of Verona is called Valentine: that is enough to make him into an archetypal lover. His beloved is called Silvia, from the Latin for the spirit of the woods and in Italian Renaissance drama a favoured name for a beautiful young woman in a love plot—besides being a frequently used name for the female lover in the *commedia dell' arte* tradition, Silvia is the heroine of Torquato Tasso's highly influential pastoral play *Aminta* (1573). The unfaithful lover, meanwhile, the cad who makes a play for his best friend's girlfriend, is called Proteus, the name in Greek myth of the son of the Ocean who could change himself into many shapes. Hence the Latin adjective *proteus*, defined in a sixteenth-century Latin dictionary as "unstable and inconstant of word and deed."[36] Early in *The Two Gentlemen*, Proteus's beloved speaks of him as an archetype of constancy, hammering the point home with reiterative rhetoric:

> His words are bonds, his oaths are oracles,
> His love sincere, his thoughts immaculate,
> His tears pure messengers sent from his heart,
> His heart as far from fraud as heaven from earth.[37]

But his name is a sign that he is the opposite of all these things.

His original girlfriend, who speaks these lines and who then disguises herself as a boy to go in pursuit of him, is called Julia. This is not so obviously a symbolic name as Proteus and Valentine, or even Silvia, but it may have had a particular association for Shakespeare and those members of his audience who knew anything about classical history and poetry: the most famous bearer of the name was Julia, the only daughter of the emperor Augustus, a figure indelibly associated with love. It was widely believed in Shakespeare's time that the poet Ovid was banished from Rome to Tomis on the Black Sea for two reasons: writing the scandalous *Ars Amatoria*, the art of love, and having an affair with the Emperor's daughter. Eliding the alleged Julia liaison with the idea of Ovid as Cupid's poet, commentators read his love poetry biographically, supposing that the "Corinna" to whom Ovid addressed many of his *Amores* was a codename for Julia. And Julia is indeed Ovid's lover in *Poetaster*, Ben Jonson's play about the Augustan poets—rather cheekily, he stages the parting scene in which Ovid says goodbye to Julia before going into exile as a rewrite of the equivalent scene in Shakespeare's *Romeo and Juliet*.

Evidence that Ovid was on Shakespeare's mind as he wrote the character of Julia comes from the most poignant moment in the play, which is also the most theatrically sophisticated. Julia is describing herself to Silvia, but in the part of the boy Sebastian, in which she is pretending that he/she was once Julia's servant. Silvia asks how tall Julia is. "About my stature," replies "Sebastian," and as proof "he" offers a memory of how during a Whitsun pageant he played "the woman's part," wearing Julia's gown, which was a perfect fit. She then goes on, unnecessarily for the proof of height but necessarily for the revelation of her interior anguish, to describe the part she played. It is a "lamentable" one, giving Shakespeare the opportunity to write one of his first descriptions of the art of tragic acting, the "Ariadne, passioning / For Theseus' perjury and unjust flight" speech.[38] As I suggested earlier, the image of the player performing tearful emotion in such a lifelike ("lively") fashion that the audience is moved to tears foreshadows the process demonstrated by the Player's speech to Hamlet. At the same time, the speech is one of Shakespeare's earliest examples of the art of "metadrama," theatrical self-consciousness: a boy actor (an apprentice in the acting company) is playing the part of a female character (Julia) playing the part of a boy character (Sebastian) fictionally remembering himself playing the part of a female character (Ariadne) in front of an audience that includes a female character (Julia), who is imagined to be moved to tears, the purpose being to move another female character (Silvia, who is of course played by another boy actor) to tears, which she duly is: "Alas, poor lady, desolate and left! / I weep myself to think upon thy words."[39] Julia/Sebastian pulls off the trick of making the "poor lady, desolate and left" into both herself and her precedent from classical mythology, Ariadne, deserted on Naxos by Theseus after he has rewarded her for assisting him into the Minotaur's labyrinth by seducing her and then deserting her.

Shakespeare learned her story from Ovid's *Heroides*, those narrative poems written in the voices of lamenting heroines who have been dumped by their lovers. The *Heroides* was one of his key sources for his art of animating "the woman's part," giving subjectivity to the female voice, albeit as a victim, yet as a victim who is given the opportunity to state her case at length in the court of audience opinion. The Petrarchan tradition of love poetry, by contrast, makes the woman into an object: beautiful but frosty, beloved but distant, anatomized part by lovely part but silent and unyielding. Her chastity is her attraction (think again of Angelo in *Measure for Measure*). The man likes a bit of resistance: the thrill of the chase, the sense that the prize is worth winning and not just an easy score. The challenge is to win the woman with words. But what happens if the verbal seduction fails? Proteus to Silvia in the woods:

> Nay, if the gentle spirit of moving words
> Can no way change you to a milder form,
> I'll woo you like a soldier, at arms' end,
> And love you 'gainst the nature of love: force ye.[40]

Silvia: "O heaven!" Proteus: "I'll force thee yield to my desire."[41] From seduction to rape. The Theseus who abandons Ariadne has form. Remember Oberon's words to Titania in *A Midsummer Night's Dream*. "Didst not thou," he says, lead Theseus

> through the glimmering night
> From Perigenia whom he ravishèd?
> And make him with fair Aegles break his faith,
> With Ariadne and Antiopa?[42]

Theseus: the serial seducer, rapist, abandoner of his conquests. His example suggests that the youthful Shakespeare had a somewhat low opinion of men in the matter of love.

Consider some of the other early works. *The Taming of the Shrew* offers two versions of courtship, with respect to the two sisters. In the Bianca plot, there is consensual seduction, achieved through role-play: Lucentio, disguised as a tutor, gives Bianca a Latin lesson in which they flirtatiously exchange lines from Ovid. But in the shrew plot, Kate is subdued through aggressive mind games and deprivation. The "induction" at the beginning frames the play as a practical joke played by a Lord on a drunken tinker, Christopher Sly, who is offered a fantasy of sexual fulfillment: as I discussed in chapter 2, he is taken to a bedroom hung with "wanton pictures" and presented with a boy dressed as a girl, only to have his pleasure withdrawn at the last minute. It was indeed a custom in aristocratic households to adorn the walls of the bedchamber with a chimneypiece or tapestries or paintings of erotic scenes, in order to set the juices flowing. Troublingly, though, the usual subject matter, as here, is coercive desire: among the pictures described to Sly are Jupiter's rape of Io and Apollo chasing Daphne through the woods, causing her legs to bleed as they are scratched with briars.

Then there is Shakespeare's earliest tragedy, *Titus Andronicus*, at the centre of which is a brutal rape, followed by mutilation of the woman's body, modelled explicitly upon the rape of Philomel in Ovid's *Metamorphoses*. And even *The Comedy of Errors*, the lightest of his early plays, has a darker dimension to its origins: though it is primarily based on the Roman dramatist Plautus's farcical comedy of the confusion of twins, *The Menaechmus Brothers*, it incorporates a plot line from a different Plautus play, *Amphitryon*, in which a husband returns to his house only to discover that his wife has been in bed with someone else. That someone else turns out to have been Jupiter, disguised as Amphitryon himself: what better way to seduce a loyal wife than to take the form of her husband?

The gods in the classical pantheon were symbols of particular qualities. Jupiter of earthly power, Apollo of the creative arts, Mars of military strength. They are images of hypermasculinity. And with their power comes their belief that they can have sex with any woman they want. If words fail them in their desire, they simply metamorphose themselves and get their way by force. As Florizel puts it in *The Winter's Tale*, when trying to reassure Perdita that he will not try to have sex with her before they marry:

> The gods themselves,
> Humbling their deities to love, have taken
> The shapes of beasts upon them: Jupiter
> Became a bull, and bellowed: the green Neptune
> A ram, and bleated: and the fire-robed god,
> Golden Apollo, a poor humble swain,
> As I seem now. Their transformations
> Were never for a piece of beauty rarer,
> Nor in a way so chaste, since my desires
> Run not before mine honour, nor my lusts
> Burn hotter than my faith.[43]

Love turns us all to beasts. The gods take the girls of their choice by assuming such forms as the bull and the ram, symbols of sexual potency. Florizel acknowledges the heat of his lust, but maintains that he will control it within the bounds of propriety and fidelity.

It should be now be abundantly clear that Shakespeare's first port of call in his anatomy of desire was Ovid. We have seen that his early comedies and the tragedy of *Titus Andronicus*, despite their diverse sources and styles, all converge on Ovid when they address the matter of *eros*. The popularity of Ovid and Ovidianism was one of the main reasons for the efflorescence of the poetry and drama of desire in the early 1590s. The court comedies of John Lyly are dramatizations of Ovidian or quasi-Ovidian myths; the prose romances of Robert Greene are steeped in allusions to the transformations of the Ovidian gods; one of the most widely practised forms of poetry was the Ovidian or neo-Ovidian narrative poem, of which the most famous examples were Marlowe's *Hero and Leander* and the poem that Shakespeare wrote during 1593, when the theatres were closed because of plague, *Venus and Adonis*, which was developed from a story in the tenth book of the *Metamorphoses* that was also an inspiration to artists such as Titian.

Venus and Adonis was not only Shakespeare's attempt to establish his classical literary credentials, perhaps as a riposte to Greene's jibe dismissing him as an ill-educated "upstart crow": it was also his distinctive anatomy of desire, and what is striking about it is the manner in which the male is put in the position of passivity. The language of seduction is given to the woman. In the sonnet tradition, the idealized female is almost always silent. In this poem, the woman speaks 531 lines and the man just 89. Venus actually speaks 45 percent of the poem, a higher proportion of her work than any other character in Shakespeare (Hamlet, the character who most dominates a play, has 37 percent of the lines). In the sonnet tradition, the enamoured poet blazons the woman's body parts. Shakespeare's Venus unashamedly blazons herself:

> I'll be a park, and thou shalt be my deer;
> Feed where thou wilt, on mountain or in dale:
> Graze on my lips; and if those hills be dry,
> Stray lower, where the pleasant fountains lie.
>
> Within this limit is relief enough,
> Sweet bottom-grass and high delightful plain,
> Round rising hillocks, brakes obscure and rough,
> To shelter thee from tempest and from rain.[44]

Adonis barely speaks until well into the poem, and when he does, he is largely monosyllabic, mumbling protestations such as "no" and "let me go."[45] At various points, he is silenced by Venus's kisses. What happens to him is analogous to what happens to the women who are forced into submission in Ovid's many tales of seduction, abduction, and rape by male gods: when he finally gets his say in a discourse contrasting the selfishness of lust with the selflessness of true love, he is cut short by Venus jumping on him, which leads him to run away and be gored to death by the boar.

The point, though, is that Venus is not any woman: she is the very embodiment of love. Cupid is her child, born of her adulterous affair with Mars, the god of war. In this poem, it is desire itself that speaks. To resist *eros*, as Adonis does, means death. Shakespeare, following Ovid, seems to be suggesting that humans have little choice but to submit to the power of love. One sees why poetry in general and Ovid in particular were regarded by Puritans as highly dangerous. In 1599, the Archbishop of Canterbury and the Bishop of London ordered the banning and burning of a number of books, among them not only a variety of "snarling satires" but also *The Metamorphosis of Pygmalion's Image*, a poem about a man having sex with a statue, Marlowe's translation of Ovid's *Amores*, a collection of extremely filthy epigrams by Sir John Davies, and a witty misogynistic work called *The XV Joys of Marriage* (the title is ironic, in that the argument is essentially that a bachelor may experience the joys of sex whereas a married man is imprisoned in a kind of hell). *Venus and Adonis* escaped the cull, perhaps because it avoided the toxic mix of satire and eroticism, perhaps because it was regarded as essentially playful, perhaps because of the patronage behind Shakespeare, or, most probably, simply because it was already in wide circulation, so could not have been easily withdrawn.[46]

Venus reacts to the moment of Adonis's death by imagining herself in the place of the boar and making the goring into an aggressive act of lovemaking: if the boar had seen Adonis's lovely face, she argues, he would have tried to kiss him. The killing was the accidental consequence of a kiss: "And nuzzling in his flank, the loving swine / Sheathed unaware the tusk in his soft groin." The double entendre in the image of sheathing a hard tusk in soft nether regions hardly needs further elaboration, though Venus provides some, just in case we have missed the point: "Had I been toothed like him, I must confess, / With kissing him I should have killed him first."[47]

This moment, the poem proposes, is the origin not merely of the association of sex with death (in Elizabethan poetry, "dying" is a frequent metaphor for orgasm, or vice-versa), but also of the idea of love as a sickness, a disease: Venus launches into a curse, prophesying that because Adonis is dead, love will always be associated with sorrow and jealousy, with "sweet beginning" and "unsavoury end," that "all love's pleasure shall not match his woe," that "It shall be fickle, false and full of fraud," striking "the wise dumb" and teaching "the fool to speak"; "It shall be raging-mad and silly-mild, / Make the young old, the old become a child"; "It shall be cause of war and dire events" (think Helen of Troy), "And set dissension 'twixt the son and sire" (or daughter and sire, one might add—think Juliet). Because death has destroyed Adonis in his prime, "They that love best their loves shall not enjoy."[48] The tone of *Venus and Adonis*, like the style of Ovid, has been light, thanks to the dazzlingly ingenious word-play, but the matter, like that of Ovid, is dark. Venus lays out a programme for the tragedy of love—*Romeo and Juliet*, *Troilus and Cressida*, *Antony and Cleopatra*—even though the main substance of the poem has been a gender-inverted parody of the tropes of the courtship comedy and the seduction sonnet.

Adonis is transformed into an anemone in order to suggest the transience of beauty. This prime of youth with an aura of androgyny that can make the lover speak, as Shakespeare does in his twentieth sonnet, of the "master-mistress" of his passion—this beauty we most desire—is as short-lived as a flower in season. When Shakespeare brings Adonis-like figures off the page of his poetry onto the stage of his theatre, it is in the form of lovely boys dressed as girls, temporarily re-dressed as boys—Portia as Balthasar, Rosalind as Ganymede, Viola as Cesario—and there is a poignancy, especially in *Twelfth Night*, that their androgynous beauty will perforce fade and die as they become wives and then mothers.

When *Venus and Adonis* was published in 1593, Shakespeare did not know how long it would be before the theatres would reopen and give him the opportunity to create those characters. Having gained the agreement of a real-life lovely boy, the Earl of Southampton, to be his patron, he set about writing a second poem, which he described in the dedication to the first as "some graver labour."[49] This notion of a progression from lighter to more serious matter was based on the so-called *cursus Virgilius*, the model of the Virgilian poetic career that began with pastoral (the *Eclogues* or *Bucolics*), proceeded to *labor* (the *Georgics*, poems about the work of farming), and climaxed in epic (the *Aeneid*, poetry of a nation). But in *Venus and Adonis*, Shakespeare had loudly trumpeted his allegiance to Ovid rather than Virgil, not only by basing his poem on a story in the *Metamorphoses* but also by plastering a quotation from the *Amores* as the epigraph on the title-page. His own "graver labour" meant, accordingly, going to a heavier poem by Ovid, the *Fasti*, an incomplete six-book poem narrating the etiology of the Roman calendar. This involved the additional labour of reading in Latin, since, in contrast to the *Metamorphoses*, for which he had Arthur Golding's English version, there was no translation.

If he did manage to plough through the entire text of the *Fasti* in search of stories about the graver labours of love, he would have found an embarrassment of riches. February, for example, offered him the festival of the Lupercalia (a calendrical moment to which he would revert in *Julius Caesar*): Ovid claims that the custom of young men running naked through the streets of Rome on that day had its origin in the humiliation of Faunus as a result of his attempt to rape Omphale, who was really the mighty Hercules cross-dressed as a girl. In March, under the influence of Mars, there was the rape of Silvia, the rape of the Sabine women, and a lament of Ariadne; in April, Venus herself puts in an appearance and upbraids Ovid for abandoning erotic elegy in favour of history; this month also includes the longest narrative in the poem, the rape of Persephone (otherwise known as Proserpina) and the anguish of her mother Ceres, a story which would haunt *The Winter's Tale* many years later in Shakespeare's career. Whereas Virgil argued that the foundation of Romanness was the heroic journey of Aeneas, which included his renunciation of *eros* in the form of Dido, Ovid seems to be suggesting that Rome was built upon the act of rape. And no legend of rape was more influential than the story of Tarquin and Lucrece, the closing section of February.

I have discussed *The Rape of Lucrece* in the contexts of Shakespeare's antiheroic idiom and of the classical shaping of his politics in the light of the fact that the story's profound influence on both Roman republican and early modern culture was that Tarquin's heinous crime in raping the virtuous Lucrece, causing her to commit suicide, gave her relatives the opportunity to drive out the Tarquins and establish the republic. The rape of a woman is, it seems, the price for the establishment of a new political order in which the people—which for most of human history has meant the men—have an electoral voice. But in the context of Shakespeare and *eros*, the point that needs to be made about *The Rape of Lucrece* is that it offers an astonishingly powerful account of the animal force of raging male desire. Furious at Lucrece's steadfast refusal to submit to his advances, Tarquin sets his foot on the light, muffles her cries by wrapping the bed linen around her face, and stains her bed with his "prone lust."[50] Rape is the extreme consequence of desire as a disease that overcomes reason and restraint. In the absence of consent, rape is masculinity's way of purging the "infirmity named *hereos.*" It is as much a form of derangement as the jealousy that turns a man to madness when he is tormented by the mental image of his beloved in bed with another man: Troilus seeing Cressida with Diomed, Othello thinking of Cassio lying on Desdemona, Posthumus imagining Iachimo mounting chaste Innogen "like a full-acorned boar," Leontes watching Hermione and Polixenes "paddling palms" and convincing himself that the child full in her womb is not his own.[51]

It was probably Shakespeare's immersion in Ovid during the closure of the theatres in 1593–94 that led him to the tragic story of Pyramus and Thisbe, lovers from rival households, in book 4 of the *Metamorphoses*, which he treated comically in the play-within-the-play in *A Midsummer Night's Dream* and which was the ultimate exemplum for the "Romeus and Juliet" story that he read in Arthur Brooke's labored 1562 poem of that title. Brooke treats the tragic love-story as an admonitory tale: *eros* is a dangerous aberration; girls should marry the person their parents think is suitable. Shakespeare, by contrast, immortalizes the star-crossed lovers. He acknowledges the dangers of passion ("These violent delights have violent ends"),[52] but he also celebrates the young girl who embraces her desire, refusing to be inhibited or to bow to her father's will. The Romeo who is superficially in love with Rosaline in the first act suffers from the symptoms of the infirmity named *hereos*, but the love of Juliet and her Romeo is both fully sexual and intensely spiritual, insofar as it lifts them to another plane:

> Come, gentle night, come, loving, black-browed night,
> Give me my Romeo, and when I shall die,

Take him and cut him out in little stars,
And he will make the face of heaven so fine
That all the world will be in love with night
And pay no worship to the garish sun.[53]

Monarchs are traditionally worshipped as the sun; Juliet proposes instead that all the world should be in love with the idea of star-crossed love. There is a famous moment in the first book of Virgil's *Aeneid* when Jupiter prophesies that Caesar—Virgil may mean Julius, he may mean Augustus, or he may mean both—will undergo an apotheosis, be raised to the heavens as a star, shining over a Roman Empire that will rule the earth and endure forever. Ovid alludes to this when the character of Pythagoras in the final book of the *Metamorphoses* prophesies that Venus will take the spirit of the emperor Augustus and turn it into a star. His fame will outshine that of Agamemnon, Achilles, and Aeneas. As Jove rules the heavens, Augustus will rule the triple-cornered earth. But there must be an element of irony here: the thrust of Pythagoras's discourse in book 15, and the whole direction of the *Metamorphoses*, has been towards transience, not endurance. The only constancy is change. This is the very opposite of Virgil's idea of an Augustan Rome that is "an empire without end" and without bound ("nec metas rerum nec tempora … imperium sine fine").[54] Ovid knows that all dynasties and dominions are transient—that was the lesson of the fall of Troy and the expulsion of the Tarquins. In his world, stellar transformation is the fate not of emperors but of victims of love such as the raped Callisto, who is doubly transformed, from nymph to bear to constellation. Besides, cheekily, the divinity who raises Augustus to the stars is not Mars the god of might but Venus the goddess of desire. In Ovid, as in *Romeo and Juliet*, it is love, not power, that brings eternal fame.

In *Antony and Cleopatra*, Shakespeare returns to the theme of "All for Love, or, the World Well Lost," as John Dryden entitled his reworked version of the play in 1677. At the climax, Cleopatra dreams of an "emperor Antony," bestriding the earth, raised god-like in the heavens:[55] this is wonderfully subversive, since the whole thrust of the play as political drama has been to tell the story of the rise of Antony's rival Octavius from one of a triumvirate into his new role as Augustus, the first Roman emperor. But now in the lover's dream it is Antony who is the emperor. Shakespeare is continuing Ovid's work

204 · CHAPTER 11

of undoing Virgil. The language of boundlessness and eternity that Virgil had ascribed to the Roman *imperium* is given by Shakespeare to the passion inspired by Cleopatra, as instanced by the glorious lines "eternity was in our lips and eyes" and the following exchange:

> CLEOPATRA. I'll set a bourn [boundary] how far to be beloved.
> ANTONY. Then must thou needs find out new heaven, new earth.[56]

Cleopatra is Venus, subduing Antony's Mars. And she is Dido to his Aeneas, but whereas Virgil tells of how Dido must be renounced in the name of empire, Shakespeare brings the forces of imagination and poetry together to reunite the lovers in death: "I come, my queen," says Antony: "Stay for me":

> Where souls do couch on flowers we'll hand in hand,
> And with our sprightly port make the ghosts gaze.
> Dido and her Aeneas shall want troops,
> And all the haunt be ours.[57]

This is at the moment when Antony is readying himself for death, following defeat in battle. But the soaring verse of his final speeches, and still more those of Cleopatra that follow, transcends defeat and apotheosizes the lovers instead of the emperor, who is left upon the dungy earth as a diminished Augustus.

In his close reading of Plutarch's life of Mark Antony, Shakespeare happened upon a little detail that must have greatly tickled his fancy. Antony's last follower, who unarms him and who bears the Roman sword that he will turn upon himself, has a very resonant name. A moment ago, I quoted Antony's words addressed to his absent beloved, imagining their reunion in Elysium, the field of the famous dead. I omitted the interjections in which he calls for his (un)armourer, whose name in Plutarch happens to be Eros. The call is also an invocation of the child of Venus, goddess of love. To quote the lines again, in full, is to see that heroic masculinity and the will to power are ultimately less powerful forces than that of *eros*:

> Eros!—I come, my queen.—Eros!—Stay for me:
> Where souls do couch on flowers we'll hand in hand,
> And with our sprightly port make the ghosts gaze.
> Dido and her Aeneas shall want troops,
> And all the haunt be ours.—Come, Eros, Eros![58]

Whereas the *Aeneid* ends with Aeneas on Italian soil, married to Lavinia and becoming the father of the Latins, inaugurating the line of command that will culminate, as prophesied by Jupiter, in the apotheosis of Augustus, Shakespeare restores Aeneas's spirit to Dido in the form of their avatars Antony and Cleopatra. Aeneas, son of Venus by Anchises, is left in the company of his half-brother Eros (Cupid), son of Venus by Mars.

Virgil's poetic imagination was sometimes at odds with his political and moral ideology. His purpose was imaginative sympathy, not only piety of the sort emphasized by his more didactic medieval and Renaissance commentators. He accordingly recognized that the virtues of Aeneas were not a given. They had to be honed through action and through choice; they involved conflicts between public duties and private desires; they necessitated sacrifices. Though Virgil devoted considerable energy to patriotic *romanitas*, praise of Augustus, and prophecy of the *pax Romana*, he also portrayed history's losers with extraordinary sympathy, directly addressing the beloved pilot Palinurus who is destined to lie naked on an unknown shore, the brave but doomed maiden-warrior Camilla, and the deserted Dido, that archetypal victim of "improbe Amor" ("scurvye Loove," as Elizabethan translator Richard Stanyhurst had it).[59] It is in this spirit that Shakespeare's most memorable allusions to Aeneas all turn on his affair with Dido and his desertion of her. During a discussion on the magical island of *The Tempest* about whether modern Tunis was synonymous with ancient Carthage, a reference to "widow Dido" leads to a tart rebuke about "widower Aeneas."[60] The exemplary classical figure is invoked by way of his marital status and his sexual entanglements, not his patriotic duty or his military virtues. *Hereos* displaces heroism.

⌒

I will return to *Antony and Cleopatra* in the next chapter. To end this one, with its argument about the double sense of "heroical love" and the way that Shakespeare's heroes are nearly always affected or infected by *hereos*, I want to offer a negative exemplum. Its source, intriguingly, is a digression within Plutarch's life of Mark Antony.

Early in his biography, Plutarch associates Antony with a life of pleasure and luxury: "In his house they did nothing but feast, daunce, and maske: and him selfe passed away the time in hearing of foolish playes, or in marrying these plaiers, tomblers, jeasters, and such sort of people."[61] By marrying, he essentially means "having sex with." Antony is also said to spend his time with whores and to enjoy having affairs with other men's wives. Later in the life, as he succumbs to the lure of Cleopatra and stops listening to the good counsel of his soldiers, he becomes an increasingly isolated figure. His followers begin to desert him (Shakespeare memorably dramatizes this in the character of Enobarbus, his principal addition to Plutarch's narrative). After the defeat at Actium, but before the return to Cleopatra, Antony's suicide, and the bite of the asp, Plutarch includes a sequence that Shakespeare omits:

> *Antonius*, he forsooke the citie and companie of his frendes, and built him a house in the sea, by the Ile of Pharos, upon certaine forced mountes which he caused to be cast into the sea, and dwelt there, as a man that banished him selfe from all mens companie: saying that he would lead *Timons* life, because he had the like wrong offered him, that was affore offered unto *Timon*: and that for the unthankefulnes of those he had done good unto, and whom he tooke to be his frendes, he was angry with all men, and would trust no man. This *Timon* was a citizen of Athens, that lived about the warre of Peloponnesus, as appeareth by *Plato*, and *Aristophanes* commedies: in the which they mocked him, calling him a vyper, and malicious man unto mankind, to shunne all other mens companies, but the companie of young *Alcibiades*, a bolde and insolent youth, whom he woulde greatly feast, and make much of, and kissed him very gladly.[62]

Plutarch's usual method was to pair a Greek life and a Roman one, and draw a comparison between them at the end. Here, exceptionally, he inserted a brief parallel within a life. His Antony compares himself to Timon because of his progression from luxury surrounded by friends and lovers to isolation far from the city.

Around the time that he was writing *Antony and Cleopatra*, Shakespeare wrote *The Life of Timon of Athens*, almost certainly in collaboration with Thomas Middleton. The title *The Life of Timon* as opposed to *The Tragedy of Timon* reads as a nod to Plutarch. The action culminates in the reading of Timon's epitaph, copied onto a tablet of wax from his grave in the woods near the sea. Plutarch records two different epitaphs, and Shakespeare duly includes them both, almost verbatim.[63] Picking up on the hint in Plutarch's Timon digression, Shakespeare (and Middleton)[64] dramatized his life in parallel with that of the Greek general and playboy Alcibiades. This was a story of which he was also aware in this phase of his career because Plutarch's "Life of Alcibiades" was the parallel to his "Life of Coriolanus." In the comparison between these two generals in the very closing pages of the *Lives*, Plutarch points out that the great difference between them was Coriolanus's abstinence. He represents the austere Roman character, devoted to mother and fatherland, chilly in his marriage. Alcibiades, by contrast, is a quintessential Greek. His beauty is emphasized throughout the "Life": he is "wonderful fair," "marvelous amiable and beloved of every man"; many great and rich men love him. He is a special friend of Socrates: Plutarch is explicit that they lie together. He is also "much given over to lust and pleasure," "incontinent of body and dissolute of life," "dainty in his fare, wantonly given unto light women, riotous in banquets, vain and womanish in apparel."[65] The "Greek" aspects of Antony, as represented by Plutarch, make him into an Alcibiades, whereas the austere Octavius is a Coriolanus.

In Plutarch, then, Alcibiades, like Antony, lives under the sign of Venus as well as that of Mars. He has plenty of time for *eros*. Indeed, at the end of the story, one of his many lovers plays a key role. Plutarch's final page finds him in a village in Phrygia with his whore Timandra.[66] He dreams of putting on "his concubines apparell, and how she dandling him in her armes, had dressed his head, friseling his heare, and painted his face, as he had bene a woman."[67] It is very like the cross-dressing of Antony and Cleopatra. He is then killed, and Timandra is the one who gives him an honourable burial.

The most striking thing about the character of Alcibiades in *Timon of Athens* is that, in sharp contrast to the way in which he was represented in Plutarch (and indeed in the entire tradition going back to Plato's *Symposium*), he has no interest in *eros*. He is only the soldier. He marches against his own city, because, as he says when denouncing the "lascivious town," the Athenian senators have "filled the time / With all licentious measure."[68] Though he is accompanied by Timandra and another whore when he visits Timon in his forest exile, there is no development of the relationship between them along the lines that could have been drawn from Plutarch. The sole purpose of Timandra's presence is for Timon to rage against the consequences of sexual desire:

TIMON. Art thou Timandra?
TIMANDRA. Yes.
TIMON. Be a whore still. They love thee not that use thee:
Give them diseases, leaving with thee their lust.
Make use of thy salt hours: season the slaves
For tubs and baths, bring down rose-cheeked youth
To the tub-fast and the diet.[69]

Whereas in *Antony and Cleopatra*, Eros guides the way to souls that couch on flowers, in *Timon* it only leads to the sweating tubs and hot baths that were the treatment for the syphilitic disease of Venus.

Timandra gives as good as she gets by way of sexual insult: she describes Timon as the "Athenian minion," a word that Shakespeare applies elsewhere to a catamite (Orsino to Olivia regarding Cesario: "But this your minion").[70] Where Plato in the *Symposium* had extolled Socrates's *eros* for the beautiful young Alcibiades as a rung on the ladder to divine love, Shakespeare removes *eros* from Alcibiades and applies it to the world of Timon before his fall. Hospitality is retrospectively painted as a transaction no different from the payment of a whore. According to the Ciceronian code of benefits, Timon's friends, upon whom he lavished such generosity, should have reciprocated his favours when he needed their assistance. Ironically, the only person to show the values of loyalty and honesty is his paid steward. Timon's rage against the world, like King Lear's, is larded with sexual disguise: he describes women's nipples as "milk-paps / That through the window-bars [of a bodice] bore at men's eyes," suggesting the petrifying stare of the Gorgon Medusa.[71] His misogyny is an intensified version of his misanthropy. It only softens when Flavius the steward visits him and weeps, a traditionally female attribute:

Then I love thee,
Because thou art a woman, and disclaim'st
Flinty mankind whose eyes do never give
But thorough lust and laughter ...
        Surely this man
Was born of woman.[72]

Even as Timon abjures things that are the making of Shakespeare—acceptance that lust is a necessity of life and celebration of release in laughter—he is forced to acknowledge that other key Shakespearean theme, the humanizing influence of woman's wit, resilience, and emotional intelligence in a male world of ambition, egotism, and violence.[73] The word "woman" occurs on only two other occasions in the entire play. The first is near the beginning, when the Fool announces his version of misanthropy: "I do not always follow lover, elder brother and woman: sometime the philosopher" (the latter being the cynic Apemantus). The second is very near Timon's end, when, all angry passion spent, he comes to the brink of tears: "Lend me a fool's heart and a woman's eyes."[74]

Timon of Athens is a bleak portrayal of a world that has very little *amicitia* and that is entirely without *eros*.[75] The play was written around the same time that Shakespeare was creating such many-dimensioned female characters as Desdemona, Isabella, Cordelia, Lady Macbeth, and Cleopatra. In the light of this, the most telling thing about it is that—other than the actor-impersonated forms of silent cross-dressed masquers of Ladies and Amazons—the two sex-workers Timandra and Phrynia are the only female characters in the play. They speak just seven lines between them. In a world without *eros*, woman is silenced.

12

THE LABOURS OF HERCULES

IN 1597, SHAKESPEARE'S WARWICKSHIRE contemporary Michael
Drayton published *England's Heroical Epistles*. In his preface, he said
that the word "heroical" was most properly applied to demigods
such as Hercules and Aeneas, "whose Parents were said to be the
one celestiall, the other mortall." He added that he had taken the
liberty of following Ovid—"whose imitator I partly professe to be"—
in applying the term to anyone "with a great and mightie spirit."[1]
Drayton's epistles, modelled on the *Heroides* of Ovid, consisted of
imaginary letters exchanged between English kings or dukes and
their lovers. The volume must have been a success, since a "newly
enlarged" edition was published the following year and reprinted
the year after. A later reprint included among its dedictory poems
one that described Drayton as "Britannia's Ovid, whose soft pen /
Transplants the Grecian Loves to English-men." It praises him for
writing about chaste courtship, for expressing "Noble Gallantry"
that is "Equal to that of *Rome*, and much above / The little Fopperies
of modern Love." The "*English* Hero," claimed the poem's author,
has a "divine" soul, just as the English heroine has a divine beauty.
"The Lover and the Brave are still the same," the encomium concludes, "The *Muses* Treasure, and Delight of *Fame*."[2]

By this account, Drayton's purpose was revisionary. Whereas the
"modern Love" of most 1590s poetry, such as the numerous sonnet sequences and the narratives of *eros* such as *Venus and Adonis*,
were about the foolishness ("fopperies") of love, his *Heroical Epistles*
will offer gentlemanly behaviour ("gallantry"). Whereas the original
Heroides of Ovid told stories of badly behaved heroes in the lamenting voices of deserted heroines damaged by the devastating force
of *amor*, Drayton will try to undo the division between the code of
hereos and that of heroism, uniting the Lover and the Brave in the
House of Fame. So, for example, in the case of "Edward the Black

Prince to Alice Countess of Salisbury," whereas Shakespeare had staged an attempted seduction in which Edward enlists the assistance of a love poet, Drayton pens an imaginary letter written after "vain desires" have been replaced by acknowledgment of the virtuous woman's "invincible Constancy."[3] Where the poetry of *eros* uses the imagery of the lover besieging the city of his beloved's chastity, in Drayton's poem, admiration for Alice's chastity is Edward's protection against the dangerous assault of Cupid's arrows:

> Love growne extreame, doth finde unlawful shifts,
> The Gods take shapes, and doe allure with gifts,
> Commaunding *Jove*, that by great *Stix* doth sweare,
> Forsworne in love, with Lovers oathes doth beare,
> Love causelesse still, doth aggravate his cause,
> It is his lawe to violate all laws;
> His reason is, in onely wanting reason,
> And were untrue, not deeply touch'd with treason;
> Th' unlawfull meanes, doth make his lawfull gaine,
> Hee speakes most true, when he the most doth faine.[4]

The lover, like the poet, is known for "faining" (that pun on lying and desiring); desire is contrary to both law and reason; when the gods are smitten with love, they resort to tricksy metamorphoses in pursuit of seduction and, if necessary, rape. *Eros* must therefore be banished in the name of reason and law.

Drayton's attempt to salvage the "heroical" from the emotional, social, and potentially political chaos caused by *hereos* reveals that there was considerable anxiety in the 1590s as to the representation of those figures from classical mythology who were heroes in the strict sense of being born of gods as well as men, most notably Aeneas and Hercules. Shakespeare, under the influence of Ovid's *Heroides*, nearly always represents Aeneas as the man who deserts Dido and causes her to commit suicide rather than as the *pius pater* of his *patria*, the heroic father of Rome. What, then, about his representation of Hercules, the figure who, it would seem, bore the Globe on his shoulders on the flag that flew above Shakespeare's theatre?[5] In this chapter, I want to explore Shakespeare's psychology of choice, of masculinity, of the will, and of anger (*furor*) by way of his allusions to the figure of Hercules.[6] In particular, I will suggest that Hercules

Figure 7. Between *Virtus* and *Voluptas*: late seventeenth-century engraving by Pietro Aquila after Annibale Carracci's painting *The Choice of Hercules* (1596)

was the principal paradigm for an essential element of Shakespeare's dramatic psychology, namely the process whereby the explosion of strong emotion, typically anger, precipitates a change of behaviour which has drastic—tragic, mortal—consequences.

For Shakespeare and his contemporaries, "Hercules at the crossroads" was the paradigm for the choice between the hard labour of duty and the easeful life of indulgence. As a young man, Hercules is confronted by two women, one representing virtue and the other representing pleasure. The story was frequently illustrated in the Renaissance, perhaps most famously in the painting by Annibale Carracci, dating from 1596, that now hangs in the Museo Nazionale di Capodimonte in Naples.[7] Hercules, leaning on his enormous club, is midpoint, at a crossroads. On one side, *Virtus* (the word is suggestive of valour and strength, as well as virtue) points towards the steep and rocky path that will lead to glory through labour and danger, while on the other, *Voluptas* lures towards the pleasures of music and play. Her naked shoulder and diaphanous drapery are such that the viewer will intuit the nature of the temptation without having to know the mythological origin of *Voluptas* as the daughter of the union between Cupid and Psyche, desire and the soul.[8]

Shortly after Shakespeare's death, Ben Jonson dramatized the choice of Hercules in his court masque *Pleasure Reconciled to Virtue*. This begins with an antimasque featuring the Bacchus-like figure of Comus; it ends with the achievement of a balance between the two paths, presided over by Mercury. The association of these two figures with the story bears interestingly on the two very different Shakespeare plays for which, I believe, the choice of Hercules served as a classical paradigm: *Love's Labour's Lost* and *Antony and Cleopatra*. The former brings together Hercules and Mercury; the latter, Hercules and Bacchus.

Love's Labour's Lost belongs to the early phase of Shakespeare's career when he was attempting to prove his classical credentials, perhaps in response to Greene's "upstart crow" insult—but at the same time, it is a glorious parody of academic pretentiousness. The punctuation in the play's title is editorial: the quarto's title-page reads *Loues labors lost* and its running header *Loues Labor's lost*; the Folio's title and running header is *Loues Labour's lost*, but the contents list has *Loues Labour lost*. Love's labour is lost? Love's labours [are] lost? Love is labour (or labours) lost? Loves [are] labour(s) lost? Whether we think of labour or labours or "labour is," the centrality of the word in the title is enough to signify the relevance of Hercules, who was even more famous for his labours than he was for his choice. In the props cupboard of Philip Henslowe, the proprietor of the rival acting company to Shakespeare's, one could find Cerberus's head, a lion skin, a club, and the apples from the garden of the Hesperides. They probably belonged to a lost two-part play, commissioned by Henslowe around the same time as *Love's Labours Lost*, on the subject of the labours of Hercules. Thomas Heywood enthused about them in his *Apology for Actors*:

> To see as I have seene, Hercules in his owne shape hunting the Boare, knocking downe the Bull, taming the Hart, fighting with Hydra, murdering Gerion, slaughtering Diomed, wounding the Stimphalides, killing the Centaurs, pashing the Lion, squeezing the Dragon, dragging Cerberus in Chaynes, and lastly, on his high Pyramides writing *Nil ultra*, Oh these were sights to make an Alexander.[9]

Figure 8. Hercules assaulting Cerberus with his club, lion's tail dangling (illustration in 1582 edition of Ovid's *Metamorphoses*)

Whether or not Shakespeare's play about the labours of love was some kind of response to these dramas, there is no doubt that the ideas of labour and of choice (virtue or pleasure, academic study or love?) give it a Herculean flavour, albeit turned to comic effect—especially when the smallest character in the academe, page-boy Moth, is cast in the role of the giant hero.

Hercules was associated above all with his strength, signified visually by his club and the skin of the Nemean lion that he killed as his first labour. The Warburg Institute's *Iconographic Database* has over a thousand images of Hercules from the sixteenth century alone; in nearly all of them, he holds his club, and in most of those in which he is not naked, he is wearing the lion skin. Its tail usually hangs to the ground.

Shakespeare wittily compares Don Armado's bombastic prose to the roar of the Nemean lion.[10] This is one of a number of occasions on which he refers to the labours. Sometimes he does so with suitable machismo, as when Coriolanus speaks in admiration of his mother's gender-bending strength:

> Nay, mother,
> Resume that spirit, when you were wont to say,
> If you had been the wife of Hercules,
> Six of his labours you'd have done, and saved
> Your husband so much sweat.[11]

In other contexts, however, the labour is translated into the world of desire. In *The Taming of the Shrew*, wooing is regarded as a Herculean task: "Leave that labour to great Hercules and let it be more than Alcides' twelve," says Gremio. In a similar vein, Don Pedro in *Much Ado about Nothing* compares the task of bringing "Signior Benedick and the Lady Beatrice into a mountain of affection the one with the other" to "one of Hercules' labours."[12] As for the individual labours, there are allusions to the rescue of Hesione from the sea monster in *The Merchant of Venice* and *King Lear*; Hippolyta in *A Midsummer's Night Dream* remembers being "with Hercules and Cadmus once, / When in a wood of Crete they bayed the bear / With hounds of Sparta"; and when Holofernes introduces the incongruous figure of impish Moth (or "Mote") playing the part of mighty Hercules, he refers to how his "club killed Cerberus, that three-headed *canus*."[13] The Pageant of the Nine Worthies, which also alludes to Hercules strangling snakes in his infancy, takes the opportunity to make jokes about the size of Moth's club ("He's not so big as the end of his club").[14]

There were numerous sources in which Shakespeare could have found out about these labours. The ninth book of the *Metamorphoses* includes a brief listing of them, spoken by Hercules shortly before his death, and when Hercules wrestles with the river-god Acheloüs at the beginning of that book, he vaunts about the chopping off the heads of the Hydra, which Shakespeare used as a metaphor in several plays.[15] Ovid offered a fuller account, which Shakespeare probably also read, in the ninth of his *Heroides*, in which Deianira goes through the labours in a retrospective narrative. But, as with the choice of Hercules, we do not need to imagine Shakespeare poring over a particular source: the twelve labours were in the common currency of classical reference throughout his lifetime.

Killing a lion, a boar, and a many-headed Hydra, cleansing the Augean stables, and capturing a hideous three-headed dog were proofs of Hercules's masculinity. The odd labour out was his theft of the apples of the Hesperides. Though this is achieved by the supremely manly means of holding up the earth while Atlas assists him in the task, a different tone is established by the paradisal garden location and the fact that the golden apple tree is guarded not only by a serpent-like dragon but also by three beautiful nymphs. This is a story associated with the temptations of the erotic, as may be seen from the way in which it is used at the beginning of *Pericles*. The play opens with the hero being given the "task" (that is to say, the labour) of solving the riddle for which the prize will be the king's daughter. Upon seeing her, Pericles addresses the gods who "have inflamed desire in my breast / To taste the fruit of yon celestial tree / Or die in the adventure." The king replies,

> Before thee stands this fair Hesperides,
> With golden fruit, but dangerous to be touched,
> For deathlike dragons here affright thee hard.
> Her face, like heaven, enticeth thee to view
> Her countless glory, which desert must gain,
> And which, without desert, because thine eye
> Presumes to reach, all the whole heap must die.[16]

The notion of a beautiful woman as a piece of "golden fruit" that is "dangerous to be touched" effectively turns the fair Hesperides into objects of erotic desire. This in turn has the effect of yoking the labours of Hercules together with the choice of Hercules: the nymphs guarding the tree become, in effect, sisters of the alluring figure of *Voluptas* at Carracci's crossroads. Traditionally, they take delight in gardening and singing, archetypal activities of leisure and pleasure as opposed to ardour and duty. Besides, once paganism has collided with Christianity, the association of garden, woman, apple, tree, and serpent can only suggest the idea of temptation.

Hercules does not only perform his serial labours. He also has a propensity to fall serially in love. With his four wives (Megara, Omphale, Deianira, and Hebe). With the fifty daughters of Thespius (he made love to them all in one night, and every one of them bore him a son). And with various boys and young men, including his charioteer Iolaus and the lovely boy Hylas. "Comfort me, boy, what great men have been in love?" lovesick Armado says to Moth. "Hercules, master," comes the reply. Armado: "Most sweet Hercules!" Then he asks for more authorities, more examples of great figures representative of masculinity and strength who have succumbed to love. This leads Armado to conclude that "Love is a familiar, love is a devil": because he has fallen in love with Jaquenetta, he is in danger of breaking the proscription on desire that is the guiding rule of the academe. "There is no evil angel but love. Yet Samson was so tempted, and he had an excellent strength. Yet was Solomon so seduced, and he had a very good wit. Cupid's butt-shaft is too hard for Hercules' club."[17] Whether or not there is a very obscene double entendre in that last image (knowing Shakespeare, there almost certainly is), it sums up the pervasive pattern of so many of the plays: the power of the arrows of desire is greater than the "club" of masculine authority and militaristic prowess.

In the longest speech in the play, Berowne acknowledges that the choice of a chaste and virtuous life of study, the project of the academe, has failed. It was the wrong choice because of its renunciation of love. Stoic philosophy offered a development of the choice of Hercules, proposing three possible paths rather than two: there was the way of duty and public service (the *vita activa*), that of retreat and academic study (the *vita contemplativa*), and the way of idleness, pleasure, and voluptuousness. In Berowne's great speech, he offers a fourth way, the choice of love. Whereas the "choice of Hercules" story and the Stoic frame of mind regarded love—and woman in particular—as a temptation to be avoided, Berowne puts forward the contrary argument. Far from being temptresses, women are the source of humanistic wisdom: "They are the books, the arts, the academes, / That show, contain and nourish all the world." It is through women that "men are men"; it is women who have the power of creativity ("the right Promethean fire"). Erotic love, sparked by "women's eyes," is accordingly a supreme virtue. And at the centre of his defence of love, he reverses the received image of Hercules: "For valour, is not Love a Hercules, / Still climbing trees in the Hesperides?"[18] Love is associated with valour, and thus virtue, as opposed to *voluptas*. Furthermore, whereas Hercules takes the golden apples and runs, Love stays in the garden, climbing the trees. Love performs the labours in super-Herculean style.

But Shakespeare is a realist. He knows that true love must combine *eros* and *caritas*. The men are accordingly tasked with more serious labours before they gain their erotic reward: a year's charitable service, ministering to the sick and moving "wild laughter in the throat of death."[19] The shadow of death, brought by the "words of Mercury" (spoken by the aptly named Mercade), forestalls the comic resolution.[20] There is a strong probability that, just as Henslowe's *Labours of Hercules* was a two-part drama, the further labours of Navarre and his fellow-lovers were explored in Shakespeare's lost sequel *Love's Labours Won*, but we will never know whether that play continued the vein of Herculean allusion.[21] What is certain is that about a decade after writing *Love's Labours*, Shakespeare returned to the paradigm of Hercules, this time in a tragedy of love.

In Plutarch's "Life of Mark Antony," the protagonist is persistently compared to Bacchus. Early in the narrative, there is a powerful contrast: while Julius Caesar in Rome wears out his strength amidst seditions and wars, Antony enjoys the fruits of peace by surrounding himself with an "Asiatic" rout of Bacchic types who indulge in license and buffoonery. We hear of how when he entered Ephesus, he was met by women dressed as Bacchants, men and boys as satyrs and fauns; spears were wreathed with ivy, and Antony was praised in song as Bacchus, giver of joy. At the climax of Plutarch's description of Antony's first sight of Cleopatra on her barge at Cydnus, Shakespeare read that "there went a rumour in the people's mouths that the goddess Venus was come to play with the god Bacchus, for the general good of all Asia." And then, as defeat looms over Antony, a "marvelous sweet harmony of sundry sorts of instruments of music" of the kind "they use in Bacchus' feasts" is heard around midnight. "The interpretation of this wonder" is that "it was the god unto whom Antonius b[o]re singular devotion to counterfeit and resemble him that did forsake them."[22]

Shakespeare, by contrast, downplays the identification of Antony as Bacchus. The god of wine is only mentioned in the drinking song during the scene on Pompey's galley. The image of a conjunction between Venus and Bacchus is omitted from Enobarbus's version of Plutarch's barge speech: what we get instead, on several occasions in the play, is a parallel with the Ovidian story of Venus and Mars.

And, most significantly, the mysterious music at night is read by the Second Soldier not as Bacchus deserting Antony but as the moment when "the god Hercules, whom Antony loved, / now leaves him."[23]

In one sense, Antony is a Herculean figure because of his great military strength. He is described as a "demi-Atlas," which is an allusion to the moment in one of the labours where Hercules is given the job of holding up the earth on behalf of Atlas.[24] But the primary significance of Hercules in this play is, it seems to me, his choice rather than his labours. Shakespeare himself is unlikely to have read the original story of the choice in Xenophon: he did not need to, since it was one of those classical influences that permeated the cultural air of his age. When Mark Antony says, "though I make this marriage for my peace, / I' the east my pleasure lies," he is demonstrably pitting Roman *virtus* (dutiful union for a political end) against Egyptian *voluptas*.[25] The association of *voluptas* with Cupid/Eros is equally clear in these lines of Antony's in the opening scene:

> Now, for the love of Love and her soft hours,
> Let's not confound the time with conference harsh:
> There's not a minute of our lives should stretch
> Without some pleasure now.[26]

The thought begins with a personification of love and ends on the idea of pleasure as immediate gratification, in the "now"—in contrast to the code of virtue, which, as the winding path in Carracci's image reminds us, is always stretching forward into the future, deferring delight for the sake of some larger end. Shakespeare's antithetical language of Rome and Egypt is his verbal equivalent of the hard and soft landscapes of Carracci's *Choice of Hercules*. Hot-blooded Egypt luxuriates on a daybed and floods with the waters of the Nile, while stone-hearted Rome is "triple pillar," "wide arch," "files and musters," "plated Mars," and "conference harsh."[27]

The opening lines of the play are spoken by a Roman soldier whose name the audience never hears and who never appears again. But in his working script Shakespeare took the trouble of giving him a name: Philo, which suggests the Greek word *philos*, meaning beloved or dear one (typically applied to a friend, but also to a lover). He and Demetrius, also unnamed in the dialogue, serve as commentators, topping and tailing the opening scene. Editors are oddly silent about the origins of these names and why Shakespeare chose them.[28] The source of "Demetrius" is obvious: Plutarch's parallel to the life of Antony is the life of Demetrius, King of Macedon. The name was readily available to stick in Shakespeare's mind.[29] If Shakespeare actually read the parallel, he would have discovered that the wife of Demetrius was called Phila. The name might alternatively have been inspired by Philotas, the physician who knew Plutarch's grandfather and gave him several colorful details that were duly included, with acknowledgment of their source, in the life of Antony. But for the Elizabethans, the most famous Philo was the Greek philosopher and rhetorician who was Cicero's teacher in Rome: Philo of Larissa.[30] The name is thus a double embodiment of the Roman code of friendship in the name of civic virtue: it both means "friend" and recalls the Ciceronian notion of mutual benefits that I discussed earlier.

We might expect a Roman soldier, especially one called Philo, to open the play with some measured Ciceronian lines, perhaps even spoken in elegiacs—which, Shakespeare would have learned in school, should never be enjambed across the couplet. But such is the spirit of voluptuous excess in Egypt that Philo immediately overflows the pentameter: "Nay, but this dotage of our general's / O'erflows the measure"; "burst / The buckles on his breast"; "the bellows and the fan / To cool a gipsy's lust."[31] His very way of speaking has been infected by the heat of passion inspired by Cleopatra. The *philos* of friendship is already giving way to the *eros* of sexual pleasure. Antony's phrase "for the love of Love" precisely evokes what we might call the play's *philo-eroticism* that breaks the Roman code of friendship embodied in the loyalty of Enobarbus and the "beneficial" marriage of Antony to the sister of Octavius.

Pleasure, which is to say *voluptas*, and its synonyms are key terms in *Antony and Cleopatra*. Octavius, the quintessential Roman, the future Augustus, speaks of Antony's "voluptuousness" and "full surfeits," his "lightness" and his "sport," his confounding of the time in "vacancy" (suggestive of leisure, *otium*, the opposite of Roman *labor*), his pawning of his "experience" to his "present pleasure."[32] When Antony tries to resist the enchantment of Cleopatra, he uses the same language: "The present pleasure, / By revolution lowering, does become the opposite of itself.... My idleness doth hatch."[33]

A whole series of Roman and neo-Roman ideas about experience, duty, and judgment are played off against the pleasure and the idleness of Egypt. In the very first scene, there is a fine example of an acting out of the choice of Hercules. A messenger comes with news from Rome, reminding Antony of his public duties, of the virtue of service. But Antony makes his choice. He will not go down that road: "Let Rome in Tiber melt and the wide arch / Of the ranged empire fall. Here is my space." *Virtus* may lead to honour—the construction of a triumphal "arch" in Rome—but arches and empires will one day fall, so why not seize the day and live in the present? "The nobleness of life," Antony continues, "is to do thus"—to kiss Cleopatra.[34] In this moment, the very idea of nobility is transferred from *virtus* to *voluptas*.

This is Antony's first capacious speech in the play. Before it, he has four one-liners in which he calls Cleopatra his love, is "grated" by news from Rome, and, in his very first utterances, attacks the Roman notion of being measured, for which another word is *decorum*:

ANTONY. There's beggary in the love that can be reckoned.
CLEOPATRA. I'll set a bourn how far to be beloved.
ANTONY. Then must thou needs find out new heaven, new earth.[35]

The decorum associated with Roman virtue requires restraint; it must be "ranged," "reckoned," held within a "bourn" (a boundary or limit). The *eros* chosen by Antony takes him instead to the infinite, the eternal. When he says, "Here is my space," he is evoking that "new heaven, new earth." The normative Shakespearean sense of the word "space" is a "space of time," as in the modern phrase "breathing space." Antony uses it for both his (leisure) time in Egypt, and in the sense of his "physical place," his location. In addition, a new sense of the word "space" was emerging in the sixteenth century, referring to the physical universe, the vacancy of the heavens—the seed of our idea of that "space" into which astronauts are propelled. John Calvin wrote of the "infinite space" of the heavens, and Hamlet says that he could count himself "a king of infinite space, were it not that I have bad dreams."[36] The trajectory of the play is towards the transcendence of Antony and Cleopatra from our "dungy earth" to this "infinite space."[37] Cleopatra imagines her lover getting there before her in "I dreamt there was an emperor Antony": an emperor not of earthly Rome but of a "new heaven."[38] She follows him there in the self-apotheosis in which she imagines herself becoming "fire and air," outstripping Charmian in the race to the empyrean where it will be her "heaven to have" a "kiss" from Antony—the image echoing that first kiss in the "here is my space" speech at the play's beginning.[39]

One of the earliest usages of the word "space" in this new sense occurs at the climax of Jasper Heywood's translation of Seneca's *Hercules Furens*: "To spaces hygh I wyll bee borne of hawghtye skyes about."[40] The Hercules story ends with an apotheosis. The gods agree, as Ovid has it, "that Hercule should become / A God." His body burns on a pyre, but his being is raised to the skies. Out of fire, he becomes air. Like a serpent casting off its "withered slough" and being rejuvenated ("And wexeth lustyer than before, and looketh crisp and bright"), he becomes a second, greater self. He finds out new heaven, is taken into space:

> so Hercules as soone as that his spryght
> Had left his mortall limbes, gan in his better part too thryve,
> And for too seeme a greater thing than when he was alyve,
> And with a stately majestie ryght reverend too appeere.
> His myghty father tooke him up above the cloudy spheere,
> And in a charyot placed him among the streaming starres.[41]

This is exactly the transcendence that Cleopatra imagines for Antony.

But what has brought Hercules to his death? *Eros*. In contrast to the comedic celebration of Love as a Hercules in *Love's Labours Lost*, the tragedy of *Antony and Cleopatra*, when seen from a Roman point of view, shows a martial hero being feminized and humiliated. For this, two Hercules stories are used as paradigms.

The first of them is one that seasoned theatregoers would have seen dramatized in the old play of *Locrine*, published in 1595 with a title page claiming that it was "newly set forth, overseen and corrected by W. S." At the beginning of each act of this neo-Senecan tragedy, there is a dumb show telling a story out of classical mythology, presented by Atë, spirit of chaos. The fourth of these derives from a story vividly told by Ovid, both in the second book of the *Fasti* (that source for *The Rape of Lucrece*) and, from a scornful rival woman's point of view, in the ninth of the *Heroides*. It shows "Omphale, daughter to the king of Lydia, having a club in her hand, and a lion's skin on her back, Hercules following with a distaff":

> Then let Omphale turn about, and taking off her panto[f]le, strike
> Hercules on the head; then let them depart, Ate remaining, saying:
>
> *Quem non Argolici mandata severa Tyranni,*
> *Non potuit Juno vincere, vicit amor.*
> Stout Hercules, the mirror of the world,

Son to Alcmena and great Jupiter,
After so many conquests won in field,
After so many monsters quelled by force,
Yielded his valiant heart to Omphale,
A fearful woman void of manly strength.
She took the club, and wear the lion's skin;
He took the wheel, and maidenly 'gan spin.[42]

The greatest of all masculine heroes is beaten over the head with a woman's shoe and exchanges his club and lion skin for a distaff. This is "great Hercules whipping a gig," as Berowne has it, when coming forward to "whip" the "hypocrisy" of his colleagues who have renounced love only to fall in love (a hypocrisy of which he is, of course, guilty himself—though at least he can claim to have been sceptical about the whole project from the start).[43]

As well as being staged in *Locrine*, the cross-dressing of Hercules and Omphale, the Lydian queen with whom he is smitten, was frequently illustrated in the sixteenth century. There is a particularly fine example, dating from about 1585, by the Flemish artist Bartholomäus Spranger: Omphale bears the club and is draped in the lion skin, while Hercules wears her female garment, fastened by a broach, as he unwinds a thread from a distaff. Cupid watches mischievously from above.

It is just such an image of emasculation that Cleopatra evokes when she remembers cross-dressing Antony:

That time? O times!
I laughed him out of patience, and that night
I laughed him into patience, and next morn,
Ere the ninth hour, I drunk him to his bed,
Then put my tires and mantels on him, whilst
I wore his sword Philippan.[44]

Here Cleopatra subverts the cardinal Stoic virtue of "patience" by associating it with drinking, sex and cross-dressing. Shakespeare does not name Hercules and Omphale: he leaves it for his more educated audience members to perceive the parallel, whilst others may simply enjoy the reversal of customary gender roles.

When it comes to the second, more drastic, Herculean love affair that parallels Antony's passion for Cleopatra, Shakespeare names the other males in the story but, again, not the *femme fatale*. "The shirt

Figure 9. Bartholomäus Spranger, *Hercules and Omphale* (c. 1585)

of Nessus is upon me," says Antony, and "Let me lodge Lichas on the horns of the moon."[45] But there is no name-check for Deianira. Hers, too, was a story that Ovid told twice, at length in book 9 of the *Metamorphoses* and in her own voice in the ninth of the *Heroides*.[46] Hercules wins the beautiful Deianira by wrestling with the river-god Acheloüs, who had taken the form of a centaur. When crossing a swollen river with his bride, he swims, but makes the error of en-

Figure 10. Two moments from the last days of Hercules: throwing Lichas (left) and, in the foreground, Hercules on his pyre (illustration in 1582 edition of Ovid's *Metamorphoses*)

trusting her to a ferryman, another centaur named Nessus, who sexually assaults her. Hercules shoots him through the heart, but Nessus takes revenge by telling Deianira, as he is dying, that his blood is a love-potion that she could use to restore Hercules's affection for her in the event of a straying in his desires. Years later, she hears a rumour that he has fallen for a girl called Iole. In the *Metamorphoses* version of the story, the rumour is false; Deianira, in her telling of her love for Hercules in the *Heroides*, believes that it is true (in some accounts, Iole is another Omphale, seducing Hercules into cross-dressed effeminacy). Deianira tries to win back his love by sending him the shirt of Nessus via a messenger called Lichas. It is, needless to say, soaked not with a love-potion but with blood tempered with the poison of the Lernean Hydra whom Hercules had slain as his second labour. Hercules's agonising death, as the poison corrodes his skin, is thus a double revenge, of the Hydra as well as Nessus. Hercules blames the messenger, flinging the hapless Lichas into the sea. He then goes to be burnt on his funeral pyre, from where he is released into the empyrean.

Shakespeare's Mark Antony, believing that Cleopatra has betrayed him in battle, identifies with the rage of Hercules:

> 'Tis well thou'rt gone
> If it be well to live. But better 'twere
> Thou fell'st into my fury, for one death
> Might have prevented many. Eros, ho!
> The shirt of Nessus is upon me. Teach me,
> Alcides, thou mine ancestor, thy rage:
> Let me lodge Lichas on the horns o' the moon,
> And with those hands, that grasped the heaviest club,
> Subdue my worthiest self. The witch shall die.
> To the young Roman boy she hath sold me, and I fall
> Under this plot; she dies for 't. Eros, ho![47]

This is Antony's most extended allusion to his "ancestor" Hercules. It is not the first time that Shakespeare has alluded to the story of the shirt of Nessus. In *The Merchant of Venice*, when Morocco has made the wrong choice of casket, he says

> If Hercules and Lichas play at dice
> Which is the better man, the greater throw
> May turn by fortune from the weaker hand:
> So is Alcides beaten by his page,
> And so may I, blind fortune leading me,
> Miss that which one unworthier may attain,
> And die with grieving.[48]

In the First Folio, the original quarto line "So is Alcides beaten by his page" reads, "So is Alcides beaten by his rage." This is an extremely felicitous misprint. The idea of being destroyed by one's own rage, by anger, is powerfully relevant to Mark Antony—as it is to Othello, King Lear, Timon of Athens, and the Coriolanus who inherits his mother's ethos that "anger's my meat."[49] For Shakespeare, the fate of Lichas at the hands of Hercules (Alcides) serves as a paradigm for the anger that both Antony and Cleopatra vent upon hapless messengers—first the unnamed one who comes to Cleopatra with news of Antony's marriage to Octavia ("Thou shalt be whipped with wire, and stewed in brine, / Smarting in lingering pickle")[50] and subsequently Thidias, whom Antony sees kissing Cleopatra's hand—and equally for the anger that Antony turns on Cleopatra, which precipitates his untimely suicide.

The idea of destructive *furor* is an aspect of classical psychology that was as important to Shakespeare as the humoral theory of psychological excess was to Ben Jonson's comedies. Jonson's dramas play out schematically: the characters are who they are; they do not suddenly *become* melancholy or choleric. Hence his favoured form of naming: Volpone is inherently cunning like a fox, Subtle is a congenital trickster, Sir Epicure Mammon is an epicure with a love of money. Shakespeare, by contrast, only occasionally names his characters by virtue of their psychology: nonsignifying names such as Jessica and Lorenzo, Beatrice and Benedick, Isabella and Helena, far outnumber psychologically pointed ones such as those of the protean Proteus in *The Two Gentlemen of Verona* or the ill-willed Malvolio in *Twelfth Night*. Shakespeare did not write with the steady-state psychology that characterized the drama of humours. He was continuously interested in psychology as process, in character being formed and changing as the action unfolds. The eruption of emotion is the extreme form of a pervasive pattern. It is striking in this regard that an examination of Shakespeare's handling of his literary sources reveals that he very often removed a prior motivation from a character. So, for example, in the old *King Leir* play, Lear wants to resign the throne because of his grief at the death of his wife (the play begins with her funeral). In the novella that is the source for *Othello*, the Ensign wants to bring down the Moor because he is in love with the Lady himself. Shakespeare likes to remove that prior motivation, and instead the psychology of the characters emerges through the process of the drama. And in that process, there is nearly always a transformational moment that comes with an eruption of passion.

These explosions of anger, I suggest, owe much more to Seneca than to Plutarch or Ovid. The story of Hercules's death is dramatized in *Hercules Oetaeus*, attributed to Seneca in the Elizabethan *Tenne Tragedies*, but widely regarded since the seventeenth century as a later imitation of his style. A much better known, and authentically Senecan, tragedy was *Hercules Furens* (*The Madness of Hercules*), which tells of an earlier incident in Hercules's eventful life when, in a frenzied fit, he murdered his first wife, Megara, and the children she had borne him. Though Antony alludes to the Deianira story in his "shirt of Nessus" speech, his language of rage would have brought the *Hercules Furens* play to the minds of classically educated audience members.

In this regard, the really interesting sequence of thought is the progression from rage to violence to suicide. Antony asks Hercules to teach him a rage that will lead him not only to throw Lichas but also to take a strong weapon into his own hands and "Subdue my worthiest self." This seems to me a fascinating moment when two Senecan traditions come together.[51] The Elizabethans were as interested in Seneca the philosopher as they were in Seneca the tragic dramatist. His epistles and his essays, in particular "The Treatise of Anger," which was translated by the dramatist Thomas Lodge, were very widely read and discussed. Crudely speaking, Seneca's ethical writings are about the control of those emotions that in his tragedies explode uncontrollably with catastrophic results.

Michel Foucault argues in *The Care of the Self*, the third volume of his *History of Sexuality*, that the writings of Seneca were of central importance to the emergence of a modern sense of the self. He suggests that it was during the first century after Christ, the Augustan and Neronian age in particular, that many modern ideas about sexual restraint, monogamy, and the dangers of sensual pleasure were first articulated—and then of course they were absorbed into Christianity. Foucault's argument is that Greek polymorphous perversity in sexual joy was expunged by first the Roman and then the Christian tradition. Why, he asks, did this occur in the first century? He proposes that it was not because of a desire on the part of Roman moralists to upbraid the emperors for their debauchery, but rather because at the centre of the philosophy of Seneca and some of the Stoics around him was a notion of the care of the self, a belief that the examined life involves a process of standing apart from oneself and then looking into oneself.

It is never too early or too late to examine and develop the self. And if the focus is on the self, then desire for the other, whether that be a woman or a boy, is a distraction from the labor of self-fashioning. This is the essence of Foucault's argument.[52] I would not go so far as to say that Seneca invented the self, but he was a key figure in the emergence of a self that took a special interest in what might be described as the second-order phenomenon of self-examination. In the words of a recent scholar of Seneca:

> The interest in second orderness, in the form of talk about self-shaping and self-knowledge, the language of self-command, the focus on self-control, especially in the face of human natural proclivities to precipitate a passionate response and the singling out of a moment of causally efficacious judgement or decision in the process of reacting to provocative stimuli: these are Seneca's contributions to the development of the will.[53]

There is an old argument among classicists about whether Seneca invented the idea of the will. The noun *voluntas* is very significant in Seneca's writings, and there is no equivalent for that word in Greek. Inventing the word and inventing the idea are not necessarily the same thing, but the notion that the process of self-shaping, self-knowledge, self-command, and the relationship of that process to the will is, I think, at the centre of what the early modern period took from Seneca.

In the philosophical and ethical writings, the Senecan self is absolutely focused on the notion of quelling the emotions through the reason: the classic Stoic idea. In Seneca the dramatist, we see the tragic outcome when the emotions are not tamed by reason, when the will fails to rein in the emotions, leading to the opposite of reason, which is madness. This opposition provides a reading of *Hamlet*: the play begins with "dramatic Seneca" in the figure of the revenger, but becomes complicated by eliding that figure with "philosophical Seneca"—the self-examining Hamlet who is absorbed in the second-order process of thinking self-consciously about self-knowledge and self-command. Eventually, Hamlet reaches *stasis*, or reconciliation between the two Senecas, when he comes to the point of Stoic resignation in his speech about the special providence in the fall of a sparrow and his acceptance that what will be will be—a speech that is essentially a Christianised version of Seneca's discourse on providence.[54] Only then is he able to release himself as a Senecan revenger and find the name of action.

The paradox faced by Hamlet is that in order to become a Senecan revenger he needs the explosion of passion that, as a Senecan philosopher, he has taught himself to resist—"Give me that man that is not passion's slave," he says in admiration of the Stoic Horatio who is ruled by reason.[55] The development of Hamlet's character is accordingly the reverse of that of Hercules in Seneca's anger play. At the climax of *Hercules Furens*, the maddened burst of rage is a form of blindness that leads Hercules to kill his entire family. He then awakens into what might be described as a reverse *anagnorisis*. Often at the end of a classical tragedy there is a moment of self-knowledge, where the character comes to see what has happened and everything makes sense. But it is too late. As Herakles says at the moment of death in Ezra Pound's translation of Sophocles's *The Women of Trachis*, the Ur-drama of the story of the shirt of Nessus, "Come at it that way, what SPLENDOUR: IT ALL COHERES."[56] In the moment of death, after the terrible action, everything seems to cohere. But in Seneca it does not cohere; it collapses. And what it collapses into is a relentless set of questions. In *Hercules Furens*, after the killing of the family, there are about twenty-eight questions in succession. What place is this? What region? Where am I? What have I done? What are these bloody bodies? What are these infernal shapes? What do I see before my eyes? And so he goes on. Where am I? Who am I? There is a complete dissolution from certainty into self-questioning.

This is the process that Hamlet reverses: he begins from questions (most famously, "To be or not to be, that is the question"), but ends in Stoic acceptance. King Lear, on the other hand, follows the path of Hercules: he moves from command to questioning: "Why should a dog, a horse, a rat have life / And thou no breath at all?"[57] Questioning, questioning.

Seneca provided Shakespeare with three different models for the climax of a tragedy. There was the *Hercules Furens* model: the explosion of anger that is replicated in the fury of Mark Antony. There was the Stoic resignation, the serenity of acceptance, to which Hamlet comes. But there was also a darker philosophy, a welcoming of death, seen especially in *Macbeth*.

> Quis Tanais, aut quis Nilus, aut quis Persica
> Violentus unda Tigris, aut Rhenus ferox,
> Tagusve Ibera turbidus gaza fluens,
> Abluere dextram poterit? Arctoum licet
> Maeotis in me gelida transfundat mare,

Et tota Tethys per meas currat manus,
Haerebit altum facinus.

What *Tanais*, or what *Nilus* els, or with his *Persyan* wave
What *Tygris* violent of streame, or what fierce *Rhenus* flood,
Or *Tagus* troublesome that flowes with *Ibers* treasures good
May my ryght hand now wash from gylt? although *Maeotis* cold
The waves of all the Northen sea on me shed out now wolde,
And al the water ther of shoulde now pas by my two handes,
Yet wil the mischiefe deepe remayne.[58]

Shakespeare compresses this elaborate fluvial and oceanic imagery into Macbeth's unforgettable lines

Will all great Neptune's ocean wash this blood
Clean from my hand? No, this my hand will rather
The multitudinous seas incarnadine,
Making the green one red.[59]

And then, as his protagonist nears his end, Shakespeare adapts the superb sequence at the end of Seneca's play when Hercules confronts the ruin of his own life. Jasper Heywood's translation is top-heavy here, so I offer my own:

Why delay my life longer in this light?
I have lost all my good things,
My mind, arms, fame, wife, children,
Even my madness: no one can be cured of a polluted mind,
Crime must be cured by death.[60]

Like both Macbeth and Othello, Hercules has lost everything: not only his arms, his fame, his military self, his wife, and his children, but his mind and even his madness.[61] No one can minister to a mind diseased. "I have lived long enough," says Macbeth.[62] The only cure is death.

13

WALKING SHADOWS

Spectrum, spectri: An image or figure in a man's imagination: a ghost.
(Thomas Cooper, *Thesaurus Linguae Romanae et Britannicae*, 1584)

AND WHAT OF HAMLET'S "UNDISCOVERED COUNTRY" (*terra incognita*) after death?[1] Did Shakespeare believe in ghosts? Alas, we have no evidence as to what Shakespeare personally believed. What we can say is that he knew that a ghost was a very effective dramatic device. So too with devils and spirits. In the early 1590s, as he was carving out his career as a player and playwright, two of the most celebrated plays in the London theatre repertoire were Thomas Kyd's *The Spanish Tragedy*, which is presided over by the Ghost of Don Andrea and a personification of Revenge, and Christopher Marlowe's *Dr Faustus*, conjuror of the devilish spirit Mephistopheles. In each case, the supernatural is the driver of the action: the demand for revenge in one case, the quest for illicit knowledge in the other.

Although *The Spanish Tragedy* is set in modern times, as Portugal attempts to secede from Spain, the Chorus consisting of Ghost and Revenge have come from the classical world. Don Andrea's long opening speech tells of his journey along "the flowing stream of Acheron," transported by "churlish Charon, only boatman there," and his arrival upon "Avernus' ugly waves" (Avernus was the lake at the entrance to the underworld). He then recalls his encounter with "Minos, Aeacus, and Rhadamanth," the three judges of the dead, and of his descent "to Pluto's court, / Through dreadful shades of ever-glooming night," where he sees two divergent paths, one of which descends to Tartarus, "the deepest hell, / Where bloody Furies shakes their whips of steel, / And poor Ixion turns an endless wheel," the other of which leads more invitingly to the meadows "Where lovers live and bloody martialists"—the destination that Virgil in *The Aeneid* called the "mourning fields" (*lugentes campi*) and "furthest plains" (*arva ultima*) that are the destination of, respectively, those such as Dido who have died for love and the heroes such as the Trojan warriors who have died in battle.[2] But Don Andrea is stopped by Pluto because he doesn't have the correct "passport," at which point he is introduced to Revenge and sent back to earth to witness the man who killed him being killed by the vengeful Bel-Imperia.[3]

Kyd's *Spanish Tragedy* was the keystone of Elizabethan revenge tragedy, but the foundations were laid by Seneca. Remember Polonius: "Seneca cannot be too heavy" for the players of tragedy at Elsinore.[4] The very idea of commencing a play with a Chorus is learned from the classical tradition and, linguistically, the long opening speech by the Ghost of Don Andrea is modelled on Seneca's *Agamemnon*, which begins with the Ghost of Thyestes:

> Departinge from the darkned dens which Dicis low doth keepe,
> Loe heere I am sent out agayne, from Tartar Dungeon deepe,
> Thyestes I, that wheather coast to shun doe stande in doubt,
> Th' internall fiendes I fly, the foalke of earth I chase about.
> My conscience lo abhors, that I should heather passage make,
> Appauled sore with feare and dread my trembling sinewes shake.[5]

Seneca's trademark was indeed the supernatural intervention that winds the plot of revenge tragedy. Thus his *Thyestes* begins, as the "Argument" of the Elizabethan translation puts it, with "Megaera one of the Hellish furies raising up Tantalus from Hell" and inciting him "to set mortall hatred betwene his two nephewes Thiestes, and Atreus being brothers."[6] The Fury and the Ghost as joint Chorus served as another model for Kyd.

The original edition of the *Thyestes* translation had a verse preface describing a dream in which the ghost of the dramatist appears to the translator, who was an Oxford don called Jasper Heywood. Seneca is wearing a "scarlet gowne" to indicate that his genre is tragedy of blood and a laurel garland in honour of his poetic greatness. He carries a book and says that he has come back from the dead

> to seeke some one that might renewe my name,
> And make me speake in straunger speeche and sette my woorks to sight,
> And skanne my verse in other tongue then I was woont to wright.[7]

This idea of an author from imperial Rome returning to pass the baton to an English successor was an essential part of the Elizabethan cultural project of dignifying the nation with a literary canon of its own.

These Senecan and neo-Senecan contexts raise a number of interesting questions that we can apply to Shakespeare. Clearly neither Kyd nor Shakespeare believed that Revenge was a real person. They trust their audience to understand that the idea—the spirit—of Revenge is being embodied in a fictional persona for dramatic purposes. Early in his career, Shakespeare doubles down on Kyd by making the figure of Revenge in *Titus Andronicus* not a discrete character but a role impersonated by Tamora:

> I am Revenge, sent from the infernal kingdom,
> To ease the gnawing vulture of thy mind
> By working wreakful vengeance on thy foes.[8]

Titus deliciously sees through the disguise and turns the vengeance back on Tamora in the most wreakful way, by dishing up her sons in a pie, self-consciously replicating Procne's revenge on Tereus in the Philomel story in Ovid's *Metamorphoses* that is explicitly displayed on the stage.

Shakespeare deploys the word "revenge" and its cognates more than two hundred times in the corpus of his works, but instead of bringing the figure on stage as a Chorus, he allows his characters to internalize the idea as a moral problem and an imperative for action. Revenge is an impulse that, as Aaron puts it in *Titus Andronicus*, hammers in the head.[9] Notice how Tamora in the guise of Revenge speaks of the "gnawing vulture" of Titus's "mind": the classical myth of Prometheus's punishment (tied to a mountainside with a vulture gnawing at his liver) is turned into a mental state. This is a typically Shakespearean move: whereas Kyd's Don Andrea comes from classical Tartarus where "Ixion turns an endless wheel," Shakespeare's Lear internalizes the fate of Ixion ("I am bound / Upon a wheel of fire that mine own tears / Do scald like molten lead").[10] The transposition of Furies and ghosts from external forces to internal mental states is a significant clue to Shakespeare's representation of the paranormal.

When Revenge is externalized, it is in the form of a human comparison, such as Pyrrhus in *Hamlet*, as opposed to an embodied spirit. Whereas self-consciously Senecan tragedians such as Kyd and Peele were content to bring on Atë, the spirit of havoc, as a prologue or in a masque between the acts, Shakespeare confines her to the rhetorical and metaphoric fabric of his plays, for example when Queen Eleanor in *King John* is described as "An Atë stirring [John] to blood and strife" or when Mark Antony speaks of "Caesar's spirit, ranging for revenge, / With Atë by his side come hot from hell."[11]

Atë does not appear on the Shakespearean stage, but Caesar's spirit does. The ghost in *Julius Caesar* is not a Senecan prologue, but a nocturnal apparition as the action builds towards its climax. Brutus is reading by the light of a flickering taper when the Ghost of Caesar enters. Brutus initially thinks that it is the "the weakness of mine eyes / That shapes this monstrous apparition." Then he asks, very much in the manner in which Hamlet interrogates the Ghost of his father,

> Art thou any thing?
> Art thou some god, some angel, or some devil,
> That mak'st my blood cold and my hair to stare?
> Speak to me what thou art.[12]

The ghost replies that he is Brutus's "evil spirit" and that he has come to tell him that they will meet at Philippi.[13] We do not witness that second meeting, but Brutus reports it after the event and acknowledges that the two visitations are a sign that his "hour is come," in other words, that he is about to die.[14] The phrase is strikingly reminiscent of the language of Jesus talking about his coming crucifixion, and in this regard it is interesting to note how the words of Roman Brutus are inflected by the Christian idea of a seeming ghost really being an angel or a devil. In an influential treatise called *Of Ghostes and Spirites walking by nyght, and of strange noyses, crackes, and sundry forewarnynges, which commonly happen before the death of menne, great slaughters & alterations of kyngdomes*, the theologian Lewis Lavater asked "What those things are which men see and hear" and which they call ghosts. He concluded "first, that good angels do sometimes appear" but that "sometimes, yea and for the most part, evil angels do appear."[15]

There are two things to notice about the ghost scene in *Julius Caesar*. First, that two fellow-soldiers, Varrus and Claudius, sleep through the entire incident and that Brutus's subsequent dialogue with his servant Lucius makes it absolutely clear that the boy has not seen or heard anything either. This strongly suggests that the ghost is a figment of Brutus's imagination. Secondly, although Brutus says that it is the Ghost of Caesar (as does the stage direction), and although at the moment Brutus kills himself he says that he is releasing the ghost that has remained restless until revenged ("Caesar, now be still"), the Ghost identifies himself not as Caesar but as Brutus's "evil spirit." He is like the Bad Angel of Marlowe's Dr Faustus or, indeed, like Prospero acknowledging that Caliban is a thing of darkness that is his own. He is a figuration of Brutus's conscience for the killing of his best friend. The idea is derived directly from Shakespeare's source, Plutarch's life of Julius Caesar:

> Brutus being … in his tent, and being yet awake, thinking of his affaires: he thought he heard a noise at his tent dore, and looking towards the light of the lampe that waxed very dimme, he saw a horrible vision of a man, of a wonderfull greatnes, and dreadful looke, which at the first made him marvellously afraid. But when he saw that it did him no hurt, but stoode by his bedside, and sayd nothing: at length he asked him what he was. The image aunswered him: I am thy ill angell, Brutus, and thou shalt see me by the city of Philippes.[16]

According to Plutarch, when the "spirit" appeared a second time, it did not speak a word—reason enough for Shakespeare to report rather than dramatize the second visitation.

Plutarch's account in the "Life of Marcus Brutus," which Shakespeare also read when scripting the play, is much fuller. Plutarch tells of how as the army marched out of Asia into Europe, a rumour spread that "a wonderful sign" had appeared to Brutus at night.[17] There is a vivid account of his sleeplessness, the result of him being a man full of cares with "his head very busily occupied." He is evoked slumbering lightly, reading "some book till the third watch of the night," until

> one night very late (when all the camp took quiet rest) as he was in his tent with a little light, thinking of weighty matters, he thought he heard one come in to him, and casting his eye towards the door of his tent, that he saw a wonderful strange and monstrous shape of a body coming towards him, and said never a word. So Brutus boldly asked what he was, a god or a man, and what cause brought him thither?

The spirit answered him, "I am thy evil spirit, Brutus: and thou shalt see me by the city of Philippes." Brutus being no otherwise afraid, replied again unto it: "Well, then I shall see thee again." The spirit presently vanished away: and Brutus called his men unto him, who told him that they heard no noise, nor saw anything at all.[18]

There is no suggestion in either "Life" that the spirit is the ghost of Caesar.

According to Plutarch, in the morning, Brutus tells Cassius about the vision. Cassius, "being in opinion an Epicurean" (a detail that Shakespeare picks up, having his Cassius say that he "held Epicurus strong / And his opinion"),[19] responds as follows:

In our sect, Brutus, we have an opinion, that we do not always feel or see that which we suppose we do both see and feel, but that our senses being credulous and therefore easily abused (when they are idle and unoccupied in their own objects) are induced to imagine they see and conjecture that which in truth they do not. For our mind is quick and cunning to work (without either cause or matter) anything in the imagination whatsoever. And therefore the imagination is resembled to clay, and the mind to the potter: who, without any other cause than his fancy and pleasure, changeth it into what fashion and form he will.[20]

I think that the cognitive scepticism articulated here struck a deep chord with Shakespeare. There are all sorts of key moments in his plays where characters do not feel or see that which they suppose they see and feel: Claudio in *Much Ado about Nothing* supposes he sees his beloved Hero with another man in her bedroom on the eve of their wedding, but he is being tricked (it is really her maid); Leontes feels like a cuckold and thinks that the girl baby he sees has been fathered by Polixenes, but he is wrong; Macbeth thinks that he sees a dagger in the air, but it is an illusion. The examples could be multiplied a hundredfold. They are the consequence of the power of imagination, for, as Plutarch's Cassius says, the human mind is "quick and cunning" to "work" all manner of things "in the imagination." *Julius Caesar* was first performed in 1599, in close proximity to *Henry V*. One or the other play was almost certainly the opening show at the newly built Globe Theatre that summer. It does not seem to me a coincidence that Cassius's argument about the "work"

of "imagination" is echoed in the Prologue to the other play: "let us
... On your imaginary forces work." In that same Prologue, the actors are referred to as "flat unraisèd spirits": that is to say, the players are the ghosts, shadows or spirits of the historical figures they
are impersonating.[21]

And for Shakespeare, a play is like a dream. Plutarch's Cassius
continues his disquisition on the power of imagination as follows:
"And this doth the diversity of our dreams shew unto us. For our
imagination doth upon a small fancy grow from conceipt to conceipt, altering both in passions and forms of things imagined. For the
mind of man is ever occupied, and that continual moving is nothing
but an imagination."[22] As with the preceding image of the mind as
a potter fashioning and forming with the clay of imagination, the
language in which Cassius describes the creativity of dreamwork is
closely akin to that in which Theseus describes the poet's art in *A
Midsummer Night's Dream* in those lines that I discussed earlier:

> And as imagination bodies forth
> The forms of things unknown, the poet's pen
> Turns them to shapes and gives to airy nothing
> A local habitation and a name.[23]

The Epicureans did not believe that divine or supernatural forces
intervene in the life of man. Cassius is therefore arguing that the
ghostly apparition is a mere effect of Brutus's fevered imagination.
It is exactly like a dream. He adds that, according to the Epicureans,
thoughtful, melancholy men such as Brutus are unusually prone to
fancies: their mental restlessness means that they "do easilier yield
to such imaginations."[24] Cicero had made a similar point in his *Tusculan Disputations*.[25] Remember, in this regard, that Shakespeare was
working on *Hamlet* in very close proximity to *Julius Caesar*—his
most thoughtful and melancholy character is also especially prone
both to vivid dreams and to the belief—is it an illusion, a delusion,
or a reality?—that he has been visited by a ghost. Dreams are visions
of the night, as are ghosts, which you never see in the daytime (the
Ghost of Old Hamlet vanishes as dawn breaks). According to this
reading, the Ghost of Caesar has the same status as Macbeth's visions
of a dagger in the air and of the Ghost of Banquo at the feast: it is the
effect of a fevered and guilty imagination. Lady Macbeth specifically

links the invisible dagger to the apparition of Banquo that is seen by Macbeth and no one else:

> This is the very painting of your fear:
> This is the air-drawn dagger which, you said,
> Led you to Duncan. O, these flaws and starts—
> Impostors to true fear—would well become
> A woman's story at a winter's fire,
> Authorized by her grandam. Shame itself!
> Why do you make such faces? When all's done,
> You look but on a stool.[26]

Some modern productions make the point by entirely confining Banquo's ghost to Macbeth's imagination, but the stage direction in the original Folio text makes clear that Shakespeare intended it to be seen by the theatre audience as well as Macbeth—just not by the other characters on stage. The audience is allowed to see through Macbeth's eyes, given access—as we are in a soliloquy—to the interior of his mind.

Several other ghosts and spirits in Shakespeare come into the category of apparitions during sleep, which is to say dreams. Towards the end of *Cymbeline*, Posthumus, captured in battle, goes to sleep in jail, at which point, to "solemn music," there is the following stage direction:

> *Enter, as in an apparition, Sicilius Leonatus, father to Posthumus Leonatus, an old man, attired like a warrior; leading in his hand an ancient matron, his wife, and mother to Posthumus, with music before them. Then, after other music, follows the two young Leonati, brothers to Posthumus, with wounds as they died in the wars. They circle Posthumus round as he lies sleeping.*[27]

Posthumus, whose name is a constant reminder that his mother died in childbirth (like Macduff, he was "ripped" by Caesarian section, which in Shakespeare's day meant death for the mother), is granted a dream in which his dead family are all restored to him. They accuse the classical gods—Mars, Juno, and Jupiter—of unfair treatment. This provokes Jupiter to descend and release them into Elysium with the prophecy that Posthumus will be restored to freedom and marry Innogen, bringing peace and good fortune to Britain. "Poor shadows of Elysium, hence," Jupiter says, "and rest / Upon your never-withering banks of flowers."[28] God and ghosts vanish, and Posthumus awakes.

There is a similar sense of divine release for the deposed and condemned Queen Katherine in *Henry VIII*, when, again to "sad and solemn music," a vision of six "spirits of peace" descends upon her as she sleeps. As with Brutus and Lucius, she asks her gentleman-usher Griffith and her woman Patience if they saw anybody enter as she slept, and is told that they did not. Griffith describes the spirits as "good dreams" that "Possess" the queen's "fancy"—figments of the imagination, that is to say.[29]

Another eve of battle vision is the celebrated scene on the night before Bosworth Field in *Richard III*. In an elegantly symmetrical piece of stagecraft, Richard sleeps in his tent on one side of the stage and Richmond (the future Henry VII) on the other. The ghosts of eleven of Richard's victims enter in quick succession, all of them cursing Richard and some blessing Richmond. After they vanish, "*Richard starts out of his dream*" and delivers a soliloquy in which his previously wholly assured sense of self begins to collapse: "Richard loves Richard: that is, I am I. / Is there a murderer here? No. Yes, I am." "What? Do I fear myself? There's none else by": the fear comes from within. The dream of ghosts has pricked his conscience and alerted him to the vengeance that will fall upon him. "*Methought* [my emphasis] the souls of all that I had murdered / Came to my tent": he believes that the ghosts are but his own thoughts. They are what Freud would have called the voice of the unconscious or the return of the repressed.[30]

Yet they have also spoken to the sleeping Richmond. Are we to believe that the ghosts have *really* returned from their graves, or is he just having a similar dream in a different key? As with Brutus and his "evil spirit," we can try to answer this question by comparing the play with its sources. In Edward Hall's *The Union of the Two Noble Famelies of Lancastre and Yorke*, Richard has "a terrible dreame" in which he "sawe diverse ymages lyke terrible develles whiche pulled and haled hym, not sufferyinge hym to take any quyet or rest." This, says Hall, both struck Richard's heart with fear and troubled his mind with "many dreadfull and busy Imaginacions"; Hall expresses his own opinion that the dream was but a "pricke of his synfull conscience."[31] The ghosts come from one of Shakespeare's other sources, either "The Tragical Life and Death of Richard III" in the long poem *A Mirror for Magistrates* or the old anonymous play from the repertoire of the Queen's Men, *The True Tragedy of Richard the Third*. In the poem, Richard dreams of "All those murderd Ghostes whome I / By death had sent to their untimely grave." In the play, which begins with a Prologue in which the Ghost of Clarence appears to Truth and Poetry, calling for Revenge ("vindicta!"), Richard speaks of how his "wounded conscience" causes him constantly to think, whether sleeping or waking, that "their ghoasts comes gaping for revenge, / Whom I have slaine in reaching for a Crowne."[32] But the ghosts do not appear on stage: that is Shakespeare's innovation, as is the idea of having the sleeping Richmond on stage at the same time. The apparitions thus serve simultaneously as agents of conscience and of nemesis for Richard, whilst being like guardian angels for Richmond.

In classical literature, ghosts have three main functions: to call for vengeance if they have been murdered, to warn society of bad times to come, and to demand proper burial, without which they cannot proceed into the underworld. The foundational example of the last of these is the appearance of Patroclus's ghost to Achilles in the twenty-third book of Homer's *Iliad*. The question of proper burial rites is a major concern in the first act of *Titus Andronicus*, but that was almost certainly written not by Shakespeare but by the more classically learned George Peele. In *Troilus and Cressida*, Achilles is finally stirred to action and vengeance by the death of his beloved Patroclus, but the ghost scene is not dramatized and the matter of burial not mentioned. In sum, then, Shakespeare's development of the figure of the ghost is to combine what could be described as the classical *nemesis* and *augury* functions—the ghost as sign that the downfall of the murderer is nigh or that something is rotten in the state—with a modern *conscience* function, the idea that the apparition is a figment of the guilty imagination of the persons who think they see it.

In the case of *Macbeth*, the ancient and modern functions are clearly split apart. The classical *nemesis* role is given to the weird sisters. Seen by both Macbeth and Banquo, they serve as classical sibyls, predictors of the future. Their prognostications, along with the unnatural events on the night of the murder of Duncan (bad weather, a falcon killed by an owl, Duncan's horses running mad), are of a

piece with those bad omens that foreshadow Caesar's assassination—
a slave unharmed by a flaming hand, an owl hooting at noon, women
swearing that they have seen "Men, all in fire, walk up and down the
streets."[33] It is signs of this kind that lead Cassius near the end of
Julius Caesar to hesitate over his Epicurean scepticism and "partly
credit things that do presage."[34] But in neither *Julius Caesar* nor
Macbeth is the audience asked to believe that the ghost is anything
other than a figment of conscience, anything other than what Macbeth calls, apropos of the dagger, "A false creation / Proceeding from
the heat-oppressèd brain."[35]

The same may be said of Shakespeare's very beautiful reported, as
opposed to staged, ghost scene. In *The Winter's Tale*, Antigonus is
commissioned to dispose of the baby that the delusional Leontes has
convinced himself is the illegitimate offspring of an adulterous union
between Hermione and Polixenes. Arriving on the fabled coast of
Bohemia, holding the baby, he speaks in soliloquy:

> I have heard, but not believed, the spirits o' th' dead
> May walk again. If such thing be, thy mother
> Appeared to me last night, for ne'er was dream
> So like a waking.[36]

He tells of how the figure of Hermione came to him "In pure white
robes, / Like very sanctity," how she wept and then told him to leave
the child in Bohemia and, since she is "counted lost for ever," name
her Perdita. "With shrieks" the figure "melted into air" (the same
phrase that Macbeth uses for the witches).[37] Antigonus then tells of
how he collected himself "and thought / This was so and no slum-
ber." He concludes,

> Dreams are toys,
> Yet for this once, yea superstitiously,
> I will be squared by this. I do believe
> Hermione hath suffered death, and that
> Apollo would, this being indeed the issue
> Of King Polixenes, it should here be laid,
> Either for life or death, upon the earth
> Of its right father.[38]

He believes that the dream-ghost is telling him the truth. But all
three of his conclusions are wrong: Hermione has not suffered death;

the child is not Polixenes's issue; and Apollo's will is for the lost one to be found and restored to Sicilia. At this point, however, the audience does not know that Hermione is alive. We are therefore, at least partially, in the position of Antigonus, and we have the option of deciding whether the dream really was a visitation from beyond the grave or whether it is a manifestation of Antigonus's guilty conscience at being party to the abandonment of the child in the wilderness, expressly against the better judgment of his wife, Paulina. Only in retrospect, when we discover that Paulina has preserved Hermione, can we be sure that it was purely a dream: Antigonus cannot have witnessed an apparition of the spirit of the dead, since Hermione is not dead.

In this instance, the theatre audience is put into the position of Macbeth at the banquet, the drowsy Brutus, and the sleeping Posthumus, Richard, and Richmond: the ghosts seem real at the time, but are subsequently discovered to be mental phantasms. Which, rationally speaking, is the experience of anybody who dreams or imagines that he or she has seen a ghost.

How, then, do these distinctions apply to Shakespeare's most loquacious and celebrated ghost, the role that, according to his first biographer, was the "top of his Performance" as an actor?[39] In the opening scene of *Hamlet*, the Ghost is initially described as a "thing."[40] Horatio, the honest companion who is the voice of sanity and the chorus to the action, initially takes the Epicurean view that it is a figment of the imagination:

> Horatio says 'tis but our fantasy,
> And will not let belief take hold of him
> Touching this dreaded sight twice seen of us.[41]

But when he sees it with his own eyes, he is forced to acknowledge that it is "something more than fantasy."[42] He then reads it as an omen akin to those aberrations of nature on the brink of Caesar's assassination: "This bodes some strange eruption to our state."[43] He explicates the Roman parallel at considerable length:

> In the most high and palmy state of Rome,
> A little ere the mightiest Julius fell,
> The graves stood tenantless and the sheeted dead
> Did squeak and gibber in the Roman streets:

As stars with trains of fire and dews of blood,
Disasters in the sun, and the moist star
Upon whose influence Neptune's empire stands
Was sick almost to doomsday with eclipse:
And even the like precurse of fierce events
As harbingers preceding still the fates
And prologue to the omen coming on,
Have heaven and earth together demonstrated
Unto our climature and countrymen.[44]

At which point the Ghost re-enters and Horatio calls it an "illusion," asking it whether it has come to predict Denmark's future or to reveal the whereabouts of some hidden treasure ("For which, they say, you spirits oft walk in death"). He charges it to speak, and it vanishes with the crowing of the cock, confirming the belief that at the first light of dawn "Th' extravagant and erring spirit hies / To his confine."[45] We will come in a moment to the nature of that confine.

When Horatio goes to tell Hamlet about the ghost, he initially gets the impression that Hamlet has seen his late father already—but what Hamlet means is that he sees him in his "mind's eye," which is to say his imagination, the place where Macbeth sees Banquo's ghost and Richard those of his victims. He is haunted by the memory of his father, not least because we may assume that he did not have a chance to say goodbye to him. Though the point is not made explicitly, the backstory clearly suggests that Hamlet was away at university in Wittenberg when his father died. The news would not have reached him until after the burial: Helsingør to Wittenberg is a journey of over five hundred kilometres each way, including a ferry crossing. Hamlet returns in mourning black to find himself at a wedding instead of a funeral. In the circumstances, it is hardly surprising that he is dreaming nightly, and imagining daily, of his father.

At the end of the scene, Hamlet is in a state of uncertainty: in one speech, he says that something is assuming his father's shape, and in the next he assumes that his father's spirit is really up in arms. There is a similar progression in the first speech he addresses to the ghost once he is up on the battlements. It begins with the assumption that the figure is either "a spirit of health or goblin damned," bringing "airs from heaven or blasts from hell"—that is to say, either a good angel like the spirits who will descend on Queen Katherine in *Henry VIII* or a devil like Marlowe's Mephistopheles, tempting him to evil. But because of the uncertainty as to its nature ("Thou com'st in such a questionable shape"), he decides to make the assumption that it genuinely is the ghost of his father. The other characters on stage remain in a state of uncertainty. Horatio says that Hamlet "waxes desperate with imagination," suggesting that he is reverting to his Epicurean line of regarding the ghost as a mental illusion of the kind to which his friend is unusually susceptible because of his melancholy disposition.[46]

The ghost only speaks when alone with Hamlet. Since this is the case, we cannot rule out the possibility that it is an illusion shared by Hamlet's friends Marcellus and Barnardo, and then Horatio—significantly, it is not seen by the other sentinel Francisco, who is not a friend of Hamlet's. Like the ill omens that are mentioned in *Julius Caesar* and cited by Horatio, the ghost might just be the embodiment of the knowledge of the Hamlet faction that something is rotten in the state of Denmark.

But when it speaks to Hamlet, it becomes another kind of ghost. It is at this point that it says where it has come from:

> I am thy father's spirit,
> Doomed for a certain term to walk the night,
> And for the day confined to fast in fires,
> Till the foul crimes done in my days of nature
> Are burnt and purged away.[47]

The word "purged" leaves little doubt that he is in Purgatory. In place of the classical idea that a figure such as Patroclus in the *Iliad* returns as a ghost because he has not had the proper burial rites that will allow him access into the underworld, we get the Roman Catholic idea that many of us will have to spend time in Purgatory, doing penance for our sins upon the earth. A principal source of income for the Roman church was the sale of indulgences, which, along with prayers for the souls of the departed, were supposed to reduce the duration of the time served in Purgatory before translation to Heaven. Corruption of this kind, together with the absence of any Biblical warrant for the idea of Purgatory, was one of the driving forces of the Protestant Reformation, which accordingly abolished Purgatory. Lavater's treatise *Of Ghostes and Spirites* was a Protestant polemic, arguing against the idea that supposed ghosts were souls returned from Purgatory because there was no such thing as Purgatory and the Bible had made clear that the dead only rise from their graves on the Day of Judgment at the end of time.

The classical ghost has turned into a Catholic ghost. Given that Hamlet is a student at Wittenberg University, birthplace of the Lutheran Reformation, this leaves him with a dilemma: if he has been trained to believe that there is no such thing as Purgatory, should he believe the Ghost? Initially, he finds the case so persuasive that he does. He swears "by Saint Patrick," the keeper of Purgatory, that "It is an honest ghost."[48] And he chides his fellow-student for his Epicurean scepticism about the supernatural: "There are more things in heaven and earth, Horatio, / Than are dreamt of in your philosophy."[49]

Subsequently, however, his own philosophical spirit of doubt and self-interrogation leads him to reconsider. Perhaps it is not an honest ghost after all:

> The spirit that I have seen
> May be the devil, and the devil hath power
> T' assume a pleasing shape, yea, and perhaps,
> Out of my weakness and my melancholy,
> As he is very potent with such spirits,
> Abuses me to damn me.[50]

As with the remarks about Brutus attributed to Cassius by Plutarch, this confirms the idea that people of a thoughtful and "melancholy" humor are especially likely to conjure up fanciful imaginings of spirits from another world.

Prompted by his fear that the ghost might actually be a devil, Hamlet comes up with the idea of staging the play within the play in order to test the veracity of the murder story by watching Claudius's reaction. Famously, when the Ghost returns to complain about the delay caused by this process, it is seen by Hamlet alone and not by Gertrude. She regards its apparent manifestation as a sign of Hamlet's madness. Her language is identical to that of Lady Macbeth chiding her husband in the banquet scene: "This is the very coinage of your brain: / This bodiless creation ecstasy is very cunning in."[51] We thus have an act 1 ghost first seeming to be a classical augury of troubled times and a Senecan revenant demanding vengeance, then announcing itself as a departed soul coming from Catholic Purgatory, but an act 3 ghost who appears to be a voicing of Hamlet's disgust at his mother's "incest" and a projection of his own "conscience," which in "To be or not to be" he has said is the cause of his delay. The act 3 ghost is more like those of Banquo and the victims of Richard III: an emanation from within the mind, not an emissary from another world.

Is Shakespeare seriously asking his audience to consider the possibility that the act 3 ghost is something different from the act 1 ghost? I would say that he might well be, not only because the act 1 ghost is seen by several characters, the act 3 ghost by Hamlet alone, but also because they wear different costumes. If we can trust the evidence of the earliest printed text of the play, which seems to be based on a shorthand or memorial reconstruction of an early performance, whereas the act 1 ghost wears full body armour, the act 3 ghost appears in his nightgown. Armour is the costume of a martial classical ghost like Don Andrea in *The Spanish Tragedy*—Shakespeare would begin his Trojan play with a prologue similarly armed. What does the nightgown suggest? Could it be a projection of Hamlet's belief that the man in Gertrude's bed should be his father, not his uncle? The costume is a visualization of his horror at the idea of Claudius coming to Gertrude in his nightgown and having sex with her.

No other ghost in early modern drama has a costume change of this sort. Furthermore, the texture of the dialogue in act 3 is very different from that in the battlement scenes of the first act, where no one doubts the ghost's presence but everyone questions what kind of a "thing" it is. Here, by contrast, the emphasis is on false perception. The ghost says,

> But look, amazement on thy mother sits.
> O, step between her and her fighting soul:
> Conceit in weakest bodies strongest works.[52]

The initial impression would seem to be that Gertrude is amazed because she has seen the ghost and she is fighting with the guilt in her soul. "Conceit" (mental illusion) is working strongly in her because she has a weak woman's body. But it is then revealed that the opposite is the case: what is amazing Gertrude is Hamlet's strange behaviour:

> That you do bend your eye on vacancy,
> And with th' incorporal air do hold discourse?

Forth at your eyes your spirits wildly peep,
And, as the sleeping soldiers in th' alarm,
Your bedded hairs, like life in excrements,
Start up and stand on end.[53]

Though his eyes are open, he is behaving like someone in a dream. (This appearance of the ghost is described as a "visitation," a word used by Shakespeare in the context of one of his most vivid dream descriptions in the near contemporary *Henry IV Part 2*.)[54] In the phrase "your spirits wildly peep," Gertrude turns the spirit of her dead husband into an emanation of her son's feelings. In her simile of "the sleeping soldiers," her soldier-husband sleeping in his orchard is replaced by a physical manifestation of a fearful dream— Hamlet's hair standing on end.

In his unique development of the ghost role, the Shakespeare of *Hamlet* may therefore be in some sense dramatizing the road to modernity. Let me explain this proposition a little more fully. As I discussed earlier, there are a number of extant references to an older *Hamlet* tragedy that clearly had a classically Senecan ghost, calling for revenge. In addition to Thomas Nashe writing of "English Seneca read by candlelight" as a source for "whole Hamlets, I should say handfuls of tragical speeches," there is an allusion in the prologue to a play called *A Warning for Fair Women* to tragedies in which "a filthy whining ghost" comes "screaming like a pig half-stickt / And cries *Vindicta*, revenge, revenge." And in Thomas Lodge's 1596 work *Wit's Misery and the World's Madness*, there is a remembrance of the ghost "which cried so miserably at the Theatre O *Hamlet revenge*."[55] The starting point, then, is the Senecan ghost calling for revenge. This is echoed in Hamlet senior's line "Revenge his foul and most unnatural murder"—though the choice of "his" as opposed to "my" is perhaps enough to sow a seed of doubt.[56]

Overlaid upon this model is the other classical idea, articulated so ably by Horatio, of the ghost as symbolic "precurse of fierce events … And prologue to the omen coming on."[57] There is then a deliberate disjunction between the desires of the classical and the Catholic ghost: solicitation to murder is hardly a good way of reducing your time in Purgatory. As the ghost departs, his refrain becomes, as was discussed in chapter 3, not "revenge" but "remember"—a mental action replaces a physical one and signals a progression towards the process of self-examination and inner exploration that characterizes Hamlet the student and speaker of soliloquies.

There is thus a progression from a Senecan ghost calling for revenge and an equally classical ghost-as-harbinger to a Catholic ghost coming from Purgatory to, in the third act, a Protestant ghost-imagining that is a mental state, the coinage of the brain. This mirrors the historical progression from ancient Rome to modern Catholic Rome to Protestant northern Europe. Denmark became an officially Lutheran state by royal decree as early as 1536, and Shakespeare knew perfectly well that he was writing for a Protestant court and city in London. The evolution of the Ghost within *Hamlet* is of a piece with that larger project whereby the drama of Shakespeare and his fellow Elizabethans was a major part of a national endeavor to create an English Protestant culture that opposed itself to modern Rome even as it drew inspiration from ancient Rome.

What is a ghost? An emanation from the past. For which another word is a memory. Remember me. What is a historical play? An emanation from the past, in which the actors are shadows—which is to say ghosts—of their historical or fictional originals. When do ghosts most frequently appear? In dreams, or dream-like nocturnal states. What is a dream? An imaginary world pieced together from memory. What is a play? An imaginary world pieced together from memory. A shared dream. "We are such stuff / As dreams are made on, and our little life / Is rounded with a sleep."[58] What is an actor? The ghost or shadow of the part that he is playing.

The recurring idea, present in all the examples I have been discussing, is that ghosts and spirits may be phantasms or mental states, not supernatural phenomena. The device for dramatizing this idea is that of having some characters see the ghosts and others not see them. This technique is also used for Shakespeare's two magical spirits, Puck in *A Midsummer Night's Dream* and Ariel in *The Tempest*. No mortal character ever sees Puck. No one but Prospero ever sees Ariel—though he is sometimes made visible in the metamorphosed form of a flame, a harpy, or a spirit in a wedding masque. His music is heard by Caliban, but he is not seen, just as neither the lovers nor Bottom in *A Midsummer Night's Dream* see Puck executing his tricks to metamorphose them.

As the agents of, respectively, Oberon and Prospero, Puck and Ariel are the engines of the plots of Shakespeare's two most magical plays. There is a sense in which Oberon and Prospero are playwrights, or directors, with Puck and Ariel as their stage managers. And it is this analogy between dreams, magic, invisible spirits, and theatre that Shakespeare persistently plays upon. Theseus's description in *A Midsummer Night's Dream* of the power of the poet is also a description of the work of Puck, who "Doth glance from heaven to earth, from earth to heaven." Shakespeare's ghosts and airy spirits are the local habitations of the trick of what Theseus, speaking just after the midsummer night's dream has come to an end at dawn, calls "strong imagination."[59]

So too, after Prospero stages his play-within-the-play—the wedding masque bringing to life the classical figures of Iris, Juno and Ceres—he makes explicit the parallel between supernatural imaginings and stage players:

> These our actors,
> As I foretold you, were all spirits and
> Are melted into air, into thin air.[60]

This is the same melting metaphor that was used for the weird sisters in *Macbeth* and the ghost in *Hamlet*.

Once one sees this analogy, one perceives another layer to the question of whether or not the ghosts in *Julius Caesar, Richard III, Cymbeline, Macbeth,* and *Hamlet,* the angels in *Henry VIII,* the sprite in *A Midsummer Night's Dream,* and the airy spirit in *The Tempest* are *real*. No, of course they are not real. They are actors, for which another word in Shakespearean usage was "shadows." Puck: "If we shadows have offended."[61] The ghosts and spirits are actors no more and *no less* than all the others characters in the plays are actors. They are "merely" actors. In Shakespearean usage, *merely* doesn't only mean *only*: it also means *absolutely, entirely, and without qualification*. To acknowledge this is to confront the full force of Jaques's reminder in *As You Like It* that "All the world's a stage, / And all the men and women merely players."[62]

This is the realization to which Macbeth eventually comes. In this respect, his tragedy has a similar but subtly different progression to that of *Hamlet*. The Danish play proceeds from a ghost seen by several characters to a ghost seen by the protagonist alone to the idea that we will all, whether a soldier like Alexander the Great or a jester like Yorick, end up as bone and dust in the grave; the Scottish play proceeds from weird sisters seen by two characters to a ghost seen by the protagonist alone to a sleepwalking woman who has become a shadow of her former self and whose imagination is racked by visions of blood and death. It is the walking shadow of the hollowed-out Lady Macbeth that leads Macbeth to meditate on life as a "poor player" (which is to say a shadow), strutting and fretting his hour on the stage, full of sound and fury (like an old-fashioned Senecan ghost), signifying not revenge but "nothing."[63] One day we will all be shadows.

14

In the House of Fame

He made his name with a highly accomplished erotic narrative poem, freely adapted from Ovid's *Metamorphoses*, in which convention is flouted and gender is bent, as a female woos a male. Among his friends and drinking companions were poets and playwrights, such as Ben Jonson and Michael Drayton, the Warwickshire man. Some of his early theatrical works had mixed success; one of them was a parody of the older conventions of drama so clever that many of the original audience members failed to see the joke. Another was a forceful study of misogyny set in Italy. His later plays pioneered a new genre of tragicomic romance, full of sea voyages, families lost and found, mistaken identities, and pastoral interludes. They worked particularly well in his acting company's intimate new indoor theatre at Blackfriars, targeted at a sophisticated and well-to-do audience of lawyers and citizens. At the end of his career, he worked closely with the prolific dramatist John Fletcher. Who knows where he would have taken the drama had he lived? But from 1613 onwards he wrote no more plays. Ill health may be presumed. He died in the spring of 1616 and was buried in Westminster Abbey, beside Geoffrey Chaucer and Edmund Spenser, the greatest writers in the language. Elegies of praise and mourning poured from the pens of the leading poets of the day, many of whom knew him intimately from their collaborations in the theatre. His immortality seemed to be assured when, after his death, his plays were gathered in a Folio volume.

I am, of course, talking about the life, work, and death of Francis Beaumont, author of the Ovidian poem *Salmacis and Hermaphroditus*, the parodic *Knight of the Burning Pestle*, and, with Fletcher, the comedy of *The Woman Hater* and the tragicomic romance of *Philaster; or, Love Lies a-Bleeding*. During the Restoration era, the plays of Beaumont and Fletcher were performed twice as often as those of Shakespeare. But fashions change. Beaumont has been eclipsed, his place in the House of Fame taken by the man from Stratford who died seven weeks later.

Having died in the provinces, Shakespeare was not immediately lauded in London. Despite this, his fame was swiftly assured: the monument in the parish church where he is buried in his own town, erected in his memory shortly after his death, proclaimed that he had the genius of Socrates, the judgment of Nestor, and the poetic art of Virgil. Before long, the writer John Weever visited the church and transcribed into his notebook both the epitaph on Shakespeare's tomb and the words on the monument. In the margin opposite the heading "Stratford upon Avon," he wrote, "Willm Shakespeare the famous poet."[1] Then in 1619, a minor poet named William Basse admired both the monument and the man in the grave below it: "Under this carved marble of thine owne / Sleep rare Tragedian Shakespeare, sleep alone."[2] Local poet Leonard Digges soon chipped in, suggesting that Shakespeare's real immortality would come through "thy works, by which, outlive / Thy tomb, thy name must: when that stone is rent, / And time dissolves thy *Stratford* Monument."[3] In the late 1620s, a book collector transcribed the poem on the monument into the margin of his copy of the First Folio, together with the epitaph on the grave and a somewhat clunky poem of his own:

Here Shakespeare lies whom none but death could Shake
And here shall lie till judgment all awake;
When the last trumpet doth unclose his eyes
The wittiest poet in the world shall rise.[4]

In 1630, the author of an anonymous pamphlet recorded "travelling through Stratford upon Avon, a town most remarkable for the birth of famous William Shakespeare."[5] Four years later, a military officer called Lieutenant Hammond wrote in his diary: "we came by Stratford upon Avon ... in the church there are some monuments ... those worth observing ... a neat Monument of that famous English Poet, Mr William Shakespeare, who was born here."[6]

These half dozen early references to the monument show that Shakespeare had quickly become Stratford-upon-Avon's favourite son. The word "famous" was attached to him, but he was no more famous than fellow-dramatists such as Beaumont—let alone Ben Jonson, who worked so hard to fashion his own fame. For all sorts of reasons, the immortality of writers is not assured. There were many successful and admired dramatists in ancient Athens, but the only unfragmented survivals in the corpus of Greek tragedy are thirty-three plays by Aeschylus, Sophocles, and Euripides. According to Jonson, in his dedicatory poem in the First Folio, Shakespeare was a worthy successor to the Roman tragedians "Pacuvius, Accius, [and] him of Cordova dead"—but the only one of these whose plays survive is the unnamed third, Seneca of Cordova. Marcus Pacuvius was known to Jonson solely by way of some admiring quotations in Horace and Cicero. The latter, in his *De Optimo Genero Oratorum* (On the best kind of orators), ranked Pacuvius first among Roman tragic poets. But all his tragedies are lost, as are the fifty or so plays of Lucius Accius. As too are the vast majority of the plays staged by producer Philip Henslowe in the Rose Theatre, home of the leading rival companies to Shakespeare's. As, for that matter, are many of the plays of the Chamberlain's/King's Men, including, it would seem, Shakespeare's *Love's Labour's Won* and Shakespeare and Fletcher's *Cardenio*.

Even when a playwright's body of work is gathered and preserved for posterity, there is no guarantee of the continuation of their fame. The Puritans closed the London theatre in 1642. Had history gone differently, the theatrical profession might not have returned to life, as it did with the restoration of the monarchy in 1660. The romantic style and monarchical sympathies of the plays attributed to Beaumont and Fletcher, collected in Folio in 1647, were more in keeping with the sensibility of the new age than those of Shakespeare. In the course of the eighteenth century, however, the taste for Beaumont and Fletcher declined as precipitously as that for Shakespeare rose exponentially. The one non-Shakespeare play of the Elizabethan and Jacobean era that remained a theatrical hit throughout the century was Philip Massinger's *A New Way to Pay Old Debts*, featuring the monstrous antihero Sir Giles Overreach, a must-play part for every leading actor. This is a nice irony, since many of the plays in the Beaumont and Fletcher canon were part-written by Massinger, but with no credit to his name.

Such are the vicissitudes of literary fame. In this final chapter, I want to ask three questions: Where did Shakespeare's idea of fame come from? Did he want to achieve posthumous fame for himself? And when, and by what means, did he become famous? The last of these questions is a very large one, which I have written about at length elsewhere, so I shall offer only the briefest of sketches, leading up to a moment of particular significance, with which I will end.

Where does the idea of fame come from? For Shakespeare's generation, the answer was, as I have sought to show it was for so many aspects of their culture, from classical antiquity. This is one of the pressure points in their dual inheritance of pagan values and the Holy Bible. In Christian terms, the only afterlife that matters is that of the soul in Heaven (or Hell—or, in the Catholic tradition, Purgatory). Worldly fame is evanescent, posthumous reputation immaterial. This could hardly be a more different attitude from that of ancient Greek and Roman literature going all the way back to the Homeric epic, the primary purpose of which was to immortalise the heroic deeds of gods, demigods, and heroes: in Homer, the frequently invoked word *kleos* denotes the idea of transcending mortality through fame. But the history of the idea is complicated. After Homer came Hesiod, who in his *Works and Days* contrasted the positive, immortalising sense of *kleos* (for which another word might be "glory" or "renown") with a negative term, *phēmē*, suggestive of rumour or gossip.[7] Fame has an unfortunate tendency to be accompanied by her dark shadow, ill repute, the blackening as opposed to the burnishing of a name. Public figures, especially military heroes, are acutely conscious of this: Othello cares so deeply about his reputation, which Iago systematically destroys through malicious gossip, because his fame has been hard won, against the odds, in voyage and battle.

In Virgil's *Aeneid*, Greek *phēmē* becomes Latin *fama*, and the word carries the double sense of fame and rumour. In the first book, Aeneas announces himself as "pius Aeneas" (pious or dutiful Aeneas), whose fame or glory is noted in the heavens above: "fama super aethera notus."[8] But in the second book, during that narration to Dido of the fall of Troy which so influenced Shakespeare's *Lucrece*, *fama* is among the watchwords applied to deceitful Sinon, the feigned deserter from the Greeks who insinuates himself into Troy, opens up the wooden horse, and brings the destruction of the city.[9] Sinon's lies are paradigmatic of *fama* as false rumour: some of the other terms that Virgil associates with him are *falsa, mendacemque improba, ficto pectore,* and *insidiis periurique arte* (false, flagrant lies, feigned feelings, insidious and skillful rhetorical art).[10] He is the Iago of the *Aeneid*. For writers such as Virgil and Shakespeare, addicted to ambivalence and complexity, the double sense of *fama* holds a peculiar attraction: they give full rein to their muse of fire when glorifying the fame of such heroic warriors as Aeneas, Othello, and Coriolanus, but they also recognize that their own fictions, their art of spinning tales, is a form of rumour that puts them in the same camp as Sinon and Iago.

In his fourth book, Virgil cuts away from Dido and Aeneas as they are making love in a cave during a storm. To what does he cut? A personification of *Fama* in her malicious guise: "Fama, malum qua non alius velocius ullum" (Rumour, the evil of the highest velocity).[11] Word spreads through all the cities of Libya that Queen Dido is having a clandestine affair. It reaches Iarbas, son of Jupiter, who was once rejected by Dido; he tells Jupiter; Jupiter tells Mercury; Mercury reminds Aeneas that his destiny is to found a city in Italy, not to waste his time with a love affair in Carthage. Rumour has ignited the chain reaction that will end with Dido on a pyre, stabbing herself with Aeneas's sword, at which point the language comes full circle and *Fama* is invoked again: "it clamor ad alta / atria; concussam bacchatur Fama per urbem" (a scream rises to the lofty roof; Rumour riots like a bacchant through the stunned city).[12]

What does Rumour look like? She is, in the words of Thomas Phaer's Elizabethan translation of Virgil, a

> Horrible monster, immense, and beneath each plume of her body
> Lurk just so many vigilant eyes—astounding to utter!
> Tattle just so many tongues, and mouths, and so many ears hear.[13]

This multilingual personification became a familiar figure in Renaissance iconography. The top half of the title page of Sir Walter Ralegh's *History of the World*, published in 1614, shows *Fama bona* and *Fama mala*, good fame with tongues on her wings, infamy spotted with them all over.

The latter image gives us a clear idea of what would have been the costume of the character who speaks the Prologue to Shakespeare's *Henry IV Part 2*, which begins (in the quarto text) with the stage direction "*Enter Rumour painted full of Tongues*":

> Open your ears; for which of you will stop
> The vent of hearing when loud Rumour speaks?
> I, from the orient to the drooping west,
> Making the wind my post-horse, still unfold

The acts commenced on this ball of earth.
Upon my tongues continual slanders ride,
The which in every language I pronounce,
Stuffing the ears of men with false reports.
　　　　　… Rumour is a pipe
Blown by surmises, jealousies, conjectures,
And of so easy and so plain a stop
That the blunt monster with uncounted heads,
The still-discordant wav'ring multitude,
Can play upon it. But what need I thus
My well-known body to anatomize
Among my household?[14]

Rumour anatomizes her own body, her props, and her motions—
those tongues, her "pipe / Blown by surmises, jealousies, conjectures,"
the wind on which she flies with winged speed—even though her
characteristics are already "well-known" to Shakespeare's audience.

Figure 11. *Fama bona* and *Fama mala*: detail of the title page of Ralegh's *The History of the World* (1614)

Figure 12. Ovid's House of Fame (illustration in 1681 edition of *Metamorphoses*)

By spreading further rumours about Rumour, Rumour is redoubling the already proved power of Rumour.

Ovid in the *Metamorphoses* gave Virgil's *Fama* a home: in his twelfth book, he describes the House of Fame, suspended between earth and sky, built of brass, the better to diffuse, as John Dryden would have it in his translation, "The spreading sounds, and multiply the news; / Where echoes in repeated echoes play."[15] Fame flew on wings borrowed from the figures of Victory and Glory, Chaucer rebuilt her House, and Petrarch in his *Triumph of Fame* bestowed upon her a trumpet as if she were an angel announcing the last judgment. Ben Jonson, in turn, staged a version of the Ovidian-Chaucerian House in his *The Masque of Queens, Celebrated from the House of Fame by the Queen of Great Britain, with her Ladies, at Whitehall, Feb 2, 1609*, which featured an anti-masque of witches spreading malice and dancing to strange music, until

> *In the heat of their* Dance, *on the sudden, was heard a sound of loud Musick, as if many Instruments had made one blast; with which not*

only the Haggs *themselves, but the* Hell, *into which they ran, quite van-*
ished, and the whole face of the Scene *altered, scarce suffering the*
memory of such a thing: But in the place of it, appeared a glorious, and
magnificent Building, figuring the House of Fame, *in the top of which,*
were discovered the twelve Masquers, *sitting upon a Throne triumphal,*
erected in form of a Pyramid, *and circled with all store of light.*[16]

There is a strong case for the argument that this *coup de théâtre* gave
Shakespeare the idea for the vanishing of the masquers in *The Tem-*
pest and Prospero's speech about the fading of the insubstantial pageant of our little lives.

The prologue to *Henry IV Part 2* is only the most elaborate of
Shakespeare's references to the corrosive power of Rumour. In *Titus*
Andronicus we hear that "The emperor's court is like the house of
Fame, / The palace full of tongues, of eyes, and ears," while in *Troilus*
and Cressida Ulysses chides Achilles on the grounds that he "Grows
dainty of his worth" because he has "his ear full of his airy fame."[17]
The collapse of fame is a key element of Shakespeare's undoing
of the heroic Homeric idiom in this play. Torn between his desire
for Patroclus, his obligation to Polyxena, and his duty as a soldier,
Achilles concludes that whatever he does he will "fail fame."[18] And
in a complex exchange, Ulysses reports to Agamemnon that Aeneas
has reported to him that the Trojans call Troilus the "second hope"
among their warriors—that is to say, the prospective successor to
Hector.[19] This report upon report is itself an example of Rumour. It
is also a knowing literary allusion. According to Ulysses, Aeneas did
"thus translate him [Troilus] to me."[20] Here we need to remember the
theory of *translatio imperii*: as part of the project to represent Rome
as a second Troy, the *Aeneid* was shaped as a *translatio* of both the
Iliad (in its martial aspect) and the *Odyssey* (in its voyaging aspect).
When Shakespeare's Aeneas speaks to his Ulysses (Odysseus) of a
"second hope," the more educated members of his audience would
hear an echo of a famous line in the final book of the *Aeneid* in which
the hero's son Ascanius is described as "Magnae spes altera Romae"
(great Rome's second hope).[21] But the image of Troilus saving Troy
in the wake of Hector's death is a false hope: shattered by Cressida's
infidelity—which will in turn lead to her historic *fama mala*—Troilus
goes willingly to his death. The audience knows that the city will not
be saved, because false Sinon will come to do his work. *Troilus and*

Figure 13. *Spes altera vitae*: inscription on lintel in Advocate's Close, Edinburgh (1590)

Cressida ends not with the trumpet of fame, but with Pandarus's images of prostitution and the spread of sexual disease.

Several early readers of Shakespeare put a more positive spin on Virgil's phrase *spes altera* by using it as the title to their manuscript copies of the sonnet "When forty winters shall besiege thy brow."[22] In the Renaissance, *spes altera vitae*, a second hope of life, became a popular emblem, motto, or inscription. For example, one finds it, dated 1590, carved above the entrance to Advocate's Close on Edinburgh's Royal Mile. Whereas the Christian conscience is focused on the second life of Heaven, the classical inheritance offers other wagers on the future, predicated upon *Fama* as the daughter of Hope: monuments, children, and poems are all created in defiance of mortality. They are bids for a second life. As noted earlier, Shakespeare's own monument in Holy Trinity church, Stratford-upon-Avon not only preserves his image in stone, with pen in hand, but also claims him as a second Virgil, a second Socrates. The frequently copied second sonnet ends with the idea that to beget a child is "to be new made when thou art old / And see thy blood warm when thou feel'st it cold." Then, as the sonnet sequence unfolds, the poems themselves become the weapon against the "bloody tyrant, Time": "So long as men can breathe or eyes can see, / So long lives this and this gives life to thee"; "Yet do thy worst, old Time: despite thy wrong / My love shall in my verse live ever young"; "And yet to times in hope my verse shall stand, / Praising thy worth, despite his cruel hand"; "Give my love fame faster than Time wastes life, / So thou prevent'st his scythe and crooked knife."[23]

Shakespeare began working on his sonnets around the time that he wrote *Love's Labour's Lost*.[24] The King of Navarre begins that play with a bid for Fame that shares many of the tropes of the sonnets:

> Let fame, that all hunt after in their lives,
> Live registered upon our brazen tombs
> And then grace us in the disgrace of death;
> When, spite of cormorant devouring Time,
> The endeavor of this present breath may buy
> That honour which shall bate his scythe's keen edge
> And make us heirs of all eternity.[25]

These words proclaim instant allegiance to the classical as opposed to the Christian tradition. The church taught that you become heir to all eternity by way of heavenly salvation, not earthly fame. Fame achieved in life is no guarantee of grace in death. The brazen tomb is but a temporary resting place, thanks to the empty tomb of the resurrected Jesus. Navarre, who goes on to suggest that his "little academe" will achieve fame through the life of the mind, is signing up himself and his team as Renaissance humanists. We must grant that the play has a lot of fun mocking their aspirations: the life of the mind is rudely interrupted by the arrival of the ladies, and by the end of the comedy the second life to which the gentlemen aspire is that which may be achieved by making babies (though the ladies deprive them of that pleasure for a year). Meanwhile, the famous heroes of both the classical and the Judaeo-Christian traditions are rendered bathetically in the farcical pageant of the Nine Worthies.

For all the subsequent deflation, there is no denying the eloquence of the king's opening speech. His language is a tissue of allusion: to the classical idea of *Fama*; to the commonest form of ancient epigraphy (namely an epitaph inscribed upon a tomb); to the Latin tag *Vivit post funera virtus* (virtue outlives death);[26] to the Ovidian image of personified Time as devourer (*Tempus edax rerum*);[27] to the Roman code of "honour"; to the Renaissance elision of *chronos*, the Greek personification of time, and Kronos, Greek equivalent of Saturn, Roman god of harvest, which created the figure of Father Time with his scythe.[28] Above all, to Horace's bold claim at the climax of his third book of *Odes*, "Exegi monumentum aere perennius" (I have made a monument more enduring than brass).[29] The essence of Horace's poem is: I will achieve immortality through my literary work. Ovid made the same brag in the final lines of his *Metamorphoses*. Whereas Virgil ended the *Aeneid* by promising immortality for the Emperor Augustus, Ovid confers it upon himself. His last word is "vivam" (I shall live), and the last word in the English translation used by Shakespeare is "fame":

> Iamque opus exegi, quod nec Iovis ira nec ignis
> nec poterit ferrum nec edax abolere vetustas ...
> ore legar populi, perque omnia saecula fama,
> siquid habent veri vatum praesagia, vivam.

> Now have I brought a woork to end which neither Joves feerce
>   wrath,
> Nor swoord, nor fyre, nor freating age with all the force it hath
> Are able too abolish quyght ...
>   ... And tyme without all end
> (If Poets as by prophesie about the truth may ame)
> My lyfe shall everlastingly been lengthened still by fame.[30]

Shakespeare uses very similar language throughout his sonnets, but gives the impression of being more interested in bestowing immortality upon his beloved than himself: "Nor Mars his sword, nor war's quick fire shall burn / The living record of your memory."[31] "This gives life to thee," not *gives life to me*. Admittedly, Thomas Thorpe, the man who saw *Shakespeare's Sonnets* into print in 1609, prefaced them with a dedication laid out in the style of a Roman monumental inscription, including the epithet "OVR. EVER. LIVING. POET," suggesting the idea of immortalization through publication. But there is a fierce debate among scholars as to whether or not this publication was authorized by Shakespeare.[32] This raises a question that William Hazlitt asked in 1814: "On Posthumous Fame,–whether Shakspeare was influenced by a love of it?"[33]

Hazlitt argued that the love of fame is culturally determined. We only crave fame if we are working in a tradition that values fame:

> When those who succeed in distant generations read with wondering rapture the works which the bards and sages of antiquity have bequeathed to them,—when they contemplate the imperishable power of intellect which survives the stroke of death and the revolutions of empire,—it is then that the passion for fame becomes an habitual feeling in the mind, and that men naturally wish to excite the same sentiments of admiration in others which they themselves have felt, and to transmit their names with the same honours to posterity.[34]

Thus, according to Hazlitt, the works of self-conscious admirers of the classics such as Dante, Chaucer, Spenser, and Milton are suffused with a desire for posthumous fame. Not so Shakespeare, he argues, on the grounds that the love of fame is a form of egotism, whereas Shakespeare "seemed scarcely to have an individual existence of his own, but to borrow that of others at will, and to pass successively through 'every variety of untried being,'—to be now Hamlet, now Othello, now Lear, now Falstaff, now Ariel."[35] This was Hazlitt's first articulation of his idea of Shakespeare's lack of positive identity, his absorption into all his characters, an idea that would eventually shape John Keats's thinking about the poet as chameleon and the opposition between the Wordsworthian "egotistical sublime" and Shakespeare's "negative capability."[36]

Hazlitt is certainly correct in saying that there is no Shakespearean equivalent to Ovid's *vivam* (I shall live). And for a long time there was a commonplace view that Shakespeare could not have been interested in posthumous fame, since he did not bother to publish his works. A contrast is often made with Ben Jonson, who in 1616 carefully oversaw the publication of his plays, poems, and court masques in *The Workes of Benjamin Jonson*, a title deliberately echoing the notion of the *Opera* of a classical author. Published in lavish Folio format, its title page was branded with a triumphal arch, sculptural figures, and Latin inscriptions all designed to suggest a classical work destined for enduring fame.

Shakespeare, so the story goes, had no such aspiration. He wrote for the theatre; half the corpus of his plays remained unpublished in his lifetime, and of the other half, many were put into print only as a way of displacing poor-quality pirated texts. Recent scholarship

Figure 14. Ben Jonson's bid for classical Fame: detail from the title page of *Workes* (1616), with quotation from Horace, figures representing different poetic kinds (satire, tragicomedy, pastoral) and "theatrum" that is at once Roman and Globe-like

has challenged this narrative, suggesting that Shakespeare was actually a much more "literary" dramatist than has customarily been supposed and indeed that in the case of his longer tragedies the editions printed in his lifetime were deliberately fashioned as "reading texts" of a length that could not have been performed in full within the time constraints of the public theatre.[37]

As with so many aspects of Shakespeare, we will never be able to recover his overt intentions on this matter. Besides, desire for print does not necessarily mean desire for posthumous fame; proprietorial rights and desire for money could equally well have played a part. What we can say, however, is that some of Shakespeare's friends sought to fashion him as a classic. The process started with his schoolfellow Richard Field, who printed *Venus and Adonis* with a title-page ornament (which he used on many of his books) portraying a tiara-adorned female figure resembling a classical goddess (possibly Juno, since she is flanked by peacocks), together with two smaller figures blowing horns suggestive of the trumpet of fame.[38] Field also included his own emblem and its motto "anchora spei" (the anchor of hope). Either he or Shakespeare himself furnished an epigraph in the form of a quotation from Ovid's *Amores*: "Vilia miretur vulgus; mihi flavus Apollo / Pocula Castalia plena ministret aqua" (Let the

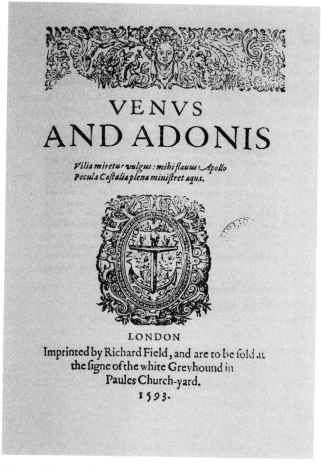

Figure 15. Opus I (*Venus and Adonis*, 1593): Shakespeare classically presented by his fellow school pupil Richard Field

rabble admire worthless things; / may golden Apollo supply me with cups full of water from the Castalian spring).[39] Shakespeare was thus ushered into print not as an author writing for the vulgar (the rabble of the public theatre), but as the successor of an admired classical exemplar, paying homage to the god of poetry and seeking inspiration from the Castalian spring on Mount Parnassus that was sacred to the Muses. Furthermore, when Field prepared that "graver labor" *Lucrece* for the press, he (or possibly Shakespeare himself?) marked a number of lines with initial inverted commas, highlighting them as *sententiae*, proverbial wisdom of the kind that was traditionally gathered from the classics and committed to memory or copied into a commonplace book.[40]

The First Folio, authorized by Shakespeare's fellow-actors John Hemmings and Henry Condell, does not have the pretensions of Jonson's title-page: it offers a simple engraving of the author as opposed to an elaborate show of classical architecture. Nevertheless, the book's arrangement by genre was a self-conscious attempt to turn Shakespeare into a classic, the author of tragedies to match those of Seneca, histories that offered a dramatic equivalent to Livy and Plutarch, comedies worthy of Plautus and Terence.

And the prefatory matter, in the creation of which Jonson himself played a leading part, fully institutes the idea of Shakespeare's posthumous fame. Jonson's dedicatory poem was entitled "To the memory of my beloved, the AUTHOR Master William Shakespeare and what he hath left us": it was common in such verses to call the writer of a book the "author," but rare to honour a maker of plays with that august title, which carried the suggestion of *auctor*, the— usually classical—*authority* for an idea. The poem returns again and again to the idea of the contemporary dramatist outdoing his antique forebears, joining them on Mount Parnassus or even displacing them from the pantheon:

> Leave thee alone for the comparison
> Of all that insolent Greece or haughty Rome
> Sent forth, or since did from their ashes come....
> The merry Greek, tart Aristophanes,
> Neat Terence, witty Plautus, now not please,
> But antiquated and deserted lie
> As they were not of nature's family.[41]

Jonson even goes so far as to compare Shakespeare with the very gods of poetry and communication, Apollo and Mercury. Similarly, in another of the prefatory poems, Leonard Digges, who was brought up in a village neighbouring Stratford-upon-Avon, attaches to Shakespeare the lines that Ovid (Naso) had written about himself at the end of the *Metamorphoses*:

> Nor fire, nor cank'ring age, as Naso said
> Of his, thy wit-fraught book shall once invade....
> Be sure, our Shakespeare, thou canst never die,
> But crowned with laurel, live eternally.[42]

Whereas Jonson's works were only reprinted once after his death, Shakespeare's Folio was reprinted three times before the end of the century.[43] And throughout the eighteenth, nineteenth, and twentieth centuries, there was a major new edition of his *Complete Works* once every twenty years or so. The creation of scholarly editions is one of the ways in which an author is inducted into the House of Posthumous Fame.

In his dedicatory poem, Jonson described Shakespeare as a "star" whose "influence" would "chide or cheer" the future course of British drama. Once the Folio was available to, in the words of its editors, "the great Variety of Readers," the plays began to influence not just the theatre, but poetry more generally. The works of John Milton, notably his masque *Comus*, were steeped in Shakespearean language. The young Milton's first published poem was an encomium prefixed to the second edition of the Folio, in which Shakespeare is said to have built himself "a live-long Monument" in the form of his plays. Shakespeare was Milton's key precedent for the writing of *Paradise Lost* in blank verse rather than rhyme. Even later seventeenth-century poets who were committed to rhyme, such as John Dryden, acknowledged the power of his dramatic blank verse; it was as an act of homage to "the Divine Shakespeare" that Dryden abandoned rhyme in *All for Love* (1678), his reworking of the Cleopatra story. As Chaucer and Petrarch had demonstrated by means of their reinventions of the figure of Fame, the exercise of inspiring influence upon later creative artists is another *gradus ad Parnassum*.

But could a writer become a classic if the style of the works was anything but neoclassical? This was the dilemma faced by Shakespeare's admirers in the late seventeenth and eighteenth centuries. On the positive side, he was invoked for his inspirational native genius, used to support claims for English naturalness as opposed to French artifice and for the moderns against the ancients. John Dryden described Shakespeare as "the man who of all Modern, and perhaps Ancient Poets, had the largest and most comprehensive soul." He brushed off charges of Shakespeare's lack of learning with the memorable judgment that "he needed not the spectacles of Books to read Nature."[44] The learned Margaret Cavendish, Duchess of Newcastle, praised Shakespeare for his extraordinary ability to enter into his vast array of characters, to "express the divers and different humours, or natures, or several passions in mankind."[45] Yet at the same time, the courtly elite had spent their years of exile in France and come under the influence of a highly refined neoclassical theory of artistic decorum, according to which tragedy should be kept apart from comedy and high style from low, with dramatic "unity" demanding obedience to strict laws. For this reason, Dryden and his contemporaries took considerable liberties in polishing and "improving" Shakespeare's plays for performance. According to the law of poetic justice, wholly innocent characters should not be allowed to die: that was why Nahum Tate rewrote *King Lear* (1681) with a happy ending in which Cordelia marries Edgar. Tate also omitted the character of the Fool, on the grounds that such a figure was beneath the dignity of high tragedy.

Thomas Betterton, leading actor of the Restoration years, so venerated the memory of Shakespeare that late in his life he travelled to Warwickshire in order to find out what he could about the dramatist's origins. He passed a store of anecdotes to the poet, playwright, and eventual Poet Laureate Nicholas Rowe, who wrote "Some Account of the Life of Mr William Shakespeare," a biographical sketch published in 1709 in the first of the six volumes of his *Works of Shakespeare*, the collection that is usually regarded as the first modern edition of the plays. The engraving opposite the title page is adorned with the trumpets of fame.

Rowe's biography offered a mixture of truth and myth, calculated to represent Shakespeare as a man of the people. It told of how young Will was withdrawn from school when his father fell on hard

Figure 16. The trumpets of fame above and below the portrait of Shakespeare on the title cut of Rowe's 1709 edition

times, how he then got into bad company and stole deer from the park of local grandee Sir Thomas Lucy. The resultant prosecution forced him to leave for London, where he became an actor and then a dramatist. Rowe's account is a symptom of how every age reinvents Shakespeare in its own image. The road from the provinces to London was a familiar one in the eighteenth century: Samuel Johnson and David Garrick walked it in real life, Henry Fielding's Tom Jones in fiction. Shakespeare served as exemplar of the writer who achieved success, and an unprecedented degree of financial reward, from his pen alone. The Earl of Southampton may have helped him on his way in his early years, but he was essentially a self-made man rather than a beneficiary of court and aristocratic patronage. For writers such as Alexander Pope and Samuel Johnson, struggling in the transition from the age of patronage to that of Grub Street professionalism, Shakespeare offered not only a body of poetic invention and a gallery of living characters, but also an inspirational career trajectory.

If we had to identify a single decade in which Shakespeare could be said to have fully entered into the House of Fame, in which his celebrity and influence grew to outstrip that of his contemporaries once and for all, it would probably be the 1730s.[46] There was a proliferation of cheap mass-market editions, while in the theatre the plays came to constitute about a quarter of the entire repertoire of the London stage, twice what they had been hitherto. The promotion of Shakespeare was driven by a number of forces, ranging from state censorship of new plays to the efforts of an influential group of female aristocratic patrons of the arts (the Shakespeare Ladies Club) to a male taste for the shapely legs of actresses in the cross-dressed "breeches parts" of the comedies. The plays were becoming synonymous with decency and Englishness, even as the institution of the theatre was still poised between respectability and disrepute. All that was then needed was for an actor to arrive in London and give new dignity to the theatrical profession by making his own fame synonymous with Shakespeare's, in a kind of celebrity feedback loop.[47]

Enter David Garrick, whose Bardolatry climaxed in the Jubilee that he organised to commemorate the bicentenary of Shakespeare's birth. The event took place in Stratford-upon-Avon in 1769, on the occasion of the opening of a new Town Hall, a mere five years later than the anniversary it was supposed to mark. It lasted for three days, during which scores of fashionable Londoners descended on the hitherto obscure provincial town where Shakespeare had been born. The literary tourist industry began here: local entrepreneurs did good business in the sale of Shakespearean relics, such as souvenirs supposedly cut from the wood of the great Bard's mulberry tree. Not since the marketing in medieval times of fragments of the True Cross had a single tree yielded so much wood. The Jubilee programme included a grand procession of Shakespearean characters, a masked ball, a horse race, and a firework display. In true English fashion, the outdoor events were washed out by torrential rain. At the climax of the festivities, Garrick performed his own poem, "An Ode upon dedicating a building and erecting a statue to Shakespeare at Stratford-upon-Avon," set to music by the leading composer Thomas Arne. In the manner of a staged theatrical "happening," Garrick had arranged for a member of the audience (a fellow-actor), dressed as a French fop, to complain—as French connoisseurs of literary taste had complained for generations—that Shakespeare was vulgar, provincial, and overrated. This gave Garrick the opportunity to voice his grand defence of Shakespeare. Though the whole business was much mocked in newspaper reports, caricatures, and stage farces, it generated enormous publicity for both Garrick and Shakespeare across Britain and the continent of Europe. The Jubilee did more than turn Stratford-upon-Avon into a tourist attraction: it inaugurated the very idea of a summer arts festival.[48]

In 1741, a statue of Shakespeare was dedicated in Westminster Abbey. He had finally fully displaced Beaumont in the national shrine. Garrick trumped this by commissioning his own secular shrine to his hero: in 1756 he completed his Temple to Shakespeare, a folly in the grounds of his villa by the Thames near Richmond. An octagonal domed building in the style of the pantheon in Rome, with an Ionic portico in the Palladian style, its centerpiece was a marble statue of the playwright by Roubiliac, for which Garrick is purported to have posed himself. There were also a number of relics, such as a chair made from the mulberry tree that the Bard was said to have planted in his garden at New Place.[49] This was Shakespeare's personal House of Fame.

In an age when orthodox religion was facing severe challenges, the cult of Shakespeare was indeed becoming a secular faith. His fecund *imagination*—his inhabiting of what Hazlitt in "On Posthumous Fame" called "every variety of untried being," natural and supernatural—became the touchstone of creativity. Thanks to the enthusiasm of poets, critics, and translators such as Samuel Taylor Coleridge, William Hazlitt, and John Keats in England, Johann Wolfgang von Goethe and the Schlegel brothers in Germany, Victor Hugo and Alexandre Dumas in France, during the era of Romanticism, the grammar-school boy from the edge of the forest of Arden became

Figure 17. Garrick's Temple by the Thames: Shakespeare's personal House of Fame (painting by Johan Zoffany, c. 1762)

the supreme deity not just of poetry and drama, but of high culture itself. Shakespeare's unique fame was assured.[50]

Perhaps the development that did more than any other to give him high cultural status, to make him *classical* as well as *popular*, was his introduction into the education system. That, after all, was the place where the canonical authors of antiquity survived. So we are brought full circle. Shakespeare's imagination had its birth in his Latin lessons in the Stratford-upon-Avon schoolroom. His memories of that education, and his subsequent reading in the classical and neoclassical tradition, shaped both his thinking and his compositional art.

Rhetoric was taught, as it had been since the time of Cicero and Quintilian, as preparation for a life of service to the state. Middle-class boys such as young Will Shakespeare and John Milton were given their training in the arts of language so that they could become lawyers or clerks or Church of England ministers or secretaries to politicians. But the Tudor educational revolution had an unintended consequence. Many of the brightest boys put their talents to very different uses: as poets, actors, and playwrights. Their plays and poems assisted in the work of nation-building by bringing alive the history and the myths that shaped the English people's sense of who they were. Simultaneously, by dramatizing the conflicts of both public and private life—tyrannical rulers being overthrown, arbiters of morality exposed as hypocrites, wives rebelling against their husbands—the poets and playwrights also made a huge contribution to the emergence of modern liberties.

English literature itself did not become the object of formal academic study until the second half of the eighteenth century. When the philosopher Adam Smith was invited to deliver a series of public lectures on "rhetoric and belles lettres" in Edinburgh in the late 1740s, he broke with tradition by speaking in the English language and using vernacular as well as ancient Roman examples of rhetorical technique and fine writing. Hugh Blair followed Smith's example when in 1760 he was appointed to the position of Professor of Rhetoric and Belles Lettres in the University of Edinburgh. Upon his retirement, Blair published his lectures, and they went through dozens of editions, remaining the standard academic introduction to the art of literary criticism for more than half a century. They were especially widely studied in the United States.

In England, meanwhile, only men who subscribed to the articles of faith of the Church of England could attend the ancient universities of Oxford and Cambridge, where the language of instruction was Latin and the humanities side of the curriculum was confined to the ancients. Religious nonconformists or "dissenters" accordingly set up academies of their own, where "polite literature" (*belles lettres*) was taught in the English language. The teaching of what we now call English Literature was one of John Aikin's duties when he took up the tutorship in *Belles Lettres* at the Warrington Academy in 1758.[51] His daughter Anna Letitia Aikin (later Barbauld) grew up to become a popular and influential poet and editor, an apologist for the French Revolution, a passionate advocate of the abolition of the slave trade, and an important early analyst of the novel—her fifty-volume anthology *The British Novelists*, published in 1810, did more than any other publication to establish the canon of English fiction.[52]

Aikin was succeeded in the literature tutorship at Warrington by the radical theologian and scientist Joseph Priestley, who also welcomed the French Revolution. From its very institutional origin, then, the discipline of English Literature was associated with dissent, with the democratization of education, and with resistance to the elitism of the established universities. It was helpful in this regard that the most sublime English poet, beside Shakespeare, was considered to be John Milton, author not only of the defining religious epic *Paradise Lost* but also of prose treatises in defence of the freedom of the press (*Areopagitica*, 1644) and the sovereign right of the people to depose their rulers (*The Tenure of Kings and Magistrates*, 1649).

The new discipline also provided educational opportunities for women. When Priestley left Warrington, the tutorship in *Belles Lettres* passed to the Unitarian minister William Enfield, who created an anthology called *The Speaker*, subtitled "miscellaneous pieces, selected from the best English writers, and disposed under proper heads, with a view to facilitate the improvement of youth in reading and speaking." First published in 1774 and reprinted on numerous occasions in subsequent years, this became the standard textbook for the teaching of eloquence and elocution in English throughout the land—at girls' schools as well as boys'. In 1811, Anna Barbauld published *The Female Speaker*, a companion volume specifically aimed at young women.[53]

Enfield's categories of literature included narrative, didactic pieces (for instance, a series of passages from Alexander Pope's *Essay on Man*), orations and harangues (political speeches, some from modern parliament, others from Shakespeare), dialogues (mostly from the drama, especially Shakespeare), descriptions (notably from eighteenth-century landscape poetry), and "pathetic" pieces (examples of strong feeling). The idea was that a thorough grounding in these four hundred pages of extracts would improve the vocabulary and articulacy of pupils, while also cultivating their emotions and their moral sense. In the early sections of the book, Shakespearean extracts are mingled among passages from the "polite" authors in the eighteenth-century tradition exemplified by Addison's *Spectator* and the works of Alexander Pope. But in the final section, devoted to the language of the emotions, Shakespeare overwhelms all others. This was the moment at which he came to the centre of what Vicesimus Knox,

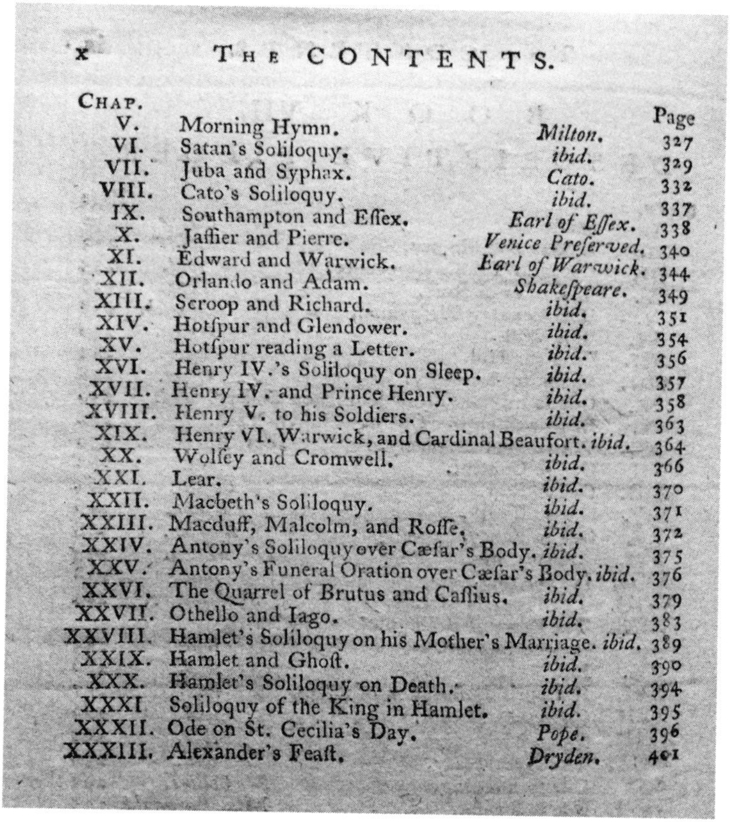

x THE CONTENTS.

Figure 18. *Ibid., Ibid., Ibid.*: contents of final section of Enfield's *The Speaker* (1774), with Shakespeare beginning to dominate the canon

compiler of a similar anthology (*Elegant Extracts*, 1783), called a "liberal education."[54]

The beneficiaries of that education were not the ruling class, who continued to be schooled in the Greek and Roman classics until well into the twentieth century, but middle-class nonconformists and women. Soon they would be joined by the working classes, through radical Chartist educational projects and more conservative workingmen's colleges, and by colonial subjects, beginning with the reform of Indian education in the 1830s.[55] Looked at from one point of view, the teaching of elocution and the emergent discipline of English were intended to instil conformity of linguistic usage and moral values. But for nonconformist pupils in the dissenting academies, for Victorian labouring-class autodidacts,[56] for the first women to gain access to universities, for colonial subjects such as Gandhi and Nehru, and for mid-twentieth-century northern working-class grammar-school boys and girls, the study of English literature was as often a crucible of liberal thought and an engine of social mobility. And, from Enfield's *Speaker* onwards, the author at the heart of that study—the one enduringly canonical writer, often the one compulsory writer—has been Shakespeare. It is the ultimate mark of his fame that he is to us what those ancient Roman authors were to him: the basis of a liberal education, the core of *studia humanitas*. He is *our* singular classic.

APPENDIX: THE ELIZABETHAN VIRGIL

WILLIAM CAXTON'S WORK TO ESTABLISH A CANON of printed classics in England would not have been complete without his *Eneydos* of 1490. This book was, however, the product of the eclectic cosmopolitanism of the Middle Ages as opposed to the humanistic nationalism that emerged in the next generation: it was a French prose translation of an Italian paraphrase of parts of the *Aeneid* mingled with sections of Boccaccio's *Fall of Princes*. The first vernacular Virgil to be produced in the British Isles was undertaken by Gavin Douglas, a leading figure in the Scottish court. His translation of the *xiii Bukes of Eneados* into the Scots tongue was completed in manuscript in 1513, the year of the Battle of Flodden where King James IV and many of his nobles were cut down.

England thenceforth had political superiority over Scotland, but its cultural development was slower. Henry VIII's leading courtier-poet, Henry Howard, Earl of Surrey, began work on an English *Aeneid*, but only completed two of the twelve books. He drew extensively on Douglas's version. His chosen books were the most renowned sequences: Aeneas's narration of the fall of Troy (book 2) and the fate of Dido (book 4). The importance of Surrey's partial translation was chiefly technical. It introduced into English poetry a new unit of composition, the verse-paragraph, and a new metre, the unrhymed pentameter—that "blank verse" which became the essential medium of Shakespeare, Milton, and Wordsworth. Latin poetry does not rhyme, so in accordance with the humanist idea of imitation, Surrey became the first English poet to abandon rhyme. He did not, however, take imitation so far as to seek to reproduce Virgil's hexameter (six metrical feet per line): he followed his admired predecessors Chaucer and Wyatt in deploying a supple five-beat line that answered to the rhythms of English speech. Seven years after its author was executed for treason, Surrey's Virgil reached print under the title *The fourth Boke of Virgill, intreating of the love between Aeneas & Dido, translated into English, and drawne into a straunge metre by Henrye late Earle of Surrey, worthy to be embraced* (1554). Books 2 and 4 were printed by Richard Tottel in 1557, the year that the same publisher produced *Songes and Sonettes*, the highly influential anthology of lyric poetry by Wyatt, Surrey, and others that was the vade mecum of such Elizabethan wooers as Abraham Slender in *The Merry Wives of Windsor*.

But Surrey's *Aeneid* was incomplete. Thomas Phaer trained for the law and then turned to medicine. In both fields, he sought to remove knowledge from the experts and offer it to the people. The aim of his much-reprinted book of "precedents" was to give a working knowledge of legal method to "every man," while his *Booke of Children* was a manual for home healthcare that has earned him a place in the annals of medical history as "the father of English paediatrics." The very act of writing about medicine and the law in the vernacular was a breach of the convention that maintained the professions as elite coteries. "I shall never cease, during my breath, to bestow my labour in removing the wall of Latin that keeps knowledge from the common man," Phaer wrote in the preface to his *Booke of Children*.[1] The translation of nine and a half books of the *Aeneid* that he undertook between 1555 and his death in 1557 was part and parcel of the same project. It provided a literary equivalent of the legal precedent book: by rendering Virgil in English, Phaer offered future writers in the vernacular what he called "large and abundant camps" of literary variety, "innumerable sorts of most beautiful flowers, figures and phrases" with which they could garnish their own verses.[2] Just as he was committed to the common law tradition of precedent, rather than the Roman system of legal codification, so Phaer transformed the *Aeneid* from a classical into a vernacular poem. As in other "Englishings," such as Arthur Golding's *Metamorphoses*, Chaucerian archaism in vocabulary domesticated the world of the poem. In book 6, Celtic "Bugges" and Middle English "Goblines" enter Virgil's underworld.

Phaer injured his hand halfway through his work on Virgil's tenth book. He died soon after. In 1573, his translation was completed by Thomas Twyne, son of a distinguished antiquarian who taught at Christopher Marlowe's school in Canterbury. William Webbe had special admiration for the style of Phaer's *Aeneid*. Phaer was, he claimed, "without doubt the best" of the gentleman translators of the classics into English.[3] If others followed this example, thought Webbe, "we shall have English Poetry at a higher price in short space: and the rabble of bald rhymes shall be turned to famous works, comparable (I suppose) with the best works of poetry in other tongues."[4]

From a strictly classical point of view, there was one deficiency in Phaer's Virgil: it was written in a seven-beat line (a "fourteener") in which the metre was determined by stress patterns, not, as in Latin verse, by the "quantitative" length of syllables. In 1582 there appeared with a Leyden imprint *The First Foure Bookes of Virgil his Aeneis Translated intoo English Heroical Verse by Richard Stanyhurst*. This new version of books 1 to 4, together with the description of Liparen from book 8, was reprinted in London the following year. The task that Stanyhurst set himself was to create an English Virgil in true hexameters, adhering as closely as possible to the quantitative metrical scheme of the original. In his own time, he was highly praised for his numbers, but roundly condemned for his diction. Here is a sample of his work, from book 1, where Aeneas makes landfall in Libya:

> Theare stands far stretching a nouke uplandish: an Island
> Theare seat, with crabknob skrude stoans hath framed an haven.
> This creeke with running passadge thee channel inhaunteth.
> Heere doe lye wyde scatterd and theare clives loftelye steaming,
> And a brace of menacing ragd rocks skymounted abydeth.
> Under having cabbans, where seas doo flitter in arches.
> With woods and thickets close couch they be clothed al upward.
> A cel or a cabban by nature formed, is under,
> Freshe bubling fountayns and stoanseats carved ar inward:
> Of Nymphes thee Nunry, wheere sea tost navye remayning
> Needs not too grapple thee sands with flooke of an anchor.[5]

The poetic feet here are not stressed and unstressed according to the sound of the syllables in spoken usage, but long or short according to a set of rules, which Stanyhurst duly laid out in his address to the reader, based on the values of diphthongs, derivatives, certain consonants, and so forth (for example, syllables ending in *b*, *d*, *t*, *n*, and *r* are short). As in the Elizabethan understanding of how Latin poetry operated, the reader is intended to scan the metrical pattern visually, not apprehend it aurally in the form of a beat. After all, the verb "to scan" pertains to the eye not the ear: it derives from Latin *scandere*, to climb, in allusion to the raising and lowering of the foot to mark rhythm. An analogous modern process might be the reading of a graph by the observation of its peaks and troughs. For the Elizabethans, the adducing of spondees, dactyls, and caesurae was conceived of as a distinct art and pleasure, not merely something intuited in the manner in which they followed the ebb, flow, and pause of English verse.

The attempt to introduce quantitative verse into English is now regarded as one of the more bizarre excrescences of the Elizabethans, but, given their desire to become the new Romans, it is perfectly understandable.[6] Since Virgil was the acknowledged master of Latin metrics, it was inevitable that he played a major role in the story of English quantitative metre. For a start, there was the example of Surrey. As we have seen, his translation had abandoned rhyme, in accordance with the absence of rhyme in Latin. He had *not* attempted to write quantitatively, nor even to reproduce the hexameter line. But because the absence of rhyme was associated with Latin poetry and because Latin poetry was quantitative, Elizabethan commentators assumed that Surrey had attempted to translate the *Aeneid* quantitatively but made a hash of it. Thus Roger Ascham: Surrey has "by good judgment avoided the fault of Rhyming" yet he has not "fully hit perfect and true versifying"; the fault was that his "feet be feet without joints, that is to say, not distinct by true quantity of syllables."[7] The irony is that, from a technical point of view, quantitative metre in English proved a dead end. The distinctive medium for the national literary tradition that began to flourish in the 1590s was what Surrey called the "strange metre" ("strange" suggesting new, different, foreign to the original) into which he had drawn two books of Virgil back in the time of Henry VIII: iambic pentameter blank verse.

One consequence of this interest in quantity was that the development of a formal "art" of English poetry took place at a distance from—and with an inevitable degree of condescension towards—the development of poetry itself as a performance art. Lyrics and sonnets written for song and recital and verse-lines written for dramatic performance were intended to be heard, not seen: they therefore could not be scanned. The fact that these forms came to dominate literary culture in the final years of the sixteenth century was one of the reasons why the vogue for quantitative metre did not endure. To put this another way: the apologists for quantitative metre misunderstood the nature of a national culture because their model was based on the schoolboy, university student, or solitary gentleman parsing and scanning a Latin text, not the actor, lover, or friend speaking verse aloud and in so doing creating a literary community.

In the case of Stanyhurst, highly classical metrical aspirations were not matched by an austere classical vocabulary. "Crabknob skrude" is symptomatic. The diction of *The First Foure Bookes of Virgil his Aeneis* was much mocked in its own time. Consider the fragment from book 8, which Stanyhurst appended at the end of his complete rendering of the first four books, *Thee description of Liparen, expressed by Virgil in thee eight booke of his Æneis, in which place, thee Poët played, as yt weare, his price, by advauncing at ful thee loftines of his veyne: doon in too English by thee translatoure for his last farewel too thee sayd Virgil*:

> Tw'ard Sicil is seated, toe the welken loftelye peaking,
> A soyl, ycleapt Liparen, from whence, with flownce furye slinging,
> Stoans, and burlye bulets, lyke tamponds, maynelye be towring.
> Under is a kennel, wheare Chymneys fyrye be scorching
> Of Cyclopan tosters, with rent rocks chamferye sharded,
> Lowd dub a dub tabering with frapping rip rap of Ætna.
> Theare stroaks stronglye threshing, yawl furth groans, stamped on
>   anvil.
> In the den are drumming gads of steele, parchfulye sparckling;
> And flam's fierclye glowing from fornace flasshye be whisking.
> Vulcan his hoate fordgharth, namde eeke thee Vulcian Island.
> Downe from the hevnlye palace travayled thee fyrye God hither.
> In this cave the rakehels yrne bars, bigge bulcked, ar hamring.
> Brotes, and Steropes, with baerlym swartye Pyracmon.

Theese thre were upbotching, not shapte, but partlye wel onward,
A clapping fyerbolt (such as oft, with rownce robel hobble,
Jove toe the ground clattreth) but yeet not finnished holye.
Three showrs wringlye wrythen glimring, and forceblye sowcing;
Three watrye clowds shymring toe the craft they rampyred hizing,
Three wheru's fyerd glystring, with Soutwynds rufflered huffling.
Now doe they rayse gastly lyghtnings, now grislye reboundings
Of ruffe raffe roaring, mens herts with terror agrysing.
With peale meale ramping, with thwick thwack sturdelye thundring.
Theyre labor hoat they folow: toe the flame fits gyreful awarding.[8]

As Stanyhurst's heading indicates, this passage is a tour de force in Virgil's original. A bravura style is needed to dramatize the eruption of Etna's volcanic matter. Stanyhurst attempts to follow his master in advancing to the full loftiness of his vein. He takes his alliterative style to an extreme as a way of bringing his Virgilian engagement to a grand finale. The sequence was therefore the easy butt of parody: Thomas Nashe in *Strange Newes* condemned his "foul lumbering boisterous wallowing measure."[9] And in his preface to Greene's *Menaphon*, Nashe surpassed himself, writing of how Stanyhurst

infired, I should say inspired, with an hexameter furie, recalled to life what ever hissed Barbarisme hath been buried this C. yeere; and revived by his ragged quill such carterly varietie as no hodge plowman in a country but would have held as the extremitie of clownerie: a patterne whereof I will propound to your judgements, as neere as I can, being part of one of his descriptions of a tempest, which is thus,

Then did he make heavens vault to rebound,
with rounce robble hobble
Of ruffe raffe roaring,
with thwicke thwacke thurlerie bouncing.[10]

Such is what Nashe calls the "Thrasonicall huffe snuffe" of barbarous Master Stanyhurst. His translation was also the specific object of satire in the sixth satire of the first book of Joseph Hall's *Virgidemiarum*: "And *Virgil* selfe shall speake the English tongue: / *Manhood & garboiles shall he chaunt* with changed feete.... If *Jove* speake English in a thundring cloud, / *Thwick thwack,* and *rif raf,* rores he out aloud."[11]

Thanks largely to Nashe's attack, Stanyhurst has come to be regarded as a kind of literary-historical bad joke. The *Cambridge History of English Literature* solemnly asked whether we can plausibly "Imagine Dido Queen of Carthage asking in fury 'Shall a stranger give me the slampam?'" and a more recent guide is characteristically dismissive in suggesting that Stanyhurst "insisted on not being mistaken for an ignoramus" but that his translation "proves, in unconscious burlesque, how bad neo-classical theory was."[12] The indecorum of high classical matter being rendered through low verbal coinages is what provokes the derision. Thus the *Cambridge History* again: "he surpassed in a fantastic eccentricity the vainest of his contemporaries. Never was there a stranger mixture of pedantry and slang than is to be found in his work."[13] Wait a minute, though: is not the juxtaposition of high and low, of kings and clowns, of soaring poetry and earthy vernacular, one of the qualities that we so value in the plays of one William Shakespeare? Do we not praise the Stratford grammar school lad to the rafters for the living sound of his lines and the astonishing array of his verbal coinages? Stanyhurst gives us: Chuff chaff, clush clash, crack-rack crashing, hob lob, hurly burly, huf puff, kym kam, muff maff, pell mell, pit pat, rags jags, swish swash, tag rag, tara-tan-tara, thwick thwack, trush trash, wig wag, yolp yalp.

Again, do we not consider the art of creating compound adjectives as one of the marks of all true poets since Homer and the ancient Greek tragedians? Stanyhurst delights in: "Herd-flock," "Frith-cops," "Blustrous huzzing with clush clash buzzing, with drooming clattered humming," "It brayeth in snorting," "The push and poke of lance," "Deep minced, far chopped," "Rapfully frapping," "With belling screech cry she roareth." One almost hears Tony Harrison's acclaimed translation of Aeschylus's *Oresteia*. Or even the sheer zany word-adoring inventiveness of another Irishman in exile on the continent: could Richard Stanyhurst be not so much a joke as a pioneer? Was he the Elizabethan James Joyce?[14]

In the *Oxford English Dictionary*, Stanyhurst is credited with the invention of a rich array of more than one hundred and fifty words, including Bepowdered, Breakvow, Carousing, Disjoincted, Distracted, Flailing, Flounce, Frolic, Gadding, Gutter, Hoblobs, Hoodwink, Makesport, Mopsy, Pertlike, Plashy, Rake, Sea-froth, Smocktoy, Spumy, Unhoused, Wanton (as a verb), and Whizling. *OED* also gives him nearly two hundred nonce-words, among them Bedgle, Bepurpled, Blastbob, Breedsleep, Crabknob, Garbroils, Gyreful, Hedgebrat, Pack-paunch, Plashbreach, Racebrood, Snarnoise, Sportbreeder, Uddered, Upvomited, and Windblast. Many of his coinages failed to make it into the *Oxford English Dictionary* at all: Bughag, Birthsoil, Foresnaffled, Hailknob, Hell-swarm, Hotlove, Lustilad, Nightfog, Rapesnatched, Seabelch, and about seventy more. And on about fifty occasions, his usage of a word predates the *OED*'s earliest citation. In the following instances, Shakespeare is cited as the earliest usage but the credit should really go to Stanyhurst: Baggage, Beldam, Eyeball, Huddle, Post-haste, Quillet.

Why was Stanyhurst condemned for his verbal invention whereas Shakespeare was praised for his? Part of the answer is that the robust vernacular was considered suitable for the stage but not for the elevated matter of Virgilian heroic verse. But there was also a certain prejudice at work, beyond the good-humoured mockery. Might such barbs as "hissed Barbarisme," "hodge plowman in a country," and "extremitie of clownerie" have been directed at Stanyhurst because he was a well-known Irishman? Born in Dublin, he went to school in Waterford. At Oxford he was a friend of Edmund Campion, the lodestone of Roman Catholicism. Developing the work of Campion, he wrote the "Description of Ireland" for Holinshed's *Chronicles*, including various passages that were censored for their criticism of a faction of the English occupiers of Ireland that was close to Queen Elizabeth. The Virgil translation was written by Stanyhurst whilst he was in exile in Leyden, where he remained for many years, a staunch Catholic with a finger in various plots in the Spanish interest. In the early 1590s, he was at the Spanish court, working on behalf of Irish and English Catholic exiles. He argued that the Spanish should invade England and Ireland in order to restore the old faith. In the late 1590s, back in the Spanish Netherlands, still in the pay of King Philip II, he became involved in plans to make the king's daughter Isabella the next queen of England and Ireland. He collaborated with the rebellion of Hugh O'Neill, Earl of Tyrone, against the Elizabethan Protestant regime in Ireland. In the light of all this, his highly inventive translation of the *Aeneid* could hardly be adopted as a "nationalist" text: much as the Elizabethan court might welcome a new vernacular Virgil in a robust Anglo-Saxon vocabulary embodying the triumph of the English language over the Latin that had long been the international tongue of Catholicism, it could hardly endorse a version coming from such a man as Stanyhurst.

Because Stanyhurst was an outlier and the Phaer version was in ponderous fourteeners, English Virgil had a curiously archaic feel in the 1590s. Nobody took it upon themselves to follow the example of the Earl of Surrey and complete an *Aeneid* in the new contemporary idiom of iambic pentameter blank verse. This association of Virgil with an archaic idiom was, I suspect, one of the reasons why he did not fire Shakespeare's imagination in the way that Ovid did—and, indeed, why there is a strong element of parody in the Player's Virgilian idiom in the Pyrrhus speech.[15]

NOTES

CHAPTER 1: THE INTELLIGENCE OF ANTIQUITY

1. His evidence in the case of *Bellott v. Mountjoy*, on which see Charles Nicholl, *The Lodger: Shakespeare on Silver Street* (Allen Lane, 2007); his gnomic remarks regarding the business of the Welcombe enclosures, of which the best account is now that in Robert Bearman, *Shakespeare's Money: How Much Did He Make and What Did This Mean?* (Oxford University Press, 2016).

2. The dedicatory epistles in *Venus and Adonis* (1593) and *Lucrece* (1594).

3. Sonnets 134–36 hint at "Will" for the "fair youth," but the "mistress" is unnamed (and does not even have a classical name along the lines of the Stella, Delia, Celia, Licia, etc. of contemporaneous sequences). There is much to be said in favour of the view of Paul Edmondson and Stanley Wells in their *Shakespeare's Sonnets* (Oxford University Press, 2004) that the "fair youth" sonnets may have been written at different times for different addressees.

4. The extent of his involvement in the publication of his Quartos remains much debated. The strongest argument against the traditional view that Shakespeare wrote his plays only for performance, not publication, is Lukas Erne, *Shakespeare as Literary Dramatist* (Cambridge University Press, 2003). See further, my discussion of posthumous fame in the final chapter.

5. I owe a particular debt to A. D. Nuttall, *Shakespeare the Thinker* (Yale University Press, 2007), a sinuous account of the development of Shakespeare's thinking about, to cite its blurb, "the nature of motive, cause, personal identity and relation, the proper status of imagination, ethics and subjectivity, language and its capacity to occlude and to communicate"— but it is a book that works very much from *within* the language and imaginative movement of the plays, not by way of reference *outward* to analogies and sources in classical thinking, which is my preferred method.

6. *King Lear*, 5. 3. 182.

7. Anne Righter (Barton), *Shakespeare and the Idea of the Play* (1962; repr., Penguin, 1967), remains indispensable more than half a century after its first publication. The *theatrum mundi* trope has a long history, which is synoptically surveyed on pp. 138–44 of *European Literature and the Latin*

Middle Ages, the great work of Curtius discussed below, and in Jean Jacquot, "Le théâtre du monde de Shakespeare à Calderon," *Revue de littérature comparée*, 31 (1957), pp. 341–72, but Shakespeare seems to have been distinctive in combining it with the equally widespread trope of "the ages of man."

8. *As You Like It*, 2. 7. 142–69.

9. *King Lear*, 4. 5. 182; *Coriolanus*, 5. 3. 196–97.

10. Proclamation of 16 May 1559, repr. in E. K. Chambers, *The Elizabethan Stage* (Oxford University Press, 1923), 4. 263.

11. For the vestigial presence of the Mystery Plays, begin with Beatrice Groves, *Texts and Traditions: Religion in Shakespeare 1592–1604* (Clarendon Press, 2006).

12. The orthodox view of the hostile relationship between Puritanism and theatre was first expounded in detail in E. N. S. Thompson, *The Controversy between the Puritans and the Stage* (Yale Studies in English, 1903); and A. M. Myers, *Representation and Misrepresentation of the Puritan in Elizabethan Drama* (University of Pennsylvania Press, 1931), both of which remain valuable resources. But, as Jonas Barish notes in *The Anti-Theatrical Prejudice* (University of California Press, 1981), the most nuanced survey of Elizabethan anti-stage polemic, "Puritan" is best regarded as a useful generic term for those who attacked the popular theatre, whether on religious, moral, political, philosophical, economic, social or public health grounds (pp. 82ff.). By no means were all the polemicists doctrinal Puritans; by no means were all Puritans antitheatrical—and "Puritanism" itself had many strands, as Patrick Collinson shows in his authoritative *The Elizabethan Puritan Movement* (Clarendon Press, 1990). For the Jacobean drama, see further, Margot Heinemann, *Puritanism and Theatre: Thomas Middleton and Opposition Drama under the Early Stuarts* (Cambridge University Press, 1980).

13. The early twenty-first century "turn to religion" in Shakespearean scholarship is exemplified by, to take a small selection of fine studies, Debora Shuger's *Political Theologies in Shakespeare's England* (Palgrave Macmillan, 2001); Jean-Christophe Mayer's *Shakespeare's Hybrid Faith: History, Religion and the Stage* (Palgrave Macmillan, 2006); Kirsten Poole's *Radical Religion from Shakespeare to Milton: Figures of Nonconformity in Early Modern England* (Cambridge University Press, 2000) and *Supernatural Environments in Shakespeare's England: Spaces of Demonism, Divinity, and Drama* (Cambridge University Press, 2011); Richard McCoy's *Faith in Shakespeare* (Oxford University Press, 2013); Elizabeth Williamson's *Religion and Drama in Early Modern England: The Performance of Religion on the Renaissance Stage* (Routledge, 2016); and the insightful essays in *Shakespeare and the Culture of Christianity in Early Modern England*, ed. Dennis Taylor and David Beau-

regard (Fordham University Press, 2003); and *Shakespeare and Religion: Early Modern and Postmodern Perspectives*, ed. Ken Jackson and Arthur F. Marotti (Notre Dame University Press, 2011). The phrase "turn to religion" was coined by Jackson and Marotti in a review essay ("The Turn to Religion in Early Modern English Studies," *Criticism*, 46 [2004], pp. 167–90); see further, Cyndia Susan Clegg's able discussion in her review essay "Shakespeare Criticism and the 'Turn to Religion,'" *Huntington Library Quarterly*, 74 (2011), pp. 599–610. My belief that Shakespeare's dramatic, imaginative, and rhetorical modes of thinking were most profoundly shaped by his engagement with classical antiquity and its afterlife means that I have more sympathy than Clegg does with the argument of Alison Shell in *Shakespeare and Religion* (Bloomsbury Academic, 2010) that Shakespeare was a dramatist whose "language is saturated in religious discourse and whose dramaturgy is highly attentive to religious precedent, but whose invariable practice is to subordinate religious matter to the particular aesthetic demands of the work in hand. For Shakespeare, as for few of his contemporaries, the Judaeo-Christian story is something less than a master narrative" (p. 3). I would say that this was precisely because his "master narratives" were the imaginative models he found in the poetry and drama of ancient Rome—that is to say, the narratives to which his masters introduced him at school. See also Shell's "Why Didn't Shakespeare Write Religious Verse?," in *Shakespeare, Marlowe, Jonson: New Directions in Biography*, ed. Takashi Kozuka and J. R. Mulryne (Ashgate, 2006), pp. 85–112.

    14. 3 & 4 Edw. VI c.10.

    15. Malvolio as "puritan" (even "The devil a puritan"): three accusations in *Twelfth Night*, 2. 3. Angelo as "precise": *Measure for Measure*, 1. 4. 53.

    16. For starting points, see "Shakespeare and Religions," *Shakespeare Survey*, 54 (2001), especially Jeffrey Knapp's essay "Jonson, Shakespeare, and the Religion of Players" (pp. 57–70). Recent, as yet unpublished, research by Peter Davidson has decisively proved the view of Robert Bearman—"John Shakespeare's 'Spiritual Testament': A Reappraisal," *Shakespeare Survey*, 56 (2003), pp. 184–202—that the so-called Spiritual Testament of Shakespeare's father is spurious.

    17. The Roman Catholic case is most strongly made by Peter Milward in a series of books including *Shakespeare's Religious Background* (Loyola Press, 1973) and *The Catholicism of Shakespeare's Plays* (Renaissance Institute, Sophia University, Tokyo, 1997), while the Protestant influence is effectively summarized in David Daniell's essay "Shakespeare and the Protestant Mind" (pp. 1–12 of "Shakespeare and Religions"). For the phrase "hot Protestant Shakespeare," see Claire McEachern's striking *Believing in Shakespeare: Studies in Longing* (Cambridge University Press, 2018).

18. For examples, see the useful survey in chapter 1 of D. C. Cattell, "Catholic-Protestant Polemic and the Shakespearean Stage: The Play of Polemic" (PhD diss., University of Exeter, 2012), https://ore.exeter.ac.uk/repository/bitstream/handle/10871/8162/CattellD.pdf?sequence=4.

19. *The Winter's Tale*, 5. 3. 45, 133. "*If* this be lawful" signals the heterodoxy.

20. *Hamlet*, 1. 2. 129–32.

21. For a useful overview of the question of Socrates and suicide in Plato's *Apology, Phaedo*, and *Crito*, see Murray Miles, "Plato on Suicide (*Phaedo* 60C–63C)," *Phoenix*, 55 (2001), pp. 244–58.

22. "I am the son of Marcus Cato, ho! / A foe to tyrants and my country's friend" (*Julius Caesar*, 5. 4. 4–5).

23. "Even by the rule of that philosophy / By which I did blame Cato for the death / Which he did give himself" (*Julius Caesar*, 5. 1. 109–11). Even here, honourably self-inflicted death is regarded as a *gift*, which it never would have been in the Christian tradition.

24. Hence Cicero's defence of Cato's suicide: *De Officiis*, 1. 112; see also his *De Finibus*, 3. 60–61. Seneca defends the right to choose one's own time to die in *Epistulae Morales*, lxx, and *De Providentia*, 2. 12.

25. For Shakespeare and suicide, begin with Rowland Wymer, *Suicide and Despair in the Jacobean Drama* (St Martin's Press, 1986).

26. Tertullian, *De praescriptione haereticorum*, vii.

27. Naseeb Shaheen, *Biblical References in Shakespeare's Plays* (University of Delaware Press, 2011); Daniel Swift, *Shakespeare's Common Prayers: The Book of Common Prayer and the Elizabethan Age* (Oxford University Press, 2012).

28. Robert Southwell, *St Robert Southwell: Collected Poems*, ed. Peter Davidson and Anne R. Sweeney (Fyfield Books, 2007), p. 63. For a survey of the arguments as to whether "*Venus*' Rose" in this passage of Southwell's dedicatory poem "From the Author to the Reader" in his *Saint Peters Complaynt* specifically evokes *Venus and Adonis* or alludes to pagan-influenced love poetry more generally, see Jason Lawrence, "'Still Finest Wits Are Stilling *Venus* Rose': Robert Southwell's 'Optima Deo,' *Venus and Adonis*, and Tasso's *canto della rosa*," *Renaissance Studies*, 27 (2013), pp. 389–406. Thomas Cooper's *Thesaurus Linguae Romanae et Britannicae* (1584) reminds the reader that Adonis is "The name of a childe, which was sonne of Cynare king of Cypres whome Venus had for hir derling, which was slaine with a Bore: whome the Poets feigned, that Venus turned into a purple flowre: some say into a Rose" (s.v. "Adonis"). That Shakespeare follows Ovid in choosing the purple flower, not the rose, perhaps tells against a direct allusion, but there is no doubt that Shakespeare was the most famous teller of the Venus and Adonis tale in the 1590s.

29. For more bullish views of Shakespeare's attitude to ancient Greece, see the essays gathered in *Shakespeare and Greece*, ed. Alison Findlay and Vassiliki Markidou (Bloomsbury, 2017).

30. *The Two Noble Kinsmen*, 5. 4. 147–53.

31. See Stephen Greenblatt, *Hamlet in Purgatory* (Princeton University Press, 2001).

32. As several critics have noticed, "Melanchthon, the great Reformation scholar of Hamlet's university of Wittenberg, [wrote] a logic textbook that went through forty-six editions before 1600, and not[ed] that God has set in our minds the principle *Quodlibet est, aut non est,* and that resistance to this law is madly to bear arms against Heaven" (Helen Cooper, "*Hamlet* and the Invention of Tragedy," *Sederi: Spanish and Portuguese Society for English Renaissance Studies,* 7 [1996)], pp. 189–200 [p. 198]).

33. Thomas Thomas, *Dictionarium linguae Latinae et Anglicanae* (1587), s. v. "*Intelligentia.*"

34. Thomas Jenkins, master of the Stratford-upon-Avon grammar school from 1575 to 1579, was actually born in London, the son of a servant to Sir Thomas White, founder of St John's College, Oxford, where he studied. Nevertheless, it is almost certain that the father was of Welsh extraction: the surname Jenkins, first recorded in Monmouthshire in the Domesday Book, was highly concentrated in south Wales.

35. The starting point for Shakespeare's schooling remains T. W. Baldwin, *William Shakspere's Small Latine and Lesse Greeke,* 2 vols. (University of Illinois Press, 1944). I have written about the subject in *Shakespeare and Ovid* (Oxford University Press, 1993), pp. 19–23; *The Genius of Shakespeare* (Oxford University Press, 1997), pp. 7–13; and especially *Soul of the Age* (Random House, 2009), pp. 69–92. Since then, there has been a spate of excellent new scholarship on the formative influence of the Elizabethan schoolroom: see especially Andrew Wallace, *Virgil's Schoolboys: The Poetics of Pedagogy in Renaissance England* (Oxford University Press, 2010); and Lynn Enterline, *Shakespeare's Schoolroom: Rhetoric, Discipline, Emotion* (University of Pennsylvania Press, 2011).

36. *The Two Gentlemen of Verona*, 4. 4. 150–56.

37. *Titus Andronicus*, 4. 1. 47–51. The argument for George Peele's involvement in the writing of the fourth act of *Titus* is much weaker than the case for his hand in the first act. See William W. Weber, "Shakespeare After All? The Authorship of *Titus Andronicus* 4.1 Reconsidered," *Shakespeare Survey,* 67 (2014), pp. 69–84; and Anna Pruitt, "Refining the *LION* Collocation Test: A Comparative Study of Authorship Test Results for *Titus Andronicus* Scene 6 (= 4.1)," in *The New Oxford Shakespeare: Authorship Companion,* ed. Gary Taylor and Gabriel Egan (Oxford University Press, 2017), pp. 92–106.

38. Claudius Holyband, *The French Littelton. A most easie, perfect, and absolute way to learne the French tongue: set forth by Claudius Holyband; Let the reader peruse the epistle to his owne instruction* (imprinted at London by Richard Field dwelling in the blacke-Friers, 1591), p. 14.

39. The most comprehensive reference work on Shakespeare's reading is Stuart Gillespie, *Shakespeare's Books: A Dictionary of Shakespeare's Sources* (Athlone, 2001), but the bibliography of the field is vast, and long has been, as witnessed by John W. Velz, *Shakespeare and the Classical Tradition: A Critical Guide to Commentary, 1660–1960* (University of Minnesota Press, 1968); and its sequel, John Lewis Walker, *Shakespeare and the Classical Tradition: An Annotated Bibliography 1961–1991* (Taylor and Francis, 2002). Yves Peyré's online *Dictionary of Shakespeare's Classical Mythology* (shakmyth.org) is an invaluable reference resource.

40. Though, to be fair to Plutarch, her lengthy oration is largely derived from him.

41. Among the many studies of Plutarch and the Roman plays, see M. W. MacCullum, *Shakespeare's Roman Plays and Their Background* (Russell and Russell, 1910); T. J. B. Spencer, *Shakespeare's Plutarch* (Penguin, 1964); Robert Miola, *Shakespeare's Rome* (Cambridge University Press, 1983); Geoffrey Miles, *Shakespeare and the Constant Romans* (Clarendon Press, 1996). The process of "feminization" is often overlooked in this context, though it is central to Coppélia Kahn's admirable *Roman Shakespeare: Warriors, Wounds and Women* (Routledge, 1997).

42. See my *Shakespeare and Ovid*; also *Shakespeare's Ovid: The Metamorphoses in the Plays and Poems*, ed. A. B. Taylor (Cambridge University Press, 2000); and *Shakespeare's Erotic Mythology and Ovidian Renaissance Culture*, ed. Agnès Lafont (Ashgate, 2016). For a more theoretically inflected treatment, see Lisa S. Starks-Estes, *Violence, Trauma and Virtus in Shakespeare's Roman Plays and Poems: Transforming Ovid* (Palgrave Macmillan, 2014).

43. Cicero, *Tusculan Disputations*, 1. 31, cited at the beginning of "That to philosophize is to learn how to die," book 1, chapter 19 of *The Essayes, or Morall, Politike, and Millitarie Discourses of Lo: Michaell de Montaigne ... Now done into English by ... John Florio* (1603).

44. This was the argument of "Shakespeare the Epicurean," the climactic chapter of my *Soul of the Age: A Biography of the Mind of William Shakespeare*, pp. 389–402; see further discussion in chapter 9. See also Tetsuo Anzai's excellent brief monograph *Shakespeare and Montaigne Reconsidered* (Renaissance Institute, Sophia University, Tokyo, 1986). More recently, Stephen Greenblatt has sketched a similar argument in "Shakespeare's Montaigne," his introduction to *Shakespeare's Montaigne: The Florio Translation of the Essays: A Selection* (NYRB Classics, 2014), pp. ix–xxxiii. For

other accounts of Shakespeare and Montaigne, see Robert Ellrodt, *Montaigne and Shakespeare: The Emergence of Modern Self-Consciousness* (Manchester University Press, 2015); and Peter Mack, *Reading and Rhetoric in Montaigne and Shakespeare* (Bloomsbury Academic, 2010).

45. Dedicatory poem in the Shakespeare First Folio. In his elegant and concise *Shakespeare and Classical Antiquity* (Oxford University Press, 2013), Colin Burrow points out the ambiguity of Jonson's "though": the line is usually interpreted as "despite the fact that you only had a smattering of Latin and less Greek," it could alternatively mean "even supposing (counterfactually) that you only had a smattering of Latin and less Greek, the major classical dramatists would still admire you" (p. 2).

46. Among the best, in addition to those cited in previous notes (I would recommend readers to begin with Burrow), are Barbara Bono, *Literary Transvaluation: From Vergilian Epic to Shakespearean Tragicomedy* (University of California Press, 1984); Gordon Braden, *Renaissance Tragedy and the Senecan Tradition: Anger's Privilege* (Yale University Press, 1985); Reuben Brower, *Hero and Saint: Shakespeare and the Graeco-Roman Heroic Tradition* (Oxford University Press, 1971); Paul Cantor, *Shakespeare's Rome: Republic and Empire* (Cornell University Press, 1983); Donna Hamilton, *Virgil and The Tempest: The Politics of Imitation* (Ohio State University Press, 1990); Heather James, *Shakespeare's Troy* (Cambridge University Press, 1997); *Shakespeare and the Classics*, ed. Charles Martindale and A. B. Taylor (Cambridge University Press, 2004); Robert Miola, *Shakespeare and Classical Comedy: The Influence of Plautus and Terence* (Oxford University Press, 1994) and *Shakespeare and Classical Tragedy: The Influence of Seneca* (Clarendon Press, 1992); Wolfgang Riehle, *Shakespeare, Plautus, and the Humanist Tradition* (D. S. Brewer, 1990). For the broader context in the period, begin with the superb compendium *The Oxford History of Classical Reception in English Literature Vol. 2: 1558–1660*, ed. Patrick Cheney and Philip Hardie (Oxford University Press, 2015).

47. James Shapiro, *Rival Playwrights: Marlowe, Jonson, Shakespeare* (Columbia University Press, 1991) remains the best starting point. For Horace and Jonson, begin with Victoria Moul, *Jonson, Horace and the Classical Tradition* (Cambridge University Press, 2010).

48. On neo-Stoicism, see Miles, *Shakespeare and the Constant Romans*, supplemented by Roland Mayer, "Personata Stoa: Neostoicism and Senecan Tragedy," *Journal of the Warburg and Courtauld Institutes*, 57 (1994), pp. 151–74. On Tacitism, see Peter Burke, "Tacitism, Scepticism and Reason of State," in *The Cambridge History of Political Thought 1450–1700*, ed. J. H. Burns (Cambridge University Press, 1991), pp. 479–98; and Mervyn James, "At a Crossroads of the Political Culture: The Essex Revolt, 1601," chap. 9 of his *Society, Politics and Culture: Studies in Early Modern England* (Cambridge

University Press, 1988). On Montaigne and Lucretius, Michael Screech's indispensable transcription of, and commentary on, *Montaigne's Annotated Copy of Lucretius* (Librairie Droz, 1998).

49. It was also the approach of my own *Shakespeare and Ovid*. Strong exemplars of a method that focuses as much on classical traditions as local links and echoes are Reuben Brower's *Hero and Saint* and Gordon Braden's *Renaissance Tragedy and the Senecan Tradition*, both cited above.

50. *Titus Andronicus*, 4.2.22–23, in response to a Latin quotation from Horace's ode "*Integer vitae*."

51. William Watson, *Decacordon: Ten Quodlibeticall Questions* (1602), p. 194; Robert Greene, "To his Gentlemanly Acquaintances," prefacing his *Groatsworth of Wit* (1592). Moth's "How canst thou part sadness and melancholy, my tender Juvenal?" in *Love's Labour's Lost* (1. 2. 8) certainly seems to be a play on "juvenile" and "Juvenal"—contextually apt, since at this point, as throughout the play, Moth is *satirizing* Don Armado's overelaborate language—and has been regarded by many commentators as an allusion to Nashe as Juvenal.

52. See further, my discussion of Iden and of the Horatianism of "Tottel's Miscellany" at the beginning of chapter 9.

53. Robert Greene, *Never too Late* (1590), p. 37.

54. Thomas Lodge, *Rosalynde: Euphues' Golden Legacie* (1590), f. 32ᵛ. The point being that the lovesickness is a pose intended to elicit the sympathy of the beloved: the lover's language of sorrow is learned from Ovid rather than felt in the heart.

55. On the basis of his name at the head of the second column of actors' names, opposite that of Burbage, who would have played Sejanus, and of the reference by John Davies of Hereford to Shakespeare playing "kingly parts" (*The Scourge of Folly*, 1610, epigram 159).

56. Ben Jonson, *Sejanus his Fall* (1605), ed. Philip J. Ayres (The Revels Plays, 1990), *Actus Secundus*, lines 303–16.

57. The flaw in the argument that Shakespeare played Tiberius is the tradition that he usually took smaller roles: there would be no more fitting part for him than Cremutius Cordus, "A gentleman of Rome; one that has writ / Annals of late, they say, and very well" (ibid., *Actus Primus*, lines 75–76).

58. On which, see my "Was Shakespeare an Essex Man?," *Proceedings of the British Academy*, 162, *2008 Lectures* (2009), pp. 1–28.

59. *A Midsummer Night's Dream*, 5. 1. 3. "Antique" is the Quarto spelling, "anticke" the Folio, the variant suggesting a pun.

60. Ibid., 5. 1. 7.

61. The key text in this respect was Richard Farmer's *Essay on the Learning of Shakespeare* (1767), which argued that Shakespeare's knowledge of

the classics was confined to translations, as witnessed by his incorporation of errors in the texts that he read.

62. *Shakespeare and the English Romantic Imagination* (Oxford University Press, 1986), *Shakespearean Constitutions: Politics, Theatre, Criticism 1730–1830* (Oxford University Press, 1989), and the second half of *The Genius of Shakespeare.*

63. Daniel Smith, "It's Still 'The Age of Anxiety.' Or Is It?," *New York Times*, January 14, 2012, http://opinionator.blogs.nytimes.com/2012/01/14 /its-still-the-age-of-anxiety-or-is-it/?_r=0.

64. And Gustav Gröber (1844–1911), a pioneer of the study of romance philology, who supervised Curtius's *Habilitationsschrift.*

65. See E. H. Gombrich, *Aby Warburg: An Intellectual Biography, with a Memoir on the History of the Library by Fritz Saxl* (Warburg Institute, 1970; rev. ed., Phaidon, 1986). Further, on the history of the Library: "The Warburg Institute: A Special Issue on the Library and Its Readers," *Common Knowledge*, 18.1 (Winter 2012). With regard to Jewishness: the Gombrich family had originally been Jewish, but converted to Lutheranism at the turn of the twentieth century. Ernst Gombrich himself never claimed any religious faith, but his profoundest intellectual and spiritual affiliation was with the Warburg Library and its Jewish origins.

66. Ernst Robert Curtius, *European Literature and the Latin Middle Ages*, trans. Willard Trask (Routledge and Kegan Paul, 1953), p. 15. In the age of digital reproduction, the argument about the "presentness" of, say, a Titian painting is more complicated than it was for Curtius. And of course the very work of the Warburg school demonstrated the "presence of the past" in paintings such as those of Titian through the analysis of allusion, *imitatio*, "set formulas," "narrative motifs," and a "wealth of figures."

67. Ibid., p. 397.

68. Ibid., p. 13.

69. Ibid., p. viii. On Curtius in his historical moment, see Colin Burrow's excellent introduction to the 2013 Princeton Univerity Press reprint, and, more fully, Arthur R. Evans, Jr., *On Four Modern Humanists: Hofmannsthal, Gundolph, Curtius, Kantorowicz* (Princeton University Press, 1970), pp. 85–145. Curtius described his research as his "intellectual alibi" during the years when he was under Nazi surveillance as a result of the critique of Hitler's cultural politics that he had published in 1932: on his decision not to leave Germany, see Jason Harding, *The Criterion: Cultural Politics and Periodical Networks in Inter-War Britain* (Oxford University Press, 2002), pp. 212–22.

70. Curtius, *European Literature and the Latin Middle Ages*, p. 437.

71. See, for an example, my discussion in chapter 11 of the transmission of the Greek term *hereos*.

CHAPTER 2: O'ER-PICTURING VENUS

1. Thomas Rogers, *Celestial Elegies of the Goddesses and the Muses* (1598), sig. B5ᵛ.

2. Poems 4, 6, 9, and 11 (the last of these was also printed in Bartholomew Griffin's *Fidessa*, 1596). On attribution, see Ward Elliott and Robert J. Valenza, "A Touchstone for the Bard," *Computers and the Humanities*, 25 (1991), pp. 199–209; and especially the analysis in Francis X. Connor, "Potential Shakespeare: Poetic Apocrypha and Methods of Modern Attribution," in Taylor and Egan, *The New Oxford Shakespeare*, pp. 113–18.

3. *The Passionate Pilgrim*, poem 4, in Shakespeare, *Sonnets and Other Poems*, ed. Jonathan Bate and Eric Rasmussen (Modern Library, 2009). Some editors emend "ears" to "ear" for the sake of the rhyme.

4. *Venus and Adonis*, lines 41–42. The metaphor of a woman "governing" a man is of a piece with the reversal of traditional gender roles throughout the poem, beginning from the simile in the first stanza of Venus as "a bold-faced suitor" (line 6).

5. *The Passionate Pilgrim*, poem 6.

6. "A never writer to an ever reader" in some copies of the 1609 quarto of *Troilus and Cressida* (*Complete Works*, p. 1534, spelling modernized).

7. *Antony and Cleopatra*, 2. 2. 229–37.

8. Plutarch, *The Lives of the Noble Grecians and Romanes*, trans. Thomas North (1579; repr., Nonesuch Press, 1930), 4. 310.

9. See E. H. Gombrich's remarkable *The Heritage of Apelles: Studies in the Art of the Renaissance* (Phaidon, 1976), usefully summarized in the blurb to its reprint as *Gombrich on the Renaissance*, vol. 3 (Phaidon, 1994): "The third volume of E H Gombrich's seminal essays on the Renaissance has the classical tradition as its central theme. Apelles, the most famous painter of ancient Greece, was said to have combined perfect beauty with supreme skill in imitating the appearances of nature. These twin ideals of perfect beauty and perfect imitation of nature, which were inherited from classical antiquity and remained unchallenged as the cornerstone of art until the twentieth century, form the starting-point for these learned and always stimulating essays."

10. Pliny the Elder, *Naturalis Historia*, 35. 36.

11. On the attribution of this, see V&A, "Venus Anadyomene," last updated 15 September 2018, http://collections.vam.ac.uk/item/O93893/venus-anadyomene-relief-lombardo-antonio/.

12. Hanna Scolnicov argues for an actual reminiscence of Pliny on Apelles, noting that "Shakespeare preserves the connection between the goddess and the water": "Both Goddess and Woman: Cleopatra and Venus," in *Shakespeare and the Visual Arts: The Italian Influence*, ed. Michele Marrapodi (Routledge, 2017), pp. 93–107.

13. *Ars Amatoria*, 3. 244, referring to a jewel incised with the image of Venus Anadyomene.

14. For this particular case, see Edgar Wind, "The Birth of Venus," chap. 8 in his *Pagan Mysteries in the Renaissance* (Faber and Faber, 1958).

15. Ibid., p. 382. On Curtius and Warburg, see further, "Curtius and the Library," pp. 65–69 of Christopher D. Johnson, *Memory, Metaphor, and Aby Warburg's Atlas of Images* (Cornell University Press, 2012). The phrase "God is in the details" is usually attributed to the architect Mies van der Rohe, who presumably derived it (with slightly adapted wording) from Warburg, probably via Curtius.

16. Anthony Grafton, "Signs of Spring," a review of Charles Dempsey, *The Portrayal of Love: Botticelli's 'Primavera' and Humanist Culture at the Time of Lorenzo the Magnificent* (Princeton University Press, 1992), *London Review of Books*, 10 June 1993, pp. 30–31.

17. Ibid.

18. Leonard Barkan, *Transuming Passion: Ganymede and the Erotics of Humanism* (Stanford University Press, 1991), p. 6.

19. Ovid, *Amores*, 1. 14, 31–34: "Formosae periere comae—quas vellet Apollo, / quas vellet capiti Bacchus inesse suo! / illis contulerim, quas quondam nuda Dione / pingitur umenti sustinuisse manu."

20. See Nicholas Penny's definitive discussion of the series in his *The Sixteenth Century Italian Paintings*, vol. 2, *Venice 1540–1600* (National Gallery Catalogues, 2008), pp. 274–86. For the dissemination of Titian's *Venus and Adonis* via engravings, see also Jonathan Bate and Dora Thornton, *Shakespeare: Staging the World* (British Museum and Oxford University Press, 2012), pp. 126–29. My knowledge of this whole subject owes much to Dora Thornton.

21. Vasari, *Lives of the Artists*, trans. George Bull (Penguin Classics, 1965), p. 36.

22. On the ancient rivalry between Christianity and classical mythology, begin with Jean Seznec's Warburgian study *The Survival of the Pagan Gods: The Mythological Tradition and Its Place in Renaissance Humanism and Art* (1953; repr., Princeton University Press, 1972): "the same conflict had existed since the first centuries of Christianity.... Nurtured upon ancient letters, the most scrupulous among [the early churchmen] cannot rid themselves of their classical memories and ways of thinking; as humanists, they continue to love what they condemn, or should condemn, as theologians. One need but recall, in this connection, St Augustine or St Jerome and their inner conflicts. Their minds are haunted by the profane poetry which they ought to denounce" (pp. 265–66). For the particular English Reformation inflection, see Marguerite A. Tassi, *The Scandal of Images: Iconoclasm, Eroticism, and Painting in Early Modern English Drama* (Susqehanna University Press, 2005), especially chap. 1; and, for the idea of visual representation as

"idolatrous," see Michael O'Connell's stimulating *The Idolatrous Eye: Iconoclasm and Theater in Early Modern England* (Oxford University Press, 2000).

23. The best synoptic account of the richness of representations of the pagan gods (and the pervasiveness of the erotic) in the visual culture of the Renaissance is Malcolm Bull, *The Mirror of the Gods: Classical Mythology in the Renaissance* (Allen Lane, 2005), though there are also fascinating thoughts on *eros* (beginning from the rape of Europa) in Roberto Calasso's highly distinctive *The Marriage of Cadmus and Harmony*, trans. Tim Parks (Jonathan Cape, 1993). The starting point on the literary side should undoubtedly be Leonard Barkan's magnificent *The Gods Made Flesh: Metamorphosis and the Pursuit of Paganism* (Yale University Press, 1986).

24. *The Merry Wives of Windsor*, 5. 5. 4, 2.

25. *A Midsummer Night's Dream*, 2. 1. 235; *The Second Part of Henry the Fourth*, 2. 2. 122–23; *Othello*, 2. 3. 15–16.

26. Sir Philip Sidney, *An Apology for Poetry*, ed. Geoffrey Shepherd (Manchester University Press, 1973), p. 138. Plutarch noted that Aristotle praised Homer for creating words of such vigour (*energeia*) that they created movement (*Moralia*, 398A), while Quintilian applied the term to the poetic art of vivid, energetic expression (*Institutio Oratoria*, VIII. 3. 89). See further, David Bradshaw, *Aristotle East and West: Metaphysics and the Division of Christendom* (Cambridge University Press, 2004), p. 54; and Wendy Olmsted, *The Imperfect Friend: Emotion and Rhetoric in Sidney, Milton, and Their Contexts* (University of Toronto Press, 2008), p. 67.

27. Quintilian, *Institutio Oratoria*, 6. 2. 32.

28. Ibid., 10. 1. 16. See further, Heinrich F. Plett, *Enargeia in Classical Antiquity and the Early Modern Age: The Aesthetics of Evidence* (Brill, 2012).

29. See further, Walter Bernhart, "Functions of Description in Poetry," in *Description in Literature and Other Media*, ed. Werner Wolf and Walter Bernhard (Rodopi, 2007), p. 134.

30. Joseph Campana, *The Pain of Reformation: Spenser, Vulnerability, and the Ethics of Masculinity* (Fordham University Press, 2012), p. 111.

31. Ovid, *Metamorphoses*, 2. 875.

32. *The xv Bookes of P. Ovidius Naso, entytuled Metamorphosis, translated oute of Latin into English meeter, by Arthur Golding Gentleman, A worke very pleasaunt and delectable* (1567), 2. 1096. Golding is quoted here, and subsequently, from Madeleine Forey's splendid modern-spelling edition: Ovid, *Metamorphoses*, trans. Arthur Golding (Penguin Classics, 2002).

33. Rachel Eisendrath, *Poetry in a World of Things: Aesthetics and Empiricism in Renaissance Ekphrasis* (University of Chicago Press, 2018) is a valuable recent study.

34. *The Taming of the Shrew*, Induction scene 2. 43–47.

35. Ibid., 48–50.

36. In *Campaspe*, the painter Apelles shows his model, Alexander's concubine, the works in his studio:

> CAMPASPE. What are these pictures?
> APELLES. This is Læda, whom Jove deceived in likenesse of a Swan.
> CAMPASPE. A faire woman, but a foule deceit.
> APELLES. This is Alcmena, unto whom Jupiter came in shape of Amphitrion her husband, and begate Hercules.
> CAMPASPE. A famous sonne, but an infamous fact.
> APELLES. Hee might doe it, because hee was a God.
> CAMPASPE. Nay, therefore it was evill done, because he was a God.
> APELLES. This is Danae, into whose prison Jupiter drizled a golden showre, and obtained his desire.
> CAMPASPE. What gold can make one yeeld to desire?
> APELLES. This is Europa, whom Jupiter ravished, this Antiopa.
> CAMPASPE. Were all the Gods like this Jupiter?
> APELLES. There were many Gods in this like Jupiter.
> CAMPASPE. I thinke in those dayes love was well ratified among men on earth, when lust was so full authorised by the Gods in Heaven.
> APELLES. Nay, you may imagine there were women passing amiable, when there were Gods exceeding amorous.
> CAMPASPE. Were women never so faire, men would be false.
> APELLES. Were women never so false, men would be fond.
> CAMPASPE. What counterfeit is this Apel[l]es?
> APELLES. This is Venus the Goddesse of love.
> CAMPASPE. What, bee there also loving Goddesses?
> APELLES. This is shee that hath power to command the very affections of the heart.
>
> John Lyly, *Campaspe*, 3. 3. 9–33, in *The Complete Works of John Lyly*, ed. R. Warwick Bond (Clarendon Press, 1902), vol. 2.

37. *Much Ado about Nothing*, 3. 3. 95–96.

38. On the availability of the visual arts in Elizabethan England, begin with Stuart Sillars's admirable *Shakespeare and the Visual Imagination* (Cambridge University Press, 2015). Further, Elizabeth Goldring's splendid *Robert Dudley, Earl of Leicester, and the World of Elizabethan Art: Painting and Patronage at the Court of Elizabeth I* (New Haven and London: Yale University Press / The Paul Mellon Centre for Studies in British Art, 2014) provides strong evidence refuting the old idea that it was only in the reign of Charles I that English collectors began importing Italian mythological paintings. And for the prevalence of Ovidian mythological scenes on tapestries and wall hangings, see Thomas Campbell's definitive *Tapestry in the*

Renaissance: Art and Magnificence (Metropolitan Museum of Art, 2002) and its sequel *Tapestry in the Baroque: Threads of Splendor* (Metropolitan Museum of Art, 2007).

39. See, for example, Richard Paul Roe's fanciful and error-strewn *The Shakespeare Guide to Italy: Retracing the Bard's Unknown Travels* (Harper, 2011). Engraving and reputation might, nevertheless, have given Shakespeare a sense of Romano's gloriously Ovidian decoration of the Palazzo Te, which was the subject of E. H. Gombrich's 1933 doctoral dissertation; see in particular his "Zum Werke Giulio Romanos: 1. Der Palazzo del Te," *Jahrbuch der Kunsthistorischen Sammlungen in Wien*, new series, 8 (1934), pp. 79–104. For a more speculative and Mantuan-focused account of Shakespeare and Romano, see Rita Severi, "Art in Shakespeare: Giulio Romano and Giovan Paolo Lomazzo" and "'This Most Sweet Paradise': Shakespeare and Mantua," chaps. 1 and 2 in *Art in Shakespeare and Other Essays* (Pàtron Editore, 2018).

40. Keir Elam notes this fact in his excellent *Shakespeare's Pictures: Visual Objects in the Drama* (Bloomsbury, 2017): see his discussion at pp. 129–40.

41. *Cymbeline*, 5. 4. 191–92; *Antony and Cleopatra*, 5. 2. 261; *The Winter's Tale*, 5. 3. 27.

42. *The Two Gentlemen of Verona*, 4. 4. 153–55.

43. *The Winter's Tale*, 5. 3. 22, 79.

44. *The Merchant of Venice*, 3. 2. 118–26.

45. For a survey of the evidence regarding this attribution, see Will Sharpe, "Authorship and Attribution: *The Spanish Tragedy* (c. 1587, revised c. 1597–98?)," in *William Shakespeare and Others: Collaborative Plays*, ed. Jonathan Bate, Eric Rasmussen, Jan Sewell, and Will Sharpe (Palgrave Macmillan, 2013), pp. 671–80.

46. For a fine meditation on the history of the rivalry between poets and painters, see Leonard Barkan, *Mute Poetry, Speaking Pictures* (Princeton University Press, 2013).

47. *The Spanish Tragedy* (1602 Quarto), 3. 13. 115–16, in *Collaborative Plays*.

48. *The Rape of Lucrece*, 400—a musical image as well as a visual one. See Lynn Enterline, *The Rhetoric of the Body from Ovid to Shakespeare* (Cambridge University Press, 2000), p. 191. Enterline's book is an especially notable treatment of the gendered aspect of Ovidian influence.

49. *Venus and Adonis*, 314–15. A painter could represent the "shadow" but not the "melting." "Look when a painter would surpass the life / In limning out a well-proportioned steed," Shakespeare has written a couple of stanzas earlier (289–90), but here he is surpassing the painter.

50. Ibid., 145–50.

51. Percy Shelley, "A Defence of Poetry," in *Shelley's Poetry and Prose*, ed. Donald Reiman and Sharon Powers (Norton, 1977), p. 504.

52. Justus Lipsius, *Sixe bookes of politickes or ciuil doctrine, written in Latine by Justus Lipsius: which doe especially concerne principalitie; Done into English by William Jones Gentleman* (1594), bk. 1, chap. 2. I am grateful to one of my anonymous Press readers for this quotation.

CHAPTER 3: RESEMBLANCE BY EXAMPLE

1. On Shakespeare and rhetoric, see especially Peter Mack, *Elizabethan Rhetoric* (Bloomsbury, 2002); and Marion Trousdale, *Shakespeare and the Rhetoricians* (University of North Carolina Press, 1984); though Sr Miriam Joseph's *Shakespeare's Use of the Arts of Language* (1947; repr., Paul Dry Books, 2008) remains valuable seventy years on. For rhetoric in relation to Renaissance literary style more generally (and Shakespeare's Ovidian poems and sonnets in particular), see Richard A. Lanham's superb study *The Motives of Eloquence: Literay Rhetoric in the Renaissance* (Yale University Press, 1976). On more specific aspects, see Raphael Lyne, *Shakespeare, Rhetoric and Cognition* (Cambridge University Press, 2011); Jenny C. Mann, *Outlaw Rhetoric: Figuring Vernacular Eloquence in Shakespeare's England* (Cornell University Press, 2012); Patricia Parker's dazzling *Shakespeare from the Margins: Language, Culture, Context* (University of Chicago Press, 1996); and Quentin Skinner's revelatory *Forensic Shakespeare* (Oxford University Press, 2014), which corrects the overemphasis of previous scholarship on Shakespeare's *elocutio* (tropes and figures of speech) at the expense of his *inventio* and *dispositio*, and in particular examines his adaptation for dramatic purposes of the techniques of *constitutio iuridicalis* (forensic rhetoric), the development of a persuasive judicial case, either in accusation or defence, notably in *The Merchant of Venice, Hamlet, All's Well that Ends Well,* and *Measure for Measure*. My argument regarding deliberative rhetoric is not intended to contest Skinner's position, but it does seem to me that whereas forensic rhetoric is indeed a key influence on many of the big set speeches and arguments in middle-period Shakespeare, deliberative rhetoric is all-pervasive as his essential compositional technique.

2. *As You Like It*, 5. 1. 32–34; *Hamlet*, 2. 2. 103–4 (Q2 variant); *The First Part of Henry the Fourth*, 1. 3. 212–13; *Love's Labour's Lost*, 4. 2. 53–56.

3. *Love's Labour's Lost*, 5. 2. 424–25, 428–32.

4. Ibid., 4. 1. 63–73 (Q1 variants).

5. Thomas Wilson, *The Art of Rhetoric* (1560), pp. 1–2.

6. Joel Altman's *The Tudor Play of Mind: Rhetorical Inquiry and the Development of Elizabethan Drama* (University of California Press, 1978)

remains the exemplary study of the ways in which early modern drama relies on the rhetorician's ability to argue *in utramque partem*.

7. The bibliography is vast: Brian Vickers, *In Defence of Rhetoric* (Clarendon Press, 1988) is an admirable starting point; Curtius, *European Literature and the Latin Middle Ages*, discussed in my opening chapter, remains exemplary, especially chap. 4 ("Rhetoric") and chap. 8 ("Poetry and Rhetoric").

8. *Hamlet*, 3. 1. 62. William James's lecture "Is Life Worth Living?" was addressed to the Harvard YMCA in 1895. Beginning with a Shakespearean quotation and steeped throughout in literary allusion, it was published in the *International Journal of Ethics* and reprinted in James's *The Will to Believe and other Essays in Popular Philosophy* (Longmans, 1897), pp. 32–62.

9. Paraphrase and quotations in this paragraph are from Thomas Wilson, *The Art of Rhetoric*, pp. 1–3.

10. Aristotle, *Rhetoric*, 1356^a, trans. W. Rhys Roberts, in *The Complete Works of Aristotle: The Revised Oxford Translation*, ed. Jonathan Barnes (Princeton University Press, 1984), p. 2156.

11. Ibid., 1358^b et seq., pp. 2159ff.

12. Ibid., 1368^a, p. 2178.

13. Ibid., 1393^a, pp. 2219–20.

14. Bk. 3, chap. 19, in George Puttenham, *The Arte of English Poesie* (1589), ed. G. D. Willcock and Alice Walker (Cambridge University Press, 1936), pp. 245–46.

15. *Henry V*, 4. 7. 22–23.

16. Ibid., 4. 7. 21–22.

17. Puttenham, *Arte of English Poesie*, p. 240. *Paradigma* is in fact Puttenham's penultimate figure in his "Of Ornament": he caps it with "the last and principal figure," namely "*Exargasia*, or The Gorgious," a term "transferred from these polishers of marble or porphirite, who after it is rough hewn and reduced to that fashion they will, do set upon it a goodly glass, so smooth and clear as ye may see your face in it": "So doth this figure (which therefore I call the *Gorgious*) polish our speech and as it were attire it with copious and pleasant amplifications" (p. 247). But in this sense, gorgeousness is not a particular figure: it is the process of polishing, the final coat of varnish.

18. Linda Bensel-Meyers does indeed say this in "Empowering the Audience: The Rhetorical Poetics of Renaissance Drama," *Style*, 23 (1989), pp. 70–86. Brian Vickers, by contrast, sees epideictic rhetoric as the principal driver: "all literature became subsumed under epideictic, and all writing was perceived as occupying the related spheres of praise and blame" (*In Defence of Rhetoric*, p. 54). Victoria Kahn, albeit focusing more on reading than theatrical spectatorship, argues that the key is a blending of deliberative and forensic rhetoric: "the written text now takes on the functions of

deliberative and judicial rhetoric" (*Rhetoric, Prudence, and Skepticism in the Renaissance* [Cornell University Press, 1985], p. 38). The theatre was at once an arena of praise/blame, of quasi-legal judgment, and of political/ public debate, so all three kinds of rhetoric were deployed, but I endorse Peter G. Platt, who writes, "I would propose the theaters as another location of Renaissance deliberative rhetoric: a place where audiences could hear and deliberate on dialogues and debates staged almost daily, and where they heard speeches in a form and forum very close to those of their ancient forebears" ("Shakespeare and Rhetorical Culture," in *A Companion to Shakespeare*, ed. David Scott Kastan [Blackwell, 1999], http://www2.idehist.uu.se /distans/ilmh/Ren/platt.htm). My particular emphasis is the centrality of "resemblance by example" and the comparison of "the past with the present," techniques which the theorists especially associated with the deliberative mode.

19. Christopher Marlowe, *The Troublesome Reign and Lamentable Death of Edward the Second* (1593), 1. 4. 391–97.

20. *Hamlet*, 1. 1. 54–56.

21. Ibid., 1. 1. 94.

22. Ibid., 1. 1. 163.

23. Robert Burton, *Anatomy of Melancholy* (1621), Third Partition, "Love and Love Melancholy," especially Memb. 3, "Symptoms or signs"; see further discussion in chapter 11.

24. *Hamlet*, 2. 2. 294–97.

25. Ibid., 1. 2. 83–85. Starting points for the much-discussed subject of Hamlet's "interiority" might be Katharine Eisaman Maus's excellent *Inwardness and the Theater in the English Renaissance* (University of Chicago Press, 1995), and, by way of contrast, Rhodri Lewis's provocative *Hamlet and the Vision of Darkness* (Princeton University Press, 2017).

26. *Hamlet*, 1. 2. 139–40.

27. Ibid., 1. 2. 149. Cf. Ovid, *Metamorphoses*, trans. Golding, 6. 394–95: "There upon a mountain's top / She weepeth still in stone; from stone the dreary tears do drop." I suspect that Shakespeare was deeply affected by Ovid's story of Niobe: though his only explicit citations of her are here and in *Troilus and Cressida* ("Hector's dead" as a word that "will Priam turn to stone; / Make wells and Niobes of the maids and wives," 5. 11. 19–20), the conjunction of tears and stone is powerfully rendered in Lear's grief ("Howl … you are men of stones," 5. 3. 264). Furthermore, when her children are all being slaughtered, her plea that just one might be saved ("O, leave me one! This little one yet save! / Of many but this only one, the least of all, I crave!" [Ovid, *Metamorphoses*, trans. Golding, 6. 379–80]) is, so to speak, a proleptic yoking of the killing of Lady Macduff's children and the reduction of Lear's train to "what need one?" (in his daughter Regan's savage riposte at 2. 2. 452).

28. *Hamlet*, 1. 2. 52–53. For further discussion of the example of Hercules, see chapter 12.

29. Thomas Cooper, *Thesaurus Linguae Romanae et Britannicae* (1584), s.v. "Hercules."

30. *Hamlet*, 1. 5. 100–108.

31. Ibid., 1. 3. 61–83 (78, 81).

32. Ibid., 1. 5. 96. See further, the nuanced chapter "'Remember Me!': Horestes, Hieronimo, and Hamlet," in John Kerrigan, *Revenge Tragedy: Aeschylus to Armageddon* (Clarendon Press, 1997), chap. 7.

33. *Hamlet*, 3. 2. 336–39.

34. *Macbeth*, 1. 7. 58–63.

35. "To the Gentlemen Students of both Universities," preface by Thomas Nashe to Robert Greene's *Menaphon (1589)*, in *The Works of Thomas Nashe*, ed. R. B. McKerrow (1958; repr., Blackwell, 1966), 3. 315.

36. Seneca, *Medea*, trans. John Studley, in *Seneca his tenne tragedies, translated into Englysh* (1581), act 4.

37. See further, Inga-Stina Ewbank, "The Fiend-like Queen: A Note on *Macbeth* and Seneca's *Medea*," *Shakespeare Survey*, 19 (1966), pp. 82–94; and Yves Peyré, "'Confusion Now Hath Made His Masterpiece': Senecan Resonances in *Macbeth*," in Martindale and Taylor, *Shakespeare and the Classics*, pp. 141–55.

38. *Hamlet*, 5. 2. 70.

39. The definitive essay on "voices" in *Coriolanus* is D. J. Gordon's "Name and Fame: Shakespeare's *Coriolanus*," originally published in 1962 and reprinted in one of the great Warburgian works, *The Renaissance Imagination: Essays and Lectures by D. J. Gordon*, ed. Stephen Orgel (University of California Press, 1975), pp. 203–19.

CHAPTER 4: *REPUBLICA ANGLORUM*

1. For Smith's treatise as a defence of the "mixed monarchy" inaugurated with Elizabeth's accession, see Anne McLaren, "Reading Sir Thomas Smith's *De Republica Anglorum* as Protestant Apologetic," *The Historical Journal*, 42 (1999), pp. 911–39.

2. Patrick Collinson, *De Republica Anglorum: Or, History with the Politics Put Back* (Inaugural Lecture, Cambridge University, 1990). For a thoughtful set of responses to Collinson's parallel argument that Elizabethan England is best understood as a "monarchical republic," see *The Monarchical Republic of Early Modern England: Essays in Response to Patrick Collinson*, ed. John F. McDiarmid (Ashgate, 2007).

3. There are numerous early allusions to *Venus and Adonis* by university readers, of which that in the Cambridge *Parnassus Plays* is only the

most celebrated; see further, Katherine Duncan-Jones, "Much Ado with Red and White: The Earliest Readers of Shakespeare's *Venus and Adonis* (1593)," *Review of English Studies*, 44 (1993), pp. 479–501, and, more generally, her *Shakespeare: Upstart Crow to Sweet Swan 1592–1623* (Bloomsbury, 2011). Also see Jean-Christophe Meyer, *Shakespeare's Early Readers* (Cambridge University Press, 2018). For *Titus* privately performed at a country residence in Rutland, see Gustav Ungerer, "An Unrecorded Elizabethan Performance of *Titus Andronicus*," *Shakespeare Survey*, 14 (1961), pp. 102–9. The *Comedy of Errors* was played as part of the Gray's Inn Christmas festivities, 28 December 1594. Nashe's reference in *Piers Penniless his Supplication to the Devil* (1592) may well have been to a pre-Shakespearean version of "Harry the Sixth."

4. Richard Helgerson's *Forms of Nationhood: The Elizabethan Writing of England* (University of Chicago Press, 1992) remains the best study of the role of imaginative writing in the creation of a sense of English national identity during the age of Shakespeare. For the role of drama in the process, see especially Ralf Hertel, *Staging England in the Elizabethan History Play: Performing National Identity* (Routledge, 2016); and Clare McEachern, *The Poetics of English Nationhood 1590–1612* (Cambridge University Press, 1996)—and indeed the long tradition of work on Shakespeare and "the Tudor myth" that is exemplified by Lily B. Campbell, *Shakespeare's Histories: Mirrors of Elizabethan Policy* (Huntington Library, 1947); and E. M. W. Tillyard, *Shakespeare's History Plays* (1946; repr., Penguin, 1991).

5. See my *Shakespeare and Ovid*, pp. 30–31, 48–49.

6. In contrast to Polydore Vergil's pre-Reformation *Anglica Historia* (drafted by 1513, printed 1534).

7. See the monumental *The Oxford Handbook of Holinshed's Chronicles*, ed. Paulina Kewes, Ian W. Archer, and Felicity Heal (Oxford University Press, 2012); also Annabel Patterson, *Reading Holinshed's Chronicles* (University of Chicago Press, 1994).

8. *1 Henry VI*, 3. 3. 81.

9. End of address to the reader ("Lectori"), which makes much of the word "patria," in William Camden, *Annales rerum Anglicarum, et Hibernicarum, regnante Elizabetha, ad annum salutis M.D.LXXXIX. Guilielmo Camdeno authore*, A5ᵛ.

10. Though historians contest Geoffrey Elton's proposition that Thomas Cromwell almost single-handedly effected a "Tudor revolution in government" during the 1530s, there is no doubting the underlying thesis that the sixteenth century witnessed a transformation from a model of government based on royal and aristocratic households to one based on a state bureaucracy and a multilayered legal system, and that this process is best described as "nation building." See, for example, *Revolution Reassessed: Revisions in the*

History of Tudor Government and Administration, ed. Christopher Coleman and David Starkey (Oxford University Press, 1986).

11. See Eamon Duffy's much-admired *The Stripping of the Altars: Traditional Religion in England, 1400–1580* (Yale University Press, 1992).

12. Quintilian, *Institutio Oratoria*, 10. 1. 19–20, in H. E. Butler's translation (Loeb, 1920–22).

13. Ibid., 10. 1. 27, alluding to Cicero's defence of the poet, *Pro Archia Poetia*, 12.

14. Ibid., 10. 1. 93 (my translation).

15. Ibid., 10. 1. 46–104.

16. Sidney, *Apology*, ed. Shepherd, p. 103; Francis Meres denominates the same eight genres in his *Palladis Tamia* (1598), which I discuss below (cited from *Elizabethan Critical Essays*, ed. G. Gregory Smith [Oxford University Press, 1904], 2. 319). Meres read Sidney's work after it was published, in two different editions, in 1595—he cites (Smith, *Elizabethan Critical Essays*, 2. 314) the edition by Henry Olney called *An Apologie for Poetrie* as opposed to the one by William Ponsonby called *The Defence of Poesie*.

17. As Shepherd points out in his edition of Sidney's *Apology* (pp. 163–64), there are also more extensive and varied lists of genres, notably in Scaliger's *Poetices*. For medieval genre theory, deriving principally from Diomedes and Donatus, see Curtius, *European Literature and the Latin Middle Ages*, pp. 440–43. See further, Madeleine Doran's enduring study, *Endeavors of Art: A Study of Form in Elizabethan Drama* (University of Wisconsin Press, 1964); and Daniel Javitch, "The Emergence of Poetic Genre Theory in the Sixteenth Century," *Modern Language Quarterly*, 59 (1998), pp. 139–69.

18. Quintilian acknowledged the "pastoral" genre, but omitted it from his list of models for the rhetorician because "Theocritus is admirable in his own way, but the rustic and pastoral muse shrinks not merely from the forum, but from town-life of every kind" (*Institutio Oratoria*, 10. 1. 55)—in other words, it is the genre of retreat from political engagement and legal debate, which are the principal domains of the public speaker. The "iambic" genre (exemplified by Archilochus) was excluded on the grounds that it "has not been popular with Roman poets as a separate form of composition, but is found mixed up with other forms of verse" (*Institutio Oratoria*, 10. 1. 96). Quintilian was thinking of Horace's mingling of the forms of iamb and epode. See further, my discussion in chapter 5 of "elegy" as both verse form and subject matter.

19. Puttenham, *Arte of English Poesie*, pp. 25–26, spelling modernized.

20. William Webbe, *A Discourse of English Poetrie* (1586), in Smith, *Elizabethan Critical Essays*, 1. 226–302 (p. 227). My modernization of spelling.

21. Ibid.

22. Ibid., 1. 239.

23. Ibid., 1. 243.

24. Ibid., 1. 255.

25. Ibid., 1. 249, spelling modernized.

26. Francis Meres, "A Comparative Discourse of our English Poets, with the Greek, Latin, and Italian Poets," part of his *Palladis Tamia, Wits Treasury* (1598), repr. in Smith, *Elizabethan Critical Essays*, 2. 308–24 (p. 318).

27. Ibid., 2. 315.

28. See Don Cameron Allen, *Francis Meres's Treatise "Poetrie": A Critical Edition* (University of Illinois Press, 1933). For Meres's method of copying and adapting preexisting sources throughout his work, see Jason Scott-Warren's splendid article, "Commonplacing and Originality: Reading Francis Meres," *Review of English Studies*, 68 (2017), pp. 902–23, which includes new research based on an examination of his books.

29. Meres, *Palladis Tamia*, in Smith, *Elizabethan Critical Essays*, 2. 315–17. Honterus was a sixteenth-century neo-Latin author.

30. Ibid., 2. 317–18.

31. On the *Sonnets* and the *Amores*, via Marlowe, see M. L. Stapleton, *Harmful Eloquence: Ovid's "Amores" from Antiquity to Shakespeare* (University of Michigan Press, 1996), though, curiously, his analysis confines itself to the "dark lady" sequence.

32. Richard Barnfield, "Poems: in divers Humors," in his *The Encomion of Lady Pecunia: or the Praise of Money* (1598), sig. E2^v.

33. On the history of bee versus ape from antiquity onwards, see G. W. Pigman III, "The Metaphorics of *Imitatio* and *Aemulatio*," Humanities Working Paper 18 (California Institute of Technology, 1979), http://authors .library.caltech.edu/14562/1/HumsWP-0018.pdf.

34. Muriel Bradbrook, "Beasts and Gods: *Greene's Groats-Worth of Witte* and the Social Purpose of *Venus and Adonis*," *Shakespeare Survey*, 15 (1962), pp. 62–72.

35. Sir Brian Vickers categorically thinks not, focusing his reading on the Aesopian origin of the image: "'Upstart Crow'? The Myth of Shakespeare's Plagiarism," *The Review of English Studies*, 68 (2017), pp. 244–67. I remain more persuaded by J. Dover Wilson, "Malone and the Upstart Crow," *Shakespeare Survey*, 4 (1951), pp. 56–68, as does John Kerrigan in chapter 1 ("Upstarts and Much Ado") of his recent and very nimble book on *Shakespeare's Originality* (Oxford University Press, 2018). Kerrigan persuasively notes "That the accusation stuck (and was linked to collaboration) is suggested by Leonard Digges' insistence that Shakespeare did not 'Plagiari-like from others gleane, / Nor begges he from each witty friend a Scene / To peece his Acts with' (dedicatory poem in *Poems: Written by Wil. Shake-speare* (1640), sig. *3^r)" (p. 115). If Greene was not accusing Shakespeare of plagiarism, or taking credit for scenes written by other dramatists

(such as himself), then someone else must have done, otherwise why would Digges leap to his fellow-Stratfordian's defence?

36. Horace, *Epistles*, 1. 3. 9–20.

37. Robert Greene, dedication to *Mirror of Modesty* (1584), cited in Dover Wilson, "Malone and the Upstart Crow," p. 67.

38. On *imitatio* as a way of understanding Shakespeare's habits of composition, see my *Shakespeare and Ovid*, passim; also Vernon Guy Dickson, *Emulation on the Shakespearean Stage* (Ashgate, 2013), and, for a specific example of the process in action, Barbara A. Mowat, " 'I tell you what mine Authors saye': *Pericles*, Shakespeare, and *Imitatio*," *Archiv für das Studium der Neueren Sprachen und Literaturen*, 240 (2003), pp. 42–59. The best general account of this key compositional practice remains Thomas M. Greene's magisterial *The Light in Troy: Imitation and Discovery in Renaissance Poetry* (Yale University Press, 1982). On the late eighteenth-century shift, begin with W. Jackson Bate's classic *The Burden of the Past and the English Poet* (Chatto & Windus, 1971) and perhaps proceed to my *Shakespeare and the English Romantic Imagination* and Robert Macfarlane's *Original Copy: Plagiarism and Originality in Nineteenth-Century Literature* (Oxford University Press, 2007). For changing attitudes to plagiarism, Robert Harold Ogden White's *Plagiarism and Imitation during the English Renaissance: A Study in Critical Distinctions* (Harvard University Press, 1935) presents a valuable repository of passages.

39. Purchased by the British Library in 2005, and now catalogued as Add. MS 81083, fols. 1–49.

Its rediscovery was announced by Stanley Wells, "By the Placing of His Words," *Times Literary Supplement*, 26 September 2003, pp. 14–15, expanded into Wells, "A New Early Reader of Shakespeare," in *Shakespeare's Book*, ed. Richard Meek, Jane Rickard, and Richard Wilson (Manchester University Press, 2008), pp. 233–40. My discussion is deeply indebted to Gavin Alexander's splendid edition, William Scott, *The Model of Poesy* (Cambridge University Press, 2013). There is an original-spelling edition online at http://www.cambridge.org/gb/files/1713/7458/6256/Original_Spelling_Edition.pdf. See also the valuable condensation of Scott's Shakespearean allusions at "The Modell of Poesye: Earliest Literary Criticism of Shakespeare," Shakespeare Documented, updated 11 June 2016, http://www.shakespeare documented.org/exhibition/document/modell-poesye-earliest-literary-criticism-shakespeare.

40. Scott, *Model of Poesy*, p. 6.

41. Ibid., p. 33.

42. Quoted in "The Modell of Poesye" along with other citations of *Richard II*. Note "the reader": Scott is working from a Quarto, treating *Richard II* as a tragedy for reading. There is no evidence that he saw it in the theatre.

43. According to Thomas Warton (*History of English Poetry* [1791], 3. 275), Webbe's *Discourse of English Poetry* was revised and reprinted in 1588 by Edward Hake under the title *The Touchstone of Wits*.

44. For sample pages, see "Shakespeare Anthologized: England's Parnassus," Shakespeare Documented, updated 25 January 2017, http://www.shakespearedocumented.org/exhibition/document/shakespeare-anthologized-englands-parnassus; and "Shakespeare Anthologized: Bel-vedére or the Garden of the Muses," Shakespeare Documented, updated 25 May 2017, http://www.shakespearedocumented.org/exhibition/document/shakespeare-anthologized-bel-vede-re-or-garden-muses. For the importance of these volumes as evidence that Shakespeare was treated as someone to be read as well as seen, see Lukas Erne, *Shakespeare as Literary Dramatist*, 2nd ed. (Cambridge University Press, 2013), pp. 98–99. On the importance of this genre more generally, see Ann Moss, *Printed Commonplace-Books and the Structuring of Renaissance Thought* (Clarendon Press, 1996).

45. Borrowed by Florio from the definition of Latin *mens* in Thomas Thomas's *Dictionarium Linguae Latinae et Anglicanae* (1587). One of the most valuable resources for the study of the language of Shakespeare and his contemporaries is the astonishingly rich *Early Modern English Dictionary Database* at https://leme.library.utoronto.ca.

46. John Florio's definition of Italian *sale* (salt or seasoning). Subsequent definitions also from Florio's *World of Wordes* (1598).

47. Such as a remarkable seventeenth-century example revealed on the BBC's *Antiques Roadshow* on 2 April 2017, but not yet transcribed (see "Shakespeare Commonplace Book on Antiques Roadshow," *The Shakespeare Blog*, 2 April 2017, http://theshakespeareblog.com/2017/04/shakespeare-commonplace-book-on-antiques-roadshow/); "wise saws": *As You Like It*, 2. 7. 159.

48. "To our English Terence, Master Will Shakespeare," in John Davies, *The Scourge of Folly* (1610), epigram 159; "To Master William Shakespeare," in Thomas Freeman, *Run and a Great Cast* (1614); Inscription on Shakespeare's monument in Holy Trinity Church, Stratford-upon-Avon ("*Obit anno domini 1616, aetatis 53, die 23 Aprilis*").

49. "To the Memory of my Beloved, the AUTHOR Master William Shakespeare and what he hath left us." In my final chapter, I discuss the poem's role in the establishment of Shakespeare's fame.

CHAPTER 5: TRAGICAL-COMICAL-HISTORICAL-PASTORAL

1. *The Two Gentlemen of Verona*, 3. 2. 70, 68–69, 70.
2. Ibid., 3. 2. 72–85.
3. Ibid., 3. 2. 87.

4. *Much Ado about Nothing*, 5. 4. 102; *As You Like It*, 3. 2. 271–72.

5. See E. K. Chambers, *William Shakespeare: A Study of Facts and Problems* (Clarendon Press, 1930), 2. 138–41, 181, and, for a more recent discussion of these and other possibly Shakespearean epitaphs and epigrams, "Poems and Inscriptions with Contemporary or Early Attributions to Shakespeare," in *Shakespeare's Poems*, ed. Katherine Duncan-Jones and H. R. Wooudhuysen (Arden Shakespeare, 2007), pp. 431–63.

6. Marianus, "The Fountain of Love," in *Select Epigrams from the Greek Anthology*, ed. J. W. Mackail (Longmans, Green, 1911), 6. 9 (p. 205). On the tradition of Renaissance imitations of this poem, see James Hutton, "Analogues of Shakespeare's Sonnets 153–54: Contributions to the History of a Theme," *Modern Philology*, 38 (1941), pp. 385–403.

7. For a good introduction to this subject, see Lawrence Danson's *Shakespeare's Dramatic Genres* (Oxford University Press, 2000). More generally, Madeleine Doran's *Endeavors of Art* remains indispensable.

8. Meres, *Palladis Tamia*, in Smith, *Elizabethan Critical Essays*, 2. 317, spelling modernized.

9. *The Rape of Lucrece*, 764–70.

10. Christopher Marlowe, *1 Tamburlaine*, 5. 2 (in which Tamburlaine wears black himself); *1 Henry VI*, 1. 1. 1 (probably written by a coauthor, not Shakespeare).

11. Thomas Nashe, preface to Robert Greene's *Menaphon*, in Nashe, *Works*, ed. McKerrow, 3. 315–16.

12. *Hamlet*, 2. 2. 353–54.

13. Though for a strong argument that Illyria in *Twelfth Night* and the island in *The Tempest* as well as the marketplace in the Ephesus of *Errors* bear resemblance to the stage space of new comedy, see Raphael Lyne, "Shakespeare, Plautus, and the Discovery of New Comic Space," in Martindale and Taylor, *Shakespeare and the Classics*, pp. 122–40.

14. The Gray's Inn festivities of 1594 were published in 1688; for the Plautus comparison, see *Gesta Grayorum: or, The history of the high and mighty Prince Henry, Prince of Purpoole, Anno Domini 1594*, ed. Desmond Bland (Liverpool University Press, 1968), p. 32. John Manningham's account of the performance of *Twelfth Night* in the Middle Temple on 2 February 1602 is in British Museum Harley MS 5353, fo. 12^v.

15. See Miola, *Shakespeare and Classical Comedy*, pp. 20–38; Riehle, *Shakespeare, Plautus, and the Humanist Tradition*, passim; John Arthos, "Shakespeare's Transformation of Plautus," *Comparative Drama*, 1 (1967–68), pp. 239–53.

16. Thomas Heywood, *An Apologie for Actors* (1612), sig. F1^v, translating Donatus.

17. Henry Cockeram, *The English Dictionarie: Or, An Interpreter of hard English Words. Enabling as well Ladies and Gentlewomen, young Schollers, Clarkes, Merchants, as also Strangers of any Nation, to the vnderstanding of the more difficult Authors already printed in our Language, and the more speedy attaining of an elegant perfection of the English tongue, both in reading, speaking and writing. Being a Collection of the choisest words contained in the Table Alphabeticall and English Expositor, and of some thousands of words neuer published by any heretofore* (1623), headwords "Tragedie" and "Comedie," spelling modernized.

18. Stephen Gosson, *Plays confuted in Five Actions* (1582), sig. C5^r.

19. See the enduring studies of Northrop Frye—"The Argument of Comedy" and *A Natural Perspective*, now helpfully gathered in *Northrop Frye's Writings on Shakespeare and the Renaissance* (University of Toronto Press, 2010), pp. 3–13, 127–225—and C. L. Barber, *Shakespeare's Festive Comedy* (Princeton University Press, 1959), together with Anne Barton, "Parks and Ardens" in her *Essays, Mainly Shakespearean* (Cambridge University Press, 1994), pp. 352–79, and *The Shakespearean Forest* (Cambridge University Press, 2017).

20. Licence for King's Men, 19 May 1603, quoted in Chambers, *William Shakespeare*, 2. 72.

21. Ibid.

22. See *Henslowe's Diary*, ed. R. A. Foakes, 2nd ed. (Cambridge University Press, 2002). Note further, the paucity of uses of "tragedy" and "comedy" in surviving sixteenth-century performance records, in contrast to records of print, in Martin Wiggins's and Catherine Richardson's extraordinarily comprehensive *British Drama 1533–1642: A Catalogue*, 8 vols. so far (Oxford University Press, 2012–).

23. None of the plays published in Shakespeare's lifetime had act divisions. The foundation for scholarly discussion of this subject remains Henry L. Snuggs, *Shakespeare and Five Acts: Studies in a Dramatic Convention* (Vantage Press, 1960), which also points out that the five-act convention derives from the closet dramas of Seneca and the treatises of neoclassical theorists, not the actual practice of Terence, as T. W. Baldwin had proposed in *Shakspere's Five-Act Structure: Shakspere's Early Plays on the Background of Renaissance Theories of Five-Act Structure from 1470* (University of Illionois Press, 1947). On the refitting of Shakespeare's plays to accommodate the act-breaks required for the trimming of candles in the indoor Blackfriars theatre, see John Jowett and Gary Taylor, "The Structure of Performance: Act-Intervals in the London theatres, 1576–1642," in Gary Taylor and John Jowett, *Shakespeare Reshaped, 1606–23* (Clarendon Press, 1993), pp. 3–50.

24. There was also Robert Yarington's *Two Lamentable Tragedies* (1601), but this was no more than a pairing of two of those "real life crime" dramas: *The one, of the murther of Maister Beech a chaundler in Thames-streete, and his boye, done by Thomas Merry. The other of a young childe murthered in a wood by two ruffi[a]ns, with the consent of his unckle.*

25. "To our English Terence, Master Will Shakespeare," in John Davies, *The Scourge of Folly*, epigram 159.

26. 138, to judge by a search on the database *Early English Books Online* (https://eebo.chadwyck.com/home).

27. A vestige of the quarto title of *Richard III* is apparent from the fact that it is "The Life and Death" in the Folio "Catalogue of Plays" and running heads, but "The Tragedy" at the top of the first page of the text.

28. Sidney, *Apology*, ed. Shepherd, pp. 135–36.

29. *Mr [Samuel] Johnson's Preface to his Edition of Shakespear's Plays* (1765), p. xiii.

30. See my introduction to *The RSC Shakespeare: Troilus and Cressida*, ed. Jonathan Bate and Eric Rasmussen (Macmillan & Modern Library, 2010), p. 1.

31. Johnson, concluding note on *Troilus* in *The Plays of William Shakespeare* (1765), 7. 547.

32. *Mr Johnson's Preface*, p. xvii.

33. *1 Henry IV*, 2. 4. 283–84.

34. *A Midsummer Night's Dream*, 5. 1. 58–62.

35. Christopher Marlowe, "The Printer to the Reader," in *Tamburlaine the Great* (1590), sig. A2^r, spelling modernized.

36. In "To the Readers" in *Sejanus his Fall* (1605), Jonson refers to the "happy Genius" of the second author—a term consonant with his praise of Shakespeare elsewhere. Edmond Malone was the first to identify the second pen as Shakespeare's—see *Plays and Poems of Shakespeare* (1821), 1. 356—but Dekker has often been proposed, and the weight of evidence favours Chapman: see Tom Cain, "*Sejanus*: Textual Essay," in *The Cambridge Edition of the Works of Ben Jonson Online*, general editor Martin Butler, https://universitypublishingonline.org/cambridge/benjonson/k/essays/Sejanus_textual_essay/.

37. *Hamlet*, 2. 2. 299, 351–55.

38. English translation of Galen, *Certaine Works* (1586), p. 72; Dolman's trans. of La Primaudaye's *French Academie* (1601), p. 50.

39. For a variorum of editorial commentary since the eighteenth century, see the relevant note on the "Hamlet Works" website, http://triggs.djvu.org/global-language.com/ENFOLDED/index.php.

40. *Henslowe's Diary*, p. 122.

41. *Hamlet*, 2. 2. 302–23 (Folio only).

42. Ibid., 2. 2. 302, 309.

43. Consideration of pastoral in relation to mixed genre in the Elizabethan period should begin with Rosalie Colie's exemplary studies *The Resources of Kind: Genre-Theory in the Renaissance* (University of California Press, 1973) and *Shakespeare's Living Art* (Princeton University Press, 1974), especially chap. 6, "Perspectives on Pastoral, Romance, Comic and Tragic," and chap. 7, " 'Nature's above Art in that Respect': Limits of the Pastoral Pattern." Louise George Clubb is excellent on the Italian context—*Italian Drama in Shakespeare's Time* (Yale University Press, 1990)—while Robert Henke argues (perhaps overstrenuously) for its influence on Shakespeare: *Pastoral Transformations: Italian Tragicomedy and Shakespeare's Late Plays* (University of Delaware Press, 1997). See also the valuable collection of essays *Early Modern Tragicomedy*, ed. Subha Mukherji and Raphael Lyne (Boydell and Brewer, 2007).

44. John Fletcher, *The Faithful Shepherdess* (1610), "To the Reader," spelling modernized.

45. Ibid.

46. Simon Forman saw *The Winter's Tale* at the Globe in May 1611 and it was performed at court in November 1611. The dance of satyrs late in the play seems to borrow from a court entertainment of January 1611, so it is a reasonable assumption that Shakespeare was working up the plot in 1610.

47. *The Winter's Tale*, 4. 4. 152–53.

48. Scott, "Modell of Poesye," British Library, Add. MS 81083, Sigs 11^r, 12^r.

49. Trans. Thomas Underdowne, 1569.

50. Orsino's simile of "th' Egyptian thief" at *Twelfth Night*, 5. 1. 114 is an allusion to the character of Thyamis in Heliodorus's tale. See further, Carol Gesner, *Shakespeare and the Greek Romance: A Study of Origins* (University Press of Kentucky, 2015); and, for the particular tale, Donald Lateiner, "Abduction Marriage in Heliodorus' *Aethiopica*," *Greek, Roman and Byzantine Studies*, 38 (1997), pp. 409–39.

51. See my introduction to *Mucedorus* in Bate et al., *Collaborative Plays*, pp. 503–6.

52. *Mucedorus*, scene 2, line 8, in Bate et al., *Collaborative Plays*, p. 514.

53. Teresa Grant, "White Bears in *The Winter's Tale* and *Oberon, The Faery Prince*," *Notes and Queries*, 48 (2001), pp. 311–13; and Barbara Ravelhofer, " 'Beasts of Recreacion': Henslowe's White Bears," *English Literary Renaissance*, 32 (2002), pp. 287–323.

54. *The Winter's Tale*, 2. 1. 33; 3. 2. 138; 5. 3. 182.

55. Ibid., 3. 3. 99.

56. Michael Drayton, "To my most dearely-loved friend HENERY REYNOLDS Esquire, of *Poets & Poesie*," in *The Minor Poems of Michael*

Drayton, ed. Cyril Brett (Clarendon Press, 1907), pp. 108–13. This poem also praises Shakespeare's comic art before his tragic.

57. The best survey of his Europe-wide influence in the sixteenth century remains the introduction to *The Eclogues of Baptista Mantuanus*, ed. Wilfred P. Mustard, Studies in the Renaissance Pastoral 1 (Johns Hopkins University Press, 1911), pp. 11–61. For more recent scholarship, see Battista Spagnoli Mantovano, *Adolescentia*, ed. and trans. Andrea Severi (Bononia University Press, 2010).

58. J. H. Lupton, A *Life of John Colet D.D., Dean of St. Paul's, and Founder of St. Paul's School* (George Bell, 1887), p. 279.

59. Charles Hoole, *A New Discovery of the Old Art of Teaching School* (1660), cited in Baldwin, *William Shakspere's Small Latine*, 1. 647.

60. Mantuan, *Adulescentia: The Eclogues of Baptista Mantuanus (1498): A Hypertext Critical Edition*, ed. and trans. Lee Piepho (The Philological Museum, University of Birmingham, 2009), Eclogue 1. 1–5.

61. *Love's Labour's Lost*, 4. 2. 72–77.

62. *Do* did not replace *Ut* in the musical gamut until the late seventeenth century. On the question of whether the misquotation of Mantuan's first word is deliberate, contrast *Love's Labour's Lost*, ed. Richard David, The Arden Shakespeare, Second Series (Methuen, 1968), pp. 81–82; and Manfred Draudt, "Holfernes and Mantuanus: How Stupid Is the Pedant of *Love's Labour's Lost*?," *Anglia*, 109 (1992), pp. 443–51.

63. Gabriel Harvey, *Foure Letters*, in *The Works of Gabriel Harvey*, ed. A. B. Grosart (Huth Library, 1884–85), 1. 195.

64. Mantuan, *Adulescentia*, 1. 41–47.

65. Ibid., 6. 1–5.

66. *Love's Labour's Lost*, 5. 2. 909–17.

67. *As You Like It*, 2. 4. 69–75. Scholarship on Shakespeare and Mantuan is sparse, with little having been added to Baldwin, *Shakspere's Small Latine*, 1. 649–52. The bibliography on Shakespeare and the longer traditions of pastoral is vast: further study might begin with Paul Alpers's capacious *What Is Pastoral?* (University of Chicago Press, 1997), and, for contrast, the sceptical take considered in Peter Lindenbaum's *Changing Landscapes: Anti-Pastoral Sentiment in the English Renaissance* (University of Georgia Press, 1986).

68. *Adulescentia*, 3. 172–74.

69. Ibid., 2. 9.

70. Virgil, *Eclogues*, 2. 1–2. Renaissance commentators did not hesitate to identify Corydon with Virgil himself: "By *Coridon* also (if we geve credit to Donate [Donatus]) is meant *Virgil*, by *Alexis* is understood *Alexander* the Lad of *Pollio*, whom he gave to *Coridon* afterward for a gyft"—"The Argu-

ment or contentes *of the second* Ecloge," in Abraham Fleming, *The bucolikes of Publius Virgilius Maro* (1575), sig. C2ᵛ. We would call this slavery and child abuse, but that is not how the Romans thought.

71. Ibid., 2. 45, 28.

72. Sonnet 126; Christopher Marlowe, "The Passionate Shepherd to his Love," first printed (untitled) in *Sonnets to sundry Notes of Musicke*, bound up with *The Passionate Pilgrim by W. Shakespeare* (1599), then in *Englands Helicon* (1600, with attribution to Marlowe). See further, "The Passionate Shepherd," chap. 3 of Bruce Smith's superb *Homosexual Desire in Shakespeare's England* (University of Chicago Press, 1991).

CHAPTER 6: S. P. Q. L

1. Chambers, *William Shakespeare*, 2. 89.

2. *Titus Andronicus*, 5. 1. 21; Sonnet 73.

3. My transcription of the Latin hexameters on the monument; my thanks to Peta Fowler for this translation.

4. See my account in *Soul of the Age*, pp. 300–303, of John Harborne as the Shakespeare family lawyer, and the inference of Shakespeare's presence in London in 1588 that may be drawn from the Bill of complainant in the Queen's Bench case of *Shakespeare v Lambert* (*Coram Rege Roll* 1311, f. 516).

5. This is an especially fine example of the kind of "kneeler monument" that became fashionable in Elizabethan England—on this phenomenon, see Nigel Llewellyn's authoritative *Funeral Monuments in Post-Reformation England* (Cambridge University Press, 2000), p. 105. There is something inherently theatrical about the pose, which makes one think of many parallels in Shakespeare, where *kneeling* is a key dramatic effect. Hamlet not killing Claudius while he is kneeling at prayer immediately comes to mind: Keir Elam nicely suggests that "Hamlet cannot kill a man whose kneeling pose reminds him of his own failed duties towards the soul of his father" (*Shakespeare's Pictures*, p. 224). On the parallels between stage tableaux and church monuments more generally, see the section on "Tomb-Sculpture and the Theatre," in Jean Wilson's admirable *The Archaeology of Shakespeare* (Sutton, 1995), pp. 81–95.

6. For a broad-ranging account of the links between representations of antiquity and the growth of early modern trade, especially with the Ottoman world of the eastern Mediterranean, see Miriam Jacobson, *Barbarous Antiquity: Reorienting the Past in the Poetry of Early Modern England* (University of Pennsylvania Press, 2014).

7. *The Merchant of Venice*, 1. 1. 163–65, 169–74.

8. Ibid., 3. 2. 243–45.

9. Arthur Golding, epistle to the Earl of Leicester, prefacing *The xv Bookes of P. Ovidius Naso, entytuled Metamorphosis, translated oute of Latin into English meter, by Arthur Golding Gentleman* (1567), lines 143–46.

10. *The Merchant of Venice*, 3. 3. 29–34.

11. Designed by Gresham himself, it was unmarked, but its occupant was readily identifiable because his funeral achievements were displayed above it. See John William Burgon, *The Life and Times of Sir Thomas Gresham, Kt., Founder of the Royal Exchange: Including Notices of Many of His Contemporaries* (R. Jennings, 1839), 2. 472.

12. It was so large that it in fact straddled the parishes of St Helen's and St Peter the Poor.

13. Paul Hentzner, in his *Travels*, in the edition cited in note 24, below.

14. Thomas Heywood, *The Second Part of, If You Know Not Me, You Know Nobody. With the Building of the Royall Exchange* (1606; repr., The Malone Society, 1935), lines 1368–76, spelling modernized.

15. See "Illustration of the trade exchange in Antwerp, 16th century, Belgium, Europe, *Historische Zeichnung*," alamy, uploaded 2018, http://www.alamy.com/stock-photo-illustration-of-the-trade-exchange-in-antwerp-16th-century-belgium-52663793.html.

16. Fernand Braudel, "Antwerp—A World Capital Created by Outside Agency," in his *Civilization and Capitalism 15th–18th Century*, trans. Siân Reynolds (University of California Press, 1983), 3. 143.

17. Effectively the signature on the tabular inscription composed by Ben Jonson, reprinted in *B. Jon: His Part of King James, His Royall and Magnificent Entertainement* (1604), sig. D3ʳ. See further, D. J. Hopkins, "Performance and Urban Space in Shakespeare's Rome, or 'S. P. Q. L.,'" in *Rematerializing Shakespeare: Authority and Representation on the Early Modern Stage*, ed. B. Reynolds and W. West (Springer, 2005), pp. 35–52.

18. The best recent overview of this broader context is Walter Chernaik, *The Myth of Rome in Shakespeare and His Contemporaries* (Cambridge University Press, 2011). For the culture of London in the period more generally, see Lawrence Manley, *Literature and Culture in Early Modern London* (Cambridge University Press, 1995); Ian W. Archer, *The Pursuit of Stability: Social Relations in Early Modern London* (Cambridge University Press, 1991); and *London in the Age of Shakespeare: An Anthology*, ed. Lawrence Manley (Pennsylvania State University Press, 1989).

19. See, among many reproductions, "Engraved View of London by C J Visscher Showing the Globe, Hand-Coloured 3rd version," British Library, accessed 18 May 2010, https://www.bl.uk/collection-items/engraved-view-of-london-by-c-j-visscher-showing-the-globe-hand-coloured-3rd-version.

20. Virgil, *Eclogues*, 1. 66.

21. Johannes de Witt, *Observationes Londiniensis* (c. 1596): the manuscript is lost, but the drawing survives in a copy by his friend Aernout van Buchel (Utrecht University Library, MS 842.1).

22. See Wilson, *Archaeology of Shakespeare*, pp. 95–96, for a good example in the form of a chest in Southwark Cathedral (where Shakespeare's actor-brother Edmund was buried and where the tomb of John Gower in all probability provided inspiration for the Chorus of *Pericles*).

23. William Camden, "The Author to the Reader," prefacing Philemon Holland's English translation of *Britannia* (1610).

24. My quotations are from the English translation by Richard Bentley, published in *Paul Hentzner's Travels in England During the Reign of Queen Elizabeth, Translated by Horace Late Earl of Orford and first printed by him at Strawberry Hill, to Which is Now Added Sir Robert Naunton's Fragmenta Regalia, or Observations on Queen Elizabeth's Times and Favourites; with Portraits and Views* (1797), Latin/English hypertext edition by Dana Sutton, The Philological Museum, uploaded 21 June 2004, http://www.philological.bham .ac.uk/hentzner/.

25. *Richard II*, 5. 1. 1–4.

26. *Richard III*, 3. 1. 68–74.

27. Quoted, as are all other passages of Hentzner, *Itinerarium Angliae*, from Dana Sutton's hypertext edition and translation for The Philological Museum, http://www.philological.bham.ac.uk/hentzner/.

28. In some sources, Cunobelan/Cymbeline is the great-nephew rather than the nephew of Cassibilan.

29. *Cymbeline*, 5. 4. 539–40, 568–69.

30. "Cymbeline's final submission to Rome, even after he has won the war against the Romans, might have had some topical value in view of James's efforts to enter into friendly negotiations with Papal Rome.... The audience must have made a complex identification: the peace is both the peace of the world at the time of Christ's birth, in which Britain participates, and also its attempted re-creation at the very time of the play's performance, with Jacobus Pacificus—who was a figure of Augustus—on the throne" (Emrys Jones, "Stuart *Cymbeline*," *Essays in Criticism*, 11 [1961], pp. 84–99, repr. in *Shakespeare's Later Comedies*, ed. D. J. Palmer [Penguin, 1971], pp. 259–600).

CHAPTER 7: BUT WHAT OF CICERO?

1. *1 Henry IV*, 1. 1. 5–6, 12–13.

2. On the limited scope of "the Wars of the Roses," see K. B. McFarlane's influential *The Nobility of Later Medieval England: The Ford Lectures for 1953 and Related Studies* (Oxford University Press, 1973), but for an argument that there were significant changes in the balance of power between

central monarchy and county nobility and gentry during the later fifteenth century, see Christine Carpenter, *The Wars of the Roses: Politics and the Constitution in England, c. 1437–1509* (Cambridge University Press, 1997).

3. Edward Hall, "An introduccion into the history of Kyng Henry the fourthe," in *The union of two noble and illustre famelies of Lancastre [and] Yorke*, fol. 1.

4. *Macbeth*, 2. 3. 59–60.

5. On the history of this idea, see David Armitage's sweeping *Civil Wars: A History in Ideas* (Yale University Press, 2017). On Cicero's use of the phrase in such key orations as *Pro Marcello* and *Pro Ligario*, see Ayelet Peer, *Julius Caesar's Bellum Civile and the Composition of a New Reality* (Routledge, 2016), p. 174; in the context of Cicero's defence of Pompey, see Armitage, *Civil Wars*, p. 66.

6. Lucan, *Civil War*, trans. Susan H. Braund (Oxford World's Classics, 1992), 1. 31–32. On the path from Caesar to Lucan, see Josiah Osgood, "Ending Civil War at Rome: Rhetoric and Reality, 88 b.c.e.–197 c.e.," *The American Historical Review*, 120 (2015), pp. 1683–95; and Osgood, *Caesar's Legacy: Civil War and the Emergence of the Roman Empire* (Cambridge University Press, 2006).

7. Christopher Marlowe, *Lucans First Book Translated Line for Line* (1600), quoted from *The Complete Poems and Translations*, ed. Stephen Orgel (Penguin Classics, 2007), p. 90. Patrick Cheney has argued that the Lucan translation signals a republican vein that reappears throughout Marlowe's short career: *Marlowe's Republican Authorship: Lucan, Liberty, and the Sublime* (Palgrave Macmillan, 2008).

8. English translation: Appian, *An Auncient Historie and Exquisite Chronicle of the Romanes Warres, both Civile and Foren*, trans. W. B. (possibly William Barker, translator of Xenophon).

9. See Gillespie, *Shakespeare's Books*, pp. 16–19, but see discussion later in this chapter for the suggestion that Cicero was more important in the shaping of Brutus's speech.

10. Roger Ascham, *Toxophilus* (1545), p. 40.

11. *Titus Andronicus*, 5. 3. 70–71.

12. Anon., *The passage of our most drad Soueraigne Lady Quene Elyzabeth through the citie of London to Westminster the daye before her coronacion Anno 1558*, sig. B2^r.

13. *Julius Caesar*, 3. 1. 282–83; *Richard II*, 1. 3. 126–27; *1 Henry IV*, 1. 1. 12–13; 4. 2. 271; *Henry V*, 5. 2. 186–87; *1 Henry VI*, 3.1. 75–76; *2 Henry VI*, 4. 8. 39–40; *3 Henry VI*, 1.1. 198–99; *Richard III*, 5. 3. 407.

14. "Concilium coetusque hominum jure sociati": Cicero, *Somnium Scipiones* (*De re publica*, vi), c3.

15. Tacitus, *De Germania*, in *The Annales of Cornelius Tacitus [and] The Description of Germanie*, trans. Richard Greneway (1598), dedicated to the Earl of Essex, who was very interested in this vein of thought.

16. John Calvin, *Institutes of the Christian Religion* (1536), 4. 20. 30, trans. Harro Höpfl, in *Luther and Calvin on Secular Authority* (Cambridge Texts in the History of Political Thought, 1991).

17. *Coriolanus*, 2. 1. 192–93; 4. 5. 92, 100.

18. Paul Cantor's *Shakespeare's Rome: Republic and Empire* (Cornell University Press, 1983) is especially good on the contrast between the republican setting of *Coriolanus* and the incipient imperial context of *Antony and Cleopatra*.

19. *Coriolanus*, 1. 1. 131–35; 3. 1. 204–5; 1. 1. 136; 3. 1. 314, 316–17; 3. 3. 1–2; 4. 2. 8.

20. See *Coriolanus*, ed. R. B. Parker (Oxford University Press, 1994), p. 172.

21. On *Libertas*, see Matthew B. Roller, "Modeling the Emperor: the Master-Slave Relationship and Its Alternatives," chap. 4 in *Constructing Autocracy: Aristocrats and Emperors in Julio-Claudian Rome* (Princeton University Press, 2001); and Duncan Kennedy, " 'Augustan' and 'Anti-Augustan': Reflections on Terms of Reference," in *Roman Poetry and Propaganda in the Age of Augustus*, ed. Anton Powell (Bristol Classical Press, 1992), pp. 26–58; as well as the influential older studies, Ronald Syme, *The Roman Revolution* (Oxford University Press, 1939); and Chaim Wirszubski, *Libertas as a Political Idea at Rome during the Late Republic and Early Principate* (Cambridge University Press, 1950).

22. *2 Henry VI*, 4. 8. 23–24.

23. Ibid., 4. 8. 24–25.

24. There is a fierce debate among historians as to whether this means that there was recognizably "republican" thought in late Elizabethan England and, if so, what relevance it might have had to Shakespeare. See especially Andrew Hadfield, *Shakespeare and Republicanism* (Cambridge University Press, 2005); and *Shakespeare and Early Modern Political Thought*, ed. David Armitage, Conal Condren, and Andrew Fitzmaurice (Cambridge University Press, 2009), in particular chap. 13, Eric Nelson, "Shakespeare and the Best State of a Commonwealth." For the wider debate, begin with Marku Peltonnen, *Classical Humanism and Republicanism in English Political Thought, 1570-1640* (Cambridge University Press, 2004); Alexandra Gajda, *The Earl of Essex and Late Elizabethan Political Culture* (Oxford University Press, 2012); and David Womersley, "Sir Henry Savile's Translation of Tacitus and the Political Interpretation of Elizabethan Texts," *Review of English Studies*, 42 (1991), pp. 313–42. For a sceptical argument, see Blair

Worden, "Republicanism, Regicide and Republic: The English Experience," in *Republicanism: A Shared European Heritage*, vol. 1, *Republicanism and Constitutionalism in Early Modern Europe*, ed. Martin van Gelderen and Quentin Skinner (Cambridge University Press, 2005), pp. 307–27.

25. *Coriolanus*, 2. 2. 76, 78–79, 79–93.

26. I take the terms from Andrew Marvell's "Horatian Ode upon Cromwell's Return from Ireland": "So restless Cromwell could not cease / In the inglorious arts of peace, / But through adventurous war / Urgèd his active star" (Andrew Marvell, *The Complete Poems*, ed. E. S. Donno with an introduction by Jonathan Bate [Penguin, 2005], p. 55).

27. *The Massacre at Paris*, 2. 6. 70–72, quoted from Christopher Marlowe, *Complete Plays and Poems*, ed. E. D. Pendry and J. C. Maxwell (Dent, 1976).

28. Plutarch, *The Lives of the Noble Grecians and Romanes,* trans. North, 3. 400.

29. Cicero, *The Fourteen Orations against Marcus Antonius (Philippics)*, trans. C. D. Yonge (1903), 2. 87.

30. Though Cicero was initially lauded for his action, the execution of Catiline without trial was subsequently regarded as an infringement of *libertas*, causing him to be temporarily exiled. For the complexity of Jonson's representation of the character of Cicero—a mixture of rhetorical bravura and otiosity, idealism and political naivite, service to Rome and personal vanity, success and failure (defeating the conspiracy, but leaving Julius Caesar free to destroy the republic many years later)—see, for example, Maurice Hunt, "Jonson vs. Shakespeare: The Roman Plays," *Ben Jonson Journal*, 23 (2016), pp. 75–100; Joseph A. Bryant, Jr., "Catiline and the Nature of Jonson's Tragic Fable," *PMLA*, 69 (1954), pp. 265–77; Michael Warren, "Catiline: The Problem of Cicero," *Yearbook of English Studies*, 3 (1973), pp. 55–73; and G. K. Hunter, "A Roman Thought: Renaissance Attitudes to History Exemplified in Shakespeare and Jonson," in *Shakespeare and History*, ed. Stephen Orgel and Sean Keilen (New York: Garland, 1999), pp. 189–211.

31. *Julius Caesar*, 1. 2. 192, 274.

32. Ibid., 1. 3. 1–2, 11, 14–28, 33–35, 39–40.

33. Ibid., 2. 1. 146–47, 150–55.

34. Ibid., 12.1. 156–58, 159, 160.

35. Plutarch, *Lives*, trans. North, 4. 443.

36. My *inventio*.

37. *Julius Caesar*, 2. 1. 53–54.

38. Ibid., 2. 1. 69.

39. Ibid., 2. 1. 229.

40. Marginal note in Plutarch, *Lives*, trans. North, "Life of Cicero," 4. 199.

41. *Julius Caesar*, 2. 1. 334–40.

42. Plutarch, *Lives*, trans. North, 4. 444.

43. Marked by him in the "Robben Island" Shakespeare: see Bate and Thornton, *Shakespeare: Staging the World*, p. 269. *Julius Caesar*, 2. 2. 33–34.

44. *Julius Caesar*, 2. 2. 34–35; Plutarch, *Lives*, trans. North, 3. 444.

45. *2 Henry VI*, 4. 1. 138.

46. Plutarch, *Lives*, trans. North, "Life of Cicero," 4. 215; Cicero, second oration against Verres (*In Verrem*, 2. 4. 55) and first oration ("quo usque") against Catiline (*Oratio in Catilinam Prima in Senutu Habita*, 2).

47. *Julius Caesar*, 3. 2. 70–249.

48. The strongest case for the influence of Appian on Shakespeare (especially by way of his preface describing the war between Octavius and Antony as the culmination of Rome's development from "common wealth" to "rule of one") is that made by Denis Feeney with respect not to *Julius Caesar* but to *Antony and Cleopatra*: "Doing the Numbers: The Roman Mathematics of Civil War in Shakespeare's *Antony and Cleopatra*," in *Citizens of Discord: Rome and Its Civil Wars*, ed. Brian Breed, Cynthia Damon, Andreola Rossi (Oxford University Press, 2010), pp. 273–92.

49. Cicero, *Philippics*, 2. 91. See further, George Kennedy, "Antony's Speech at Caesar's Funeral," *Quarterly Journal of Speech*, 54 (1968), pp. 99–106. The case for Appian is summarized by Gillespie, *Shakespeare's Books*, pp. 16–19.

50. *Julius Caesar*, 2. 1. 225–26.

51. Plutarch, *Lives*, trans. North, 4. 229.

52. Plutarch, *Lives*, trans. North, 4. 228–29. Here he calls Ligarius by the forename Quintus, whereas in the "Life of Brutus" he calls him Caius, which Shakespeare follows, but the context makes clear that it is the same man.

53. *Julius Caesar*, 3. 2. 201; 3. 3. 33. It is possible that I am overreading here and that Shakespeare merely forgot to include Ligarius's name in the entry direction of 3. 1 (or had an insufficiently large cast to include him), but the omission seems purposeful, given that he makes room for Trebonius, who is a noncharacter in comparison.

54. *Julius Caesar*, 2. 1. 347.

55. Far more men than women, of course, though for some examples of educated women reading Cicero, see Gemma Allen, *The Cooke Sisters: Education, Piety and Politics in Early Modern England* (Oxford University Press, 2016), pp. 19, 24–25, 37–38. For starting points on the vast subject of Cicero's pervasive influence in the period, see Howard Jones, *Master Tully: Cicero in Tudor England* (De Graaf, 1998); and David Marsh, "Cicero in the Renaissance," in *The Cambridge Companion to Cicero*, ed. Catherine Steel (Cambridge University Press, 2013), pp. 306–17.

56. Cicero, *Pro Ligario*, trans. C. D. Yonge (1891), 11.

57. *The Merchant of Venice*, 4. 1. 184–205.

58. Cicero, *Pro Ligario*, trans. Yonge, 37–38.

59. See Ernst H. Kantorowicz's celebrated *The King's Two Bodies: A Study in Medieval Political Thought* (1957), with new introduction by Conrad Leyser (Princeton University Press, 2016).

60. *Julius Caesar*, 4. 2. 59–61.

61. Ibid., 4. 2. 63.

62. Ibid., 4. 2. 68.

63. Cicero, *De Officiis*, 2. 75–77.

64. Ibid., 1. 91.

65. *Julius Caesar*, 4. 2. 129–46.

CHAPTER 8: PYRRHUS'S PAUSE

1. Sir John Harington, "A Preface, or rather a Brief Apology of Poetry, and of the Author and Translator," in Smith, *Elizabethan Critical Essays*, 2. 211.

2. Sir Thomas Elyot, *The Boke named the Governour* (1531), bk. 1, chap. 10.

3. Edmund Spenser, "Letter of the Authors expounding his *whole intention in the course of this worke, which* for that it giveth great light to the Reader, for the better understanding is hereunto annexed," in *The Faerie Queene* (1590), http://www.luminarium.org/renascence-editions/ralegh.html.

4. Barbara A. Mowat, "Constructing the Author," in *Elizabethan Theater: Essays in Honor of S. Schoenbaum*, ed. R. B. Parker and Sheldon P. Zitner (University of Delaware Press, 1996), p. 96.

5. He is the most highly praised of the six poets whose lives are recorded in the surviving text, the other five being Horace, Lucan, Perseus, Terence, and Tibullus.

6. Suetonius, "Vita Vergili," in *De Viris Illustribus* (Lives of Illustrious Men), trans. J. C. Rolfe (Loeb Classical Library, Harvard University Press, 1914), p. 465.

7. Thomas Twyne, "Virgils life, set foorth, as it is supposed, by Aelius Donatus, and done into English," in *The whole xii. Bookes of the Aeneidos of Virgill* (1573), A2ᵛ. Donatus's extra material is usually assumed to derive from a longer, now lost, version of Suetonius.

8. There are numerous studies of Virgil's *Nachleben*: perhaps begin with David Scott Wilson-Okamura, *Virgil in the Renaissance* (Cambridge University Press, 2010), and the same author's "Virgil in Late Antiquity, the Middle Ages, and the Renaissance: An Online Bibliography," accessed 1 June 2018, http://www.virgil.org/bibliography/. For a wider chronological span:

Philip Hardie, *The Last Trojan Hero: A Cultural History of Virgil's "Aeneid"* (I. B. Tauris, 2014).

9. See "Appendix: The Elizabethan Virgil."

10. Spenser, *The Faerie Queene*, 3. 9. 38.

11. For example, King Arthur's lineage in book 1, canto 9, and the genealogy of the British kings in book 2, canto 10.

12. Nashe, preface to Greene's *Menaphon*, in Works, ed. McKerrow, 3. 324; Meres, *Palladis Tamia*, in Smith, *Elizabethan Critical Essays*, 2. 319, 317.

13. William Warner, *Albions England* (1586), dedictory epistle and bk. 1, chap. 1, line 4.

14. Ibid., prose "Addition" at the end of 1586 edition.

15. Ibid., p. 113.

16. Warner, *Albions England . . . The third time corrected and augmented . . . With the chiefe alterations and accidents therein happening, untill her nowe Majesties moste blessed Raigne* (1592), chap. 39, p. 173.

17. *Richard II*, 5. 1. 11–12.

18. *3 Henry VI*, 4. 8. 25.

19. *2 Henry VI*, 3. 2. 89–119.

20. *Titus Andronicus*, 5. 3. 80–87. See *The Arden Shakespeare: Titus Andronicus*, rev. ed., ed. Jonathan Bate (Bloomsbury, 2018), p. 310, for the case for the ascription of this speech to the Quarto's "Romane Lord" as opposed to Marcus, as in the editorial tradition. Alternatively, if the Goths are regarded as the true descendants of the good old primitive ways, as suggested below, then maybe there is a case for the Folio's ascription to a Goth.

21. On the possible ambivalence of Shakespeare's representation of Lucius, see A. B. Taylor, "Lucius, the Severely Flawed Redeemer of *Titus Andronicus*," *Connotations*, 6 (1996–97), pp. 138–57; but also, Jonathan Bate, "Lucius, the Severely Flawed Redeemer of *Titus Andronicus*: A Reply," *Connotations*, 6 (1996–97), pp. 330–33.

22. "IVDICIO PYLIVM, GENIO SOCRATEM, ARTE MARONEM, / TERRA TEGIT, POPVLVS MÆRET, OLYMPVS HABET."

23. *Julius Caesar*, 1. 2. 118–20.

24. *2 Henry VI*, 5. 2. 61–65.

25. *Cymbeline*, 3. 4. 57 (Dido repeatedly calls Aeneas *perfide*, "false one" [Virgil, *Aeneid*, 4. 305, 366]); *The Tempest*, 2. 1. 64–65.

26. *The Merchant of Venice*, 5. 1. 11–14. The farewell wave across the sea is not in Virgil: it is probably inspired by Ariadne on Naxos, known to Shakespeare from Ovid's *Heroides* and perhaps Chaucer's *Legend of Good Women*.

27. Recent Virgil scholarship has emphasized the tradition of "pessimistic" readings of *The Aeneid*, suggesting that Virgil himself in certain respects had an antiheroic imagination, insofar as the emotional sympathy and elegiac qualities of the poem are at their most intense in the representation

of female figures such as Dido in book 4 and Camilla in book 11. In *The Other Virgil: "Pessimistic" Readings of the Aeneid in Early Modern Culture* (Oxford University Press, 2007), Craig Kallendorf argues for the presence of such readings in Shakespeare's time (including Marlowe and Nashe's *Dido Queen of Carthage*), but my sense is that Shakespeare's recuperation of Dido came primarily from the voice given to her by Ovid in *Heroides* 7.

28. William Scott, *The Modell of Poesye* (1599), fo. 11^r.

29. Dedication to *Venus and Adonis*. Patrick Cheney argues that through the many agricultural metaphors in this dedication ("ear," "barren a land," "harvest," "yield") Shakespeare is "presenting himself as a Virgilian author of pastoral" on his way to a higher form, following the Virgilian *cursus* from pastoral to epic, a progression self-consciously imitated by Spenser: *Shakespeare, National Poet-Playwright* (Cambridge University Press, 2004), p. 94.

30. See Scott Goins, "Two Aspects of Virgil's Use of *Labor* in the *Aeneid*," *The Classical Journal*, 88 (1993), pp. 375–84.

31. Virgil, *Eclogues*, 10. 69; *Georgics*, 1. 145.

32. Patrick Cheney has argued consistently that the Ovidianism of Shakespeare and Marlowe constitutes a "counter-nationhood," consciously setting the amorous and theatrical traditions against the heroic idiom of, for example, Spenser and Chapman (though the opposition runs the risk of underplaying the importance of romance and the erotic in Spenser). See Cheney's *Shakespeare, National Poet-Playwright* and *Shakespeare's Literary Authorship* (Cambridge University Press, 2012); also his *Marlowe's Counterfeit Profession: Ovid, Spenser, Counter-Nationhood* (University of Toronto Press, 2011).

33. *The Rape of Lucrece*, 176–82, 505.

34. Ibid., 199, 542.

35. Ibid., 1424–26.

36. *Titus Andronicus*, 5. 3. 81–82. For Virgil's use of *ekphrasis*, see Michael C. J. Putnam, *Virgil's Epic Designs: Ekphrasis in the Aeneid* (Yale University Press, 1998). The bibliography on the *ekphrasis* in *Lucrece* is substantial: one might begin with Catherine Belsey, "Invocation of the Visual Image: Ekphrasis in *Lucrece* and Beyond," *Shakespeare Quarterly*, 63 (2012), pp. 175–98; and Marion A. Wells, "'To Find a Face Where All Distress Is Stell'd': Enargeia, Ekphrasis, and Mourning in *The Rape of Lucrece* and the *Aeneid*," *Comparative Literature*, 54 (2002), pp. 97–126. See also Cheney, *National Poet-Playwright*, p. 134, and, linking this passage to Shakespeare's other allusions to Aeneas's tale to Dido, Heather James's fine "Dido's Ear: Tragedy and the Politics of Response," *Shakespeare Quarterly*, 52 (2001), pp. 360–82.

37. *The Rape of Lucrece*, 1564–77.

38. Thomas Nashe, *Pierce Penniless, His Supplication to the Devil*, in Nashe, *Works*, ed. McKerrow, 1. 212.

39. *1 Henry VI*, 4. 3. 45–56.

40. *Henry V*, 3. 1. 31–34.

41. *Coriolanus*, 5. 6. 129–32.

42. Modern scholarship begins from Gary Taylor's influential "Shakespeare and Others: The Authorship of *Henry the Sixth, Part One*," *Medieval & Renaissance Drama in England*, 7 (1995), pp. 145–205; but see also Marcus Dahl, "Did Shakespeare Write *Henry VI Part One*? Or: Gary Taylor and Rhetoric of Attribution: A Prelude to Statistical Analysis and the Justification of an 'Initial Pattern,'" *Postgraduate English: A Journal and Forum for Postgraduates in English*, 1 (March 2000), http://community.dur.ac.uk/post graduate.english/ojs/index.php/pgenglish/article/view/3/2.

43. *1 Henry VI*, 4. 7. 23–32.

44. *3 Henry VI*, 2. 5. 114–22.

45. The first critic to make full sense of the speech, and the link between Hamlet and Pyrrhus, was Harry Levin in his enduring study *The Question of Hamlet* (Oxford University Press, 1959). See also Heather James's suggestive reading in "Dido's Ear: Tragedy and the Politics of Response": "In Hamlet's vision the tragic theater forges a link between commiseration and consent—even, or perhaps especially, to the revolutionary content of regicide" (p. 381); *Hamlet*, 2. 2. 380.

46. *Hamlet*, 2. 2. 381, 383–84, 390–91.

47. Ibid., 2. 2. 395–407.

48. Ibid., 2. 2. 410–34.

49. Virgil, *Aeneid*, 2. 510.

50. *Hamlet*, 2. 2. 411–13, 415–16; Virgil, *Aeneid*, 2. 509–11; Christopher Marlowe and Thomas Nashe, *Dido Queen of Carthage*, 2. 1. 253–54, quoted from Marlowe, *Complete Plays and Poems*, ed. Pendry and Maxwell. The triangulation of the Player's speech, Virgil's original, and the play by Marlowe and Nashe has produced much debate ever since these parallels were first noticed by eighteenth-century editors. The best discussion is James Black, "Hamlet Hears Marlowe, Shakespeare Reads Virgil," *Renaissance and Reformation*, 18 (1994), pp. 17–28.

51. Virgil, *Aeneid*, 2. 551–52; *The Aeneid of Thomas Phaer and Thomas Twyne: A Critical Edition*, ed. Steven Lally (Taylor and Francis, 1987), 2. 557–58.

52. Marlowe and Nashe, *Dido Queen of Carthage*, 2. 1. 255–56; *Macbeth*, 1. 2. 24.

53. Virgil, *Aeneid*, 2.471–75, as translated in Phaer/Twyne, ed. Lally.

54. *Hamlet*, 2. 2. 440–41.

55. *Hamlet*, 3. 4. 83–84, 100–101.

56. Ibid., 2. 2. 422.

57. Ibid., 3. 1. 62–94.

58. Ibid., 3. 1. 89.

59. *Troilus and Cressida*, 1. 2. 19; *Macbeth*, 5. 7. 1–2; *3 Henry VI*, 5. 6. 83; *Richard III*, 5. 3. 181–210.

60. See the exemplary treatment in Bruce R. Smith, *Shakespeare and Masculinity* (Oxford Univesity Press, 2000), especially pp. 11, 27, 47–48; *Troilus and Cressida*, 5. 11. 1, 3–23.

61. "A never writer to an ever reader" in some copies of the 1609 quarto of *Troilus and Cressida* (*Complete Works*, p. 1534).

62. Horace, *Epistulae*, 1. 1. 14–15, my translation.

CHAPTER 9: THE GOOD LIFE

1. For Spenser and Virgil, see Merritt Y. Hughes, *Virgil and Spenser* (University of California Press, 1969); also Jane Tylus, "Spenser, Virgil, and the Politics of Poetic Labor," *ELH*, 55 (1988), pp. 53–77. For Shakespeare, Marlowe, and Ovid, see William Keach, *Elizabethan Erotic Narratives: Irony and Pathos in the Ovidian Poetry of Shakespeare, Marlowe, and Their Contemporaries* (Hassocks, 1977); and my own *Shakespeare and Ovid*. For Jonson and Horace, see Robert B. Pierce, "Ben Jonson's Horace and Horace's Ben Jonson," *Studies in Philology*, 78 (1981), pp. 20–31; Katharine Eisaman Maus, *Ben Jonson and the Roman Frame of Mind* (Princeton University Press, 1984); Joanna Martindale, "'The Best Master of Virtue and Wisdom': The Horace of Ben Jonson and His Heirs," in *Horace Made New: Horatian Influences on British Writing from the Renaissance to the Twentieth Century*, ed. Charles Martindale and David Hopkins (Cambridge University Press, 1993), pp. 50–85; and especially Victoria Moul, *Jonson, Horace and the Classical Tradition*.

2. I have not encountered any substantial attempt to offer a "Horatian" reading of Shakespeare. The most detailed treatment of particular echoes remains the relevant chapter in T. W. Baldwin's *William Shakspere's Small Latine*, 2. 497–525. Stuart Gillespie summarizes the existing scholarship in his admirable *Shakespeare's Books*, coming up with relatively thin pickings and the conclusion that "A fairly good knowledge of the text of Horace's *Odes*, with more mixed levels of awareness of his other works, is evident in Shakespeare, but he is, *tout court*, no Horatian writer" (pp. 259–68). The bibliography to the Horace entry in Gillespie lists little more than some dozen noticings of local echoes, while the online *World Shakespeare Bibliography* has more than three hundred entries for Ovid and fewer than ten for Horace (rather more appear if one types "Horace" into the search box,

but most of the results concern either the influence of the Shakespearean Gothic on Horace Walpole or the editorial work of Horace Howard Furness!).

3. Elizabeth Jane Weston, *Parthenicôn* (c. 1608), 1. 13, in Elizabeth Jane Weston, *Collected Writings*, ed. and trans. Donald Cheney and Brenda M. Hosington (University of Toronto Press, 2000), p. 25. Originally published in her *Poëmata* (1602), fol. B2ʳ, with a variant in line 2, "celebris" for "assidua." The neglect of Weston's superbly crafted neo-Latin poetry is one of the more shameful stories in twentieth-century English literary history and criticism, attributable more to the decline of the classics than to her gender. Recovery began with the research of Susan Bassnett (e.g., "Revising a Biography," *Cahiers élisabéthains*, 37 [1990], pp. 1–8) and J. W. Binns's monumental survey of neo-Latin texts, *Intellectual Culture in Elizabethan and Jacobean England* (Francis Cairns, 1990), pp. 110–13.

4. See *Songs and Sonettes by Henry Howard, Earl of Surrey, Sir Thomas Wyatt the Elder, Nicholas Grimald and Uncertain Authors*, ed. as *Tottel's Miscellany* in the English Reprints of Edward Arber (1870; repr., AMS Press, 1966), pp. 27, 85, 161.

5. Ibid., "Of the courtiers life, written to John Poins," pp. 88–90.

6. Thomas Cooper, *Thesaurus Linguae Romanae et Britannicae* (1584), s.v. "Horatius."

7. Suetonius, *Q. Horatii Flacci Vita, per Suetonium Tranquillum Conscripta* (this trans. by Alexander Thomson, 1796). Not included in Philemon Holland, trans., *The historie of tvvelve Caesars emperours of Rome: written in Latine by C. Suetonius Tranquillus, and newly translated into English. With a marginall glosse, and other briefe annotations there-upon* (1606), but available in some early modern editions of Horace, such as *Quinti Horatii Flacci Poemata scholijs siue annotationibus, quae breuis commentarij vice esse possint à Ioanne Bond illustrata. Impensis Georgij Bishop* [Printed by Shakespeare's friend Richard Field] (1608).

8. Horace, *Epistles*, 1. 4. 15–16 (Loeb trans.), a deliberately parodic image of an Epicurean life of bodily pleasure, targeted at the self-mortifying elegiac poet Tibullus (who is probably the Albius of that poem).

9. *Love's Labour's Lost*, 4. 3. 92; *A Midsummer Night's Dream*, 5. 1. 57–58.

10. *Timon of Athens*, 1. 2. 30–31, with respect to Apemantus, quoting Horace, *Epistles*, 1. 2. 62.

11. *Love's Labour's Lost*, 4. 2. 77–78.

12. *Titus Andronicus*, 3. 1. 51–56.

13. *Cymbeline*, 3. 3. 56–58.

14. *2 Henry VI*, 4. 10. 11–18.

15. *3 Henry VI*, 2. 5. 1–54 (21–22, 41, 40, 54).

16. *2 Henry IV*, 3. 1. 30–31, 38–39, 45–46, Quarto-only passage following 3. 1. 53 (*Complete Works*, p. 1024).

17. Rebecca Yearling, *Ben Jonson, John Marston and Early Modern Drama: Satire and the Audience* (Springer, 2016) is a good starting point for the image of such 1590s writers as Joseph Hall and John Marston as "whipping satirists" or "snarling satirists"; Jonson's *Poetaster* is well contextualized in the Revels Plays edition of Tom Cain (Manchester University Press, 1996).

18. See my discussion in *Soul of the Age*, pp. 354–59.

19. *Timon of Athens*, 5. 1. 22–24.

20. Ibid., 1. 1. 26–31.

21. At *Odes*, 4. 2. 26–32, Horace is the busy bee, laboriously collecting the materials for his *operosa carmina*; at *Epistles*, 1. 19. 44, *manare poetica mella* is put in the mouth of a hostile and sarcastic critic of him (I owe this point to one of my anonymous Press readers).

22. *Timon of Athens*, 1. 1. 54–56.

23. Bate, "Shakespeare the Epicurean," chap. 24 in *Soul of the Age*. For a counterargument that there is an anti-Epicurean vein of thought in Shakespeare, especially in *Hamlet*, see Patrick Gray, " 'HIDE THY SELFE': Montaigne, Hamlet, and Epicurean Ethics," in *Shakespeare and Renaissance Ethics*, ed. Patrick Gray and John D. Cox (Cambridge University Press, 2014), pp. 213–36.

24. On this, see further Robert Pogue Harrison, *Gardens: An Essay on the Human Condition* (University of Chicago Press, 2008), passim.

25. See Cicero, *De Finibus*, passim, and Epicurus, "Principal Doctrines," in book 10 of Diogenes Laërtius, *Lives and Opinions of Eminent Philosophers*.

26. *Titus Andronicus*, 2. 4. 36–37.

27. *Love's Labour's Lost*, 1. 1. 207.

28. *Much Ado about Nothing*, 3. 1. 174; George Chapman, "Eugenia; or, True Nobility's Trance," in *Works*, ed. A. C. Swinburne (Chatto and Windus, 1875), 1. 336.

29. *Henry V*, 4. 7. 26.

30. Horace, *Satires*, 2. 6.

31. Horace, *Odes*, 4. 10, not among the odes translated by John Ashmore in 1621; in my pocket edition of Horace, *Satires, Epistles, Art of Poetry and Odes: The Latin Text with Conington's Translation* (Bell, 1931), there is a prim note opposite the Latin text of 4. 10: "[This Ode is not included in Professor Conington's translation]."

32. Sonnet 94. There is an excellent, albeit brief, discussion of Horace and Shakespeare's homoerotic sonnets in Bruce Smith, *Homosexual Desire in Shakespeare's England* (University of Chicago Press, 1991), pp. 228–30: "Horace's love lyrics must have startled, bothered, and intrigued Renaissance readers. The Roman poet writes about love, not as an idealistic young suitor eager for ungranted favors and untasted delights, but as a jaded man

of the world, someone who has traversed Venus's myrtle groves and come out the other side. Nothing could be less like Petrarch praising Laura or Astrophel gazing upon Stella. Furthermore, Horace writes about sexual desire between males with a matter-of-factness that avoids romanticizing that desire no less than it refuses to be embarrassed by it. He drops all the masks. There, simply, it is" (p. 228). As Smith remarks, this is exactly the tone of Shakespeare's sonnets, and the thing that makes them so different from all the other Elizabethan sonnet sequences.

33. *Twelfth Night*, 2. 3. 23–25.

34. Ibid., 2. 3. 34–39.

35. Final verse of "It was a lover and his lass" in *As You Like It*, 5. 3, 10–27, with words supplied from extratextual survival of the song.

36. *As You Like It*, 2. 1. 2–4, 10, 15, 17; 2. 7. 178–80, 193.

37. Ibid., 2. 1. 60–65.

38. Ibid., 4. 1. 15.

39. Ibid., 3. 2. 12.

40. Ibid., 3. 2. 24, 18–23.

CHAPTER 10: THE DEFENCE OF PHANTASMS

1. John Bodenham, *Politeuphuia: Wit's Commonwealth* (1598), p. 48.

2. Ibid., pp. 49–50.

3. Puttenham, *The Arte of English Poesie*, bk. 1, chap. 31, ed. Willcock and Walker, p. 60. My modernization of spelling.

4. Herbert's early sonnet "My God, where is that ancient heat towards thee," lines 4–5. This poem was sent to his mother in 1610; excluded from *The Temple*, Herbert's collected poems, it was first printed in Walton's *Life*— see *The English Poems of George Herbert*, ed. C. A. Patrides (Dent, 1974), p. 205. For numerous further examples of the assault on poetry as both full of lies and dangerously sexual, see Russell A. Fraser's underrated studies *The War against Poetry* (Princeton University Press, 1970) and *The Dark Ages and the Age of Gold* (Princeton University Press, 1973).

5. Johan Huizinga, "Art and Life," chap. 19 in *The Waning of the Middle Ages: A Study of the Forms of Life, Thought and Art in France and the Netherlands in the XIVth and XVth Centuries* (1924; repr., Doubleday, 1956). For a balanced retrospective on this influential book, see William J. Bouwsma, "Twentieth-Century Classics Revisited: *The Waning of the Middle Ages* by Johan Huizinga," *Daedalus*, 103 (1974), pp. 35–43.

6. On the basis of the number of reprints and frequency of allusion, the most influential works published during those years might be the following: the English Bibles of Tyndale (1534, 1536) and Coverdale (1535); William Lily's grammar (*An Introduction of the Eyght Partes of Speche, and*

the Construction of the Same, numerous editions); the 1543 edition of John Harding's verse *Chronicle of England*, with prose continuation by Richard Grafton, including the first printed text of Sir Thomas More's *Life of Richard III*; John Bale's martyrological *Brief Chronicle* concerning Sir John Oldcastle, Lord Cobham (1544) and his *Examinations of Anne Askew* (1546–47); *Certain Sermons or Homilies, appointed by the King's Majesty to be declared and read by all Parsons, Vicars, or Curates, every Sunday in their Churches* (1547) and *The Book of the Common Prayer* (1549), both by Thomas Cranmer and others; Edward Hall's *Union of the Two Noble and Illustrious Families of Lancaster and York* (1548); Hugh Latimer's sermon on the plough (1548; repr. in his *Sermons* of 1555); Thomas Chaloner's English translation of Erasmus's *Praise of Folly* (1549); Thomas Sternhold's metrical versions of nineteen of the *Psalms* (1549); Robert Crowley's edition of *The Vision of Pierce Plowman* (1550) and his poem *Philargyrie of Great Britain* (1551); More's *Dialogue of Comfort against Tribulation* (1553) and the English version of his *Utopia* (translated by Ralph Robinson, 1551); Thomas Wilson's *The Art of Rhetoric* (1553); the first (1554–55) edition of the work which became known as *A Mirror for Magistrates*. Many of these works, notably the various chronicles and the *Mirror for Magistrates*, were valuable sources for Shakespeare and his fellow dramatists and poets, but the intention of the original authors was anything but the provision of popular entertainment. My list is restricted to publicly disseminated and thus in some sense propagandistic works, the printing press during this period being frequently an instrument of control and rarely a vehicle for play. In the manuscript poetry of courtiers such as Wyatt and Surrey, one does find a sheer delight in "poesy"—but their lyrics were not disseminated in print prior to the publication of Tottel's *Songes and Sonettes* in 1557. That is one of the reasons why Tottel—beloved of Shakespeare's Abraham Slender—was such an important book. For a polemical reading of the literature of the reign of Henry VIII as monolithic and in many senses propagandistic, in contrast to the variegated forms of the so-called Middle Ages, see James Simpson, *Reform and Cultural Revolution*, The Oxford English Literary History, vol. 2, *1350–1547* (Oxford University Press, 2002).

7. Sidney, *Apology for Poetry*, ed. Shepherd, p. 102.

8. Puttenham, *Arte of English Poesie*, p. 3.

9. Sidney, *Apology for Poetry*, ed. Shepherd, p. 103. The most sophisticated recent account of Sidney's treatise is Catherine Bates, *On Not Defending Poetry: Defence and Indefensibility in Sidney's 'Defence of Poesy'* (Oxford University Press, 2017).

10. Sidney, *Apology for Poetry*, ed. Shepherd, pp. 101, 103.

11. Ibid., p. 103.

12. Harry Berger Jr., *Second World and Green World: Studies in Renaissance Fiction-Making* (University of California Press, 1988), pp. 11–12.

13. Webbe, *A Discourse of English Poetry*, in Smith, *Elizabethan Critical Essays*, 1. 252, where it is argued that such works are indeed "very Poetry" but that the potential harm in them comes not from the poetry "but the abuse of the users, who, undamaging their own dispositions by reading the discoveries of vices, resemble foolish folk who, coming into a garden without any choice or circumspection, tread down the fairest flowers and willfully thrust their fingers among the nettles."

14. Stephen Gosson, *A pleasant invective against Poets, Pipers, Players, Jesters and such like Caterpillars of a Commonwealth* (1579). Gosson, the most influential of antistage polemicists, was a former playwright, poacher turned gamekeeper; he was not, it must be acknowledged, in doctrinal sympathy with the more extreme versions of Puritanism.

15. *Hamlet*, 3. 2. 15–17.

16. *As You Like It*, 3. 3. 12. Having said this, it must be acknowledged that recent scholarship has broken down the duality between "religious" and "secular" styles in the sixteenth century. See in particular the immensely learned and insightful work of Brian Cummings: *The Literary Culture of the Reformation: Grammar and Grace* (Oxford University Press, 2002) and *Mortal Thoughts: Religion, Secularity and Identity in Shakespeare and Early Modern Culture* (Oxford University Press, 2013).

17. Batman's mythography relied to a large degree on Georg Pictorius's *Apotheseos* (1558), but the examples of how "the Poets fayne" are his own: see Anna-Maria Hartmann, "Stephen Batman, Edmund Spenser, and Myth as an Art of Discernment," chap. 2 in *English Mythography in Its European Context, 1500–1650* (Oxford University Press, 2018), where it is argued that this is Batman's method of recuperating positive morals from irreligious falsehoods—in this sense, he was working in the tradition of the *Ovide moralisé*, as was his fellow-protestant contemporary Arthur Golding.

18. All Batman quotations are from *The golden booke of the leaden goddess* (1577), pages unnumbered, quoted from Early English Books Online: Text Creation Partnership, https://quod.lib.umich.edu/e/eebo/A05703.000 1.001/1:6?rgn=div1;view=toc.

19. Stephen Greenblatt offers an influential reading of *The Faerie Queene*, book 2, canto 12, in the context of Reformation hostility to images in "To Fashion a Gentleman: Spenser and the Destruction of the Bower of Bliss," chap. 4 in *Renaissance Self-Fashioning: From More to Shakespeare* (University of Chicago Press, 1980).

20. *A Midsummer Night's Dream*, 4. 1. 197–206, garbling 1 Corinthians 2:9–10.

21. *3 Henry VI*, 1. 2. 31; *The Merchant of Venice*, 5. 1. 85–86; *A Midsummer Night's Dream*, 1. 1. 31–32; *Twelfth Night*, 1. 5. 142–43.

22. Now generally regarded as a collaboration with Thomas Middleton, but there is a consensus that accepts Shakespeare's authorship of the Poet/ Painter scene.

23. *Timon of Athens*, 1. 1. 74–75.

24. Ibid., 1. 1. 237–49.

25. *Cymbeline*, 4. 2. 300–303.

26. Ibid., 4. 2. 327–28.

27. Ibid., 4. 2. 333–34.

28. Ibid., 4. 2. 346; Horace, *Odes*, 2. 20. 1, imitated in Shakespeare's Sonnet 55 ("Not marble nor the gilded monuments / Of princes shall outlive this powerful rhyme"). Compare also the opening speech of *Love's Labour's Lost*. See further, the discussion in my final chapter.

29. *Cymbeline*, 4. 2. 341–42.

30. Tertullian, *De Spectaculis*, XXIII, in *Tertullian: Apology and De Spectaculis. Minucius Felix: Octavius*, trans. T. R. Glover and G. H. Rendall, Loeb Classical Library 250 (Harvard University Press, 1931), p. 287.

31. Plato, *Sophist*, 236a–c.

32. Plato, *Republic*, 514a–520a.

33. See especially Plotinus, *Enneads*, 1. 3. 1–2.

34. Sidney, *Apology for Poetry*, ed. Shepherd, p. 125.

35. Puttenham, *Arte of English Poesie*, bk. 1, chap. 8, ed. Willcock and Walker, p. 19.

36. Thomas Blount, *Glossographia: Or A Dictionary, Interpreting all such Hard Words, whether Hebrew, Greek, Latin, Italian, Spanish, French, Teutonick, Belgick, British or Saxon; as are now used in our refined English Tongue. Also the Terms of Divinity, Law, Physick, Mathematicks, Heraldry, Anatomy, War, Musick, Architecture; and of several other Arts and Sciences Explicated. With Etymologies, Definitions, and Historical Observations on the same. Very useful for all such as desire to understand what they read* (1656), s.v. "Phantasm."

37. *A Midsummer Night's Dream*, 4. 1. 197–98; *Romeo and Juliet*, 2. 3. 22, 16; *Love's Labour's Lost*, 4. 1. 90; 5. 1. 13.

38. *Julius Caesar*, 2. 1. 63–69.

39. *Macbeth*, 2. 1. 40ff.

40. *A Midsummer Night's Dream*, 5. 1. 18.

41. Quintilian, *Institutio Oratoria*, 6. 2. 29–30. There is a valuable discussion in Ronald Levao, *Renaissance Minds and Their Fictions: Cusanus, Sidney, Shakespeare* (University of California Press, 1985), p. 118. In *Proteus Unmasked: Sixteenth-Century Rhetoric and the Art of Shakespeare* (Lehigh University Press, 2004), p. 55, Trevor McNeely notes the importance of this

passage for Elizabethan ideas of the actor's power to generate emotion—the matter upon which Hamlet reflects in his "How all occasions" soliloquy. John D. Lyons argues that the passage is also crucial for the emergence of the Romantic and modern idea of the power of "imagination," even though Quintilian does not have the actual word (the English translation "things absent are presented to our imagination" unhelpfully merges *imagines* and *animo* in Quintilian's "imagines rerum absentium ... ita repraesentantur animo"). See Lyons, *Before Imagination: Embodied Thought from Montaigne to Rousseau* (Stanford University Press, 2005), p. 25.

42. *Twelfth Night*, 4. 2. 34, 65.

43. Ibid., 5. 1. 361.

44. *The Tempest*, 1. 2. 30, 33, 340, 434; 2. 2. 307; 4. 1. 43, 130; 5. 1. 55, 369.

45. *A Midsummer Night's Dream*, 5. 1. 2–20.

46. See, for example, Aristotle, *De Anima*, 3. 3.

47. Not noted in Variorum, Oxford, or 2nd or 3rd series Arden editions.

48. *OED* "compact," adj. (2), "Joined in compact, leagued," citing Samuel Daniel, *First Fowre Bks. Civile Warres* (1595), i. liii. sig. D², "The chiefe of those you find / Were of his faction secretly compact," and Shakespeare, *Measure for Measure* (c. 1604), 5. 1. 240, "Thou pernicious woman / Compact with her that's gone." All *OED* citations are from http://www.oed.com.

49. *Hamlet*, 1. 1. 27–28.

50. *Timon of Athens*, 1. 1. 39–41.

51. The attribution was first made by Edward Capell in 1760. The current state of scholarship is expertly reviewed in the Arden edition, *King Edward III*, ed. Richard Proudfoot and Nicola Bennett (Bloomsbury, 2017), pp. 49–89; and by Sharpe, "Authorship and Attribution."

52. The Arden editors propose (pp. 69–80) that the surviving text of *Edward III* may well be Shakespeare's revision of an earlier version, in which case he probably wrote the part of Lodowick in close proximity to the composition of *A Midsummer Night's Dream*.

53. *Edward III*, 2. 1. 1–8 (quoted from Bate et al., *Collaborative Plays*).

54. "It is impossible to think without an image [*phantasma*]" (Aristotle, *De Memoria*, 450a. 1). Furthermore, "Aristotle's views about imagery (*phantasmata*) cannot be fully understood in isolation from his views about imagination (*phantasia*), which he defined as '(apart from any metaphorical sense of the word) the process by which we say that an image [*phantasma*] is presented to us' (*De Anima* 428a. 1–4). Aristotle has been accredited with the very invention of the concept of imagination ... and certainly it seems fair to say that the roots of most subsequent discussions of the concept can be traced back to his work (even though, for him, it did not have the strong association with creativity and aesthetic insight that it has since acquired, mostly through the influence of the Romantic movement)"

(Nigel J. T. Thomas, "Mental Imagery," in *The Stanford Encyclopedia of Philosophy*, ed. Edward N. Zalta, Spring 2018 ed., https://plato.stanford.edu /archives/spr2018/entries/mental-imagery).

55. *Edward III*, 2. 1. 66–67.

56. Ibid., 2. 1. 76–79.

57. Ibid., 2. 1. 106, 111.

58. Ibid., 2. 1. 152–54.

59. *Measure for Measure*, 2. 4. 163–79.

60. *The Comedy of Errors*, 1. 2. 98–100.

61. *Antony and Cleopatra*, 1. 2. 124; *As You Like It*, 3. 2. 255–60; *Henry V*, 5. 2. 232–33.

62. *Henry V*, 5. 2. 234–39.

63. *A Midsummer Night's Dream*, 3. 2. 158, 160–61.

64. *Othello*, 1. 3. 78.

65. Ibid., 1. 3. 102.

66. *The Winter's Tale*, 5. 3. 45–47.

67. Ibid., 5. 3. 132–34.

68. *As You Like It*, 5. 3. 70–71; *Romeo and Juliet*, 1. 4. 100–102.

69. *A Midsummer Night's Dream*, 5. 1. 25–26.

70. Marsilio Ficino, *Commentarium in Convivium Platonis De Amore* (1484), 6. 10; repr. in *Marcilii Ficini Florentini Opera Omnia* (Bottego d'Erasmo, 1959). English translation from quotation by Ioan P. Couliano in his *Eros and Magic in the Renaissance*, trans. Margaret Cook (University of Chicago Press, 1987), p. 87.

71. Ficino as paraphrased by Couliano, *Eros and Magic in the Renaissance*, p. 88.

72. "Vinculum quippe vinculorum amor est" (Giordano Bruno, *De vinculis in genere* [c. 1588], art. XVI, http://www.esotericarchives.com/bruno /vinculis.htm).

73. D. P. Walker, *Spiritual and Demonic Magic: From Ficino to Campanella* (Penn State Press, 2000), pp. 82–83.

74. Couliano, *Eros and Magic in the Renaissance*, pp. 93–95.

75. Ibid., pp. 88–90.

76. Richard Baines, in "A Folio containing Papers chiefly relating to Ecclesiastical Affairs," British Library Harley MS 6848, https://www.bl.uk /collection-items/accusations-against-christopher-marlowe-by-richard -baines-and-others.

77. Giordano Bruno, *Theses De Magia*, LVI, http://www.esotericarchives .com/bruno/theses.htm, English translation from Couliano, *Eros and Magic in the Renaissance*, p. 91.

78. Ibid., English translation from Couliano, *Eros and Magic in the Renaissance*, p. 90.

79. Frances Yates, *A Study of Love's Labour's Lost* (1936; repr., Cambridge University Press, 2013). The force of Yates's broad argument about Neoplatonism versus humanism in the play is much stronger than her suggestions that Holofernes is a portrait of John Florio and that the name Berowne somehow alludes to Bruno. Yates's *Giordano Bruno and the Hermetic Tradition* (1964; repr., Routledge, 2002) remains essential reading, even though no direct connection with Shakespeare can be proven. Similarly, one does not have to read Prospero *as* John Dee or Cornelius Agrippa to discover a Brunoesque nexus of *eros* and magic in *The Tempest*, as Yates did in her (very Warburgian) 1974 Lord Northcliffe Lecture on "Magic in the Last Plays," published in her *Shakespeare's Last Plays: A New Approach* (Routledge, 1975), pp. 101–14.

80. *Love's Labour's Lost*, 4. 3. 346–47.

81. Ibid., 4. 3. 367.

82. Colossians 3:5, 14 (Geneva translation).

83. *The Tempest*, 5. 1. 368–73.

84. Ibid., 5. 1. 374–75.

CHAPTER 11: AN INFIRMITY NAMED *HEREOS*

1. *Hamlet*, 4. 4. 24; 4. 4. 187.

2. *As You Like It*, 5. 3. 10. Good starting points for this subject are David Lindley, *Shakespeare and Music* (Arden Shakespeare, 2006); and Suzanne Lord, *Music from the Age of Shakespeare: A Cultural History* (Greenwood, 2003).

3. Anon., *The Return from Parnassus Part 1*, 3. 1, 4. 1, in *The Three Parnassus Plays (1598–1601)*, ed. J. B. Leishman (Nicholson and Watson, 1949).

4. *The Merry Wives of Windsor*, 1. 1. 140.

5. Giles Fletcher, "To the Reader," in *Licia, or Poemes of Love* (1593).

6. Robert Greene, *Groats-worth of Witte* (1592), sig. C3ʳ.

7. John Rainolds, *Th-overthrow of stage-plays, by the way of controversy betwixt D[octor] Gager and D[octor] Rainolds wherein all the reasons that can be made for them are notably refuted; th'objections answered, and the case so cleared and resolved, as that the judgement of any man, that is not forward and perverse, may easily be satisfied. Wherein is manifestly proved, that it is not only unlawful to be an actor, but a beholder of those vanities* (1599), p. 7, https://open.library.ubc.ca/media/download/pdf/52383/1.0074 609/46, alluding to Genesis 39:7.

8. W. S., *The Tragedy of Locrine* (1595), 1. 3. 8–11, in Bate et al., *Collaborative Plays*.

9. *As You Like It*, 4. 1. 145–46.

10. Henry Crosse, *Vertues Common-wealth: Or the High-way to Honour* (1603), sig. Q1ʳ. The title reads as a riposte to Bodenham and Meres's *Wits Commonwealth*.

11. For surveys of the current state of scholarship regarding this attribution, see pp. 650–57 of Will Sharpe's "Authorship and Attribution" in Bate et al., *Collaborative Plays*, and pp. 123–93 of Taylor and Egan, *The New Oxford Shakespeare: Authorship Companion*.

12. *Arden of Faversham*, 1. 60–66, in Bate et al., *Collaborative Plays* (scene and line numbers only; no act divisions).

13. See, e.g., Nashe, "Choice of Valentines" (line 296), in Nashe, *Works*, ed. McKerrow, 3. 414.

14. Marlowe's expansion of Ovid's "lente currite, noctis equi" (*Amores*, 1. 13. 40).

15. *Romeo and Juliet*, 3. 2. 1–5.

16. *Arden of Faversham*, 1. 101–2.

17. Sidney, *Apology for Poetry*, p. 125.

18. Richard Bright, *A Treatise of Melancholie* (1586), p. 254.

19. Robert Burton, *The Anatomy of Melancholy what it is. With all the kindes, causes, symptomes, prognostickes, and severall cures of it. In three maine partitions with their severall sections, members, and subsections. Philosophically, medicinally, historically, opened and cut up. By Democritus Junior. With a satyricall preface, conducing to the following discourse* (1621), Third Partition, sec. 2, mem. 1, subsec. 2, "How love tyranniseth over men. Love or heroicall melancholy, his definition, part affected."

20. Ibid., p. 543.

21. *Hamlet*, 2. 1. 82–85, 99–101.

22. *Trolius and Cressida*, 1. 1. 46–47; 3. 2. 15, 20–22; 2. 3. 50–51.

23. Ibid., 1. 1. 48.

24. Andrew Boord, *The Breviarie of Health wherin doth folow, remedies, for all maner of sicknesses & diseases, the which may be in man or woman. Expressing the obscure termes of Greke, Araby, Latin, Barbary, and English, concerning phisick and chirurgerie. Compyled by Andrew Boord, Doctor of phisicke: an English-man* (1587), chap. 174.

25. *The workes of our antient and learned English poet, Geffrey Chaucer, newly printed*, ed. Thomas Speght (1598), in the list of "The Hard Words of Chaucer Explained" that Speght compiled for his edition.

26. 1598 note emended to "*Eros*, fol. 3, p. 1 g. Whereas some copies have Hereos, some Hernes, and some such like coounterfait word, whereof can be given no reason; I have set doune Eros, *i*. cupid." See further, John Livingston Lowes, "The Loveres Maladye of Hereos," *Modern Philology*, 11 (1941), pp. 491–546 (pp. 492–93).

27. Ad-Damîrî, *Hayât al-Hayawân* (late fourteenth century), trans. A. S. G. Jayakar (London and Bombay, 1906), quoted in Lowes, "The Loveres Maladye of Hereos," p. 517. Mary Wack notes that "Constantine the African's translations disseminated a medical view of love that helped to shape the European experience of *eros* during the high Middle Ages. He was the first, as far as we know, to endow the Arabic word for passionate love or lovesickness—*isq*—with a Latin equivalent, and thus to give Western physicians a diagnostic term for the malady of love" ("Alī ibn al-'Abbās al-Maǧūsī and Constantine on Love, and the Evolution of the Practica Pantegni," in *Constantine the African and 'Alī ibn al-'Abbās al-Maǧūsī: The "Pantegni" and Related Texts*, ed. Charles Burnett and Danielle Jacquart [Brill, 1994], p. 161). On *amor hereos* in the high Middle Ages, see further Roger Boase, *The Origin and Meaning of Courtly Love* (Manchester University Press, 1977), appendix 1.

28. Sonnet 130.

29. See Erwin Panofsky, "Blind Cupid," chap. 4 in *Studies in Iconology: Humanistic Themes in the Art of the Renaissance* (Oxford University Press, 1939; repr., Harper & Row, 1962).

30. *A Midsummer Night's Dream*, 2. 1. 168–75.

31. *A Midsummer Night's Dream*, 5. 1. 2–22. See my discussion of Theseus's speech in chapter 10.

32. On this subject, one might begin with *Plato and the Poets*, ed. Pierre Destrée and Fritz-Gregor Herrmann (Brill, 2011), especially chap. 5, F. J. Gonzalez, "The Hermeneutics of Madness: Poet and Philosopher in Plato's *Ion* and *Phaedrus*," pp. 93–110.

33. Sonnet 116; Sonnet 129.

34. For the many editions and translations that evidence the status of *Diana* as one of the foundational pastoral romances of the age, see Julián Arribas, "Estudio Bibliográfico: Catalogo de Ejemplares," in Jorge de Montemayor, *Los Siete Libros De La Diana* (Tamesis, 1996), pp. 19–83. John Hoskins regarded it as one of the three key influences on Sidney's *Arcadia*, the apogee of Englished pastoral romance: "For the web, as it were, of his story, he followed three: Heliodorus in Greek, Sannazarius' *Arcadia* in Italian, and *Diana* by Montemayor in Spanish" (Hoskins, *Directions for Speech and Style* [1599; repr., Princeton University Press, 1935], p. 41).

35. This does not necessarily mean that Shakespeare could read Spanish: there were many French translations of Montemayor, and an English one (completed by 1582) may have circulated in manuscript prior to its publication in 1598. J. L. Chamosa González argues that Shakespeare used Nicolas Collin's French translation (1578): "La versión de la historia de Félix y Felismena que Shakespeare utilizó para su *The Two Gentlemen of Verona*,"

in *Actas del X Congreso Nacional de AEDEAN* (AEDEAN, 1988), pp. 257–67. He could alternatively have been reworking the plot of *Felix and Feliomena*, a now-lost dramatization of it performed by the Queen's Men in the 1580s.

36. Richard Howlet, *ABCEdarium Anglico Latinum, Pro Tyrunculis* (1552), s.v. "Proteus."

37. *The Two Gentlemen of Verona*, 2. 7. 75–78.

38. Ibid., 4. 4. 142–56.

39. Ibid., 4. 4. 158–59.

40. Ibid., 5. 4. 57–60.

41. Ibid., 5. 4. 60–61.

42. *A Midsummer Night's Dream*, 2. 1. 77–81.

43. *The Winter's Tale*, 4. 4. 29–39.

44. *Venus and Adonis*, 231–38.

45. E.g., ibid., 185, 379, 587, 611, 785.

46. On the ban, Richard A. McCabe, "Elizabethan Satire and the Bishops' Ban of 1599," *Yearbook of English Studies*, 11 (1981), pp. 188–93, emphasizes the libelous and seditious nature of some of the banned books, while John Peter, *Complaint and Satire in Early English Literature* (Clarendon Press, 1956), focuses on the obscenity and indecency of others; Andrew S. Keener, "Robert Tofte's *Of Mariage and Wiving* and the Bishops' Ban of 1599," *Studies in Philology*, 110 (2013), pp. 506–32, notes anxiety about Aretino-influenced Italian debauchery, and Lynda Boose detects fear of homoerotic imagery: "The 1599 Bishop's Ban, Renaissance Pornography, and the Sexualization of the Jacobean Stage," in *Enclosure Acts: Sexuality, Property and Culture in Early Modern England*, ed. Richard Burt and John Michael Archer (Cornell University Press, 1994), pp. 185–200. Bryan Herek provides a summary overview in "Reconsidering the 1599 Bishops' Ban on Satire," in *Renaissance Papers 2011*, ed. Andrew Shifflett and Edward Gieskes (Boydell and Brewer, 2012), pp. 131–40.

47. *Venus and Adonis*, 1115–18.

48. *Venus and Adonis*, 1138, 1140, 1141, 1146, 1151–52, 1159–60, 1164.

49. Dedicatory letter to Henry Wriothesley, 3rd Earl of Southampton, prefacing *Venus and Adonis*, *Complete Works*, p. 2398.

50. *The Rape of Lucrece*, 673–86 (684).

51. *Cymbeline*, 2. 4. 209; *The Winter's Tale*, 1. 2. 139. There has been a wealth of scholarship on Shakespeare and rape in recent years: further reading could begin with Jean E. Howard, "Interrupting the Lucrece Effect?: The Performance of Rape on the Early Modern Stage," in *The Oxford Handbook of Shakespeare and Embodiment: Gender, Sexuality, and Race*, ed. Valerie Traub (Oxford University Press, 2016), pp. 657–72; and, for an Ovidian inflection, Lisa Starks-Estes, *Violence, Trauma, and Virtus in Shakespeare's Roman Poems and Plays: Transforming Ovid* (Palgrave, 2014).

52. *Romeo and Juliet*, 2. 5. 9.

53. Ibid., 3. 2. 20–25. The invocation to night and its erotic opportunity also functions, as does the nightingale versus lark duologue of Romeo and Juliet at the beginning of 3. 5, as an *imitatio* of Ovid's *Amores*, 1. 13 (described by Christopher Marlowe in his translation as "Ad Auroram, ne properet," "To the dawn, not to hurry"), with its famous line "lente currite, noctis equi!"—which is quoted in Latin by Dr Faustus in the very different context of his damnation speech (Ovid, *Amores*, 1. 13. 40; Marlowe, *Ovid's Elegies*, 1. 13, heading; *Dr Faustus*, 5. 2. 143, with an additional "lente" for emphasis).

54. Virgil, *Aeneid*, 1. 278–79.

55. *Antony and Cleopatra*, 5. 2. 92.

56. Ibid., 1. 3. 43; 1. 1. 16–17.

57. Ibid., 4. 14. 58–62.

58. Ibid.

59. Virgil, *Aeneid*, 4. 412, trans. Stanyhurst (1582), L4^v.

60. *The Tempest*, 2. 1. 63–65. The allusion has led to much scholarly discussion of the broader correspondences between *The Aeneid* and *The Tempest*: see, for example, Hamilton, *Virgil and "The Tempest"*; Jan Kott, "*The Aeneid* and *The Tempest*," *Arion*, 3 (1978), pp. 425–51; John Pitcher, "'A Theatre of the Future': The *Aeneid* and *The Tempest*," *Essays in Criticism*, 34 (1984), pp. 193–215; and Leah Whittington, "Shakespeare's Virgil: Empathy and *The Tempest*," in *Shakespeare and Renaissance Ethics*, ed. Patrick Gray and John D. Cox (Cambridge University Press, 2014), pp. 98–120. Despite the best efforts of these and other critics, I have never been able to see a coherent pattern to the allusions and parallels, beyond the particular context of the contrast between King Alonso's daughter Claribel remaining in North Africa, married to the King of Tunis, and Aeneas leaving Dido Queen of Carthage to fulfil his destiny in Italy.

61. Plutarch, *Lives*, trans. North, 4. 298.

62. Ibid., 4. 347–48.

63. *Timon of Athens*, 5. 4. 80–83. A. B. Dawson and G. E. Minton argue in their Arden edition (Bloomsbury, 2008), p. 338, that Shakespeare's intention would have been for one of the two to be omitted.

64. Who may have been the partner with access to the other apparent sources: Lucian's second-century Greek satirical dialogue "Timon the Misanthrope" (available in Latin but not English) and perhaps the anonymous (Inns of Court?) comedy *Timon*.

65. Plutarch, *Lives*, trans. North, 5. 348–60.

66. Phrygia presumably gave Shakespeare the name of his second whore, Phrynia.

67. Plutarch, *Lives*, trans. North, 5. 389.

68. *Timon of Athens*, 5. 4. 1, 3–4.

69. Ibid., 4. 3. 85–91.

70. Ibid., 4. 3. 83; *Twelfth Night*, 5. 1. 113.

71. *Timon of Athens*, 4. 3. 124–25.

72. Ibid., 4. 3. 487–90, 498–99.

73. That is a generalization, of course, but one I am happy to share with Marilyn French's underrated if overschematic *Shakespeare's Division of Experience* (Simon and Schuster, 1981).

74. *Timon of Athens*, 2. 2. 118–19; 5. 1. 159. There are also five passing, mildly sententious, mentions of "women."

75. Joseph Lane argues that "almost all the differences" between Shakespeare's Alcibiades and the figure in Plato's dialogues and Plutarch are "attributable to a single most enormous revision": "Shakespeare's Alcibiades lives among erotic Athenians and yet is not possessed by *eros* ... it is this lack of *eros* that makes the 'happy' ending, the unhoped for peaceful resolution of Athens' political turmoil, possible," but that Shakespeare thought it was most unlikely that there would ever be such a leader: "Alcibiades beyond Eros: The Unlikely Reform of the Ancient City in Shakespeare's *Timon of Athens*," paper presented at the annual meeting of the American Political Science Association, Hilton Chicago and the Palmer House Hilton, Chicago, IL, 2 September 2004, http://www.allacademic.com/meta/p60918_index.html. Given the role of what might be described as Alcibiadean homoerotic bonds in the court of King James, it might have been ill-advised of Shakespeare and Middleton to propose that such a leader was desirable.

CHAPTER 12: THE LABOURS OF HERCULES

1. Michael Drayton, *Englands Heroicall Epistles* (1597), "To the Reader," sig. A2^r.

2. J. W., "On the Authour MICHAEL DRAYTON, Esq and his *Heroick Epistles*," in 1695 reprint of *Englands Heroicall Epistles*, sig. A3^r.

3. Michael Drayton, "Edward the blacke Prince to Alice Countesse of Salisburie," in *Englands Heroicall Epistles*, 2nd ed. (1603, printed with *The Barrons Wars in the raigne of Edward the second*), "The Argument."

4. Ibid., sig. E4^v.

5. The evidence is not irrefutable, but there is a strong likelihood that Rozencrantz's line "Hercules and his load" (*Hamlet*, 2. 2. 323) alludes to Hercules standing in for Atlas as globe-bearer on the "sign" (probably the flag, like the one flying in the de Witt drawing of the Swan) of the Globe. See Richard Dutton, "*Hamlet, An Apology for Actors*, and the Sign of the Globe," *Shakespeare Survey*, 41 (1989), pp. 35–43. For scepticism, see Tiffany Stern, "Was TOTUS MUNDUS AGIT HISTRIONEM Ever the Motto of the Globe

Theatre?," *Theatre Notebook*, 51 (1997), pp. 122–27; but see also Richard Abrams, "Oldys, Motteux and 'The Play'rs Old Motto': The 'Totus Mundus' Conundrum Revisited," *Theatre Notebook*, 61 (2007), pp. 122–31.

6. For other approaches to Shakespeare and Hercules, see Charlotte Coffin, "Hercules," in *A Dictionary of Shakespeare's Classical Mythology*, ed. Yves Peyré (2009–), http://www.shakmyth.org/myth/111/hercules; M. T. Jones-Davies, "Shakespeare and the Myth of Hercules," in *Reclamations of Shakespeare*, ed. A. J. Hoenselaars (Editions Rodopi, 1994), pp. 57–74; Jeffrey Shulman, "At the Crossroads of Myth: The Hermeneutics of Hercules from Ovid to Shakespeare," *ELH*, 50 (1983), pp. 83–105; Eugene M. Waith, *The Herculean Hero in Marlowe, Chapman, Shakespeare, and Dryden* (Chatto and Windus, 1962).

7. See Edgar Wind, "Virtue Reconciled with Pleasure," chap. 5 in his *Pagan Mysteries in the Renaissance*; and Erwin Panofsky, *Hercule à la croisée des chemins*, trans. D. Cohn (1930; repr., Flammarion, 1999).

8. J. J. M. Tobin argues for Shakespeare's direct knowledge of Apuleius, the classical source that transmitted the Cupid and Psyche myth to the Renaissance, but I am by no means persuaded: *Shakespeare's Favorite Novel: A Study of The Golden Ass as Prime Source* (University Press of America, 1984).

9. Thomas Heywood, *An Apologie for Actors* (1612), sig. B4^r. Douglas Arrell interestingly revives an old argument that Heywood's own plays *The Silver Age* and *The Brazen Age* were derived from the lost Henslowe plays: "Heywood, Henslowe and Hercules: Tracking *1* and *2 Hercules* in Heywood's *Silver* and *Brazen Ages*," *Early Modern Literary Studies*, 17 (2014), pp. 1–21.

10. *Love's Labour's Lost*, 4. 1. 79–80.

11. *Coriolanus*, 4. 1. 17–21.

12. *The Taming of Shrew*, 2.1, 247–48; *Much Ado about Nothing*, 2. 1. 250–52.

13. *A Midsummer Night's Dream*, 4. 1. 104–6; *Love's Labour's Lost*, 5. 2. 605. Shakespeare was not alone among his contemporaries in getting the eleventh labour wrong: the task was not to kill Cerberus but to capture him and bring him up from the underworld.

14. *Love's Labour's Lost*, 5. 1. 89–90.

15. Ovid, *Metamorphoses*, 9. 182–204, 69–72; *Coriolanus*, 3. 1. 113; 2. 3. 10–11; *1 Henry IV*, 5. 3. 25; *2 Henry IV*, Induction, 18; 4. 1. 272; *Henry V*, 1. 1. 36; *Othello*, 2. 3. 279.

16. *Pericles*, 1. 1. 20–23, 28–34. The scene is by Shakespeare's collaborator, George Wilkins, but Shakespeare would obviously have known it: he could not have written the second half of the play without being familiar with the first.

17. *Love's Labour's Lost*, 1. 2. 49–52, 130–33.

18. Ibid., 4. 3. 354–55, 362, 353, 352, 342–43.

19. Ibid., 5. 2. 854.

20. Ibid., 5. 2. 927.

21. Though the absence of *Love's Labours Won* from the First Folio suggests that it *may* have been an alternative name for one of the surviving comedies, the suspended ending of *Love's Labours Lost*, together with the evidence of both Francis Meres's naming of the two plays in succession in 1598 and the stationer's catalogue of 1603 listing "marchant of vennis, taming of a shrew … loves labor lost, loves labor won," strongly support the hypothesis that it was a sequel. See T. W. Baldwin, *Shakspere's Love's Labour's Won: New Evidence from the Account Books of an Elizabethan Bookseller* (Southern Illinois University Press, 1957).

22. Plutarch, *Lives*, trans. North, 4. 292, 308, 310–11, 352.

23. *Antony and Cleopatra*, 4. 3. 21–22.

24. Ibid., 1. 5. 27.

25. Ibid., 2. 3. 43–44.

26. Ibid., 1. 1. 48–51.

27. All these epithets occur in the first fifty lines of the play: ibid., 1. 1. 12, 35, 3, 4, 49.

28. The Arden third series edition, for example, omits them from its lengthy discussion of characters' names: *Antony and Cleopatra*, ed. John Wilders (Routledge, 1995), pp. 87–89.

29. And of course he had already used it for the changeable lover in *A Midsummer Night's Dream*.

30. For Cicero's admiration of him, see *Epistulae ad Familiares*, 13. 1; *Academica*, 1. 4; *Brutus*, 89; *Tusculanae Quaestiones*, 2. 3.

31. *Antony and Cleopatra*, 1. 1. 1–10.

32. Ibid., 1. 4. 24–34.

33. Ibid., 1. 2. 120–26.

34. Ibid., 1. 1. 35–39.

35. Ibid., 1. 1. 15–17.

36. In a chapter called "In the creation of the world, and all things in it, the true God distinguished by certain marks from fictitious gods," Calvin refers to "infinite space … vacant space" (*Institution of the Christian Religion*, trans. John Norden [1599], 14. 22. 1). *Hamlet*, 2. 2. 247–48.

37. *Antony and Cleopatra*, 1. 1. 37.

38. Ibid., 5. 2. 92, 1. 1. 17.

39. Ibid., 5. 2. 325, 339–40.

40. *Hercules Furens*, trans. Jasper Heywood, in *Seneca His Tenne Tragedies* (1581), iv. sig. I8.

41. Ovid, *Metamorphoses*, trans. Golding, 9. 323–28.

42. *Locrine*, 4. 1. 1–10, in Bate et al., *Collaborative Plays.*

43. *Love's Labour's Lost*, 4. 3. 160, 144.

44. *Antony and Cleopatra*, 2. 5. 21–26.

45. Ibid., 4. 12. 45, 47.

46. For an excellent account of the Englishing of this story in Shakespeare's time, in the context of early modern attitudes to women, see Richard Rowland, "The Desperation of Deianira: *Heroides* 9 and Early Modern Translation," *Translation and Literature*, 22 (2013), pp. 1–24.

47. *Antony and Cleopatra*, 4. 12. 41–51.

48. *The Merchant of Venice*, 2.1. 33–39.

49. *Coriolanus*, 4. 3. 63.

50. *Antony and Cleopatra*, 2. 5. 79–80.

51. This subject is very well analysed in Braden, *Renaissance Tragedy and the Senecan Tradition.*

52. Michel Foucault, *The History of Sexuality: Volume 3: The Care of the Self*, trans. Robert Hurley (Allen Lane, 1988).

53. Brad Inwood, *Reading Seneca: Stoic Philosophy at Rome* (Clarendon Press, 2005), p. 155.

54. Lodge's translation of Seneca's works included the "arguments" of Justus Lipsius, the neo-Stoic philosopher who did more than anybody else to reconcile Stoicism and Christianity in the sixteenth century (an attempted reconciliation that was as old as Boethius).

55. *Hamlet*, 3. 2. 56–57.

56. Ezra Pound's translation of Sophocles, *Women of Trachis* (New Directions, 1985), p. 50.

57. *King Lear*, 5. 3. 323–25.

58. Seneca, *Hercules Furens*, 1323–29, trans. Heywood. There is another parallel in Seneca, *Phaedra* (lines 1715–18; the translation in *Seneca His Tenne Tragedies* is by John Studley), but the "hand" is not present there, suggesting that *Hercules Furens* is the primary source for the sequence in *Macbeth.*

59. *Macbeth*, 2. 2. 71–74.

60. "Cur animam in ista luce detineam amplius / morerque nihil est: cuncta iam amisi bona, / mentem arma famam coniugem gnatos manus, / etiam furorem, nemo polluto queat / animo mederi: morte sanandum est scelus" (Seneca, *Hercules Furens*, 1258–62).

61. For a reading of Othello's farewell to arms in relation to *Hercules Furens*, see Robert S. Miola, "Othello *Furens*," *Shakespeare Quarterly*, 41 (1990), pp. 49–64.

62. *Macbeth*, 5. 3. 25.

CHAPTER 13: WALKING SHADOWS

1. *Hamlet*, 3. 1. 85.
2. Virgil, *Aeneid*, 6. 440, 477.
3. Thomas Kyd, *The Spanish Tragedy*, ed. Philip Edwards (Revels Plays, Methuen, 1959), 1. 1. 1–91 (19, 20, 29, 33, 55–56, 64–66, 61, 77).
4. *Hamlet*, 2. 2. 353–54.
5. Seneca, *Agamemnon*, trans. John Studley in *Seneca His Tenne Tragedies*, p. 141.
6. Ibid., p. 21.
7. Jasper Heywood, *The seconde tragedie of Seneca entituled Thyestes faithfully Englished by Iasper Heywood fellowe of Alsolne College in Oxforde* (1560), sig. *¶ 2ʳ.
8. *Titus Andronicus*, 5. 2. 30–32.
9. Ibid., 2. 3. 39.
10. *King Lear*, 4. 6. 46–48.
11. *King John*, 2. 1. 63; *Julius Caesar*, 3. 1. 289–90.
12. *Julius Caesar*, 4. 2. 366–71.
13. Ibid., 4. 2. 372.
14. Ibid., 5. 5. 23.
15. Johann Caspar Lavater, *De spectris, lemuribus et magnis atque insolitis fragoribus* (1569), trans. Robert Harrison as *Of ghostes and spirites walking by nyght . . .* (1572).
16. Plutarch, *Lives*, trans. North, 3. 454 (dramatically, this is in the closing paragraph of the "Life of Julius Caesar").
17. Ibid., 4. 464.
18. Ibid.
19. Ibid. *Julius Caesar*, 5. 1. 83–84.
20. Plutarch, *Lives*, trans. North, 4. 464.
21. *Henry V*, Prologue, 17–18, 9.
22. Plutarch, *Lives*, trans. North, 4. 465.
23. *A Midsummer Night's Dream*, 5. 1. 14–17.
24. Plutarch, *Lives*, trans. North, 4. 465.
25. Cicero, *Tusculanae Disputationes*, 3. 28–31.
26. *Macbeth*, 3. 4. 71–78.
27. *Cymbeline*, 5. 3. 132.
28. Ibid., 5. 3. 200–201.
29. *Henry VIII*, 4. 2. 86–102 (86, 89, 101, 102).
30. *Richard III*, 5. 3. 121–210 (180, 187–88, 186, 208–9).
31. Hall's *Union of the Two Noble Famelies*, repr. in Geoffrey Bullough, *Narrative and Dramatic Sources of Shakespeare* (Routledge and Kegan Paul, 1966), 3. 291. Hall was the main source for Holinshed's *Chronicles*, from

which Shakespeare worked. In the light of my subsequent discussion about Catholic ghosts from Purgatory as opposed to Protestant manifestations of "conscience," it is significant that Hall's history is a work of Tudor Protestant polemic.

32. *The True Tragedy of Richard III* (1594), repr. in Bullough, *Narrative and Dramatic Sources of Shakespeare*, 3. 247, 338.

33. *Julius Caesar*, 1. 3. 25.

34. Ibid., 5. 1. 85.

35. *Macbeth*, 2. 1. 45–46.

36. *The Winter's Tale*, 3. 3. 19–22.

37. Ibid., 3. 3. 25–26, 36, 39–40; cf. *Macbeth*, 1. 3. 83–84.

38. Ibid., 3. 3. 41–49.

39. Nicholas Rowe, "Some Account of the Life, etc. of Mr William Shakespear," in his *The Works of Mr William Shakespear* (1709), 1. vi.

40. *Hamlet*, 1. 1. 35.

41. Ibid., 1. 1. 27–29.

42. Ibid., 1. 1. 62.

43. Ibid., 1. 1. 78.

44. Second Quarto only: *Hamlet*, cut passage following 1. 1. 117 (*Complete Works*, p. 2000).

45. *Hamlet*, 1. 1. 118–49 (119, 129, 147–48).

46. Ibid., 1. 4. 21, 24, 69.

47. Ibid., 1. 5. 13–17.

48. Ibid., 1. 5. 150, 152; on this dimension, see Stephen Greenblatt's *Hamlet in Purgatory*, pp. 73–101; this superb study also has an excellent chapter on the variety of Shakespeare's stage ghosts (pp. 151–204).

49. Ibid., 1. 5. 184–85. "Your" in the Quarto text, "our" in the Folio.

50. *Hamlet*, 2. 2. 530–35.

51. Ibid., 3. 4. 142–43.

52. Ibid., 3. 4. 114–16.

53. Ibid., 3. 4. 120–25.

54. Ibid., 3. 4. 112; *2 Henry IV*, 3. 1. 21.

55. Nashe, preface to Robert Greene's *Menaphon*, in Nashe, *Works*, ed. McKerrow, 3. 315–16. Anon., *A Warning for Fair Women* (1599), Induction, lines 54–57; Thomas Lodge, *Wit's Misery and the World's Madness* (1596), p. 56.

56. *Hamlet*, 1. 5. 29.

57. Quarto-only passage following *Hamlet*, 1. 1. 117 (*Complete Works*, p. 2000). Could Horatio's speech with the Julius Caesar comparison have been cut from the Folio text of the play because Shakespeare or his actors thought that it was overcomplicating matters to have quite so many contradictory interpretations of the nature of the ghost?

58. *The Tempest*, 4. 1. 169–71.
59. *A Midsummer Night's Dream*, 5. 1. 13, 18.
60. *The Tempest*, 4. 1. 161–63.
61. *A Midsummer Night's Dream*, 5. 1. 393.
62. *As You Like It*, 2. 7. 142–43.
63. *Macbeth*, 5. 5. 19–28 (24, 28).

CHAPTER 14: IN THE HOUSE OF FAME

1. Society of Antiquaries, MS 127.
2. British Library, Lansdowne MS 777, f. 67^v.
3. Dedicatory poem in 1623 First Folio.
4. Folger Shakespeare Library, MS 26.
5. *A Banquet of Jeasts* (1630), p. 157.
6. British Library, Lansdowne MS 213, f. 332^v. For other evidence of Shakespeare's early fame, see *The Shakspere Allusion-Book: A Collection of Allusions to Shakespere from 1591 to 1700*, ed. John James Munro, Clement Mansfield Ingleby, Lucy Toulmin Smith, and Frederick James Furnivall (Oxford University Press, 1932).
7. See Philip Hardie's magnificent *Rumour and Renown: Representations of Fama in Western Literature* (Cambridge University Press, 2012), especially chapters 1 ("Introduction") and 3 ("Virgil's *Fama*"), to which my whole discussion is deeply indebted. For an equally splendid history of the idea of fame, see Leo Braudy, *The Frenzy of Renown: Fame and Its History* (New York, 1997).
8. Virgil, *Aeneid*, 1. 378–79.
9. See Hardie's discussion of Sinon, *Rumour and Renown*, pp. 73–77. Also Elena Giusti, *Carthage in Virgil's Aeneid: Staging the Enemy under Augustus* (Cambridge University Press, 2018), pp. 167–70.
10. Virgil, *Aeneid*, 2. 82, 83, 80, 107, 195.
11. Ibid., 4. 174.
12. Ibid., 4. 665–66, my translation.
13. Ibid., trans. Phaer, 4. 183–85.
14. *2 Henry IV*, Induction, 1–22. See further, Frederick Kiefer, *Shakespeare's Visual Theatre: Staging the Personified Characters* (Cambridge University Press, 2003), pp. 89–92.
15. Lines 67–68 of Dryden's translation, in *The Poems of John Dryden*, ed. Paul Hammond and David Hopkins (Longman, 2005), 5. 432.
16. Ben Jonson, *Masque of Queens* (1609), The Holloway Pages, http://www.hollowaypages.com/jonson1692fame.htm.
17. *Titus Andronicus*, 2. 2. 133–34; *Troilus and Cressida*, 1. 3. 145–46.

18. *Troilus and Cressida*, 5. 1. 36.

19. Ibid., 4. 5. 121.

20. Ibid., 4. 5. 124.

21. Virgil, *Aeneid*, 12. 168.

22. Sonnet 2, copied as "Spes altera" in several manuscripts: see Gary Taylor, "Some Manuscripts of Shakespeare's Sonnets," *Bulletin of the John Rylands Library*, 68 (1985), pp. 210–46.

23. Sonnets 16, 18, 19, 60, 100. The best treatment of the theme of immortality and the defeat of time in the sonnets remains J. B. Leishman, *Themes and Variations in Shakespeare's Sonnets* (Routledge, 1961), but see also Ramie Targoff's fine recent study, *Posthumous Love: Eros and the Afterlife in Renaissance England* (University of Chicago Press, 2014), with its persuasive argument that the pursuit of immortality in the Elizabethan sonnet tradition "differs from both its classical and Petrarchan counterparts in its explicit self-understanding as compensation for the fact that earthly love is mortal (for the Latin elegists there is very little of this sentimental strain, whereas for Petrarch immortal fame complements, rather than compensates for, a shared heavenly future). Within the English love sonnet, the afterlife of love gets displaced from eschatology onto the literary artifact itself" (p. 5).

24. This is evident from the fact that *The Passionate Pilgrim by William Shakespeare* (1599) includes both two sonnets from *Love's Labour's Lost* and two sonnets that will later appear in *Shakespeare's Sonnets* (1609).

25. *Love's Labour's Lost*, 1. 1. 1–7.

26. A common tag, which Shakespeare might have noticed at the very end of *The first parte of the Mirour for Magistrates* (1574), fol. 74ᵛ.

27. Ovid, *Metamorphoses*, 15. 234.

28. On which, see Erwin Panofsky's "Father Time," chap. 3 in *Studies in Iconology*.

29. Horace, *Odes*, 3. 30. 1.

30. Ovid, *Metamorphoses*, 15. 871–72, 878–79; trans. Golding, 15. 984–86, 993–95.

31. Sonnet 55.

32. Thorpe has often been considered a "pirate" publisher, but modern scholarship has tended towards the view that the 1609 volume was authorized by Shakespeare: see Katherine Duncan-Jones "Was the 1609 *Shakespeares Sonnets* Really Unauthorized?," *The Review of English Studies*, 34 (1983), pp. 151–71. The strongest supporting evidence for authorization is Thomas Heywood's comment in his *Apology for Actors* (1612) that Shakespeare objected to his name appearing on the title page of *The Passionate Pilgrim* (which included poems by other writers) "and hee to doe himself right hath since published them in his owne name" (sig. G4ʳ⁻ᵛ).

33. William Hazlitt, "On Posthumous Fame,–whether Shakspeare was influenced by a love of it?," *The Examiner*, 22 May 1814, repr. in *The Round Table* (1817), pp. 21–24.

34. Hazlitt, "On Posthumous Fame," quoted from *The Romantics on Shakespeare*, ed. Jonathan Bate (Penguin, 1992), p. 164.

35. Ibid., p. 166.

36. See "Shakespeare to Hazlitt to Keats," chap. 8 of my *Shakespeare and the English Romantic Imagination*.

37. See especially Lukas Erne, *Shakespeare as Literary Dramatist*, 2nd ed.; and Richard Dutton, "The Birth of the Author," in Parker and Zitner, *Elizabethan Theater*, pp. 71–92.

38. On this ornament, which also appears at the head of *The Rape of Lucrece*, see Douglas Bruster's excellent "Shakespeare's Lady 8," *Shakespeare Quarterly*, 66 (2015), pp. 47–88.

39. Ovid, *Amores*, 1. 15. 25–26.

40. Henry Woudhuysen is one of the few scholars to note this, in his exemplary British Academy Lecture, "The Foundations of Shakespeare's Text," *Proceedings of the British Academy*, 125 (2004), pp. 77–78.

41. Ben Jonson, "To the memory of my beloved, the AUTHOR Master William Shakespeare and what he hath left us," in Shakespeare, *Complete Works*, pp. lxii–lxiii.

42. Leonard Digges, "To the memory of the deceased author Master W. Shakespeare," quoted from Shakespeare, *Complete Works*, p. lxiii.

43. Or perhaps we should say four times, since the Third Folio went through two distinct editions, with the addition of what came to be known as the "apocryphal" plays, on which, see Peter Kirwan's admirable *Shakespeare and the Idea of Apocrypha* (Cambridge University Press, 2015). For the broader history of Shakespeare in print in this period, see Andrew Murphy's authoritative *Shakespeare in Print: A History and Chronology of Shakespeare Publishing* (Cambridge University Press, 2003); Sonia Massai's fine *Shakespeare and the Rise of the Editor* (Cambridge University Press, 2007); and Emma Depledge, *Shakespeare's Rise to Cultural Prominence: Politics, Print and Alteration, 1642–1700* (Cambridge University Press, 2018).

44. John Dryden, *Essay of Dramatick Poesie* (1668), p. 47.

45. Margaret Cavendish, *Sociable Letters*, ed. James Fitzmaurice (Broadview Press, 2004), p. 177.

46. See my *Shakespearean Constitutions*, pp. 23–27; and Robert D. Hume, "Before the Bard: 'Shakespeare' in Early Eighteenth-Century London," *ELH: A Journal of English Literary History*, 64 (1997), pp. 41–75.

47. I have offered accounts of Garrick along these lines in *Shakespearean Constitutions*, especially pp. 27–35, and "The Shakespeare Phenomenon," in *Shakespeare in Art*, ed. Jane Martineau (Merrell, 2003), especially pp. 11–13.

See also Peter Holland, "The Age of Garrick," in *Shakespeare: An Illustrated Stage History*, ed. Jonathan Bate and Russell Jackson (Oxofrd University Press, 1996), pp. 69–91; and, more fully, Vanessa Cunningham, *Shakespeare and Garrick* (Cambridge University Press, 2008).

48. I borrow this paragraph from my *Shakespeare: Staging the World*, cowritten with Dora Thornton, p. 266. On the Jubilee, see further Christian Deelman, *The Great Shakespeare Jubilee* (Joseph, 1964); Michael Dobson, *The Making of the National Poet: Shakespeare, Adaptation and Authorship, 1660–1769* (Clarendon Press, 1992); and Andrew McConnell Stott, *What Blest Genius? The Jubilee That Made Shakespeare* (Norton, 2018).

49. See further, "Local History Notes. Garrick's Villa and Temple to Shakespeare," London Borough of Richmond upon Thames, http://www .richmond.gov.uk/media/6314/local_history_garricks_villa.pdf, and references therein.

50. See my *Shakespeare and the English Romantic Imagination* and Peter Davidhazi, *The Romantic Cult of Shakespeare* (Palgrave Macmillan, 1998).

51. For the broader history, see P. O'Brien, *Warrington Academy, 1757– 86: Its Predecessors and Successors* (Owl Books, 1989).

52. See William McCarthy's magisterial biography, *Anna Letitia Barbauld: Voice of the Enlightenment* (Johns Hopkins University Press, 2008).

53. My discussion here draws on my *English Literature: A Very Short Introduction* (Oxford University Press, 2010), pp. 63–65. See further, Janet Bottoms, " 'Doing Shakespeare': How Shakespeare Became a School 'Subject,' " *Shakespeare Survey*, 66 (2013), pp. 96–109.

54. See Vicesimus Knox, *Liberal Education, or a Practical Treatise on the Methods of acquiring Useful and Polite Learning* (1780).

55. See Gauri Viswanathan, *Masks of Conquest: Literary Study and British Rule in India* (Columbia University Press, 1989).

56. See Jonathan Rose's inspirational *The Intellectual Life of the British Working Classes* (Yale University Press, 2001).

APPENDIX: THE ELIZABETHAN VIRGIL

1. Thomas Phaer, *The Booke of Children* (1544), sig. A4ᵛ.

2. Thomas Phaer, "Address to the Reader," in 1558 edition of *The Seven First Bookes of the Eneidos*.

3. Webbe, *A Discourse of English Poetry*, in Smith, *Elizabethan Critical Essays*, 1. 243.

4. Ibid., 1. 301: "Epilogue to the *Discourse*."

5. *The First Foure Bookes of Virgil his Aeneis: Translated intoo English heroical verse by Richard Stanyhurst, wyth oother Poëtical divises theretoo annexed* (Leiden, 1582), bk. 1, lines 159–71; "with" in the second line is

probably a printer's error for "where," due to compositorial eyeskip to "with" in the next line.

6. As Derek Attridge points out in his fine *Well-Weighed Syllables: Elizabethan Verse in Classical Metres* (Cambridge University Press, 1974), pp. 89–90.

7. Ascham, *The Scholemaster*, ed. R. J. Schoeck (Dent, 1966), bk. 2, p. 128.

8. *The First Foure Bookes of Virgil his Aeneis*, pp. 94–95.

9. Nashe, *Works*, ed. McKerrow, 1. 299, in the context of Nashe's confutation of Gabriel Harvey's *Foure Letters*—Harvey, being a proponent of classical metrics, had praised Stanyhurst.

10. Nashe, *Works*, ed. McKerrow, 3. 319–20.

11. *The Poems of Joseph Hall*, ed. Arnold Davenport (Liverpool University Press, 1949), p. 17.

12. Charles Whibley, "Translators," in *The Cambridge History of English Literature*, ed. A. W. Ward and A. R. Waller (Cambridge University Press, 1919), 4. 18; J. W. Saunders, *A Biographical Dictionary of Renaissance Poets and Dramatists, 1520–1650* (Harvester, 1983), p. 155.

13. Whibley, "Translators," 4. 17.

14. There is a good account of the Irishness of Stanyhurst's language in Patricia Palmer, *The Severed Head and the Grafted Tongue: Literature, Translation and Violence in Early Modern Ireland* (Cambridge University Press, 2014), pp. 125–32.

15. For further discussion of the Elizabethan translations of Virgil, with particular emphasis on Protestant ideology, see Sheldon Brammall's admirable *The English Aeneid: Translations of Virgil 1555–1646* (Edinburgh University Press, 2015).

INDEX